PEARSON LONGMAN
KEYSTONE
C

PEARSON English Learning System

Anna Uhl Chamot

John De Mado

Sharroky Hollie

PEARSON

Upper Saddle River, New Jersey • Boston, Massachusetts • Chandler, Arizona • Glenview, Illinois

PEARSON LONGMAN
KEYSTONE C

PEARSON English Learning System

Staff credits: The people who made up the *Longman Keystone team,* representing editorial, production, design, manufacturing, and marketing, are John Ade, Rhea Banker, Liz Barker, Danielle Belfiore, Virginia Bernard, Kenna Bourke, Anne Boynton-Trigg, Johnnie Farmer, Patrice Fraccio, Geraldine Geniusas, Charles Green, Henry Hild, Lucille M. Kennedy, Ed Lamprich, Emily Lippincott, Tara Maceyak, Maria Pia Marrella, Linda Moser, Laurie Neaman, Sherri Pemberton, Liza Pleva, Edie Pullman, Monica Rodriguez, Tania Saiz-Sousa, Chris Siley, Lynn Sobotta, Heather St. Clair, Jennifer Stem, Jane Townsend, Marian Wassner, Lauren Weidenman, and Adina Zoltan.

Smithsonian American Art Museum contributors: Project director and writer: Elizabeth K. Eder, Ph.D.; Writer: Mary Collins; Image research assistants: Laurel Fehrenbach, Katherine G. Stilwill, and Sally Otis; Rights and reproductions: Richard H. Sorensen and Leslie G. Green; Building photograph by Tim Hursley.

Text design and composition: Kirchoff/Wohlberg, Inc., TSI Graphics, Quarasan

Text font: 11.5/14 Minion
Acknowledgments: See page 471.
Illustration and Photo credits appear on page 473, which constitute an extension of this copyright page.

Library of Congress Cataloging-in-Publication Data
Chamot, Anna Uhl.
  Longman Keystone / Anna Uhl Chamot, John De Mado, Sharroky Hollie.
    p. cm. — (Longman Keystone)
  Includes index.
  ISBN 1-42-843492-5 (v. 8)
  1. Language arts (Middle school)—United States. 2. Language arts (Middle school)—Activity
    programs. 3. Language arts (Secondary)—United States. 4. English language—Study and
    teaching. I. Demado, John II. Hollie, Sharroky III. Title.
LB1631.C4466 2008
428.0071'2—dc22

                    2007049279

ISBN-13: 978-1-4284-3492-9
ISBN-10: 1-4284-3492-5

Printed in the United States of America
2 3 4 5 6 7 8 9 10 V063 16 15 14 13

About the Authors

Anna Uhl Chamot is a professor of secondary education and a faculty advisor for ESL in George Washington University's Department of Teacher Preparation. She has been a researcher and teacher trainer in content-based second-language learning and language-learning strategies. She co-designed and has written extensively about the Cognitive Academic Language Learning Approach (CALLA) and spent seven years implementing the CALLA model in the Arlington Public Schools in Virginia.

John De Mado has been an energetic force in the field of Language Acquisition for several years. He is founder and president of John De Mado Language Seminars, Inc., an educational consulting firm devoted exclusively to language acquisition and literacy issues. John, who speaks a variety of languages, has authored several textbook programs and produced a series of music CD/DVDs designed to help students acquire other languages. John is recognized nationally, as well as internationally, for his insightful workshops, motivating keynote addresses, and humor-filled delivery style.

Sharroky Hollie is an assistant professor in teacher education at California State University, Dominguez Hills. His expertise is in the field of professional development, African-American education, and second-language methodology. He is an urban literacy visiting professor at Webster University, St. Louis. Sharroky is the Executive Director of the Center for Culturally Responsive Teaching and Learning (CCRTL) and the co-founding director of the nationally acclaimed Culture and Language Academy of Success (CLAS).

Reviewers

Dear Student,

Welcome to LONGMAN
KEYSTONE

Longman Keystone has been specially designed to help you succeed in all areas of your school studies. This program will help you develop the English language skills you need for language arts, social studies, math, and science. You will discover new ways to use and build upon your language skills through your interactions with classmates, friends, teachers, and family members.

Keystone includes a mix of many subjects. Each unit has four different reading selections that include literary excerpts, poems, and nonfiction articles about science, math, and social studies. These selections will help you understand the vocabulary and organization of different types of texts. They will also give you the tools you need to approach the content of the different subjects you take in school.

As you use this program, you will discover new words, use your background knowledge of the subjects presented, relate your knowledge to the new information, and take part in creative activities. You will learn strategies to help you understand readings better. You will work on activities that help you improve your English skills in grammar, word study, and spelling. Finally, you will be asked to demonstrate the listening, speaking, and writing skills you have learned through fun projects that are incorporated throughout the program.

Learning a language takes time, but just like learning to skateboard or learning to swim, it is fun! Whether you are learning English for the first time, or increasing your knowledge of English by adding academic or literary language to your vocabulary, you are giving yourself new choices for the future, and a better chance of succeeding in both your studies and in everyday life.

We hope you enjoy *Longman Keystone* as much as we enjoyed writing it for you!

Good luck!

Anna Uhl Chamot
John De Mado
Sharroky Hollie

Smithsonian American Art Museum

Dear Student,

At the end of each unit in this book, you will learn about some artists and artworks that relate to the theme you have just read about. These artworks are all in the Smithsonian American Art Museum in Washington, D.C. That means they belong to you, because the Smithsonian is America's collection. The artworks were created over a period of 300 years by artists who responded to their experiences in personal ways. Their world lives on through their artworks and, as viewers, we can understand them and ourselves in new ways. We discover that many of the things that concerned these artists still engage us today.

Looking at an artwork is different from reading a written history. Artists present few facts or dates. Instead, they offer emotional insights that come from their own lives and experiences. They make their own decisions about what matters, without worrying if others agree or disagree. This is a rare and useful kind of knowledge that we can all learn from. Artists inspire us to respond to our own lives with deeper insight.

There are two ways to approach art. One way is through the mind—studying the artist, learning about the subject, exploring the context in which the artwork was made, and forming a personal view. This way is deeply rewarding and expands your understanding of the world. The second way is through the senses—letting your imagination roam as you look at an artwork, losing yourself in colors and shapes, absorbing the meaning through your eyes. This way is called "aesthetic." The great thing about art is that an artwork may have many different meanings. You can decide what it means to you.

This brief introduction to American art will, I hope, lead to a lifetime of enjoyment and appreciation of art.

Elizabeth Broun
The Margaret and Terry Stent Director
Smithsonian American Art Museum

Glossary of Terms

You will find the following words useful when reading, writing, and talking about art.

abstract a style of art that does not represent things, animals, or people realistically

acrylic a type of paint that is made from ground pigments and certain chemicals

background part of the artwork that looks furthest away from the viewer

brushstroke the paint or ink left on the surface of an artwork by the paintbrush

canvas a type of heavy woven fabric used as a support for painting; another word for a painting

composition the way in which the different parts of an artwork are arranged

detail a small part of an artwork

evoke to produce a strong feeling or memory

figure the representation of a person or animal in an artwork

foreground part of the artwork that looks closest to the viewer

geometric a type of pattern that has straight lines or shapes such as squares, circles, etc.

mixed media different kinds of materials such as paint, fabric, objects, etc. that are used in a single artwork

oil a type of paint that is made from ground pigments and linseed oil

paintbrush a special brush used for painting

perception the way you understand something you see

pigment a finely powdered material (natural or man-made) that gives color to paint, ink, or dye

portrait an artwork that shows a specific person, group of people, or animal

print an artwork that has been made from a sheet of metal or a block of wood covered with a wet color and then pressed onto a flat surface like paper. Types of prints include lithographs, etchings, aquatints, etc.

symbol an image, shape, or object in an artwork that represents an idea

texture the way that a surface or material feels and how smooth or rough it looks

tone the shade of a particular color; the effect of light and shade with color

watercolor a type of paint that is made from ground pigments, gum, and glycerin and/or honey; another word for a painting done with this medium

Contents

UNIT 1

How can change improve people's lives?

Contents

UNIT 2

What are the benefits of facing challenges?

Contents

Contents

UNIT 5

What is the human spirit? **302**

Contents

UNIT 6

 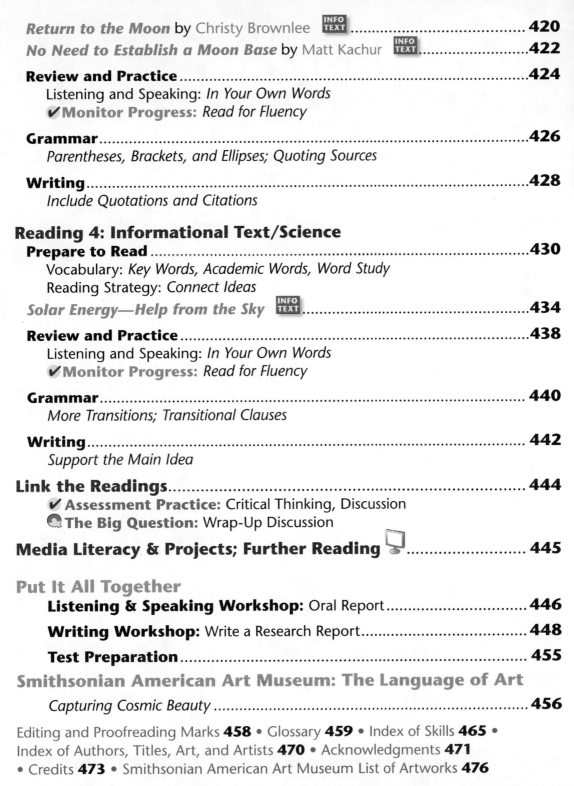

THE BIG QUESTION

How can change improve people's lives?

This unit is about change. You will read informational texts that describe how inventions and activities can improve people's lives. You will also read literature about the first woman to vote and a girl who begins a community garden. Reading, writing, and talking about these topics will give you practice using academic language and will help you become a better student.

Reading

1 Novel	**2** Science	**3** Novel

From *Riding Freedom* by Pam Muñoz Ryan	"Early Inventions"	From *Seedfolks* by Paul Fleischman
Reading Strategy: Analyze historical context	**Reading Strategy:** Recognize sequence	**Reading Strategy:** Visualize

Listening and Speaking—Descriptive

At the end of this unit, you will choose a topic and give a team **presentation** about it.

Writing—Descriptive

In this unit you will practice **descriptive writing.** This type of writing describes things, or tells what things look, sound, feel, smell, or taste like. After each reading you will learn a skill to help you write a descriptive paragraph. At the end of the unit, you will use these skills to help you write a descriptive essay.

Quick Write

In your notebook, write the word *change.* List some words or phrases that you associate with this word. Then share your list with a partner.

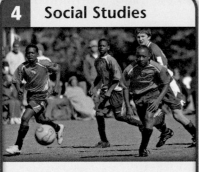

4 **Social Studies**

"From Refugees to Fugees"

Reading Strategy: Preview

DVD **VIEW AND RESPOND**
Watch the DVD for Unit 1 and answer the questions at www.LongmanKeystone.com.

Prepare to Read

What You Will Learn

Reading
- Vocabulary building: *Literary terms, word study*
- Reading strategy: *Analyze historical context*
- Text type: *Literature (novel excerpt)*

Grammar
Sequence words and phrases; Appositives

Writing
Describe an event or experience

▶ THE BIG QUESTION

How can change improve people's lives?
In most places, people are supposed to follow rules and obey laws. What rules and laws do you follow? Are there any rules or laws that you would like to see changed? How would your life improve if these rules or laws changed? Use your prior experience to discuss with a partner.

LEARNING STRATEGY

Compare new information to your prior experiences. This will make the new information more meaningful to you, and it will be easier to understand.

▶ BUILD BACKGROUND

In this section, you will read an excerpt from the historical fiction novel ***Riding Freedom***. Historical fiction uses real events, places, or people in a fictional story.

The story is about Charlotte Parkhurst, a real person who lived during the 1800s. As a young girl, Charlotte loved horses, but girls weren't supposed to work in the stables. Taking care of horses was a boy's job. Girls were expected to cook and clean.

As an adult, Charlotte lost the use of one eye after a horse kicked her in the face. But she loved horses so much that she became an expert horse rider and a stagecoach driver. In her time, women weren't allowed to do these things. In fact, there were many things that women weren't permitted to do, such as voting and owning property. However, Charlotte found ways to do the things she wanted.

▲ A stagecoach in the Old West

► VOCABULARY

Learn Literary Words

Literary Words

plot
conflict

Audio

A **plot** is the sequence of related events in a story. Most plots include a problem, or **conflict**, the events that lead toward solving the conflict, and the solution to the conflict. Plots usually move forward in time. They have a beginning, a middle, and an end.

A conflict is a struggle that can occur between the following forces:

- Character versus self
- Character versus another character
- Character versus society
- Character versus nature

Conflict is important in stories because it sets the plot in motion and makes the story interesting and suspenseful.

Practice

Workbook
Page 1

Work with a partner. Read the following paragraph. Identify the conflict, the events leading to the solution, and the solution itself.

> Frank looked up to see three women enter the building. A group of men began complaining loudly. Frank knew the men were behaving badly; he reminded the men that it was now legal for women to vote. The men looked at one another. They respected Frank and his opinions and slowly stopped calling out to the women. Instead, they stood by quietly and watched as the women cast their ballots and left the building.

◄ Women voting at the polls

Listening and Speaking: Academic Words

Study the **red** words and their meanings. You will find these words useful when talking and writing about literature. Write each word and its meaning in your notebook, then say the words aloud with a partner. After you read the excerpt from *Riding Freedom*, try to use these words to respond to the text. Ask your peers and teacher for their feedback and support.

achieved = succeeded in doing something, especially by working hard	⇒	Women **achieved** the right to vote in 1920.
attitudes = thoughts or feelings about something or someone	⇒	In the 1800s, some men had negative **attitudes** about women and their desire to vote.
discrimination = unfair treatment of some people because of their race, ethnic group, religion, or gender	⇒	In the 1800s, **discrimination** kept women from voting and purchasing land.
illegal = not allowed by law	⇒	A long time ago, it was **illegal** for women to vote in presidential elections.

Practice

Workbook Page 2

Work with a partner to answer these questions. Try to include the **red** word in your answer. Write the sentences in your notebook.

1. What goals have you **achieved** in your lifetime?

2. Are people's **attitudes** toward women today different from the way they were years ago? If so, how?

3. Do you think **discrimination** affects people today? If so, who and why?

4. What do you think should happen to someone who does something **illegal**?

▲ What does this magazine cover from the 1920s refer to?

Word Study: Double Consonants

Adding an ending, such as *-ed* or *-ing*, to a word can change its meaning. When endings are added to a single-syllable word that ends in a vowel + a consonant, the final consonant is doubled. For words with more than one syllable, the consonant doubles only if the stress is on the final syllable of the word.

Base Word	+ Ending	= New Word
grin	-ed	grinned
run	-ing	running
occur	-ed	occurred
begin	-ing	beginning

Practice  Workbook Page 3

Work with a partner. Copy the chart above into your notebook. Add four blank rows. Then add *-ed* and *-ing* to the words below and add them to the chart.

clap	rebel	regret	visit

READING STRATEGY | ANALYZE HISTORICAL CONTEXT

Analyzing the historical context of a story or text can make it more meaningful and easier to understand. Historical context includes the political and cultural changes that happened during a particular time period. To analyze historical context, follow these steps:

- As you read, pay attention to the events in the text.
- Think about how the location of the story affects the characters.
- Consider what you already know about the place or the time of the story.
- Notice how the characters are reacting to the events as they happen.

As you read *Riding Freedom*, think about the time and place of the story. What new historical information do you learn?

 Workbook Page 4

Set a purpose for reading Read the excerpt to find out how Charlotte Parkhurst made it possible for a woman to vote in the 1868 presidential election. How did her actions change people's perceptions of women?

from RIDING FREEDOM

Pam Muñoz Ryan

Dressed as a man, Charlotte "Charley" Parkhurst bought land in California. Her friend Hayward comes to her new home for a visit. In this scene, Charlotte prepares to say good-bye to him—and to reveal her secret plan.

Hayward stayed for a month of Sundays, and Charlotte couldn't bear thinking about him leaving again.

The morning he left she said, "Hay, you can **stock tender** for me as long as you like."

"Charlotte, I'm beginning to think you like having me around," he teased. "I never thought I'd see the day. But first, I got work to finish in Missouri. Then I got to help my **folks** move out here."

He hesitated, then said, "Charlotte, come with me."

"It'll take me over a year, Charlotte. You could get someone to watch the place. Won't you come?"

She turned and looked at him. "I can't, Hay. I don't want to leave. I worked my whole life for this. I belong *here*. I want to build up my horse stock, and I got apples to pick, and things I got to do. Besides, there's something I been thinking on for some time that I feel real strongly about."

She knew she could tell Hay anything but she wasn't sure how he'd react to this. "I **registered** to vote in Santa Cruz County. The election's in a few weeks, and I don't want to miss it."

Hayward stared at her and shook his head. "Charlotte, you'll be going against the law."

---

stock tender, take care of horses and cattle
folks, parents
registered, officially enrolled

Reading Skill

To understand the words in bold type, read the definitions at the bottom of the page. Later, use the words in your own sentences.

"Hay, I know more about who to vote for than most. Women are citizens of this country just like you. They work hard and make decisions **sound** as a man's."

"There's a lot of folks who don't agree."

"There's a lot of *men* who don't agree," said Charlotte.

Hayward grinned at her.

"I ain't one of them," he said. "I just don't understand what you'll be provin' if no one *knows* you're a woman."

"I guess I'm proving that here I am, a member of this county that most folks respect. Most of them ask *me* who *I'm* voting for! And the only reason I can walk in and vote is because they *think* I'm a man. Sooner or later, they'll all know I was a woman and my point will be made."

"So, someday you're gonna let people know you're a lady?" he asked.

"Maybe. But whether I let them know or not, I'll be wearin' these same clothes and tendin' my horses and runnin' this ranch, same as always."

He considered what she said and shook his head. "You know your mind, Charlotte, and that's fine by me. You know how I feel about you."

"I know."

He gave her a big hug and acted like he was never going to let go. Then he got on his horse and rode down the lane, past the **corral**. Charlotte stood on the porch and watched him ride away. He stopped halfway down the road and waved his hat.

Charlotte waved back.

---

sound, practical, based on good judgment
corral, pen for horses or cattle

✔ **LITERARY CHECK**

With whom does Charlotte have a conflict?

BEFORE YOU GO ON

1 Why doesn't Charlotte want to leave with Hayward?

2 Why does Charlotte feel women should have the right to vote?

On Your Own
Do you think Charlotte's plan is a good one? Why or why not?

It was sprinkling when Charlotte rode into town that November afternoon, but a little rain couldn't stop her. She hoped it wouldn't stop other folks from getting out and doing what they had to do, either. Luckily, by the time she got to town, the sun had come out. She **hitched** the **mustang** and walked down the street and nodded to the people walking by. A big sign in the window of the hotel said **POLLS**. Some of the ladies in town went about their **errands** and didn't seem to give a second thought to the long line of men in front of the hotel. Others gathered out front, in twos and threes, waiting for their men-folk, and acted like there was nothing special going on inside. Charlotte wondered if they really didn't care. Or if they were going about playing their roles like she was playing hers.

One man came up and clapped her on the back.

"Glad to see ya, Charley," he said.

Another man said, "Pretty excitin' day, ain't it, Charley?"

Charlotte didn't say much. She shook hands all around and got in line with the men. She listened to them banter and joke around her.

"Heard Wyoming's gonna give women the right to vote. I thought I'd heard everything."

"What's this country comin' to?"

"What do you think, Charley?"

hitched, tied
mustang, small wild horse
polls, place for voting
errands, short trips to buy something

Charlotte said, "I don't think it hurts nothin'. Guess they know their minds as well as us."

"Don't hurt nothin'! Them women fightin' for this is just plain crazy, stirrin' up trouble all over. They'll be the **ruination** of this country. I told my wife that she wouldn't ever be votin' as long as she's married to me, no matter what the law says. What does she know about **politics**?"

Several other men added their opinions.

The line inched up the hotel steps.

A little boy ran up, found his father in line, and tugged on his hand.

"Papa, Papa! The Tayor boy said Sarah and I can't play ball 'cause I'm little and she's a girl. And she's fightin' him in the street and he's twice as big as her. Hurry, Papa!"

The father shook his head. "We told her and told her about fightin'. When's that girl gonna learn?"

The men chuckled, and the father and the little boy left.

The line moved closer to the desk.

Charlotte got to the front and signed the book.

The **registrar** handed her the **ballot**. She studied the names. Horatio Seymour or Ulysses S. Grant, the conservative **Democrat** or the much talked-about **Republican**. She had listened to the talk and heard people's debates. She had heard good things and bad things about both men but she knew her own mind and what she thought was right.

---

ruination, destruction, downfall
politics, the issues of running a country
registrar, official who records votes
ballot, piece of paper that you use to vote
Democrat, member of one of the two major political parties in the United States, the Democratic party
Republican, member of the other major political party, the Republican party

BEFORE YOU GO ON

1 Which state was the first to give women the right to vote?

2 What does the boy report about his sister, Sarah?

On Your Own
Why do you think the men had negative **attitudes** about the idea of women voting?

Reading 1 **11**

"You know who you're votin' for, Charley?" asked the man next to her.

"Yes, I do," said Charlotte.

"Old Jake couldn't make it today because he's ailin'. Felt real bad about not comin', but I told him one vote won't make no difference."

Charlotte nodded to the man. Would her one vote make a difference? Why was she doing this? Someday when people found out, would they just think she had been crazy, too? Or would they wonder that she had a good reason?

Yes, she told herself. She had a good reason.

This was something she could do for those women out front who were pretending they didn't mind that they couldn't vote. And for that little girl outside who was already standing up for herself.

She smiled. And for me, she thought. Because I'm as **qualified** as the next man.

She marked her choice for president of the United States.

She turned in her ballot, then faced the crowd of men still waiting in line. She tipped her hat.

"Gentlemen," she said, "may the best man win."

Then she walked out of the hotel, got on her horse, and rode home.

---

qualified, capable

12 Unit 1

> ✔ **LITERARY CHECK**
> Which line best expresses the turning point, or climax, in the **plot**?

From the Author

This fictional novel is based on the true story of Charlotte Darkey Parkhurst.

Posing as a male, by the 1860s, she was a noted "whip" or "jehu" (a Biblical term referring to a **charioteer**) of the time. Charlotte retired from driving at a ranch near Watsonville, California.

After Charley's death, it was discovered that she was a woman. **Deeds** and records confirm that Charlotte, disguised as Charles

▲ A stagecoach station

Parkhurst, owned property in Watsonville. Charlotte's cabin was near the Seven Mile House, a former stagecoach stop and hotel. This **way station** for travelers on the Santa Cruz to Watsonville stage line was located on a road that was later named Freedom Boulevard. Charlotte also registered to vote in Santa Cruz County, fifty-two years before any woman would be allowed to vote in **federal** elections in the United States.

We will never really know Charlotte's motives for choosing to live her life the way she did. Possibly, she did what she had to do to survive during a time when there were very few opportunities for young women. I suspect that she stumbled upon the chance to become a stage driver, that she was good at it, and that it gave her personal freedoms that she would have never experienced as a girl. That freedom would have been very hard for anyone to give up once they had experienced it.

---

charioteer, driver of an ancient vehicle called a chariot
deeds, official papers that say who owns a piece of land
way station, rest stop
federal, governmental

ABOUT THE **AUTHOR**

Pam Muñoz Ryan has written numerous award-winning novels and picture books for young readers. She started her career as a teacher and later began writing on the advice of a friend. Today she lives in Southern California with her husband and four children.

BEFORE YOU GO ON

1 What motivated Charlotte to place her vote?

2 When did people discover that "Charley" was actually a woman?

💡**On Your Own**
Imagine yourself "in Charlotte's shoes." Would you have acted similarly in order to gain your personal freedoms?

Reading 1 **13**

➤ **READER'S THEATER**

Act out the following scene between Charlotte and a man at the polls.

Man: I was hoping to see you here, Charley.

Charlotte: I wouldn't miss voting today.

Man: Yeah, all the *men* should come and vote. But have you heard the news? Women in Wyoming are going to be allowed to vote soon, too. Can you imagine what would happen if we let women vote?

Charlotte: Why shouldn't women vote? They can make up their own minds.

Man: No, they can't. Women don't know what to think, and they don't know anything about politics.

Charlotte: You might be surprised. The women I know can think for themselves.

Man: If we let women vote, the country will be ruined.

Charlotte: I don't agree with you at all. I think you're mistaken.

Man: I don't think so. I hope I'm not alive to see the day a woman in this country is allowed to vote.

Charlotte: [*grinning*] Something tells me you'll be here to see it happen. Just wait.

Speaking SKILL

Speak clearly and loudly enough for everyone to hear.

➤ **COMPREHENSION**

Workbook Page 5

Recall

1. What were the other ladies in town doing while Charlotte stood in line to vote?

2. What did the men think would be the ruination of the country?

Comprehend

3. How are Sarah (the little girl who was fighting) and Charlotte similar?

4. Who was Charlotte referring to when she said, "May the best man win"?

Analyze

5. How do you think the men in town would have reacted if they had known Charlotte was a woman? Support your answer by evaluating information in the story.

6. What is the author's attitude about personal freedom? Support your answer by evaluating information in the story. Do you agree with the author? Why or why not?

Connect

7. Have you ever voted? Who or what did you vote for and why?

8. Do you think **discrimination** against women still exists today? Why or why not?

➤ DISCUSSION

Discuss in pairs or small groups.

1. How do you think Charlotte felt after she turned in her ballot?

2. Do you think Charlotte was right to disguise herself as a man in order to vote? Explain.

Q How can change improve people's lives? What other rights have women **achieved** over the past century? How have their lives improved?

Listening SKILL
Give the speaker your full attention. Don't talk to your classmates.

➤ RESPONSE TO LITERATURE
Workbook Page 5

Utilize How do you think *Riding Freedom* would have ended if someone had discovered Charlotte's secret? Work with a partner to rewrite the story's ending. Write a paragraph that explains how Charlotte gets caught voting as a woman and who discovers her secret. Then share your version of events with the class.

Grammar

Sequence Words and Phrases

It is important to be able to express the sequence, or order, of events. Sequence words and phrases help a reader understand the events in a story.

> But **first**, I got work to finish in Missouri. **Then** I got to help my folks move out here.

Sequence words and phrases follow a certain order. A sequence of events always begins with *first* and often ends with *finally* or *last. However, then, next, now,* and *after that* can be used in any order within the sequence. Use a comma after all these sequence words and phrases except for *then* and *now.*

> **First,** Charlotte got to the front.
> **Then** she signed the book.
> **Next,** the registrar handed her the ballot.
> **After that,** she studied the names.
> **Now** she knew what she had to do.
> **Finally, / Last,** she marked her choice for president of the United States.

Notice in the examples above that there is parallel structure. This means that all the sentences use the same word order and verb tense.

Practice  Workbook Page 6

Work with a partner. In your notebook, copy the events below. Put the events in the correct sequence.

_____ Then he drove to the restaurant.

_____ Last, he met his date, Jane.

_____ Then he got dressed.

_____ Next, he got in his car.

_____ Now he was ready to go.

_____ First, Mike took a shower.

___3___ After that, he put on some aftershave.

Apply

Work with a partner. Using sequence words, tell your partner a story.

Example: *First, we packed the car . . .*

Appositives

An appositive is a noun or noun phrase that renames another noun next to it. The appositive can be a short or long combination of words.

> Horatio Seymour or Ulysses S. Grant, **the conservative Democrat** or **the much talked-about Republican**.
> [first phrase renames *Horatio Seymour;* second phrase renames *Ulysses S. Grant*]

When a comma is used with an appositive, it means that it gives extra information, and it is called a nonrestrictive appositive. When there is no comma, the information is essential, and it is called a restrictive appositive.

> Charlotte's cabin was near Seven Mile House, **a former stagecoach stop and hotel**.
> Charlotte's cabin was near the former stagecoach stop and hotel **Seven Mile House**.

Grammar SKILL

An appositive must agree with the noun it renames. If the noun is singular or plural, the appositive must be as well.

Practice

Workbook
Page 7

Work with a partner. Copy the sentences below into your notebook. Then underline the appositive in each.

Example: <u>My sister</u> Sue just got a puppy.

1. Charlotte felt it was necessary to perform the **illegal** act voting.
2. Mexico City, the biggest city in the world, is very interesting.
3. On Venus, the closest planet to Earth, there is no water.
4. Pam Muñoz Ryan's book *Paint the Wind* is very interesting.
5. Pam Muñoz Ryan, my favorite author, signed this book.

✔ GRAMMAR CHECK

When do you use a comma with an ***appositive?***

Apply

Work with a partner. Look at the sentences in the Practice exercise. Decide if the appositives are restrictive or nonrestrictive.

Writing

Ongoing Writing Skills Practice

Describe an Event or Experience

At the end of this unit you will write a descriptive essay. To do this, you will need to learn some of the skills writers use in descriptive writing.

> **Writing Prompt**
>
> Write a descriptive paragraph about an exciting event you participated in or attended, for example, a sports event, a party, or a family celebration. Before you write, list the events in chronological order, using a graphic organizer. Be sure to use sequence words in your description.

1 **PREWRITE** Begin by choosing a real event or experience that happened to you.

- Think of a title for your description.

- Make a list of the steps that were part of the main event.

- List the steps of the event in a sequence-of-events organizer.

  Workbook Page 8

- Decide which sequence words you can use with each step.

Here's a sequence-of-events organizer created by a student named Haley. She is describing how she got ready for her first school formal.

My First School Formal

First, I had my hair done at a professional salon.

↓

Next, I put on makeup and small amounts of glitter.

↓

Then I put on my black dress and high heels.

↓

Finally, my escort arrived to pick me up.

2 **DRAFT** Use your organizer to help you write a first draft.

- Remember to use chronological sequence.
- Add details to make each step of your description more vivid.
- Make sure to use sequence words.

3 **REVISE** Read over your draft. Look for places where the writing is unclear or needs improvement. Use the Writing Checklist to help you identify problems. Then revise your draft, using the editing and proofreading marks listed on page 458.

4 **EDIT** Check your work for errors in grammar, usage, mechanics, and spelling. Trade papers with a partner to obtain feedback. Use the Peer Review Checklist on Workbook page 8. Edit your final draft in response to feedback from your partner and your teacher.

5 **PUBLISH** Prepare a clean copy of your final draft. Share your descriptive paragraph with the class. Save your work. You'll need to refer to it in the Writing Workshop at the end of the unit.

Here is Haley's description of her first school formal.

Writing Checklist

ORGANIZATION:
☑ I used chronological order.

WORD CHOICE:
☑ I used sequence words to make the order of events clear to the reader.

Haley Coy

My First School Formal

Getting ready for my first school formal was hectic and exciting. First, I had my hair done at a professional salon. Countless bobby pins and squirts of hairspray were used before the style was complete. The updo gave me an elegant look. Next, I applied gentle brush strokes of makeup and small amounts of glitter on my cheeks. Then it was time to put on my black dress and high heels. The heels gave me enough height so that my dress just grazed the floor. Finally, my escort arrived to pick me up. He looked great in his elegant black tuxedo. As he placed a yellow rose corsage on my wrist, my parents started snapping pictures of us. Now, I'll have plenty of photographs to remember just how incredible we looked on that memorable night.

Prepare to Read

What You Will Learn

Reading
- Vocabulary building: *Context, dictionary skills, word study*
- Reading strategy: *Recognize sequence*
- Text type: *Informational text (science)*

Grammar
Simple past: regular and irregular verbs

Writing
Describe an object

➤ ◯ THE BIG QUESTION

How can change improve people's lives? What kinds of tools or machines do you use on a daily basis? A toothbrush? Television? Computer? Pen? Copy the chart below into your notebook. List objects that you use every day. Include a brief description of how you use each item. Then share your chart with a small group. Discuss how people's everyday lives have been changed by these items. Ask your peers and teacher for their feedback and support in order to develop background knowledge about this topic.

Tool or Machine	How I Use It

➤ BUILD BACKGROUND

"Early Inventions" is a science article about inventions, or things that people design to improve their lives. Many of these inventions have made a big difference in how we live.

Inventions are created for various reasons. Some are created so people can do things they couldn't do before. For example, the music cylinder allowed people to record music and listen to it whenever they wanted. Some inventions, like the microwave oven, are designed to make the things we already do easier. Some inventions are made just for fun, like cotton candy. And some, as you will discover in "Early Inventions," are created purely by accident.

◀ An Edison gramophone

► **VOCABULARY**

Listening and Speaking: Key Words

Key words are important, topic-related vocabulary. Read aloud and listen to these sentences. Use the context to figure out the meaning of the highlighted words. Use a dictionary to check your answers. Then write each word and its meaning in your notebook.

1. The designer sketched a picture of the tool he wanted to make.
2. The device opens metal cans.
3. Scientists haven't discovered any new elements, or simple chemical substances made of only one type of atom, since 1939.
4. The invention of the vacuum cleaner made cleaning the house faster and easier.
5. The inventor applied for a patent from the government. He didn't want anyone else to make or sell his invention.
6. Students study the periodic table to learn more about chemical elements.

Key Words

designer
device
elements
invention
patent
periodic table

Audio

Audio

Practice  **Workbook Page 9**

Write the sentences in your notebook. Choose a key word from the box above to complete each sentence. Then take turns reading the sentences aloud with a partner. Ask your peers and teacher for their feedback and support.

1. All the chemical elements in the world are listed on the _____.
2. Max will sell the new video game he invented after he receives a _____ from the government.
3. The stapler is a _____ that fastens papers together.
4. The clothing _____ created all the costumes for the play.
5. Similar _____ are grouped together on the periodic table.
6. The _____ of the Internet allowed people to find information quickly.

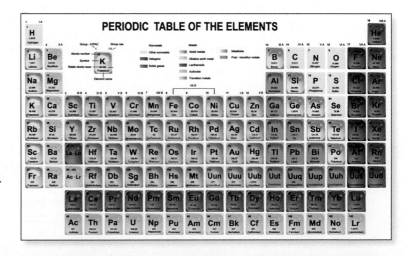

▲ The periodic table of chemical elements, invented in 1869

Listening and Speaking: Academic Words

Study the **red** words and their meanings. You will find these words useful when talking and writing about informational texts. Write each word and its meaning in your notebook, then say the words aloud with a partner. After you read "Early Inventions," try to use these words to respond to the text.

created = made or invented		Alexander Graham Bell **created** a new way for people to communicate with each other— the telephone.
function = the purpose of something		The **function** of a washing machine is to clean clothes.
significant = noticeable or important		The invention of the computer had a **significant** impact on society. We will see the effects of this invention for many years to come.
technology = all the knowledge and equipment used in science		As **technology** has improved, scientists have been able to develop many new products.

Practice

Work with a partner to answer these questions. Try to include the **red** word in your answer. Write the sentences in your notebook.

1. Have you ever **created** something you were proud of? If so, what?
2. What is the **function** of an airplane?
3. In your opinion, what is one of the most **significant** inventions ever created?
4. What kinds of new **technology** might be invented in the future?

▼ The airplane is one of the most significant inventions of the twentieth century.

Word Study: Nouns That Modify Nouns

A noun is a person, place, or thing. Sometimes, a noun is used to decribe, or modify, another noun. For example, two nouns make up the phrase *bear cub*. However, the first noun acts as an adjective— *bear* gives you more information about the *cub*. Look at the sentences below for examples of other nouns that modify nouns.

She placed the tea bag in the mug.	➡	*tea* modifies *bag*
I cooked dinner in the microwave oven.	➡	*microwave* modifies *oven*
The first telegraph lines were built in the 1850s.	➡	*telegraph* modifies *lines*
I poured the juice into a paper cup.	➡	*paper* modifies *cup*

Practice  **Workbook** Page 11

Work with a partner. Copy the sentences below into your notebook. Circle each noun modifier and underline the noun being modified.

1. The lie detector said that he wasn't telling the truth.
2. The telephone wire was sticking out of the wall.
3. Ben spilled juice on his computer keyboard.
4. She snapped her bubble gum loudly.
5. The ice pop melted in the sun.

LEARNING STRATEGY

Use a concept map to acquire new vocabulary. Adding words or phrases to a Venn diagram, a timeline, or a chart will help you see the relationships between words and their meanings.

READING STRATEGY | RECOGNIZE SEQUENCE

Recognizing sequence in a text is important because it helps you to understand the order in which things happen. To recognize sequence, follow these steps:

- As you read, look for words that the author uses to show sequence, for example, *first*, *then*, *next*, *finally*, *last*, *while*, *during*, and *after*.
- Look for dates and times, for example, *morning* and *Wednesday*.
- It may help you to draw a timeline of the events described.

As you read "Early Inventions," make a note of the sequence in which things were invented. What happened first, next, and last?

 **Workbook** Page 12

Set a purpose for reading As you read about inventions, consider how our ancestors' lives were different from ours today. What impact did these inventions have on us?

Early Inventions
Audio

The Nineteenth Century

In the nineteenth century, many new products and industries developed because of advances in science. Plastic, **synthetic** fabrics, electric light, telephones, photography, cars, and radio were just a few of the inventions that would change people's lives.

---

synthetic, not natural

▲ A woman wearing bloomers

Bloomers
c. 1853
Amelia Bloomer

In the nineteenth century, people thought pants for women were outrageous. This may have been why American women's rights **reformer** Amelia Bloomer liked them. She believed that long, baggy pants **gathered** at the ankle would **liberate** women. When she appeared in her pants in about 1853, there was more laughter than liberation. But within thirty-five years, another invention made "bloomers" seem like a good idea—they were ideal for women who wanted to ride bikes.

Safety elevator
1853
Elisha Otis

Knowing that people were scared of elevators, Elisha Otis invented a safety **hoist** with arms that shot out and grabbed the sides of the **elevator shaft** if the supporting cable broke. In New York City, he demonstrated his invention's effectiveness by having the cable cut while he was in it. He installed his first passenger safety elevator in 1857 in a New York store.

---

reformer, person who tries to change society
gathered, tied or tightened
liberate, free
hoist, device that lifts and lowers
elevator shaft, chamber an elevator moves in

Transatlantic telegraph
1858
Cyrus Field, Charles Bright, William Thomson

By the 1850s, there were several short underwater **telegraph lines**. American **financier** Cyrus Field wanted to go further. He wanted to link the United States and Britain with a cable across the Atlantic Ocean. Field hired many engineers and scientists, including Charles Bright and William Thomson. After heroic efforts, a transatlantic cable was laid in 1858. However, there were problems, which made the cable fail within weeks. But it proved that the idea worked. A permanent link between the two countries was finally established in 1866.

Periodic table
1869
Dmitry Mendeleyev

In 1866, Russian **chemist** Dmitry Mendeleyev listed the elements by **atomic weight**. He found that the list showed a pattern: similar elements appeared at regular intervals, or periods. Mendeleyev published his periodic table in 1869. In 1871, he created a version with gaps where there were breaks in the pattern. He said that the gaps represented undiscovered elements. Most chemists did not see the importance of this until at least twenty years later.

---

telegraph lines, electric wires used to carry messages
financier, person who lends large amounts of money
chemist, scientist who studies the interaction of atoms and molecules
atomic weight, the mass of a single atom of a certain element

▲ **What is this advertisement for?**

Jeans
1873
Jacob Davis, Levi Strauss

In the 1850s, the Gold Rush in California attracted people from everywhere. Levi Strauss had a business that supplied people with everything they needed, including pants. **Tailor** Jacob Davis started making denim pants with **riveted** pockets, to make them strong for hard work. He suggested to Strauss that they could make lots of money. So Strauss provided the cash to get started, and Davis supplied the know-how. In 1873, they got the first patent for jeans.

---

tailor, someone who makes clothes that are measured to fit exactly
riveted, fastened by small metal bolts

BEFORE YOU GO ON

1 Why did Amelia Bloomer believe wearing pants would help women?

2 How did both Jacob Davis and Levi Strauss contribute to the invention of jeans?

On Your Own
Which of these inventions have you heard of before?

The Twentieth Century

In the first fifty years of the twentieth century, new inventions and discoveries transformed both everyday life and the world of science. Ordinary people got radios, lifesaving drugs, and cars. Scientists created a new **physics**, which revealed the awesome energy hidden in **matter**. The modern world was nearly here.

Vacuum cleaner
1902
Hubert Booth

Early devices for removing dust just tried to blow it away. One day, British engineer Hubert Booth put a handkerchief over his mouth and sucked the **upholstery** of a chair. The dirt he collected convinced him that vacuum cleaning would be much better. He started a company to make vacuum cleaners in 1902. But the cleaners were so big they had to be parked outside the houses they cleaned.

---

physics, study of the basic laws of nature
matter, material that everything is made of
upholstery, material that covers furniture

Teddy bear
1902
Morris Mitchtom, Margarete Steiff

Popular American president Theodore "Teddy" Roosevelt became even more popular in 1902, when he went on a hunting trip but refused to shoot a defenseless bear cub. Cashing in on this, New York **retailer** Morris Mitchtom began selling cuddly toy bears. They had shoe-button eyes and jointed limbs. Mitchtom called them "Teddy's Bears." They were a huge success, and their name soon became "teddy bears." At about the same time, German designer Margarete Steiff started making similar bears. Although they weren't exactly like Mitchtom's bears, Steiff bears became the number one best-sellers.

▲ A Steiff bear

---

retailer, person who sells goods from a store

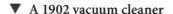
▼ A 1902 vacuum cleaner

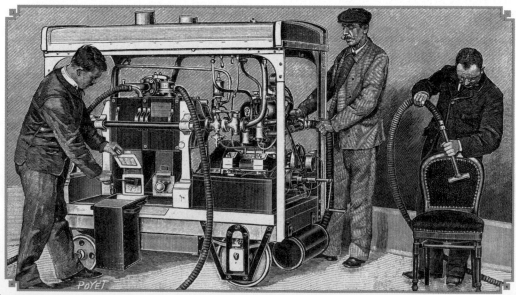

Electric washing machine
1907
Alva Fisher

For years, inventors tried to find a way of reducing the hours spent over a steaming washtub. Women spent many hours washing the family's clothes by hand. The first electric washing machine was designed in 1907 by American engineer Alva Fisher. It had a drum that turned back and forth to tumble clothes clean. Its motor was simply bolted on to the outside of the machine. It wasn't very safe, but it saved women many hours of work.

Ice pop
1923
Frank Epperson

Refreshing, flavored ice on a stick was patented by American salesman Frank Epperson in 1924. The **legend** is that Epperson invented the ice pop by accident in 1905, when he was a boy, by leaving a drink with a stirrer in it out on a cold night. His patent describes **cylindrical** ice pops made in ordinary test tubes.

---

legend, popular, probably untrue, story
cylindrical, round, but flat at top and bottom

◀ An early washing machine

Bubble gum
1928
Walter Diemer

Walter Diemer, a young **accountant** working for the Fleer Chewing Gum Company in Philadelphia, Pennsylvania, thought he could improve on the company's product. In 1928 he produced a gum that was so stretchy he could blow bubbles with it. He had created bubble gum. His company started selling it as Dubble Bubble. Diemer taught the sales force how to blow the perfect bubble, and the gum became a favorite worldwide.

Cat's eyes
1935
Percy Shaw

Cat's eyes are the little **reflectors** set in the road that make driving at night safer. Possibly inspired by real cats' eyes, British engineer Percy Shaw invented them in 1934, but they were not used until the following year. Their secret was in the **rubber** that housed the reflectors. Whenever a car ran over a cat's eye, a flexible "eyelid" wiped the reflectors clean, ready for the next driver. Shaw became a millionaire.

---

accountant, person who keeps track of money
reflectors, pieces of plastic that reflect light
rubber, stretchy, durable substance used in things like car tires

---

BEFORE YOU GO ON

1 Which invention was **created** by accident? How was it invented?

2 Who was Mitchtom's teddy bear named after?

On Your Own
If you could be the first to invent something, what would you invent?

► **COMPREHENSION**  Workbook Page 13

Recall

1. Who invented the electric washing machine?

2. What pattern did Mendeleyev find in his list of chemicals?

Comprehend

3. What is the same about the invention of the vacuum cleaner and the invention of the teddy bear?

4. Why did Cyrus Field want to build a transatlantic telegraph?

Analyze

5. Why do you think the author chose to write about these particular inventions?

6. Did the author use chronological order in the article? If so, how?

Connect

7. What characteristics do you think an invention must have in order for it to be **significant**? Why?

8. In general, what positive effects has **technology** had on everyday life? Has technology had any negative effects? Explain.

Reading Skill
Make sure you understand different types of sentences. Questions are used routinely to ask for information. They often include words such as *who, what, where, why, when,* or *how.*

► **IN YOUR OWN WORDS**

Review the reading. Choose the four inventions that you think are the most significant. Look at the date of each invention. In your notebook, draw a timeline like the one below. Add the dates to the timeline in chronological order. Then write a sentence describing each of the four inventions. Present your timeline and summaries to the class.

1873

Jacob Davis and
Levi Strauss create the
first pair of jeans.

A replica of the first lightbulb ►

▶ DISCUSSION

Discuss in pairs or small groups.

1. The majority of the inventors that you read about were men. Why do you think that is?

2. What qualities do you think a person must have in order to be an inventor?

Q How can change improve people's lives? Name new technologies that have been invented during your lifetime. What was your life like before these inventions existed? How have they changed your life for the better?

»⌯ Listening SKILL

Look at the speaker as he or she speaks.

▶ READ FOR FLUENCY

When we read aloud to communicate meaning, we group words into phrases, pause or slow down to make important points, and emphasize important words. Pause for a short time when you reach a comma and for a longer time when you reach a period. Pay attention to rising and falling intonation at the end of sentences.

Work with a partner. Choose a paragraph from the reading. Discuss which words seem important for communicating meaning. Practice pronouncing difficult words. Give each other feedback.

▶ EXTENSION  Workbook Page 13

Utilize Choose an object that you use every day. Use the library or the Internet to research that object. Describe the **function** of the object and find out who invented it and when and how it was invented. Then complete the chart below. Use as many academic words as possible. Then share the results with your class.

Object:
Function:
Inventor:
Year object was invented:
How object was invented:

LEARNING STRATEGY

To better acquire and understand new academic language, use and reuse these words in meaningful ways in your writing.

Grammar

Simple Past: Regular Verbs

Use the simple past to talk about actions that happened in the past. There are rules for forming the simple past of regular verbs.

Grammar SKILL

The base form of a verb is also called the simple form. There are no endings (-s, -es, -d, -ed) on the base form.

Rule	Base Form	Simple Past
Add -ed if base form ends in two consonants, C-V-C* pattern, C-V pattern + -y, or double consonant.	want develop stay install	Cyrus Field **wanted** to go further. They **developed** new inventions. The cat's eye **stayed** clean. He **installed** it in 1857.
If base form ends in -e, just add -d.	prove create	It **proved** her theory was correct. Scientists **created** a new physics.
For one-syllable words with C-V-C pattern, double final consonant and add -ed.	stop plan stir	The cable **stopped** working. He **planned** to link the two countries. He **stirred** his drink.
If base form ends in -y, change y to i and add -ed.	try supply	Inventors **tried** to find a way. His business **supplied** everything.

*C stands for *consonant* and V stands for *vowel*.

Form questions with the auxiliary verb *did*. Use *did not* (*didn't*) with negatives. Use the base form of the verb with questions and negatives.

> **Did** Teddy Roosevelt **invent** the Teddy Bear? No, he **didn't**.

Practice

Workbook Page 14

Work with a partner. Copy the paragraph below into your notebook. Complete the paragraph using the simple past form of the verb in parentheses.

The Hungarian journalist Laszlo Biro (invent) _invented_ the ballpoint pen in 1938. Biro (**1.** notice) _____ that the type of ink used in newspaper printing (**2.** dry) _____ quickly. As the pen (**3.** move) _____ along the paper, the ball (**4.** rotate) _____, picking up ink from the ink cartridge and leaving it on the paper. Biro's invention (**5.** change) _____ the way people write.

Apply

Write five sentences telling what you did yesterday, using the simple past. Use a dictionary if necessary. Then talk to a partner about what you did last weekend.

30 Unit 1

Simple Past: Irregular Verbs

Many verbs have an irregular form in the simple past. Their simple past form is not made by adding -d or -ed. You will need to memorize them. Form questions with *did* and the base form of the verb. Form the negative with *did not* (*didn't*) and the base form of the verb. For the verb *be*, form the negative with *wasn't* or *weren't*; form questions by switching the verb *was* or *were* with the subject.

Grammar SKILL

Don't use the auxiliary verb *did* with the simple past of *be* (*was / were*).

Base Form / Simple Past			Example
be	→	was/were	**Was** the first electric washing machine safe?
think	→	thought	People **didn't think** pants for women was appropriate.
say	→	said	He **said** they represented undiscovered elements.
get	→	got	Did they **get** the first patent for jeans?
put	→	put	Hubert Booth **put** a handkerchief over his mouth.

Look at the chart for more irregular verbs in the simple past.

Irregular Past Verbs											
catch	→	caught	hide	→	hid	send	→	sent
come	→	came	keep	→	kept	sleep	→	slept
fly	→	flew	lose	→	lost	tell	→	told
give	→	gave	run	→	ran	win	→	won

Practice
Workbook Page 15

Work with a partner. Copy the sentences into your notebook. Complete the sentences with the simple past of the verb in parentheses. Use a dictionary if necessary.

Example: Sammy *didn't come* (not come) to school today.

1. Val _____ (leave) the party early.

2. I _____ (not tell) anyone your secret.

3. _____ you _____ (give) Sharon the letter?

4. Maya _____ (not catch) the ball.

5. Rhea _____ (send) me a postcard from Santiago.

Apply

In your notebook, write five regular or irregular verbs. Work with a partner. Take turns, using your verbs to tell a story.

Example: *It was a cold and dark night . . .*

✔ GRAMMAR CHECK

How do you form the negative of be *in the* **simple past**?

Writing

Ongoing Writing Skills Practice

Describe an Object

In this lesson you will write a description of an object. A good description includes sensory details to appeal to the reader's five senses. This helps the reader to imagine how an object sounds, smells, looks, feels, or tastes.

> **Writing Prompt**
>
> Write a descriptive paragraph about an object that you have used, eaten, or worn, such as a computer, an apple, or a sweater. List related sensory details in a graphic organizer. Include these details in your paragraph. Be sure to use regular and irregular verbs in the simple past correctly.

1 **PREWRITE** Begin by choosing a story to tell.

- Write the name of the object in the center bubble of your graphic organizer.

- Ask yourself how this object sounds, smells, looks, feels, or tastes.

- Add details for each sense in each of the other five bubbles.

Workbook
Page 16

- Think of interesting adjectives and verbs to describe your experience.

Here's a word web created by a student named Pablo for a description of a faucet:

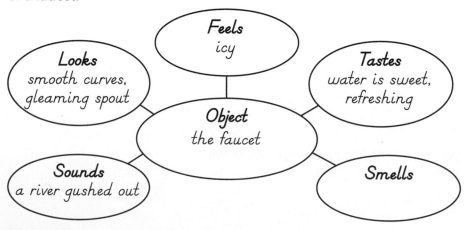

2 DRAFT Use your word web to help you write a first draft.

- Remember to describe the object using different senses.

- Use a variety of adjectives and verbs to make your description vivid.

- As you write, try to make your audience feel your experience of the object.

3 REVISE Read over your draft. Look for places where the writing is unclear or needs improvement. Use the Writing Checklist to help you identify problems. Then revise your draft, using the editing and proofreading marks listed on page 458.

4 EDIT Check your work for errors in grammar, usage, mechanics, and spelling. Trade papers with a partner to obtain feedback. Use the Peer Review Checklist on Workbook page 16. Edit your final draft in response to feedback from your partner and your teacher.

5 PUBLISH Prepare a clean copy of your final draft. Share your descriptive paragraph with your class. Save your work. You'll need to refer to it in the Writing Workshop at the end of the unit.

Here is Pablo's description. Notice how he contrasts the hot day and the cool water to make his description more vivid.

Pablo Espínola

The Faucet

It had to be 100 degrees in the kitchen. As I stood at the sink, the reflection of the sun on the faucet's metal hurt my eyes. I noticed the faucet's smooth curves, the knobs, and the gleaming spout. When I turned the cold-water knob, a river gushed out of the spout and hit the sink. Small droplets of water bounced out, leaving little wet marks along my arms. When I placed my hand on the metal spout, it felt icy from the cold water running through it. I got a glass from the cupboard and filled it. On a hot day, the water from the faucet tasted sweet and refreshing. After washing my hands and face, I felt cool and comfortable in my house on that hot, hot day.

Prepare to Read

▶ 🄠 THE BIG QUESTION

How can change improve people's lives? Do you know someone who has a garden? What kinds of plants grow there? What kind of changes take place in a garden? How could you benefit from having a garden? Discuss with a partner.

▶ BUILD BACKGROUND

You will read an excerpt from the novel **Seedfolks**. It is a work of fiction about an empty lot that becomes a community garden. In some city neighborhoods, people plant gardens in vacant lots or empty areas of land. Each person plants flowers or vegetables in one part of the garden and then they take care of that area.

   In *Seedfolks*, a different character narrates each chapter, telling about the garden from his or her point of view. Each chapter is like a short story. Short stories usually present a short sequence of events, and the main character usually experiences a problem or conflict. A girl named Kim narrates the first chapter you will read. She tells why she decided to plant beans in an empty city lot.

▲ A community garden

Learn Literary Words

Imagery is descriptive language used in literary works. Writers use sensory details to create imagery. This helps the reader see, feel, taste, touch, and smell what the writer is describing. Try to identify the use of imagery in the excerpt from *Seedfolks* below.

> The sidewalk was completely empty. It was Sunday, early in April. An icy wind teetered trash cans and turned my cheeks to marble. In Vietnam we had no weather like that. Here in Cleveland people call it spring. I walked half a block, then crossed the street and reached the vacant lot.

Notice how the words *icy* and *marble* appeal to your sense of touch, and the words *empty*, *teetered,* and *vacant* appeal to your sense of sight.

The **setting** of *Seedfolks* is an old, abandoned lot in Cleveland, Ohio. The setting of a literary work is the time and place of the action. *Time* can be a specific year, season, or time of day. *Place* can be a specific location on a map, such as a town, state, or country. *Place* can also be a specific environment, such as a garden or a junkyard.

Practice  Workbook Page 17

Work with a partner. Choose a setting from the box below. Create imagery by listing sensory details that describe the setting. Then rewrite your list, placing the most important details first. Read your list to the class. Ask your peers and teacher for their feedback and support.

beach	favorite restaurant
bedroom	house
classroom	local park

Literary Words

imagery
setting

Audio

LEARNING STRATEGY

Use words that you already know to learn new and essential language, or words that you must know in order to understand your schoolwork.

▲ Sensory details such as *empty* and *cold* could be used to describe this building.

Listening and Speaking: Academic Words

Study the **red** words and their meanings. You will find these words useful when talking and writing about literature. Write each word and its meaning in your notebook, then say the words aloud with a partner. After you read the excerpt from *Seedfolks*, try to use these words to respond to the text.

goal = something you want to do in the future	➡	She's a new and inexperienced gardener. Her **goal** is to grow prize-winning flowers.
involved = included in a project or situation	➡	She got **involved** in a garden club at school. She goes to their meetings every Friday.
located = in a particular place or position	➡	The bean plants are **located** at the back of the garden.
reacted = behaved in a particular way because of what someone has said or done	➡	Juan **reacted** with joy and excitement when the seeds began to grow.

 Audio

Practice  **Workbook Page 18**

Work with a partner to answer these questions. Try to include the **red** word in your answer. Write the sentences in your notebook.

1. What is one **goal** you hope to accomplish before next summer?

2. What community service project would you like to become **involved** in?

3. Where is your house **located**?

4. How would you **react** if someone suggested a community garden for your neighborhood?

Prize-winning flowers ▶

Word Study: Apostrophes

As you read the excerpt from *Seedfolks*, you will see words that include an apostrophe ('). Use an apostrophe to make a noun show possession or to take the place of missing letters, as in a contraction.

To show possession:

- Add ' + *s* to the end of a singular noun.
- Add an apostrophe (') to the end of a plural noun.

I found the **girl's plants**. [the plants that belong to the girl]
The **plants' leaves** were wilting. [the leaves of the plants]

A contraction is two words combined into one with an apostrophe. Use the apostrophe to take the place of a missing letter or letters.

I'd never entered the lot before.	[I + had = I'd]
There's a garden in the lot.	[there + is = there's]

Practice  Workbook Page 19

Work with a partner. Read aloud the phrases in the box below. Combine the words in each phrase to make contractions or possessive nouns. Then, in your notebook, write a sentence using those words.

can not	seeds of the beans	had not	father of the girl	it is

READING STRATEGY   VISUALIZE

When you visualize, you make pictures in your mind of what you are reading. To visualize, follow these steps:

- As you read, think about what the author wants you to see.
- Pay attention to descriptive words and figurative language.
- Stop from time to time and visualize the story's characters, setting, and events.

As you read *Seedfolks*, ask yourself, "What language is the author using to create a picture of the characters, setting and events?"

 Workbook Page 20

Set a purpose for reading As you read, pay attention to Kim's actions. How do they affect other characters in the story?

from

Seedfolks

Audio

Paul Fleischman

Kim

I stood before our family **altar**. It was dawn. No one else in the apartment was awake. I stared at my father's photograph—his thin face stern, lips latched tight, his eyes peering permanently to the right. I was nine years old and still hoped that perhaps his eyes might move. Might notice me.

The candles and incense sticks, lit the day before to mark his death anniversary, had burned out. The rice and meat offered him were gone. After the evening feast, past midnight, I'd been wakened by my mother's crying. My oldest sister had joined in. My own tears had then come as well, but for a different reason.

I turned from the altar, tiptoed to the kitchen, and quietly drew a spoon from a drawer. I filled my lunch **thermos** with water and reached into our jar of dried lima beans. Then I walked outside to the street.

The sidewalk was completely empty. It was Sunday, early in April. An icy wind teetered trash cans and turned my cheeks to **marble**. In Vietnam we had no weather like that. Here in Cleveland people call it spring. I walked half a block, then crossed the street and reached the **vacant** lot.

I stood tall and **scouted**. No one was sleeping on the old couch in the middle. I'd never entered the lot before, or wanted to. I did so now, picking my way between tires and trash bags. I nearly stepped on two rats **gnawing** and froze. Then I told myself that I must show my bravery. I continued farther and chose a spot far from the sidewalk and hidden from view by a rusty refrigerator. I had to keep my project safe.

---

altar, table used for religious purposes
thermos, container that keeps liquids warm or cold
marble, hard, smooth stone
vacant, empty
scouted, looked around
gnawing, biting or chewing on something continuously

I took out my spoon and began to dig. The snow had melted, but the ground was hard. After much work, I finished one hole, then a second, then a third. I thought about how my mother and sisters remembered my father, how they knew his face from every angle and held in their fingers the feel of his hands. I had no such memories to cry over. I'd been born eight months after he'd died. Worse, he had no memories of me. When his spirit **hovered** over our altar, did it even know who I was?

I dug six holes. All his life in Vietnam my father had been a farmer. Here our apartment house had no yard. But in that vacant lot he would see me. He would watch my beans break ground and spread, and would notice with pleasure their pods growing plump. He would see my **patience** and my hard work. I would show him that I could raise plants, as he had. I would show him that I was his daughter.

My class had sprouted lima beans in paper cups the year before. I now placed a bean in each of the holes. I covered them up, pressing the soil down firmly with my fingertips. I opened my thermos and watered them all. And I **vowed** to myself that those beans would **thrive**.

---

hovered, floated in the air
patience, willingness to wait
vowed, made a promise
thrive, live well

BEFORE YOU GO ON

1 What kind of seeds did Kim plant?

2 Where did Kim plant her seeds? Describe the area where her garden was **located**.

💡 **On Your Own**
Have you ever planted seeds before? If so, what kind and why?

Reading 3 **39**

Wendell

My phone doesn't ring much, which suits me fine. That's how I got the news about our boy, shot dead like a dog in the street. And the word last year about my wife's car wreck. I can't hear a phone and not jerk inside. When Ana called I was still asleep. Phone calls that wake me up are the worst.

"Get up here quick!" she says. I live on the ground floor and watch out for her a little. We're the only white people left in the building. I ran up the stairs. I could tell it was serious. I prayed I wouldn't find her dead. When I got there, she looked perfectly fine. She dragged me over to the window. "Look down there!" she says. "They're dying!"

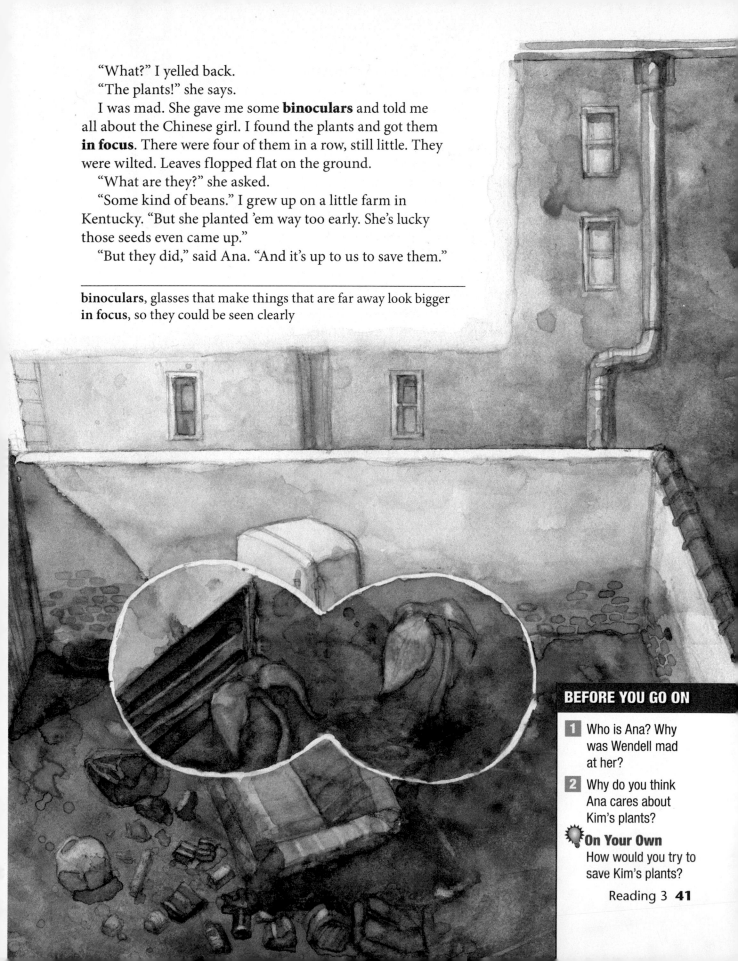

"What?" I yelled back.

"The plants!" she says.

I was mad. She gave me some **binoculars** and told me all about the Chinese girl. I found the plants and got them **in focus**. There were four of them in a row, still little. They were wilted. Leaves flopped flat on the ground.

"What are they?" she asked.

"Some kind of beans." I grew up on a little farm in Kentucky. "But she planted 'em way too early. She's lucky those seeds even came up."

"But they did," said Ana. "And it's up to us to save them."

---

binoculars, glasses that make things that are far away look bigger
in focus, so they could be seen clearly

BEFORE YOU GO ON

1 Who is Ana? Why was Wendell mad at her?

2 Why do you think Ana cares about Kim's plants?

On Your Own
How would you try to save Kim's plants?

Reading 3 **41**

It was a weekend in May and hot. You'd have thought that those beans were hers. They needed water, especially in that heat. She said the girl hadn't come in four days—sick, probably, or gone out of town. Ana had twisted her ankle and couldn't manage the stairs. She pointed to a **pitcher**. "Fill that up and soak them good. Quick now."

School janitors take too much bossing all week to listen to an extra helping on weekends. I stared at her one long moment, then took my time about filling the pitcher.

I walked down the stairs and into the lot and found the girl's plants. You don't plant beans till the weather's hot. Then I saw what had kept her seeds from freezing. The refrigerator in front of them had bounced the sunlight back on the soil, heating it up like an oven. I bent down and gave the dirt a feel. It was hard packed and light colored. I studied the plants. Leaves shaped like **spades** in a deck of cards. Definitely beans. I scraped up a ring of dirt around the first plant, to hold the water and any rain that fell. I picked up the pitcher and poured the water slowly. Then I heard something move and spun around. The girl was there, stone-still, ten feet away, holding her own water jar.

She hadn't seen me behind the refrigerator. She looked afraid for her life. Maybe she thought I'd jump up and grab her. I gave her a smile and showed her that I was just giving her plants some water. This made her eyes go even bigger. I stood up slowly and backed away. I smiled again. She watched me leave. We never spoke one word.

---

pitcher, container used to hold liquid
spades, symbols shaped like pointed leaves

I walked back there that evening and checked on the beans. They'd picked themselves up and were looking fine. I saw that she'd made a circle of dirt around the other three plants. Out of nowhere the words from the **Bible** came into my head: "And a little child shall lead them." I didn't know why at first. Then I did. There's plenty about my life I can't change. Can't bring the dead back to life on this earth. Can't make the world loving and kind. Can't change myself into a millionaire. But a patch of ground in this trashy lot—I *can* change that. Can change it big. Better to put my time into that than moaning about the other all day. That little girl showed me that.

The lot had buildings on three sides. I walked around and picked myself out a spot that wouldn't be shaded too much. I dragged the garbage off to the side and tossed out the biggest pieces of broken glass. I looked over my plot, squatted down, and fingered the soil awhile.

That Monday I brought a shovel home from work.

Bible, holy book of Christians

ABOUT THE **AUTHOR**

Paul Fleischman was born in Monterey, California, and grew up in Santa Monica. Today he lives in Aromas, California. Fleischman is the author of many books about music and natural history.

✔ **LITERARY CHECK**
Why is the setting especially important in this story?

BEFORE YOU GO ON

1 Why didn't Kim's seeds freeze in the cold weather?

2 What did Wendell realize after his encounter with Kim and her plants?

💡 **On Your Own**
What changes did you read about in this story?

► READER'S THEATER

Act out the following scene between Ana and Wendell.

Ana: [*impatiently*] It's about time you got up here!

Wendell: What's the problem? I was afraid you were sick.

Ana: Quick, come over to the window. Look down there. They're dying.

Wendell: What are you talking about? What's dying?

Ana: The plants. The plants! Here, take my binoculars.

Wendell: [*looking through the binoculars*] Okay, I see them. So what?

Ana: Do you know what kind of plants they are?

Wendell: They look like beans. I used to grow beans on my farm.

Ana: They don't look good, do they? What's wrong with them?

Wendell: They were planted way too early. I can't even believe they came up.

Ana: Well, they did. And now it's our job to save them.

Wendell: Our job? What are we going to do?

Ana: *You* are going to water those plants. I can't because I twisted my ankle. Now, take this pitcher—fill it up with water. Quickly!

► COMPREHENSION

Workbook
Page 21

Did you understand the story? If not, reread it with a partner. Then answer the questions below.

Recall

1. In what city does this story take place?

2. Where did Kim live before she moved to Cleveland?

Comprehend

3. Why did Kim plant lima beans? What was her **goal**?

4. How did the location of Kim's plants help them grow?

Analyze

5. How does the author want the reader to feel about Kim?
6. Why did Kim plant her seeds in the early morning hours?

Connect

7. Is there a community garden in your neighborhood? If so, describe it.
8. Describe a time in your life when you experienced a change. What was it? How did it make you feel?

Listening SKILL

If you can't hear the speaker, you may say, "Excuse me, could you speak louder, please?"

▶ DISCUSSION

Discuss in pairs or small groups.

1. Why do you think Ana **involved** herself in helping Kim and her plants?
2. What was Wendell's life like before he became involved in helping Kim's plants grow?
- **Q** **How can change improve people's lives?** Have you ever helped a stranger without being asked to do so? What did you do? How did you feel afterward? Do you think that small acts of kindness can change people's lives? If so, how?

▶ RESPONSE TO LITERATURE

Workbook Page 21

Utilize At the end of *Seedfolks*, Wendell decides to make a change in his life. How did Kim and her plants inspire this new beginning? What do you think this means for Wendell? What will he do? Write a paragraph that explains what you think Wendell will do and why. Trade papers with a partner and read each other's paragraphs aloud.

Grammar

Comparison Structures: Adjectives

To compare people or things, you can use comparison structures such as comparative and superlative adjectives. A comparative adjective compares two things. A superlative adjective compares one thing in a group to two or more things in that group. Form comparative adjectives with *-er* or *more*; form superlative adjectives with *-est* or *most*. Comparative and superlative adjectives can come after a linking verb or before the noun they modify.

> These flowers are **more beautiful than** those. [after linking verb *are*]
> It's **the most beautiful** flower I've seen. [before noun *flower*]

A comparative adjective is usually followed by *than*, but if the comparison is understood, *than* is often omitted. A superlative adjective is usually preceded by *the*. Possessive pronouns can also precede superlatives.

> The garden is **dryer than** last year.
> I am **younger** (than she is).
> I tossed out **the biggest** pieces of broken glass.
> **My oldest** sister joined in.

Practice  Workbook Page 22

Work with a partner. Copy the sentences into your notebook. Then complete each sentence with the correct form of the adjective in parentheses.

Example: Oranges are _sweeter_ (sweet) than lemons.

1. The black cat is _____ (friendly) than the white cat.
2. This car is _____ (good) than my last one.
3. This exercise is the _____ (easy) one I've ever done.
4. Peg is the _____ (interesting) person I know.
5. My cousin is a _____ (fast) driver than I am.

Apply

Work with a partner. In your notebook, write down some adjectives to describe a person or thing. Then describe this person or thing to your partner, using comparative and superlative adjectives.

Example: smart *"My father is the smartest person I know."*

Grammar SKILL

Remember that there are spelling changes when you make comparative and superlative adjectives. Also, some adjectives have irregular comparative and superlative forms, for example, *good / better / best.*

STRENGTHEN YOUR SOCIAL LANGUAGE

Making comparisons means communicating well. Go to www.LongmanKeystone.com and do the activity for this unit. This activity will help you use specific learning strategies to acquire basic vocabulary words necessary for describing people and objects.

Comparison Structures: Adverbs

To compare two actions, you can use comparison structures such as comparative and superlative adverbs. For one-syllable adverbs, use *-er* and *-est*. For two- or more syllable adverbs, plus adverbs that end in *-ly*, use *more* and *most*. Some adverbs have irregular comparative and superlative forms.

Grammar SKILL

Some words are both adjectives and adverbs, for example, *early / earlier / earliest* and *hard / harder / hardest*.

fast → faster → fastest	She ran **faster** than last time, but I ran **the fastest**.
deeply → more deeply → most deeply	I planted the beans **more deeply** in the ground. Of all her sisters, she felt his death **the most deeply**.
well → better → best	I knew **better than** to plant that early. She gardened **the best** when she was alone.
badly → worse → worst	She felt **worse than** ever. It was **the worst** she'd ever felt.
far → farther/further → farthest/furthest	I continued **farther** and chose a spot far from the sidewalk. I had traveled **the furthest** I'd ever traveled before.

Practice

Workbook Page 23

Work with a partner. Copy the sentences below into your notebook. Then complete each sentence with the correct form of the adverb in parentheses.

Example: He works *more quickly* (quick) than she does.

1. You can get to New York _____ (fast) by plane than by train.
2. He studies _____ (good) with music playing.
3. I drive _____ (carefully) than I used to.
4. Rick **reacted** _____ (bad) of everyone I know.
5. Martin speaks _____ (fluently) than he did before.

✔ GRAMMAR CHECK

When forming a **superlative adverb,** *when do you use* most?

Apply

Work with a partner. Tell him or her about something you can do well now that you couldn't in the past. Use comparative and superlative adverbs.

Example: *I speak English better now than I did last year.*

Writing

Ongoing Writing Skills Practice

Describe a Place

In this unit, you have learned how to describe an event and an object. Now you will learn how to describe a place. One way to write a description of a place is to present the details in spatial order, or in order of location. For example, to describe your classroom, you might start at the back of the room and make your way toward the front, describing all the important features along the way. Words such as *inside, outside, on top of, underneath,* or *next to* can tell readers the position of people or things.

> **Writing Prompt**
>
> Write a paragraph describing a place you are familiar with, such as a room in your home, a park, or your neighborhood. List your details in a graphic organizer. Present them in spatial order. Be sure to include comparison structures such as comparative and superlative adjectives.

1 **PREWRITE** Begin by choosing the place you wish to describe.

- Close your eyes and try to visualize the place in your mind's eye.

- First, get a picture of the whole scene.

- Then look carefully at each part of the place: the back, the middle, and the front.

- List your ideas in a graphic organizer like the one below.

 **Workbook Page 24**

Here's a three-column chart created by a student named Nicole.

The Garden		
Back	Middle	Front
corn stalks	tomatoes, eggplants	squash, carrots

2 **DRAFT** Use your graphic organizer to help you write a first draft.

- Give an overview of the scene.
- Describe the specific details of the place in spatial order.
- Keep in mind your purpose for writing.

3 **REVISE** Read over your draft. Look for places where the writing is unclear or needs improvement. Use the Writing Checklist to help you identify problems. Then revise your draft, using the editing and proofreading marks listed on page 458.

4 **EDIT** Check your work for errors in grammar, usage, mechanics, and spelling. Trade papers with a partner to obtain feedback. Use the Peer Review Checklist on Workbook page 24. Edit your final draft in response to feedback from your partner and your teacher.

5 **PUBLISH** Prepare a clean copy of your final draft. Share your description with the class. Save your work. You'll need to refer to it in the Writing Workshop at the end of the unit.

Here is Nicole's description. What does it tell us about her family?

Writing Checklist

ORGANIZATION:
☑ I presented details in spatial order.

WORD CHOICE:
☑ I used comparison structures such as comparative and superlative adjectives correctly.

Nicole Siley

The Garden

As I walked outside, I noticed my grandparents' garden. Looking at it, the first thing I noticed were the beautiful colors—red, yellow, purple, green, and orange. Then I noticed how the vegetables were arranged from back to front according to the size of the plants. In the far back, there were corn stalks, the tallest plants in the garden. Next, there were the biggest tomato plants I had ever seen. They sat in the middle of the garden with the eggplants. My favorite vegetables, the squash and the carrots, were in the front rows. Looking at these vegetables made me remember all the wonderful Sunday night dinners I've shared with my family. I never imagined that looking at vegetables could trigger such pleasant memories.

Prepare to Read

What You Will Learn

Reading
- Vocabulary building: *Context, dictionary skills, word study*
- Reading strategy: *Preview*
- Text type: *Informational text (social studies)*

Grammar
Order of adjectives; Compound adjectives

Writing
Describe a group of people

THE BIG QUESTION

How can change improve people's lives? People play sports for many different reasons. Sometimes they just enjoy playing the game—it's fun, and great exercise. Professional players take sports very seriously because it is their career. Whatever the reason, sports can change people's lives for the better. In team sports such as basketball, baseball, and soccer, players must learn to work together to be successful and win.

Work with a partner. Think about sports you have played. What did you most like about the game? Did learning to play a game change your life in some way? If so, how?

BUILD BACKGROUND

"From Refugees to Fugees" is a social studies article about how soccer changed the lives of one group of very special boys. The boys were refugees from war-torn countries such as Sudan, Bosnia, and Afghanistan who immigrated to the United States with their families. Since 1980, more than 2.5 million refugees from more than 66 countries have settled here. Many of these refugees are young people. They often don't speak English and have little education. They must learn a new language, understand new customs, and make new friends.

Though the boys in the article you will read came from different countries, they had two things in common: a past they wanted to forget and a love of soccer. One woman, a soccer coach, brought the boys together to form a team called the Fugees. It was a new beginning for these brave boys.

▼ The Fugees soccer team

► VOCABULARY

Listening and Speaking: Key Words

Read these sentences aloud with a partner. Use the context to figure out the meaning of the highlighted words. Use a dictionary to check your answers. Then write each word and its meaning in your notebook.

Key Words

athletes
boundaries
professional
responsibilities
sacrifice
uniforms

Audio

1. Each team has many fine athletes. These players are good at sports.

2. The coach marked the field's boundaries with chalk. The players can't kick the ball outside of these lines.

3. Professional players get paid for being on a team. It is their job.

4. The players have many responsibilities. There are many things that they must do.

Audio

5. Players sacrifice things in order to have time to practice. They give up TV, or school clubs, or time with friends.

6. You can tell the teams apart by the color of their uniforms. Each team wears a different outfit.

Practice  **Workbook Page 25**

Write the sentences in your notebook. Choose a word from the box above to complete each sentence. Then take turns reading the sentences aloud with a partner.

1. There are many _____ baseball players. They are paid to play ball.

2. The team's new _____ are blue and white. They have the players' names and numbers on the back.

3. The sports team has five new _____ who all play soccer well.

4. Players often must _____ sleeping late on weekend mornings.

5. Luisa has many _____ as the team captain. There are many things she must do.

6. The _____ of the playing field are clearly marked.

▲ Professional soccer player Mia Hamm goes for the ball at the Olympics, 2004.

Listening and Speaking: Academic Words

Study the **red** words and their meanings. You will find these words useful when talking and writing about informational texts. Write each word and its meaning in your notebook, then say the words aloud with a partner. After you read "From Refugees to Fugees" try to use these words to respond to the text.

Academic Words

element
focus
positive
require

Audio

element = one part of a plan, system, piece of writing, and so on	→	Teamwork is an important **element** in baseball, soccer, and football.
focus = give all your attention to a particular person or thing	→	Baseball players must **focus** on the ball at all times.
positive = good or useful	→	Team sports can have a **positive** effect. Players learn to help one another.
require = need something	→	The team will **require** new uniforms. Their old ones are torn.

Audio

Practice

Workbook Page 26 ▶

Work with a partner to answer these questions. Try to include the **red** word in your answer. Write the sentences in your notebook.

1. What is the most important **element** that makes a team successful?

2. What do you **focus** on when you watch a baseball game?

3. Why is playing sports a **positive** experience?

4. What items do tennis players **require**?

Soccer players must focus on the ball. ▶

Word Study: Spelling Long *a* and Long *e*

The text you are going to read contains words with long vowel sounds, such as *a* (change) and *e* (see). There are different ways to spell each of these sounds. Look at the chart below.

Long *a*		Long *e*	
Spelling	Examples	Spelling	Examples
a	danger	e	b**e**gan
a_e	g**a**m**e**	ee	refug**ee**
ai	tr**ai**ning	ea	t**ea**m
ay	pl**ay**ers	eo	p**eo**ple
ea	gr**ea**t	y	bod**y**

Practice  Workbook Page 27

Work with a partner. Copy the chart below into your notebook. Take turns reading the words in the box. Then write each word in the correct chart column. Circle the letters that stand for the long *a* and long *e* sounds.

arrange	east	trains	flurry
crayon	remember	feet	lake

Long *a*		Long *e*	

READING STRATEGY | PREVIEW

Previewing a text helps you understand the content more quickly. To preview, follow these steps:

- Look at the title and headings.
- Look at the visuals and read the captions or labels.
- Think about your purpose for reading the text.
- Read the first and last sentences of each paragraph.

Before you read "From Refugees to Fugees," think about what you already know about this subject. What more would you like to know?

 Workbook Page 28

Set a purpose for reading How did the game of soccer change the lives of a special group of boys?

From Refugees to Fugees

Audio

Jane Schwartz

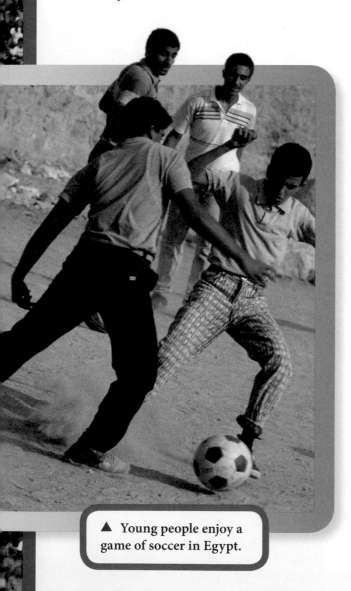

▲ Young people enjoy a game of soccer in Egypt.

Americans call the game *soccer*. The British, and almost everyone else in the world, call it *football*. Under either name, soccer has become the most popular sport in the world. It is played almost everywhere. More than 200 countries have national professional teams. Every four years, more people watch the final game of the World Cup **tournament** on TV than any other sporting event.

The Simplest Sport

Soccer is often called "the simplest sport." That's probably one reason for its wide appeal. It requires very little **equipment**. You don't use bats, racquets, clubs, paddles, or sticks. You don't wear gloves, mitts, helmets, or **goggles**. You don't need skis, sleds, anything that floats, or anything with an engine in it. All you need is a round ball and some space. Even the youngest kids in the poorest parts of the world can usually put together those two things.

There is an old saying: "**Necessity** is the mother of invention." This means that if people need something, they will find a way to invent it. The rules of soccer took away the use of the players' hands. This forced soccer players to "invent" new ways to use their feet. Soccer players don't just *pass* the ball with their feet.

Reading Skill

To help you understand the reading, study the title and headings. This will help you identify the most important ideas.

---

tournament, sports competition
equipment, things needed for a
    particular activity
goggles, special glasses that protect the eyes
necessity, being in need

They *protect* it, *block* it, and *steal* it from their opponents. Their footwork is so fast and so skillful that sometimes it's hard to follow without replaying the action in slow motion. In addition, players often **dazzle** audiences with leaping kicks that are as awesome as the flying dunks of professional basketball players.

A Little History

No one knows exactly where or when soccer began. Written records from 2,000 years ago in China describe games in which a ball was kicked into a goal. Other records have been found in Japan, Greece, and Italy.

The modern game of soccer was developed from the eighth to the nineteenth century in England. In 1863, a formal set of rules was adopted. Other countries accepted these rules, and soon international matches were held. At this time, Great Britain ruled colonies all over the world, and British **traders**, soldiers, and sailors introduced the game to many parts of Asia, Africa, and the Americas.

The *Fédération Internationale de Football Association* (FIFA) was formed in 1904. It is still the governing body of the sport. By 1930, there were professional football leagues in many countries. The first World

▲ The Fugees soccer team

Cup tournament was held in Uruguay in 1930. It has been held every four years since then.

A Big Boom

Today, about 20 million people in the United States play soccer, and about 80% of players are under the age of 18. It is the fastest growing team sport in the country.

The wave of immigrants to the United States in the last ten to fifteen years has been a big part of the soccer boom. These newcomers have arrived from Central and South America, Africa, and parts of Asia. Many have come from countries torn

---

dazzle, amaze with an inspiring display
traders, people who buy and sell goods

◄ Pele was one of the best soccer players of all time.

BEFORE YOU GO ON

1 What two things do you need to play soccer?

2 About how many people play soccer in the U.S. today? How many are young people?

On Your Own
Have you ever invented something out of necessity?

Reading 4 **55**

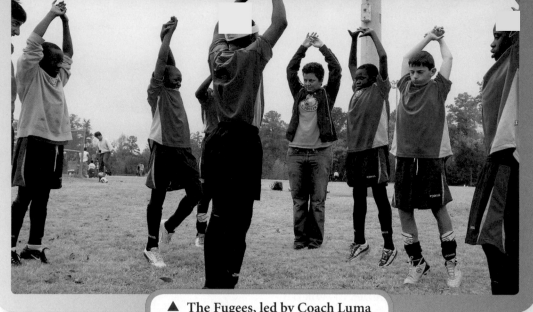

▲ The Fugees, led by Coach Luma Mufleh, stretch before a game.

apart by war, poverty, and natural disasters. Soccer is important to people already in the United States, but it has an even deeper meaning to many recent refugees. For them, soccer can sometimes be a **lifeline**.

Something Bigger Than Winning

In 2004, a soccer team was organized in Clarkston, Georgia, a small town outside of Atlanta. Over 60,000 refugees have resettled in Georgia since 1981. It is made up entirely of refugees. The team called itself the Fugees (as in re**fugees**). The players are all in this country legally, brought by a **resettlement agency** because of housing and low-paying jobs nearby.

The reporter Warren St. John wrote about the Fugees in the *New York Times*. The boys, all between eight and thirteen, have come from Sudan, Somalia, Bosnia, Iraq, Afghanistan, Burma, Cuba, Congo,

and Eritrea. Some lived for years in refugee camps. Some have been separated from their families. Some watched their loved ones taken away to prison. One boy saw his father murdered in their home. They have been through a lot in their young lives.

One day a young coach named Luma Mufleh put up a sign announcing **tryouts** for a soccer team. The team was to be for refugees only, and she was going to be the coach. Those who made the team had to sign a contract accepting certain responsibilities on and off the field. They were going to have to work really hard and sacrifice their free time, but they would have the chance to do something they loved. Before they played their first game, the boys had already "won" several important things: respect, a group they could belong to, and the chance to do really well at something.

---

lifeline, something that someone depends on completely
resettlement agency, organization that helps refugees adjust to life in the United States

tryouts, times when people who want to be on a sports team are tested so that the best can be chosen

The season wasn't perfect. The Fugees did not win every game. The **tragedies** they had experienced in the past did not suddenly disappear. But other teams admired the way the Fugees played. Parents from the **wealthier** teams helped the Fugees buy balls, uniforms, and **cleated shoes**. The boys on the team learned to work together. They had come from different countries, but they all shared a love of soccer. They got to know one another through the sport, and the sport is helping them all to **bridge the gap** from their old world to their new one.

In 2006, Luma Mufleh started a **nonprofit** organization called the Fugees Family. The organization provides soccer for 86 boys age 10 to 18, as well as after-school tutoring and an academic

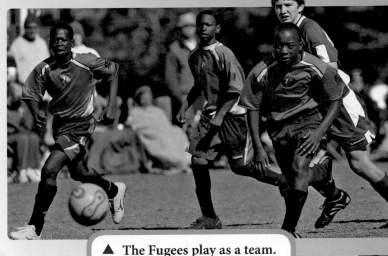

▲ The Fugees play as a team.

camp. The Fugees Family focuses on helping young survivors of war heal from **traumatic** past experiences. Their goal is to ensure young refugees have the same opportunities as other young athletes and to provide the skills required to graduate from high school, go to college or job training, and lead successful, positive lives.

Throughout U.S. cities and towns soccer is working its magic. It may be "the simplest game," but soccer can have a powerful effect on people's lives. No other sport crosses over so many cultural, racial, and ethnic boundaries as soccer.

---

tragedies, events that cause a lot of sadness
wealthier, richer, having more money
cleated shoes, sneakers that have short pieces of rubber, plastic, or metal attached to the bottom of them, in order to prevent someone from slipping
bridge the gap, reduce or get rid of the difference between two things
nonprofit, not money-making

---

traumatic, very difficult and upsetting

ABOUT THE **AUTHOR**

Jane Schwartz writes on many subjects and in many different genres. She is best known for *Ruffian: Burning from the Start*, a nonfiction book about a famous racehorse who suffered a fatal injury. She has also written *Caught*, a novel about a young girl growing up in Brooklyn during the 1950s, and *Grammar Power*, a humorous grammar book. In addition, she writes articles for the *New York Times* and *Sports Illustrated*, and she writes poetry. When she is not busy writing, Schwartz loves to travel.

BEFORE YOU GO ON

1 Who is Luma Mufleh and what did she do?

2 What is the goal of the Fugees Family?

On Your Own
Why do you think soccer is significant for many recent refugees?

Reading 4 **57**

Review and Practice

► **COMPREHENSION**  Workbook
Page 29

Recall

1. Why is the team called the Fugees?
2. What countries do the members of the Fugees come from?

Comprehend

3. Why is soccer called "the simplest sport"?
4. What helped cause the soccer boom in the United States?

Analyze

5. How is soccer different from baseball, or basketball, or tennis?
6. What is the author's attitude toward the Fugees? How can you tell?

Connect

7. If you could meet the Fugees, what would you say?
8. What is your favorite sport? Why do you like to play or watch it?

► **IN YOUR OWN WORDS**

Writers of informational texts often use clues to help readers follow the main idea. Section headings, or subheadings, are helpful clues. Imagine that you are telling a partner about "From Refugees to Fugees." Use the subheadings to help you identify the main idea of each section. Complete the chart below to help you organize your ideas. Then share your summary with a classmate. See how they compare.

🔊 *Speaking* TIP

Use notes and pictures to help you remember and explain the main ideas clearly.

Part of the Text	Summary of Main Ideas
Introduction (no subheading)	Soccer/Football is the most popular sport in the world.
The Simplest Sport	
A Little History	
A Big Boom	
Something Bigger Than Winning	

► DISCUSSION

Discuss in pairs or small groups.

▲ Fans celebrate after a win during the World Cup.

1. What is the history of soccer?

2. How do sports bring different kinds of people together?

3. What does the expression "It's not whether you win or lose, it's how you play the game" mean to you?

Q **How can change improve people's lives?** In what ways does moving to the United States improve the lives of refugees?

Listening SKILL

Listen carefully to other people's ideas.

► READ FOR FLUENCY

Reading with feeling helps make what you read more interesting. Work with a partner. Choose a paragraph from the reading. Read the paragraph. Ask each other how you felt after reading the paragraph. Did you feel happy or sad?

Take turns reading the paragraph aloud to each other with a tone of voice that represents how you felt when you read it the first time. Give each other feedback.

► EXTENSION

Learn more about a member of the Fugees or about a famous soccer star. Choose a player. Use magazine stories, newspaper articles, and websites to find information. Copy and complete the following chart to organize your ideas. Share your findings with the class.

Player	Team	Country of Birth	Important Games	Outstanding Skills

Grammar

Order of Adjectives

Adjectives describe nouns. A phrase that uses more than one adjective to describe a noun is called an adjectival phrase. Most adjectival phrases come before the noun they describe. There are different categories of adjectives, which describe different qualities. When you use an adjectival phrase before a noun, place the adjectives in the order shown in the chart below.

Grammar SKILL

When a noun is used to describe another noun, it functions as an adjective, for example, **toy** store, **paper** doll.

Determiner	Opinion	Size	Age	Shape	Color	Origin	Material	Purpose	NOUN
a few	smart		young			local			players
the		small				Sudanese		support	group
some		big		round	white		plastic	soccer	balls

When you use adjectives from the same category, separate the adjectives with commas.

> The refugees want to have **successful, positive** lives. [both *opinions*]

Practice

Workbook
Page 30

Work with a partner. Copy the sentences into your notebook, putting the adjectives in parentheses in the correct order. Use commas where necessary.

✔ **GRAMMAR CHECK**
When do you use commas within adjectival phrases?

Example: Jane is wearing *a pretty black wool* (wool, a, black, pretty) skirt.

1. I just bought _____ (new, several, interesting) books to read.
2. Ann ate _____ (delicious, huge, a) plate of mussels.
3. Gene likes _____ (old, his, lovely, charming) house.
4. Barb finished _____ (colorful, tiny, a) painting.
5. Rob is going to stay in _____ (mountain, quiet, a, relaxing) cabin.

Apply

Write five sentences using adjectival phrases about some of the pictures in your textbook. Then read your sentences to a partner.

Example: There is a nervous young Asian girl on page 98.

Compound Adjectives

A compound adjective is formed when two or more words work together to modify the same noun. The first word modifies the second, and the two together modify the noun. Some common compound adjectives are written as one word, but those that are less common are hyphenated.

> The children had come from **war-torn** countries.
> The story of the Fugees is much better than any **make-believe** story.

When more than one adjective modifies a noun separately, it is not a compound adjective. If you can use one of the adjectives alone to modify the noun, do not use a hyphen.

> **Correct:** A large **immigrant** community lives in Atlanta.
> **Incorrect:** A large-immigrant community lives in Atlanta.

Do not use a hyphen to combine an adverb and an adjective. The adverb modifies the adjective, and the adjective modifies the noun.

> **Correct:** The **incredibly lucky** boy won the prize.
> **Incorrect:** The incredibly-lucky boy won the prize.

Grammar **SKILL**

Remember that an adverb modifies a verb, an adjective, or another adverb. Adverbs often end in *-ly*, but not always.

Practice  **Workbook Page 31**

Work with a partner. Copy the sentence starters on the left into your notebook. Complete them with the phrase containing the compound adjective on the right.

Example: *The mountain goat is a sure-footed animal.*

The mountain goat is	a ten-dollar bill.
1. Don't go the wrong way down	the northwest part of town.
2. Last night we watched	a middle-aged man.
3. My friend gave me	a three-hour movie.
4. Our teacher is	a one-way street.
5. She lives in	a sure-footed animal.

Apply

Work with a partner. Find three more compound adjectives in the reading. Write sentences with them in your notebook.

Writing

Ongoing
Writing
Skills
Practice

Describe a Group of People

At the end of this unit, you will write a descriptive essay. To do this, you will need to learn some of the skills writers use to describe people, places, and things. To describe a group of people, writers include details and adjectives to describe the group's traits, or characteristics, such as their values, relationships, customs, and/or activities.

> **Writing Prompt**
>
> Write a descriptive paragraph about a group of people. Be sure to use compound adjectives correctly, and put adjectives in the correct order.

1 **PREWRITE** Begin by choosing a group of people to describe.

- Ask yourself what is special and interesting about this group of people.

- Think about their appearance, their homes, their crafts, and their traditions.

- List your ideas in a graphic organizer like the one below.

Workbook
Page 32

Here's a T-chart created by a student named Katie. She used the T-chart to list traits that describe the Cherokee people.

Group Cherokee	
Trait	Example
good builders	constructed houses of river cane and plaster built larger seven-sided buildings for ceremonies
created wonderful artwork	made beautiful baskets out of river cane carved wooden masks for ceremonies and battles

2 **DRAFT** Use your organizer to help you write a first draft.

- Keep in mind your purpose for writing.
- Remember to include details to describe the special characteristics of the people.
- Use adjectives to make your description clear and vivid.

3 **REVISE** Read over your draft. Look for places where the writing is unclear or needs improvement. Use the Writing Checklist to help you identify problems. Then revise your draft, using the editing and proofreading marks listed on page 458.

4 **EDIT** Check your work for errors in grammar, usage, mechanics, and spelling. Trade papers with a partner to obtain feedback. Use the Peer Review Checklist on Workbook page 32. Edit your final draft in response to feedback from your partner and your teacher.

5 **PUBLISH** Prepare a clean copy of your final draft. Share your description with the class. Save your work. You'll need to refer to it in the Writing Workshop at the end of the unit.

Here is Katie's description. Notice her use of details and adjectives.

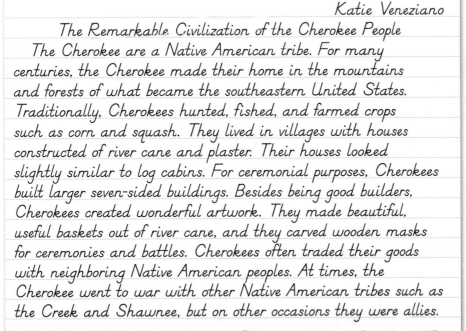

Katie Veneziano

The Remarkable Civilization of the Cherokee People

The Cherokee are a Native American tribe. For many centuries, the Cherokee made their home in the mountains and forests of what became the southeastern United States. Traditionally, Cherokees hunted, fished, and farmed crops such as corn and squash. They lived in villages with houses constructed of river cane and plaster. Their houses looked slightly similar to log cabins. For ceremonial purposes, Cherokees built larger seven-sided buildings. Besides being good builders, Cherokees created wonderful artwork. They made beautiful, useful baskets out of river cane, and they carved wooden masks for ceremonies and battles. Cherokees often traded their goods with neighboring Native American peoples. At times, the Cherokee went to war with other Native American tribes such as the Creek and Shawnee, but on other occasions they were allies.

Writing Checklist

IDEAS:
☑ I described a group's characteristics.

WORD CHOICE:
☑ I used details and adjectives to support and develop my description.

CONVENTIONS:
☑ I used compound adjectives correctly, and put adjectives in the correct order.

Link the Readings

Critical Thinking

Look back at the readings in this unit. Think about what they have in common. They all tell about changes. Yet they do not all have the same purpose. The purpose of one reading might be to inform, while the purpose of another might be to entertain or persuade. In addition, the content of each reading relates to changes differently. Now copy the chart below into your notebook and complete it.

Title of Reading	Purpose	Big Question Link
From *Riding Freedom*		*It describes the first American woman to vote in a presidential election.*
"Early Inventions"		
From *Seedfolks*		
"From Refugees to Fugees"	*to inform*	

Discussion

Discuss in pairs or small groups.

- How is Charlotte in *Riding Freedom* similar to the inventors in "Early Inventions"?

- Q **How can change improve people's lives?** Compare and contrast the ways in which each of the readings in this unit describes change. Think critically about the people in the readings. How were their lives improved by the changes they experienced? Does change always improve people's lives? Explain.

Media Literacy & Projects

Work in pairs or small groups. Choose one of these projects.

1 American women called suffragettes began to fight for the right to vote in the 1820s. They were rewarded for their work in 1920, when women won the right to vote. Use the Internet to research a suffragette and how her actions helped women. Share your results with the class.

2 Think of an invention that you would like to create. Illustrate your invention, showing how it works and what it does. Include descriptive labels and captions. Then refer to your visual(s) as you share your ideas with a partner.

3 Create a community garden. Map out an area on a piece of posterboard. Draw and label the plants you want to include in your garden. Then take your classmates on a "tour," describing each plant as you do so.

Further Reading

Choose from these reading suggestions. Practice reading silently with increased ease for longer and longer periods.

Inventions that Changed the World, David Maule
This Penguin Reader® looks at some of the most important inventions from ancient times to the present day. Topics include printing, mathematics, navigation, weapons, flight, communications, and computers.

Give Me Liberty: The Story of the Declaration of Independence, Russell Freedman
The author describes the events before, during, and after the American Revolution. We get to know the people whose views helped shape a new nation and to understand the significance of the Declaration of Independence, both then and now.

The Story of Thomas Alva Edison, Margaret Cousins
Here is the life story of the man who brought us the phonograph, motion pictures, and the electric light bulb—revolutionary inventions that forever changed the way we live.

Put It All Together

Team Presentation

You will give a team presentation describing a person, place, object, or experience that has changed your school or community for the better.

1 **THINK ABOUT IT** Look back over the readings in this unit. Talk in teams about change. Think of changes that have occurred in your school or community recently.

Work together to develop a list of beneficial changes that have taken place, for example:

- The new hire of an inspirational teacher
- A new community center
- The purchase of new school equipment
- The development of a new recycling plan

2 **GATHER AND ORGANIZE INFORMATION** As a team, choose a topic from your list. Then write down everything you know about that topic. Include any questions you have about it.

Research Use the library and/or the Internet to get more information. You may also wish to interview school or community leaders or fellow students. Remember to use appropriate language during your interview. If you are speaking to a person you have not met before or the interview occurs in a serious setting, use formal language. Formal language includes complete sentences, correct grammar, and few contractions. If you are speaking to someone you know well, use informal language. Informal language includes more conversational words, simple phrases and sentences, and contractions. Take notes on what you find.

Order Your Notes Share your notes with the team. Discuss which sensory details could be used within the presentation to create a picture in the minds of the audience members. Write them in a graphic organizer, such as a word web. Choose a logical order in which to present this information.

Use Visuals Make or use existing visual aids such as photos, maps, and illustrations to enhance your presentation. Make sure they are large enough for audience members to see easily.

3 **PRACTICE AND PRESENT** Keep your graphic organizer nearby as you practice your presentation as a group. Speak clearly and confidently, and use your visual aids to support key ideas. Make sure each team member has a part, and work on making smooth transitions from one speaker to the next. Keep practicing until you no longer need to look at your graphic organizer.

Deliver Your Group Presentation Look at your audience as you speak. Emphasize key ideas by pointing to your visual aids. Slow down when you come to the most important points, or restate them at the end of your presentation.

4 **EVALUATE THE PRESENTATION**
You will improve your skills as a speaker and a listener by evaluating each group presentation you give and hear. Use this checklist to help you judge your group's presentation and the group presentations of others.

- ☑ Was the team's topic clear?
- ☑ Did the speakers use sensory details to help listeners create a picture in their minds?
- ☑ Could you hear and understand each speaker easily?
- ☑ Were the transitions between speakers smooth and logical?
- ☑ What suggestions do you have for improving the team presentation?

 Speaking SKILL

Learning Strategy: Request assistance. Ask a friend or classmate to listen and give feedback as your team practices. Or record your rehearsal, if possible. Listen to the recording together, and find places where you can improve your presentation.

 Listening SKILLS

As you listen, identify the team's topic. Listen for the general meaning, main ideas, and important details. After each presentation, exchange this information with a partner to confirm that you have understood it correctly.

Take notes as you listen. Write down key details, and use them to picture what the speakers are describing.

 STRENGTHEN YOUR SOCIAL LANGUAGE

Describing a process means communicating well. Go to www. LongmanKeystone.com and do the activity for this unit. This activity will help you expand your vocabulary using high-frequency English words necessary for identifying and describing people, places, objects, and processes.

WRITING WORKSHOP

Descriptive Essay

Write a Descriptive Essay

In this workshop, you will write a descriptive essay. An essay is a group of paragraphs that focus on one topic. Most essays begin with a paragraph that introduces the topic. Two or more body paragraphs develop the topic by adding ideas and details. A concluding paragraph sums up what the essay is about.

> **Writing Prompt**
>
> Write a five-paragraph descriptive essay about an experience or change in your life that had a big effect on you. Describe the places, people, and events surrounding this experience. Include adjectives and sensory details that appeal to the senses and will help the reader understand your experience. Use sequence words to show what happened and how you changed after this experience.

1 **PREWRITE** Review your previous work in this unit. Now brainstorm ideas. What experiences had an impact on your life, feelings, or ideas? You might write about meeting a new friend, moving to a new place, or trying a new activity. Choose an experience that you can describe clearly and vividly.

Ongoing Writing Skills Practice

In your notebook, answer these questions:

- What was the main experience?

- What were the details?

- What effect did this experience have on me?  **Workbook** Page 33

After selecting a topic, use a graphic organizer such as a word web or a sequence of events chart to develop your essay. A student named Nicole wrote about going to middle school. She used a word web to gather ideas and details for her essay.

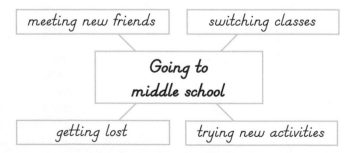

2 **DRAFT** Use your graphic organizer and the model on pages 71–72 to help you write a first draft

- Include an introductory paragraph, three body paragraphs, and a concluding paragraph.

- Use sequence words to show chronological development.

- Describe your feelings and explain how they changed.

3 **REVISE** Read over your draft. Think about how well you have addressed questions of purpose, audience, and genre. Your purpose is to describe. Is your description vivid? Does it help the reader to imagine your experience?

Keep these questions in mind as you revise your draft. Use the Writing Checklist below to help you identify additional issues that may need revision. Mark your changes on your draft using the editing and proofreading marks listed on page 458.

SIX TRAITS OF WRITING CHECKLIST

☑ **IDEAS:** Does my essay describe an experience that had an important effect on me?

☑ **ORGANIZATION:** Are my ideas organized logically?

☑ **VOICE:** Does my writing express who I am?

☑ **WORD CHOICE:** Do I use words that describe events and feelings?

☑ **SENTENCE FLUENCY:** Do my sentences flow smoothly?

☑ **CONVENTIONS:** Does my writing follow the rules of grammar, usage, and mechanics?

LEARNING STRATEGY

Monitor your written language production. Using a writing checklist will help you assess your work. Evaluate your essay to make sure that your message is clear and easy to understand.

Here are the revisions Nicole plans to make to her first draft.

A Big Step

In my town, three elementary schools ~~go~~ [combine] into one middle school. I used to think my elementary school was the larg~~er~~[est] school in town, with the most students. [Now] I realize that the middle school is so much larger! Going there has been a [n]ew, ~~exciting~~ experience that has changed me in many ways.

[At first,] I had feelings of concern about going to middle school. I ~~worryed~~ [worried] about the responsibility of getting my own locker and remembering the combination. I also ~~worryed~~ [felt nervous] about getting lost There were so many[, busy] [long] classrooms and ~~hallways~~! Getting lost is a scary thing to think about[, when you're young].

For a while, other things bothered me too. There were lots of strangers. [When I started,] I didn't know many of the students or any of the teachers. Also I had to switch classes for the first time, so I had to learn the schedule. Different classes began on different days at different times. ~~It seemed very confusing!~~

[Finally,] I realized that everything was going to be fine. The teachers in the school helped us find our way during the first week, so we didn't get too lost. I began to like having my own locker to keep my stuff[, private and safe.] switching classes gave everybody a chance to meet up with old friends and to make new friends from other schools. [Also there are tons of fun clubs to join.]

Revised to improve word choice and correct use of superlative adjective.

Revised to include sequence word and correct order of adjectives.

Revised to include a transition word and to correct spelling according to spelling patterns for simple past.

Revised to improve specific details.

Revised to improve flow of ideas.

Revised to add a sequence word and specific details.

The step from elementary school to middle school changed me. I adjusted very well to the challenges. I learned that students are given more freedom as they get older but that they still have people there  to watch over them and help them ^. Best of all, middle school expanded my horizons by allowing me to experience new activities and to meet new friends.

4 **EDIT** Check your work for errors in grammar, usage, mechanics, and spelling. Then trade essays with a partner and use the Peer Review Checklist below to give each other constructive feedback. Edit your final draft in response to feedback from your partner and your teacher.

Workbook
Page 33

PEER REVIEW CHECKLIST

- ☑ Does the first paragraph introduce the topic?
- ☑ Does the concluding paragraph sum up the main ideas?
- ☑ Does the essay describe the experience clearly?
- ☑ Is the description organized chronologically?
- ☑ Is there a development in the writer's feelings before and after the experience?
- ☑ Is it clear why the experience changed the writer?
- ☑ What changes could be made to improve the essay?

Here are the changes Nicole decided to make to her final draft as a result of her peer review.

Nicole Siley

A Big Step

In my town, three elementary schools combine into one middle school. I used to think my elementary school was the largest school in town, with the most students. Now I realize that the middle school is so much larger! Going there has been an exciting new experience that has changed me in many ways.

At first, I had feelings of concern about going to middle school. I worried about the responsibility of getting my own locker and remembering the combination. I also felt nervous about getting lost. There were so many busy classrooms and long hallways! Getting lost is a scary thing to think about when you're young.

Revised to correct an error in mechanics.

For a while, other things bothered me, too. There were lots of strangers. When I started, I didn't know many of the students or any of the teachers. Also I had to switch classes for the first time, so I had to learn the schedule. It seemed very confusing! Different classes began on different days at different times.

Finally, I realized that everything was going to be fine. The teachers in the school helped us find our way during the first week, so we didn't get too lost. I began to like having my own locker to keep my stuff private and safe. switching classes gave everybody a chance to meet up with old friends and to make new friends from other schools. Also, there are tons of fun clubs to join.

Revised to improve word choice and to correct errors in mechanics.

The step from elementary school to middle school changed me. I adjusted very well to the challenges. I learned that students are given more freedom as they get older, but that they still have people there to watch over them and help them. Best of all, middle school expanded my horizons by allowing me to experience new activities and to meet new friends.

5 **PUBLISH** Prepare a clean copy of your final draft. Share your essay with the class.

Workbook
Page 34

Test Preparation

PRACTICE

Read the following test sample. Study the tips in the boxes.
Work with a partner to answer the questions.

Jing and Sarah are in Mrs. Sampson's class. They have to do a report about where refugees settle in the United States. Jing is very excited when he finds this chart. He thinks it will help them for the report.

Refugee Settlement by State in 2009

State	Rank	Number of Refugees
Arizona	4	4,320
California	1	11,278
Florida	5	4,193
Michigan	6	3,500
New York	3	4,412
Texas	2	8,212

1 Which state receives the most refugees?

    A Arizona
    B California
    C New York
    D Texas

2 Which state is ranked third?

    F Texas
    G Michigan
    H Florida
    J New York

3 Who wants Sarah to do a report?

    A Jing
    B Her father
    C The class
    D Mrs. Sampson

Taking Tests
You will often take tests that help show what you know. Study the tips below to help you improve your test-taking skills.

Tip
Eliminate answers that you know are wrong. Look at the remaining answers. Choose the best answer from those that are left.

Tip
Review the test when you are finished. You may find questions you skipped or mistakes you made.

Workbook
Pages 35–38

Invention and Change

The United States has always been a country of invention and change. When the first European settlers arrived in the 1500s, they called their new homeland the New World. Since then, the country has grown and changed in ways the first settlers could never have imagined. The theme of change runs throughout the work of many American artists.

Hans Hofmann, *Fermented Soil* (1965)

In *Fermented Soil*, Hans Hofmann did not paint faces or objects that you would recognize. Instead, he used thick and thin brushstrokes. He also used the flat edge of a knife to apply layers of color. Hofmann purposely used paints made from colors that come from the earth. Then he layered these colors one on top of another until he created a field of yellows, golds, and browns. Hofmann even tried to "turn" the paint with the flat knife as though he were turning dirt. The end result is a "garden" of paint on a huge canvas.

When something *ferments*, it breaks down and then changes into something new. Hofmann called this work *Fermented Soil* because he began with simple brown paint. Then he had the brown paint "ferment" with other layers of color until it became something new.

▲ Hans Hofmann, *Fermented Soil*, 1965, oil, 48 × 60 in., Smithsonian American Art Museum

▲ Samuel Colman, *Storm King on the Hudson*, 1866, oil,
32⅛ × 59⅞ in., Smithsonian American Art Museum

Samuel Colman, *Storm King on the Hudson* (1866)

In *Storm King on the Hudson*, Samuel Colman shows the
new world of steam-powered engines. These great ships arrived
on American rivers in the mid-1800s. On the left side of this
painting, steam-powered boats move down the mighty Hudson
River in New York State. The rowboats in their path look very
small and weak. In the distance, on the right side of the canvas,
the white sails of several sailboats stand out against the sides of
Storm King Mountain. Colman wanted to show the two worlds
that existed on the Hudson River at the time: the new and the
old, or the new steam-powered ships versus boats powered by
people, such as the sailboat and rowboat.

But this change came with a price, as Colman shows in his
painting. Dirty air from the smokestacks on the steamers fills
the sky. The artist shows this in contrast with the clean white
color of the clouds in the background. Sometimes change also
signals the end of good things.

Hofmann's work captures the exciting side of change,
while Colman's painting shows both the good and the bad.
Even though Colman's painting is more realistic, both artists
capture a tension that all of us connect with change.

Discuss What You Learned

1 In what way are these
artworks about inventing
something new?

2 How do both Colman and
Hofmann show tension in
their paintings?

Big Question
How could you capture
the idea of change in an
artwork? Explain.

Workbook
Pages 39–40

THE BIG QUESTION

What are the benefits of facing challenges?

This unit is about challenges. You will read texts that describe people who faced various challenges and the benefits they experienced as a result. Reading, writing, and talking about these topics will help you practice the language you need to use in school.

Reading

1 Social Studies/Song

- "The Train to Freedom"
- "Follow the Drinking Gourd"

Reading Strategy:
Skim

2 Memoir/Poem

- "Five New Words at a Time" by Yu-Lan (Mary) Ying
- "Quilt" by Janet S. Wong

Reading Strategy:
Identify problems and solutions

3 Interview/Novel

- "An Interview with Gary Paulsen" by Leonard S. Marcus
- From *Hatchet* by Gary Paulsen

Reading Strategy:
Predict

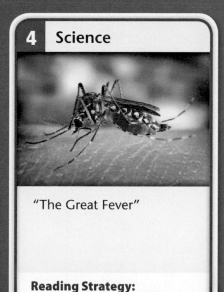

4 **Science**

"The Great Fever"

Reading Strategy:
Recognize cause and effect

Listening and Speaking—Narrative

At the end of this unit, you will choose a topic and present a **personal narrative.**

Writing—Narrative

In this unit you will practice **narrative writing,** or writing that tells a story. After each reading you will learn a skill that will help you write a narrative paragraph. At the end of the unit, you will use these skills to write a fictional narrative.

Quick Write

What does *challenge* mean to you? Write your own definition. Share it with a partner.

VIEW AND RESPOND
Watch the DVD for Unit 2 and answer the questions at <u>*www.LongmanKeystone.com*</u>*.*

Prepare to Read

What You Will Learn

Reading
- Vocabulary building: *Context, dictionary skills, word study*
- Reading strategy: *Skim*
- Text type: *Informational text (social studies) and song*

Grammar
Prepositions; Present and past progressive

Writing
Write a story with a starter

▶ ◉ THE BIG QUESTION

What are the benefits of facing challenges? When you "face a challenge," you try something even though you might fail. Some challenges are worth accepting; others can be dangerous. Have you ever accepted a difficult challenge? What was it? Was the outcome beneficial? Share your experience with your peers and teacher. Ask for their feedback and support in order to develop background knowledge about this topic.

▶ BUILD BACKGROUND

"The Train to Freedom" is a nonfiction article about the secret routes that escaping slaves followed to freedom.

In the mid-1800s, slavery was illegal in the northern states, but it was still legal in the South. Many slaves in the South tried to escape. Their journeys were filled with challenges and dangers.

For example, discussing escape routes could be dangerous for the escaping slaves and others. Sometimes slaves hid this information in the songs they sang. You will read one of these songs called **"Follow the Drinking Gourd."**

Escape routes slaves used to travel north ▶

Reading Skill

To help you understand the challenges that escaping slaves faced, use the map to trace the routes that they took in their journey north. Name some of the states they escaped to.

➤ VOCABULARY

Listening and Speaking: Key Words

Read aloud and listen to these sentences. Use the context to figure out the meaning of the highlighted words. Use a dictionary to check your answers. Then write each word and its meaning in your notebook.

Key Words

fugitive
heritage
network
runaway
shelter
Underground Railroad

1. The fugitive slaves were caught and sent back to where they came from.

2. The discoveries, art, events, and accomplishments of our country's past make up our national heritage.

3. Many people created a network to help escaping slaves find food and a safe place to sleep.

4. Some people received rewards for catching and returning runaway slaves.

5. People who were against slavery offered their homes as shelter to slaves.

6. We learned that thousands of slaves escaped to freedom using the Underground Railroad.

Practice  **Workbook Page 41**

Write the sentences in your notebook. Choose a key word from the box above to complete each sentence. Then take turns reading the sentences aloud with a partner.

1. The police looked all over the city for the _____ woman.

2. The fugitives found _____ in an old barn during the storm.

3. The woman was only one of many in the _____ who provided fugitive slaves with supplies.

4. Fugitive, or _____, slaves often became ill from traveling on foot.

5. Freedom is a part of America's _____.

6. Many people supported the _____ , helping slaves escape to freedom.

What is the purpose of this poster? ▶

RAN AWAY!

FROM THE SUBSCRIBER. My Mulatto Boy, GEORGE. Said George is 5 feet 8 inches in height, brown curly Hair, dark coat. I will give $400 for him alive, and the same sum for satisfactory proof that he has been killed.
Vide ANTHONY & ELLIS' MAMMOTH "UNCLE TOM'S CABIN." WM. HARRIS.

Listening and Speaking: Academic Words

Study the **red** words and their meanings. You will find these words useful when talking and writing about informational texts. Write each word and its meaning in your notebook, then say the words aloud with a partner. After you read "The Train to Freedom" and "Follow the Drinking Gourd," try to use these words to respond to the texts.

accompanied = went somewhere with someone	→	She **accompanied** slaves on their journeys to freedom.
aid = help or support given to someone	→	The slaves received **aid**, such as food and shelter, from people who opposed slavery.
challenge = something difficult that you need skill or ability to do	→	The trip was a **challenge**. The weather was bad, and the slaves were in constant danger.
code = a way to use words, letters, or numbers to send secret messages	→	The song contained a **code**. It told the slaves where to go.

Audio

Practice  Workbook Page 42

Work with a partner to answer these questions. Try to include the **red** word in your answer. Write the sentences in your notebook.

1. Who **accompanied** you to school this morning?
2. Have you ever received **aid** from a classmate? Explain.
3. What is your biggest **challenge** at school?
4. Have you ever sent a message that contained a secret **code**? If so, what kind of code did you use?

Word Study: Words with *ch* and *tch*

Ch and *tch* are consonant clusters. They sound the same but are spelled differently. Look at the words *which* and *scratch*. The final sound in each word is the same, but the words are spelled differently. English words may begin with the letters *ch*, but never with the letters *tch*. Read the examples in the chart below and pronounce each word aloud.

Spelling	Initial Position	Final Position
ch	**ch**allenge **ch**ance	mu**ch** ea**ch**
tch		ma**tch** fe**tch**

Practice  Workbook Page 43

Copy the sentences below into your notebook. Fill in the missing letters of each word and check the spelling in a dictionary. Then read the sentences aloud with a partner.

1. We gave him a _____eese and tomato sandwi_____ for lun_____.
2. They took a _____ance offering shelter to fugitives.
3. Dogs were used to ca_____ the fugitive. They _____ased him for many miles.
4. He hid in a deep di_____.

READING STRATEGY | SKIM

Skimming a text helps you get a general understanding of what the text is about before you read it more carefully. It also helps you set a purpose for reading. To skim a text, follow these steps:

- Look at the title and visuals to get an idea of what the text is about.
- Read the first paragraph quickly. Then read the first sentence of the paragraphs that follow.
- Don't stop at any words you don't know—skip over them.
- After you skim the text, try to summarize what you learned before you go back and read it again.

Before you read "The Train to Freedom," skim the text quickly. Then stop and think about what you read. What do you already know about the subject? What more do you think you will learn?

 Workbook Page 44

INFORMATIONAL TEXT

SOCIAL STUDIES AND SONG

Set a purpose for reading As you read, think about how slaves traveled on the Underground Railroad. What challenges did they face? Who gave them aid along the way?

The Train to Freedom

Audio

Risk Takers

People who tried to escape from slavery in the United States took a dangerous chance. Slave catchers and their dogs **continually** hunted runaway slaves. When they were caught, they might be beaten. Sometimes they were hanged. Even if runaways did not get caught, they often became ill from traveling on foot while tired, cold, wet, and hungry.

continually, constantly

◄ Slaves picking cotton

Many free African Americans and others also took risks to help slaves who were running away. People who helped runaways could be punished. Yet many people did not think slavery was right, and they found ways to help the slaves escape.

The Underground Railroad

The Underground Railroad wasn't really underground, and it was not a real railroad. It was called "underground" because it was secret. And it was called a "railroad" because it helped fugitive slaves travel to places where they could be free. A network of people supported the Underground Railroad, helping the slaves escape.

Many of the words connected to the Underground Railroad were railway terms. For example, slaves on the Underground Railroad were called "passengers." The homes, businesses, and churches where they could stop for food or shelter were known as "stations" and "depots." The people who lived in these homes or ran these businesses were called "stationmasters."

▲ Harriet Tubman

"Conductors" were courageous people who went with slaves on their journeys. Levi Coffin, a white **Quaker** from Cincinnati, was a well-known conductor. But the most famous conductor was Harriet Tubman, a woman who had been a slave herself.

Harriet Tubman

Harriet Tubman knew the evils of slavery. She was born a slave and worked as a maid, a children's nurse, and a field worker. When she was in her early teens, she tried to help a runaway slave. When she was caught trying to help, she was hit in the head with a heavy weight and almost died. As a result of this injury, she suffered from **blackouts** throughout her life.

Quaker, member of a Christian religious group that opposes all forms of violence
blackouts, periods of unconsciousness

BEFORE YOU GO ON

1 What was the Underground Railroad?

2 Why were stations important to slaves on the Underground Railroad?

On Your Own
If you worked on the Underground Railroad, would you rather have worked as a stationmaster or a conductor? Why?

▲ Harriet Tubman (left) helped many slaves escape to freedom.

Harriet Tubman was twenty-nine years old when she made her own escape from slavery. Her journey was difficult, but she was successful and settled in Philadelphia. She worked as a dishwasher and began to make plans to rescue her family. Over the next few years, she brought her sister's family and her brothers to the North, where they were free.

However, Harriet Tubman was still not satisfied. Over a ten-year period, she traveled back to the South nineteen times to help more than 300 slaves escape. She was known along the Underground Railroad as Moses because, like Moses in the story of **Exodus**, she led her people to freedom.

Harriet Tubman became a hero among slaves and among **abolitionists**, but others hated her. Large rewards were offered for her capture. She wore clever disguises so no one would recognize her.

Harriet Tubman's accomplishments were not limited to her work on the Underground Railroad. During the Civil War, she became a **spy** for the **Union** army. She later worked in Washington, D.C., as a government nurse. She died at the age of ninety-three.

Exodus, Bible story in which people escape from slavery
abolitionists, people who wanted to end slavery
spy, person who watches other people secretly to discover information about them
Union, northern states during the Civil War

Travel on the Underground Railroad

What was it like traveling to the North on the Underground Railroad? Although it was different for each person, it was never easy. Slaves had to find out how to escape from the slaveholders' property. Sometimes they had to leave family members or friends and risk never seeing them again. Slaves who wanted to escape could not talk about their plans. Discussing escape plans could be dangerous for the escaping slave or for others.

It was often a challenge for fugitives to find their way from one stop to the next. Sometimes fugitive slaves had a conductor with them from the beginning of the journey, but sometimes they didn't. Runaway slaves had to trust strangers to help them. They often spoke in code, using one word to mean another. (Some of these code words can be found in the spirituals and other slave songs that have become part of our American heritage. The codes used by travelers and helpers on the Underground Railroad could be hidden in these songs.)

Runaway slaves often tried to **cover** between 10 and 20 miles a night. During daylight, they rested at depots or stations—homes, shops, and churches—when they could. Sometimes they slept in barns or in the woods.

The Underground Railroad operated in many states. Ohio, especially, had numerous Underground Railroad stations. Thousands of runaway slaves followed the Underground Railroad into Ohio. To do this they had to cross the Ohio River.

---

cover, travel

Free States		Slave States	
California	New Hampshire	Alabama	Mississippi
Connecticut	New Jersey	Arkansas	Missouri
Illinois	New York	Delaware	North Carolina
Indiana	Ohio	Florida	South Carolina
Iowa	Oregon	Georgia	Tennessee
Maine	Pennsylvania	Kentucky	Texas
Massachusetts	Rhode Island	Louisiana	Virginia
Michigan	Vermont	Maryland	
Minnesota	Wisconsin		

◄ The free states and the slave states in 1860

BEFORE YOU GO ON

1 Who was Harriet Tubman?

2 What is a **code**?

On Your Own
What would be the hardest thing for you to leave behind if you were a runaway slave? Why?

Reading 1 **85**

Other Supporters of the Underground Railroad

Slavery did not occur only in the South of the United States. Many of the slaves brought to North America arrived at northern cities and were sold to slave owners in the North. However, slavery was more **widespread** in the South, and it lasted much longer there.

More and more people in the North heard about the Underground Railroad. They formed groups to raise money and provide food and shelter for runaway slaves. These groups, known as "vigilance committees," helped settle fugitive slaves, who were faced with a very different climate and environment in the North. The vigilance committees helped the former slaves find jobs.

We do not have a complete history of the Underground Railroad. There are few written **accounts** of the Underground Railroad or the experiences of former slaves. Because of this, no one knows exactly how many slaves escaped on the Underground Railroad to free states, Canada, or Mexico. We also don't know how many people took the risk of helping the fugitive slaves on their way, or who these people were. But some **historians estimate** that as many as 100,000 slaves rode the Underground Railroad to freedom.

widespread, common
accounts, descriptions
historians, people who study history
estimate, guess, based on available information

Who published these pamphlets?
What is their purpose? ▶

Follow the Drinking Gourd

*This song contains a secret code. The "drinking gourd" is what the fugitive slaves called the **Big Dipper**. One of the stars in the Big Dipper points to the North Star, which the fugitive slaves used as a guide to the North.*

When the sun comes back and the first **quail** calls,
Follow the Drinking Gourd.
For the old man is waiting for to carry you to freedom,
If you follow the Drinking Gourd.

Chorus:
Follow the Drinking Gourd. Follow the Drinking Gourd.
For the old man is awaiting to carry you to freedom if you
Follow the Drinking Gourd.

The river bank makes a very good road,
The dead trees show you the way,
Left foot, **peg foot**, traveling on
Follow the Drinking Gourd.

Chorus
The river ends between two hills,
Follow the Drinking Gourd.
There's another river on the other side,
Follow the Drinking Gourd.

Chorus
Where the great big river meets the little river,
Follow the Drinking Gourd.
For the old man is awaiting to carry you to freedom,
If you follow the Drinking Gourd.

▲ A dipper is a cup with a long handle. It is used to collect drinking water. The slaves thought of the Big Dipper as a dipper made from a gourd, like this one.

Big Dipper, group of stars in the shape of a bowl with a long handle
quail, wild, fat bird with a short tail
peg foot, refers to Peg Leg Joe, who went from farm to farm teaching the song to slaves

BEFORE YOU GO ON

1. How did the vigilance committees help fugitive slaves?

2. What information is hidden in "Follow the Drinking Gourd"?

On Your Own
What do you think it would have been like to travel at night, following the North Star?

► **COMPREHENSION**

Workbook
Page 45

Recall

1. Where did fugitive slaves rest during daylight?
2. What happened to fugitive slaves who were caught?

Comprehend

3. Why was the North Star important to escaping slaves?
4. In what ways did people offer **aid** to fugitive slaves?

Analyze

5. Why do you think Harriet Tubman became a spy for the Union army?
6. Some slaves did not escape when they had the chance. Why?

Connect

7. Would you risk your life in order to obtain freedom? Explain your answer.
8. Would you risk your life in order to help another person in need? Why or why not?

▲ Graue Mill in Oak Brook, Illinois, is believed to have been an Underground Railroad station.

► **IN YOUR OWN WORDS**

The chart below lists the section headings from "The Train to Freedom." Write the main idea of each section in the chart. Then use this information to summarize the article for a classmate.

Heading	Main Idea
Risk Takers	Fugitive slaves, and the people who helped them escape, took a dangerous chance.
The Underground Railroad	
Harriet Tubman	
Travel on the Underground Railroad	
Other Supporters of the Underground Railroad	

➤ DISCUSSION

Discuss in pairs or small groups.

1. Do you think it would have been more dangerous to be a stationmaster or a conductor on the Underground Railroad? Why?

2. Do you think the people who aided fugitive slaves gained anything from the experience? Explain.

Q **What are the benefits of facing challenges?** Do you know of other groups of people who faced **challenges** as they tried to achieve freedom? Who are they? What did they do? Do you think any benefits (other than freedom) are gained from facing such challenges?

➤ READ FOR FLUENCY

It is often easier to read a text if you understand the difficult words and phrases. Work with a partner. Choose a paragraph from the reading. Identify the words and phrases you do not know or have trouble pronouncing. Look up the difficult words in a dictionary.

Take turns pronouncing the words and phrases with your partner. If necessary, ask your teacher to model the correct pronunciation. Then take turns reading the paragraph aloud. Give each other feedback on your reading.

➤ EXTENSION  Workbook Page 45

Utilize Imagine that you are a conductor on the Underground Railroad. You are helping a group of fugitive slaves travel north to the Ohio River. You know how to find the Big Dipper, the North Star, and stations where people will help you. It is a cold winter night. The river is frozen, making it easier for you to cross. In your notebook, write a journal entry that describes your experience. Try to use as much academic language as possible in your entry.

Grammar

Prepositions

A preposition is always followed by a noun or noun phrase. Together these words are called a prepositional phrase. Prepositions are used to show time, show place or direction, or provide details. Here are some of the most common prepositions.

> **SHOW TIME: ANSWER "WHEN?"**
> She died **at the age of ninety-three**.
> When she was **in her early teens**, she tried to help a runaway slave.
>
> **SHOW PLACE: ANSWER "WHERE?"**
> The codes used by travelers and helpers could be hidden **in these songs**.
> It helped slaves travel **to places** where they could be free.
> A Quaker **from Cincinnati** was a well-known conductor.
>
> **PROVIDE DETAILS: ANSWER "WHO?," "HOW?," OR "WHAT?"**
> The codes used **by travelers and helpers** could be hidden in these songs.
> "Conductors" went **with slaves on their journeys**.
> They became ill **from traveling on foot**.
> Large rewards were offered **for her capture**.
> Many **of the words** connected to it were railway terms.

Grammar SKILL

A prepositional phrase can appear at the beginning or at the end of a sentence. When at the beginning, use a comma after a prepositional phrase.

Practice

Workbook Page 46

Work with a partner. Write the sentences in your notebook. Circle the correct preposition to complete each sentence.

Example: She helped many slaves escape (to / at / in) freedom.

1. (From / In / By) 1865, slavery was abolished.
2. Fugitive slaves traveled (on / of / to) places of freedom.
3. They rested (at / with / on) the church.
4. Sometimes fugitive slaves slept (for / to / in) the woods.
5. There is a river (on / by / for) the other side.

✔ GRAMMAR CHECK

What always follows a preposition?

Apply

Work with a partner. Read the sentences in the chart above. Then find other examples in the reading of prepositions that show time, show place or direction, or provide details.

Present and Past Progressive

The present progressive shows an action in progress now. It can also show some future actions. Form the present progressive with *is*, *am*, or *are* and a present participle.

> The old man **is waiting** to carry you to freedom.
> Tomorrow I**'m running** away.

The past progressive shows an action that continued during a period of time in the past. Form the past progressive with *was* or *were* and the present participle. To show that the action was interrupted, use the simple past. You can use the adverbs *while* with the present progressive and *when* with the simple past. If the adverb clause begins the sentence, use a comma.

> **While** Harriet Tubman **was helping** a slave escape, a slave catcher **caught** her.
> Harriet Tubman **was helping** a slave escape **when** a slave catcher **caught** her.

For questions in the present or past progressive, switch the *be* verb and the subject. For the negative, use a negative *be* verb.

> **Are** they **traveling** tomorrow?   No, they**'re not**. / No, they **aren't**.
> **Was** she **traveling** with a conductor?   No, she **wasn't**.

Grammar SKILL

The present participle is formed by adding *-ing* to the base form of the verb: *help +* *-ing* → *helping*. If the base form ends in *-e*, drop the *e*: *giving*.

Practice

Workbook Page 47

Work with a partner. Copy the sentences. Complete each sentence with the correct form of the verb in parentheses.

Example: ___*Is*___ she *arriving* (arrive) this week or next week?

1. I _____ (sit) in class yesterday when the fire bell _____ (ring).
2. She _____ (leave) on a trip tomorrow, **accompanied** by her aunt.
3. While they _____ (work) in the garden, it _____ (start) to rain.
4. _____ you _____ (go) camping next weekend?
5. I _____ (not study) last night when you _____ (call).

Apply

Work with a partner. Write five sentence starters that use the past progressive. Take turns finishing each other's sentences with adverb clauses in the simple past.

Example: I was riding my bike . . . when a car hit me.

Writing

Write a Story with a Starter

At the end of this unit you will write a fictional narrative. To do this, you will need to learn some of the skills writers use to write narratives, or stories. An important aspect of a story is its setting. To describe a setting, you need to include details about the time (year, month, time of day) and place (country, state, neighborhood, home) of a story's action.

Writing Prompt

Write a fictional narrative. Begin your story with the following starter: *The view was unlike anything I had ever seen before.* Use prepositions that describe when and where the action in the story takes place. Use the present and past progressive correctly.

1 **PREWRITE** Begin by thinking of a setting for your story.

- Close your eyes and visualize the setting: Where is it? What time of day or night is it? What can you see?

- Name the setting in the top bubble of your word web.

- Add details about the time and the place in the lower bubbles.

Workbook Page 48

Here's a word web created by a student named Madeline. She used this story starter: *The moon was glowing brightly in the dark of night.* Then she used a word web to organize details about the setting.

Setting
the underground
railroad

Details about time
night, autumn, long
and difficult journey

Details about place
bright moon, warm
breeze, river, forests,
barns, basements

2 **DRAFT** Use your word web to help you write a first draft.

- Use the story starter to lead into the description of your setting.
- Describe the place and the time.
- Use prepositions to describe the location and time of actions.
- Use the present and past progressive correctly.

3 **REVISE** Read over your draft. Look for places where the writing is unclear or needs improvement. Use the Writing Checklist to help you identify problems. Then revise your draft, using the editing and proofreading marks listed on page 458.

4 **EDIT** Check your work for errors in grammar, usage, mechanics, and spelling. Trade papers with a partner to obtain feedback. Use the Peer Review Checklist on Workbook page 48. Edit your final draft in response to feedback from your partner and your teacher.

5 **PUBLISH** Prepare a clean copy of your final draft. Share your story with the class. Save your work. You'll need to refer to it in the Writing Workshop at the end of the unit.

Writing Checklist

IDEAS:
☑ I used an interesting story starter.

WORD CHOICE:
☑ I used words that clearly establish the setting.

Here is Madeline's story. Notice how she first establishes the setting before going on to narrate the events in the story.

Madeline Shaw

A Journey on the Underground Railroad

The moon was glowing brightly in the dark of night. A warm autumn breeze rustled the remaining leaves on the trees as we escaped and ran towards the river. The water was cold as we waded through it. It was the beginning of a journey that would take us to the North, where we could be free. Each night, we traveled anywhere from 10–20 miles a night, always reaching the next stop as daylight approached. Then caring, decent people provided us with places to rest. We slept in old barns, in cold basements, or even in the woods that surrounded their properties. We continued to travel in this way for a long time. It was a long and difficult journey, but well worth it, as we were finally rewarded with freedom.

Prepare to Read

What You Will Learn

Reading

- Vocabulary building: *Literary terms, word study*
- Reading strategy: *Identify problems and solutions*
- Text type: *Literature (personal narrative and poetry)*

Grammar

Gerunds as subjects and subject compliments; Gerunds as objects

Writing

Rewrite a familiar story

THE BIG QUESTION

What are the benefits of facing challenges? Moving to a new city, state, or country can be overwhelming. You have to say good-bye to your friends, you might have to go to a new school, and you might live among people who speak a different language or have different beliefs or customs than your own.

Have you ever moved to a new place? Where did you move? What challenges did your family face there? How was the move beneficial for your family? Use your prior experiences to discuss these questions with a partner.

▲ A family moves into their new home.

BUILD BACKGROUND

In this section, you will read a personal narrative called **"Five New Words at a Time"** and a poem, **"Quilt."** In a personal narrative, the writer tells about something he or she experienced. In the narrative you are about to read, the writer tells about moving to a new country and having to learn a new language.

➤ VOCABULARY

Learn Literary Words

Literary Words
characters
point of view

Audio

As you have learned, a plot is a sequence of related events within a story. The people or animals involved in those events are called **characters**. You can learn about characters' traits, feelings, and actions by paying attention to their involvement in story events, what they say, and what other characters in the story say about them.

   Point of view refers to the narrator, or person telling the story. When a person tells a story using the pronouns *I, me, my,* or *we,* the story is in the first-person point of view. Personal narratives use the first-person point of view.

> **First-person point of view:**
> Today is my first day at this school. I'm nervous. I don't know English that well, and I'm afraid this will keep me from making new friends.

In other stories, the narrator uses the pronouns *he, she,* or *they* to refer to the characters. These stories are told from the third-person point of view.

> **Third-person point of view:**
> Leila was nervous on her first day of school in the United States. She missed her friends and teachers in Ecuador.

Practice

Workbook
Page 49

Write the sentences below in your notebook. Identify the point of view in each sentence. Then change those sentences in the first-person point of view to the third person, and those sentences in the third person to the first person. Take turns reading the sentences aloud with a partner.

1. I moved to America earlier this year.
2. His English tutor was very friendly.
3. We meet every day after school.
4. "How do you like your tutor?" my teacher asked.
5. I answered, "He is very helpful."

▲ A student works with his tutor.

Listening and Speaking: Academic Words

Study the **red** words and their meanings. You will find these words useful when talking and writing about literature. Write each word and its meaning in your notebook, then say the words aloud with a partner. After you read "Five New Words at a Time" and "Quilt," try to use these words to respond to the texts.

approach = a way of doing something or dealing with a problem	➡	Our teacher's **approach** was a lot of fun. She encouraged us to play word games every day.
communicate = express your thoughts or feelings so other people understand them	➡	When I came to America, it was difficult to **communicate** with my classmates because I did not speak English.
resources = a supply of materials used to complete a task	➡	I used **resources**, like a dictionary and a thesaurus, to complete my homework.
response = something that is said, written, or done as a reaction or reply to something else	➡	My **response** to the teacher's question was correct.

Audio

Practice

Workbook
Page 50

Work with a partner to answer these questions. Try to include the **red** word in your answer. Write the sentences in your notebook.

1. What **approach** do you use when trying to make new friends?

2. How do you **communicate** with someone who does not speak your language?

3. What kinds of **resources** do you use in school?

4. What is your **response** to the idea of an extended school year?

▲ This student uses resources, such as a microscope and a slide, in her science class.

Word Study: Prefixes *im-*, *over-*, *un-*, *after-*

Prefixes are groups of letters added to the beginning of base words to change their meanings. Learning how to quickly identify and pronounce prefixes will help you as you sound out words. Memorizing the meanings of prefixes will help you understand new and unfamiliar words.

Prefix	Meaning	Base Word	New Word
im-	not	perfect	imperfect
over-	too much	do	overdo
un-	not	equal	unequal
after-	after	noon	afternoon

Practice
Workbook Page 51

Work with a partner. Look through "Five New Words at a Time" and find words with the prefixes shown above. Write a definition for each word. Then use a dictionary to check your work.

READING STRATEGY | **IDENTIFY PROBLEMS AND SOLUTIONS**

Identifying problems and solutions helps you understand a text better. Many texts include a problem that a person or character has to solve. To identify these problems and solutions, follow these steps:

- What problem or problems does the person or character have?
- Think about your own experience and what you would do to solve the problem.
- Remember that there may be more than one solution to a problem.
- Read on and find out how the person solves or tries to solve the problem.

As you read "Five New Words at Time," ask yourself what problems the characters experience. How do they try to solve their problems? Are they able to find solutions, or not?

Workbook Page 52

Set a purpose for reading As you read, pay attention to the families described in the texts. What is the **response** of each family to challenging situations?

Five New Words at a Time

Audio

Yu-Lan (Mary) Ying

My family came to America in 1985. No one spoke a word of English. In school, I was in an English as a Second Language class with other foreign-born children. My class was so overcrowded that it was impossible for the teacher to teach English properly. I **dreaded** going to school each morning because of the fear of not understanding what people were saying and the fear of being laughed at.

At that time, my mother, Tai-Chih, worked part time in a Chinese restaurant from late afternoon till late in the night. It was her unfamiliarity with the English language that forced her to work in a Chinese-speaking environment. Although her job **exhausted** her, my mother still woke up early in the morning to cook breakfast for my brother and me. Like a hen guarding her chicks, she never **neglected** us because of her **fatigue**.

Reading Skill

Identify the words you don't understand *as you read* and ask your teachers or peers for help with those words.

---

dreaded, worried about
exhausted, tired
neglected, failed to take care of
fatigue, tiredness

So it was not surprising that very soon my mother noticed something was troubling me. When I said nothing was wrong, my mother answered, "You are my daughter. When something is bothering you, I feel it too." The pain and care in her moon-shaped eyes made me burst into the tears I had held back for so long. I explained to her the fear I had of going to school. "Learning English is not impossible," my mother said. She cheerfully suggested that the two of us work together to learn the language at home with books. The **confidence** and **determination** my mother had were **admirable** because English was as new to her as it was to me.

That afternoon I saw my mother in a different light as she waited for me by the school fence. Although she was the shortest of all the mothers there, her face with her welcoming smile and big, black eyes was the most promising. The afternoon sun shone brightly on her long, black hair creating an **aura** that distinguished her from others.

My mother and I immediately began reading together and memorizing five new words a day. My mother with her encouraging attitude made the routine fun and interesting. The fact that she was sacrificing her resting time before going to work so that I could learn English made me see the strength she possessed. It made me admire my mother even more.

---

confidence, belief in oneself
determination, strong desire to succeed
admirable, worthy of respect
aura, quality or feeling

✔ **LITERARY CHECK**

Who are the **characters** *in this story?*

🎧 *Listening* **SKILL**

Follow along in your book as you listen to the Audio CD. Notice the words in bold type. To understand them, read the definitions at the bottom of the page. Knowing the meanings of these words will enhance and confirm your comprehension of the story.

BEFORE YOU GO ON

1 Why was Yu-Lan afraid to go to school?

2 What did her mother suggest to help Yu-Lan learn English?

💡 **On Your Own**
Have you ever felt like Yu-Lan? What was your experience?

Reading 2 **99**

Very soon, I began to comprehend what everyone was saying and people could understand me. The person solely responsible for my accomplishment and happiness was my mother. The reading also helped my mother learn English so that she was able to pass the postal entrance exam.

It has been seven years since that reading experience with my mother. She is now forty-three and in her second year at college. My brother and I have a strong sense of who we are because of the strong values my mother established for herself and her children. My admiration and **gratitude** for her are endless. That is why my mother is truly the guiding light of my life.

---

gratitude, thankfulness, appreciation

ABOUT THE **AUTHOR**

Yu-Lan (Mary) Ying received her medical degree from the University of Pittsburgh Medical School. She practices in otology and neurotology in Pittsburgh, Pennsylvania.

> ✔ **LITERARY CHECK**
> *From which character's **point of view** is this story told? How do you know?*

Quilt

Janet S. Wong

Our family
is a quilt

of odd **remnants**
patched together

in a strange
pattern,

threads **fraying**,
fabric wearing thin—

but made to keep
its warmth

even in bitter
cold.

---

remnants, parts of something that
remain after the rest of it is gone
fraying, becoming loose

ABOUT THE POET

Janet S. Wong was educated at UCLA and
Yale Law School. After several years practicing
law, she began writing poetry and books for
young readers. She lives in New Jersey with
her husband and son.

BEFORE YOU GO ON

1 How did Yu-Lan's
mother benefit
from reading with
Yu-Lan?

2 What object does
the speaker of the
poem liken her
family to? Why?

On Your Own
What object would
you liken your
family to? Explain.

Reading 2 **101**

Review and Practice

▶ READER'S THEATER

Audio

Act out the following scene between Yu-Lan and her mother.

Yu-Lan: This is impossible! I'll never learn English.

Mother: What's the matter? You look so upset!

Yu-Lan: Nothing, I'm fine. How was work?

Mother: I can tell you're upset. What's wrong?

Yu-Lan: Oh, Mother, I'm so frustrated! I can't learn English. It's too difficult for me.

Mother: Don't they teach you English in school?

Yu-Lan: The class is so large. The teacher has no time to answer my questions.

Mother: I'm sorry to hear that, but learning English is not impossible. I need to learn English, too. Why don't we study together? Every day we will learn five new words.

Yu-Lan: Oh, Mother, do you really think we could?

Speaking SKILL
Speak naturally and with feeling.

▶ COMPREHENSION

Workbook
Page 53

Recall

1. Why was it impossible for Yu-Lan's teacher to teach English properly?
2. Why was Yu-Lan's mother forced to work in a Chinese-speaking environment?

Comprehend

3. Why was it important for Yu-Lan and her mother to learn English?
4. What do the actions of Yu-Lan's mother tell you about her character?

Analyze

5. What did Yu-Lan's mother teach her daughter about facing challenges?
6. In the poem "Quilt," the speaker says the following about her family: *but made to keep/its warmth/even in bitter/cold*. What does this mean?

▲ A Chinese restaurant

Connect

7. Have you ever had to learn another language? If so, what was your **approach**? What **resources** did you use?

8. Do you think learning a new language is challenging? Why or why not?

► DISCUSSION

Discuss in pairs or small groups.

1. Are the family relationships described in the personal narrative and in the poem similar in any way? If so, how?

2. Yu-Lan's mother encourages her daughter to learn English. Do you think it is easier to face challenges with the help and encouragement of other people? Explain.

Q **What are the benefits of facing challenges?** Have you ever helped someone overcome a challenge? What did you do? How did the experience make you feel?

► RESPONSE TO LITERATURE

Workbook Page 53

Utilize Can you think of a recent challenge you've had to face? Compare your experience to Yu-Lan's. Copy the chart below into your notebook. Complete the right column with information about your experience. Share your chart with your peers and teacher. Ask for their feedback about how your experience compares with Yu-Lan's.

Experience	Yu-Lan	Me
Challenge	learned to **communicate** in English	
Feelings about challenge	scared, frustrated	
Approach to challenge	read with her mother and learned five new words a day	
Outcome	both mother and daughter learned English	

Grammar

Gerunds as Subjects and Subject Complements

A gerund is the *-ing* form of the verb that functions as a noun. A gerund or gerund phrase is often the subject of a sentence. A gerund is singular. It is followed by a third-person-singular verb. A possessive noun or a possessive pronoun is often used before a gerund. Form the negative of a gerund with *not*.

> "**Learning English** is not impossible," my mother said.
> **Our reading** also helped my mother learn English.
> **Not finishing** the assignment would be bad.

A gerund can also be a subject complement. A subject complement is a noun following a linking verb that defines or describes the subject.

> My favorite pastime is **reading**. [*reading* defines subject *my favorite pastime*]

Practice  Workbook Page 54

Work with a partner. Copy the sentences below into your notebook. Complete the sentences with the gerund form of the word in parentheses.

Example: (draw) *Drawing* is my favorite part of art class.

1. Kyle's (piano play) —————— is wonderful.
2. The best thing for your health is (eat) —————— small meals.
3. (sleep) —————— too much isn't good for you.
4. (not know) —————— a language can be difficult.
5. (watch) —————— TV can help you learn English.

Apply
Work with a partner. Think of some activities that end in *-ing* that you like to do. Take turns telling your partner about these activities, using gerunds as subjects.

Example: Playing video games is my favorite thing to do.

Grammar SKILL

The *-ing* ending occurs in many English words. Be careful not to mistake the gerund with the present progressive form or the present participle:

Studying English is fun. (gerund)
We **are studying** English. (present progressive)
Our English class is **interesting**. (present participle)

✔ **GRAMMAR CHECK**

*What is often used before a **gerund**?*

Gerunds as Objects

Gerunds and gerund phrases are often used as the object of a
sentence. Gerunds are used after certain verbs. These include verbs
that express preferences (*like, hate, avoid*); the verbs *begin, finish,* and
delay; verbs that give advice (*consider, discuss, suggest*); and verbs that
describe thoughts (*recall, miss, remember*).

Grammar SKILL

A gerund with its
objects, complements,
and modifiers is called
a gerund phrase. For
example, *dreaded going
to school each morning*
is a gerund phrase.

> I **dreaded going** to school each morning.
> My mother and I **began reading** together.

Gerunds often follow prepositions and verb-preposition combinations.

> I explained to her the fear I had **of going** to school.
> She was sacrificing her resting time **before going** to work

> My mother **believed in taking** care of her children.
> She never **complained about having** to work hard.

Practice
**Workbook
Page 55**

Work with a partner. Copy the sentences below into your notebook.
Complete the sentences with the gerund form of the verbs from
the box.

| swim   fly   drive   work   hike   watch |

Example: Cindy enjoys *swimming* in the ocean.

1. Neal began _____ the movie an hour ago.
2. She started _____ for the bank in 2003.
3. Jemma worried about _____ to Copenhagen.
4. They finally completed _____ the Appalachian Trail.
5. She can't stand _____ in traffic.

Apply

Work with a partner. Write down five sentence starters using the verbs
on this page. Take turns completing them with gerunds and your own
ideas and opinions.

Example: I can't stand . . . taking tests.

Writing

Rewrite a Familiar Story

The point of view from which a story is told is an important story element. In this lesson you will retell a story from a different point of view. Stories may be written from different characters' points of view. For example, the personal narrative you just read is told from Yu-Lan's point of view. Yu-Lan describes the characters and events in the story and how she felt about them. But the same events could be narrated from another character's point of view, such as Yu-Lan's mother. How would her version of the story be different from her daughter's version?

> **Writing Prompt**
>
> Think about a story you know well. Rewrite it from a different character's point of view. Use the pronouns *I, me, my,* or *we* if you write in the first-person. Use *he, she,* or *they* if you write in the third-person. Try to use gerunds as the subject of a sentence, the object of a verb, and/or the object of a preposition.

1 PREWRITE Begin by choosing a story to rewrite.

- What point of view was used in the story you chose?
- Whose point of view will you choose to retell the story?
- How will this change the interpretation of the events?
- How will you need to change the pronouns?
- List your ideas in a T-chart.  **Workbook Page 56**

Here's a T-chart created by a student named Austin for retelling the story about Yu-Lan from her mother's point of view:

Yu-Lan's POV	Mother's POV
mother unfamiliar with English— forced to work in a Chinese restaurant	like working in a Chinese restaurant because I am able to understand others
mother never neglected us	working long hours made it difficult to spend time with my children
dreaded going to school each morning	noticed Yu-Lan seemed unhappy

2 **DRAFT** Use your T-chart to help you write a first draft.

- Remember to change the pronouns.

- Keep in mind the feelings and opinions of the new person telling the story.

- As you write, think about how to convey the character's point of view in your choice of words and expressions.

3 **REVISE** Read over your draft. Look for places where the writing is unclear or needs improvement. Use the Writing Checklist to help you identify problems. Then revise your draft, using the editing and proofreading marks listed on page 458.

4 **EDIT** Check your work for errors in grammar, usage, mechanics, and spelling. Trade papers with a partner to obtain feedback. Use the Peer Review Checklist on Workbook page 56. Edit your final draft in response to feedback from your partner and your teacher.

5 **PUBLISH** Prepare a clean copy of your final draft. Share your story with your class. Save your work. You'll need to refer to it in the Writing Workshop at the end of the unit.

Writing Checklist

VOICE:
☑ I used a voice that captured the character's point of view.

WORD CHOICE:
☑ I used pronouns that correctly conveyed the character's point of view.

SENTENCE FLUENCY:
☑ I used gerunds as subjects and objects.

Here is Austin's paragraph. Notice the changes in the story because of the new point of view.

Austin Saiz

Five New Words at a Time

Although we didn't speak English, my children and I moved to America in 1985. I quickly found a job at a Chinese restaurant. I like working there because I am able to understand what people are saying. But working long hours makes it difficult for me to spend time with my children. I am usually exhausted when I help them get ready for school in the morning. Even so, I noticed my daughter seemed unhappy. One day, I asked her what was wrong. She looked at me and burst into tears. She told me that learning English at school was impossible. I reassured her that learning a new language could be fun. In fact, I promised her that we would read books and learn the language together—five new words at a time.

Prepare to Read

What You Will Learn

Reading

■ Vocabulary building: *Literary terms, word study*

■ Reading strategy: *Predict*

■ Text type: *Literature (interview and novel excerpt)*

Grammar

Simple and compound sentences; Agreement in simple and compound sentences

Writing

Write a personal letter

▶ 🅠 THE BIG QUESTION

What are the benefits of facing challenges? Imagine that you are on a camping trip. You become separated from your friends and now you are alone in the woods. What would you need in order to survive? List these items in your notebook. Then think about the challenges you would face while trying to obtain those items. Discuss your ideas with a partner.

▶ BUILD BACKGROUND

In this section, you will read **"An Interview with Gary Paulsen."** In it, Paulsen, now an author, describes his challenging childhood experiences.

Remembering these times helped Paulsen write the fictional novel ***Hatchet.*** It is about a thirteen-year-old boy named Brian Robeson. Before Brian flies to Canada to visit his father, Brian's mother gives him a hatchet, or a small ax. Brian takes the hatchet with him as he boards a single-engine plane. During the flight, the pilot suffers a heart attack and dies. The plane crashes into the Canadian wilderness, leaving Brian alone with nothing more than his hatchet and the clothes on his back. Will this be enough to help Brian survive?

▲ A single-engine plane flying over a heavily wooded area

► VOCABULARY

Learn Literary Words

Author's influences are factors that may affect an author's writing. These factors include the author's date and place of birth and cultural background, personal experiences, and world events that took place during the author's lifetime. Such influences can contribute to the kinds of conflict an author writes about.

Conflict, or a struggle between opposing forces, is an important story element because it causes the action. One kind of conflict takes place within the character's mind. The character struggles with his or her own thoughts and feelings.

Another kind of conflict is between a character and an outside force. The outside force might be another person or a force of nature, such as a wild animal or a hurricane. This kind of conflict is called an **external conflict**.

Literary Words
author's influences
external conflict

Audio

LEARNING STRATEGY

Use words that you already know to learn new and essential language, or words that you must know in order to understand your schoolwork.

Practice  Workbook Page 57

Work with a partner. Read the paragraph below. Then answer the following questions: What kind of conflict is described? What is causing the conflict? Who is affected?

The sun was shining as Theo left the farm. Soon after, a large, dark cloud passed over the sun's bright rays. A chilly wind whipped across the sky. Theo pulled the collar of his jacket up around his neck and continued to trudge towards town. He was used to cold weather, but he wasn't prepared for the driving snow that showered from the sky minutes later. The road quickly became covered in white, the path to town no longer visible. Theo lost his sense of direction. Worse yet, the damp cold began to seep through his clothing.

Listening and Speaking: Academic Words

Study the **red** words and their meanings. You will find these words useful when talking and writing about literature. Write each word and its meaning in your notebook, then say the words aloud with a partner. After you read "An Interview with Gary Paulsen" and the excerpt from *Hatchet*, try to use these words to respond to the texts.

available = able to be used or seen	→	The boy looked for the closest **available** food source he could find.
injured = hurt	→	The fall from the ledge hurt his leg and left him badly **injured**.
structure = a building or something that has been built	→	He built a **structure** to live in. It is made of wood.
survive = continue to live after an accident or illness	→	The boy had one goal—to **survive** until someone came to rescue him.

Audio

Practice  **Workbook Page 58**

Work with a partner to answer these questions. Try to include the **red** word in your answer. Write the sentences in your notebook.

1. If you were lost in the wilderness, what kinds of food do you think would be **available** to you?

2. Have you ever been **injured**?

3. What kind of **structure** do you live in?

4. Would you be able to **survive** in unfamiliar surroundings? Why or why not?

▲ Wild berries can be a source of food in the wilderness.

Word Study: Closed Compound Nouns

Compound nouns are formed by combining two or more nouns together. Some compound nouns are written as one word. They are called closed compound nouns. The word *basketball* is a closed compound noun. It is made up of two nouns: *basket + ball*. Look at the chart below for more examples.

Noun	+ Noun	= Compound Noun
note	book	notebook
fire	fly	firefly
day	light	daylight

Practice  Workbook Page 59

Work with a partner. Copy the sentences below into your notebook. Use the words in the box to form a closed compound noun to complete each sentence. Then take turns reading the sentences aloud.

door	fire	stone	week
end	sand	way	wood

1. He bumped his head as he walked through the _____.
2. _____ is a kind of rock.
3. We are going on a trip to the mountains this _____.
4. He lit the _____ to keep himself warm.

READING STRATEGY | PREDICT

Predicting helps you better understand a text and focus on a story. Before you read, predict (or guess) what the story will be about. You can also make new predictions as you're reading. To predict, follow these steps:

- Stop reading from time to time and ask yourself, "What will happen next?"
- Look for clues in the story and in the illustrations. Think about what you already know. Make a prediction.

As you read the excerpt from *Hatchet*, stop and check to see if your prediction was correct. Make a new prediction if necessary.

 Workbook Page 60

Reading 3 **111**

Set a purpose for reading As you read, think about the kinds of challenges Gary Paulsen faced during his childhood. Then look for evidence of these experiences when you read the excerpt from *Hatchet*.

An Interview with Gary Paulsen

Leonard S. Marcus

Gary Paulsen first learned survival skills as a child growing up in a deeply troubled home. By the age of twelve, the future author of *Hatchet* (1987) had taught himself to keep house, make his own fun, and live for weeks at a time in the wilderness.

Leonard Marcus (LM): *What kind of child were you?*

Gary Paulsen (GP): I had a really rough childhood. So to me, childhood was mainly something to get through alive. Now, though, I'm actually grateful for some of those early experiences.

LM: *Grateful in what way?*

GP: Because I was pretty much on my own by the age of seven or eight, I learned about **tenacity** and **independence** and the willingness to fight. And I can go back now to some of the things that happened to me and write about them. They're like a **mine** that I can **harvest**.

---

tenacity, determination
independence, the freedom to take care of yourself without needing other people
mine, a deep hole in the ground from which gold, coal, etc., is dug
harvest, gather from

▼ Gary Paulsen plays with his dog on a hillside.

LM: *How did you survive?*

GP: At one time, when we were living in an apartment in a small Minnesota town, I moved down into the basement of our building by myself. I had found a place in back of the furnace, a sort of **alcove**, with a half-sized couch and a light hanging from the ceiling. That became my home. Half the time my parents wouldn't know I was gone.

LM: *Did you enjoy spending time alone in the woods, as so many of your characters do?*

GP: I fostered myself to the woods. Whenever I went into the woods, all the **hassles** of life were very quickly forgotten. It's still that way for me.

LM: *What kind of student were you?*

GP: A miserable one! I flunked ninth grade and barely got through high school.

LM: *When did you decide to become a writer?*

GP: Not until years later. I don't know why, but one night when I was about twenty-seven, it just came to me that I wanted to write. I had never thought of writing before then. I didn't even know what a **manuscript** was.

LM: *What do you tell kids who want to write?*

GP: Read. Read like a wolf eats! You can't learn anything watching television. It's very important to turn the box off—and carry a book with you all the time.

▲ Gary Paulsen often spent time in the woods as a child.

---

alcove, small space
hassles, troubles
manuscript, book before it is published

ABOUT THE **INTERVIEWER**

Leonard S. Marcus works in the field of children's literature as an author, critic, magazine editor, and professional lecturer. In fact, Marcus travels around the world speaking to teenagers in different countries. When he's not traveling, Marcus lives in Brooklyn, New York.

BEFORE YOU GO ON

1 How does Paulsen describe his childhood?

2 Does Paulsen enjoy spending time alone in the woods today? Why or why not?

On Your Own
What do you do to **survive** difficult times in your life?

from Hatchet

Gary Paulsen

Brian Robeson was traveling to Canada to visit his father when the pilot of the single-engine plane in which he was flying had a heart attack. The plane crashed into a lake, leaving Brian alone in the Canadian wilderness. That was two days ago. Bruised and battered, Brian must find a way to survive in the wilderness alone, with nothing more than a thin jacket and a hatchet.

Using the sun and the fact that it rose in the east and set in the west, he decided that the far side was the northern side of the ridge. At one time in the far past it had been scooped by something, probably a **glacier**, and this scooping had left a kind of sideways bowl, back in under a **ledge**. It wasn't very deep, not a **cave**, but it was smooth and made a perfect roof and he could almost stand in under the ledge. He had to hold his head slightly tipped forward at the front to keep it from hitting the top. Some of the rock that had been scooped out had also been **pulverized** by the glacial action, turned into sand, and now made a small sand beach that went down to the edge of the water in front and to the right of the overhang.

It was his first good luck.

No, he thought. He had good luck in the landing. But this was good luck as well, luck he needed.

---

glacier, large, slow-moving mountain of ice
ledge, surface of rock
cave, deep hollow area in rock
pulverized, crushed

All he had to do was wall off part of the bowl and leave an opening as a doorway and he would have a perfect shelter—much stronger than a **lean-to** and dry because the overhang made a watertight roof.

He crawled back in, under the ledge, and sat. The sand was cool here in the shade, and the coolness felt wonderful to his face, which was already starting to **blister** and get especially painful on his forehead, with the blisters on top of the swelling.

He was also still weak. Just the walk around the back of the ridge and the slight climb over the top had left his legs **rubbery**. It felt good to sit for a bit under the shade of the overhang in the cool sand.

And now, he thought, if I just had something to eat.

Anything.

When he had rested a bit he went back down to the lake and drank a couple of swallows of water. He wasn't all that thirsty but he thought the water might help to take the edge off his hunger. It didn't. Somehow the cold lake water actually made it worse, sharpened it.

---

lean-to, shelter with a sloped roof, made by leaning fallen branches against a tree, a rock, or other branches
blister, swell with a clear liquid
rubbery, weak and unsteady

BEFORE YOU GO ON

1 Describe Brian's surroundings. What kind of area is he in?

2 Why does Brian consider himself lucky?

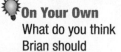 **On Your Own**
What do you think Brian should do next?

Reading 3 **115**

He thought of dragging in wood to make a wall or part of an overhang, and picked up one piece to pull up, but his arms were too weak and he knew then that it wasn't just the crash and injury to his body and head, it was also that he was weak from hunger.

He would have to find something to eat. Before he did anything else he would have to have something to eat.

But what?

* * *

At first he was too far away to see what they were doing, but their color drew him and he moved toward them, keeping the lake in sight on his right, and when he got closer he saw they were eating berries.

He could not believe it was that easy. It was as if the birds had taken him right to the berries. The slender branches went up about twenty feet and were heavy, drooping with **clusters** of bright red berries. They were half as big as grapes but hung in bunches much like grapes and when Brian saw them, glistening red in the sunlight, he almost yelled.

His pace quickened and he was in them in moments, scattering the birds, grabbing branches, stripping them to fill his mouth with berries.

---

clusters, groups or bunches

He almost spit them out. It wasn't that they were **bitter** so much as that they lacked any sweetness, had a **tart** flavor that left his mouth dry feeling. And they were like cherries in that they had large **pits**, which made them hard to chew. But there was such a hunger on him, such an emptiness, that he could not stop and kept stripping branches and eating berries by the handful, grabbing and jamming them into his mouth and swallowing them, pits and all.

He could not stop and when, at last, his stomach was full he was still hungry. Two days without food must have shrunken his stomach, but the drive of hunger was still there. Thinking of the birds, and how they would come back into the berries when he left, he made a carrying **pouch** of his torn **windbreaker** and kept picking. Finally, when he judged he had close to four pounds in the jacket he stopped and went back to his camp by the ridge.

Now, he thought. Now I have some food and I can do something about fixing this place up. He glanced at the sun and saw he had some time before dark.

---

bitter, bad tasting
tart, sharp, sour
pits, hard fruit centers, which hold the seeds
pouch, small bag
windbreaker, thin jacket that protects from wind and rain

BEFORE YOU GO ON

1 Why is Brian unable to collect wood for his shelter?

2 What food does Brian find in the woods?

On Your Own
Do you know how to find food in the woods? If so, what kind(s)?

Reading 3 **117**

If only I had matches, he thought, looking **ruefully** at the beach and the lakeside. There was driftwood everywhere, not to mention dead and dry wood all over the hill and dead-dry branches hanging from every tree. All firewood. And no matches. How did they used to do it? he thought. Rub two sticks together?

He tucked the berries in the pouch back in under the overhang in the cool shade and found a couple of sticks. After ten minutes of rubbing he felt the sticks and they were almost cool to the touch. Not that, he thought. They didn't do fire that way. He threw the sticks down **in disgust**. So no fire. But he could still fix the shelter and make it—here the word "safer" came into his mind and he didn't know why—more livable.

Kind of close it in, he thought. I'll just close it in a bit.

He started dragging sticks up from the lake and pulling long dead branches down from the hill, never getting out of sight of the water and the ridge. With these he **interlaced** and wove a wall across the opening of the front of the rock. It took over two hours, and he had to stop several times because he still felt a bit weak and once because he felt a strange new **twinge** in his stomach. A tightening, rolling. Too many berries, he thought. I ate too many of them.

But it was gone soon and he kept working until the entire front of the overhang was covered save for a small opening at the right end, nearest

---

ruefully, with regret
in disgust, with a strong feeling of dislike or disapproval
interlaced, joined together by crossing over each other
twinge, sudden pain

the lake. The doorway was about three feet, and when he went in he found himself in a room almost fifteen feet long and eight to ten feet deep, with the rock wall sloping down at the rear.

"Good," he said, nodding. "Good. . . ."

Outside the sun was going down, finally, and in the initial coolness the mosquitos came out again and clouded in on him. They were thick, terrible, if not quite as bad as in the morning, and he kept brushing them off his arms until he couldn't stand it and then dumped the berries and put the torn windbreaker on. At least the sleeves covered his arms.

Wrapped in the jacket, with darkness coming down fast now, he crawled back in under the rock and **huddled** and tried to sleep. He was deeply tired, and still aching some, but sleep was slow coming and did not finally settle in until the evening cool turned to night cool and the mosquitos slowed.

Then, at last, with his stomach turning on the berries, Brian went to sleep.

---

huddled, brought his knees to his chest

ABOUT THE **AUTHOR**

Gary Paulsen has worked as a ranch hand, an engineer, a sailor, and a dog-sled racer. Since becoming a writer, he has published more than 175 books for young readers. Many include characters that face challenges.

✔ **LITERARY CHECK**

*What may have **influenced** the author, Gary Paulsen, to write* Hatchet?

BEFORE YOU GO ON

1 Is fire important to Brian's survival? Why?

2 How does Brian make his shelter "safer"?

💡 **On Your Own**
What do you think Brian's efforts say about his personality?

Reading 3 **119**

Review and Practice

► DRAMATIC READING

A good way to understand the flow of spoken conversation is to act out or recite an interview. Read "An Interview with Gary Paulsen" again with a partner. Work together to interpret any difficult or unknown words or phrases. Take turns reading the parts of the interviewer, Leonard S. Marcus, and Gary Paulsen. After you have practiced, recite the second page of the interview for the class.

 Speaking SKILL

Face your fellow students during your recitation.

► COMPREHENSION Workbook Page 61

Demonstrate your understanding of the story by responding to the questions.

Recall

1. What led Brian to the berries?
2. What does Brian use to protect himself from mosquitoes?

Comprehend

3. What does the **structure** that Brian uses as a shelter look like?
4. What does Brian try to achieve by rubbing two sticks together?

Analyze

5. What caused Brian's bodily injuries?
6. How do you think the hatchet will be helpful to Brian in the wilderness?

Connect

7. Do you like spending time in the wilderness? Why or why not?
8. Have you ever been lost in the wilderness? If so, what did you do?

▲ A hatchet

► DISCUSSION

Discuss in pairs or small groups.

1. In your opinion, what is the greatest challenge Brian must overcome in the wilderness?

2. What does Gary Paulsen mean when he says that he "fostered" himself to the woods?

Q What are the benefits of facing challenges? How did Gary Paulsen benefit from his childhood challenges later in life? Could Brian benefit in the same way? Explain.

Workbook
Page 61

► RESPONSE TO LITERATURE

Utilize Work with a partner. Describe what you think will happen to Brian next. Can he make a fire? Does he survive in the wilderness? Is he ever rescued? Try to use as much academic language as possible. Then share your ideas with the class.

»)) Listening SKILL

Think about the points others are making. Try to relate their ideas to what you already know.

LEARNING STRATEGY

Monitor your written language production. Ask a classmate for feedback. If necessary, use different words, place thcm in a different order, or reorganize your sentences to make your message clear.

▲ A campfire on the shore of a lake

Grammar

Simple and Compound Sentences

A complete sentence has a subject and a predicate. The subject is what or whom the sentence is about. The predicate tells something about the subject and contains either an action verb or a linking verb.

A simple sentence contains one subject and one verb. A simple sentence may also contain an object, predicate adjective or predicate noun, prepositional phrases, adverbs, or adjectives.

| action verb | prepositional phrase | | linking verb | adverb | prepositional |
| subject | object | | noun | adjective | phrase |

He tucked the berries in the pouch.   The sand was cool here in the shade.

A compound sentence joins two simple sentences or independent clauses with a conjunction. Don't use a comma when the subject is the same for both clauses.

> They were thick, **and** he kept brushing them off his arm.
> The sand was cool in the shade, **so** he sat for a while.
> It wasn't very deep **but** it was smooth and made a perfect roof.

Practice

Workbook Page 62

Work with a partner. Copy the pairs of simple sentences below into your notebook. Rewrite them as compound sentences, using the conjunction in parentheses. Use a comma when necessary.

Example: He ate the berries. Then he saved some. (and)
            He ate berries and then he saved some.

1. I went to the library. I checked out the book *Hatchet*. (and)
2. The book was interesting. I finished it quickly. (so)
3. He can rest. He can try to find his way home. (or)
4. He hit his head. It started to swell. (so)
5. He had to find something to eat. He didn't know what. (but)

Apply

Work with a partner. Find three simple sentences and three compound sentences in the reading. Compare your sentences with your partner's.

Agreement in Simple and Compound Sentences

In a sentence, the verb must agree in number with the subject. If the subject is singular, then the verb must be singular. If the subject is plural, then the verb must be plural. Be sure you are consistently using the correct form of the verb (present, past, etc.)

singular subject and verb

SIMPLE SENTENCE: The doorway was about three feet.

singular subject and verb, simple past   plural subject and verb, simple past

COMPOUND SENTENCE: He felt the sticks, and **they were** almost cool.

Be careful that all nouns and pronouns agree. Each pronoun should correctly refer to its antecedent, or the noun that comes before it.

He had to hold **his head** slightly tipped forward to keep **it** from hitting the top. [*His* refers to antecedent *he*; *it* refers to antecedent *head*.]

Practice  Workbook Page 63

Work with a partner. Copy the sentences below into your notebook. Choose the word in parentheses that best completes each sentence.

Example: We opened ___our___ books. (our / my)

1. She likes tea, and they _____, too. (does / do)
2. My friend lent me _____ car. (my / his)
3. She was **injured**, but they _____ fine. (were / was)
4. He hit _____ head. (his / her)
5. They fished, and then they _____.(swim / swam)

Apply

Write four sentences describing a member of your family. Then tell a partner about the person. Be sure your sentences follow the rules of agreement you have learned.

Example: My cousin Amelia is a ballet dancer. Her . . .

Writing

Ongoing
Writing
Skills
Practice

Write a Personal Letter

In this unit, you have been learning about narrative writing. In this lesson, you will write a narrative in the form of a personal letter. In a personal letter, you tell the reader a story about a memorable event or experience in your life. A personal letter has five parts: the date, the greeting, the body, the closing, and the signature. It is in the body of the letter that you include memories, ideas, and sensory details to make your story interesting to the reader.

> **Writing Prompt**
>
> Write a personal letter to a friend about a memorable event you've experienced. Be sure to include the five main parts of a letter. Include simple and compound sentences in the body of your letter.

1 **PREWRITE** Begin by choosing the person you wish to write to and an event that you want to tell him or her about.

- Try to recall an interesting event from your recent past.
- What was the detailed sequence of events?
- How did you feel about this event?
- List your ideas in a graphic organizer like the one below.

Workbook
Page 64

Here's a graphic organizer created by a student named George for a letter describing his camping trip.

Date: *October 1, 2010*

Greeting: *Dear Joe,*

Body: *I went on a camping trip with my cousins.*
It took us almost six hours to get to the campsite.
We put up the tent and it rained.
The next day, we hiked to the other side of the mountain.

Closing: *Best,*
Signature: *George*

2 **DRAFT** Use your graphic organizer to help you write a first draft.

- Remember to tell what happened in chronological order.
- Add sensory details to make the story interesting.
- Use a variety of simple and compound sentences.
- Be sure to include all five parts of the letter.

3 **REVISE** Read over your draft. Look for places where the writing is unclear or needs improvement. Use the Writing Checklist to help you identify problems. Then revise your draft, using the editing and proofreading marks listed on page 458.

4 **EDIT** Check your work for errors in grammar, usage, mechanics, and spelling. Trade letters with a partner to obtain feedback. Use the Peer Review Checklist on Workbook page 64. Edit your final draft in response to feedback from your partner and your teacher.

5 **PUBLISH** Prepare a clean copy of your final draft. Share your personal letter with the class. Save your work. You'll need to refer to it in the Writing Workshop at the end of the unit.

Writing Checklist

WORD CHOICE:
☑ I included vivid sensory details and memories in my narrative.

SENTENCE FLUENCY:
☑ I used simple and compound sentences in the body of my letter.

CONVENTIONS:
☑ I included all five parts of a personal letter.

Here is George's letter. Notice how he included simple and compound sentences in the body of his letter.

October 1, 2010

Dear Joe,

Hi, how are you? I've had many tests to study for recently and I have been really stressed out. So last weekend I tried to relax. I went on a camping trip in the mountains with my cousins. It took us almost six hours to get to the campsite! We were exhausted by the time we got there and we still had to pitch the tent. We were almost finished when it started to rain. Luckily, we stayed dry and we got a good night's rest. The next day, we hiked to the other side of the mountain. We found a big, clear lake and jumped into it to cool off. Then we ate lunch. Before long, it was time to go home. I enjoyed spending time with my cousins. Maybe next time, you can come with us.

Best,
George

What You Will Learn

Reading

■ Vocabulary building: *Context, dictionary skills, word study*

■ Reading strategy: *Recognize cause and effect*

■ Text type: *Informational text (science)*

Grammar
Passive voice: simple past; regular and irregular past participles; Passive voice: review

Writing
Write a personal narrative

THE BIG QUESTION

What are the benefits of facing challenges? Think about a challenging problem you solved in the past. Why was it challenging? How did you benefit from the experience? Discuss with a partner.

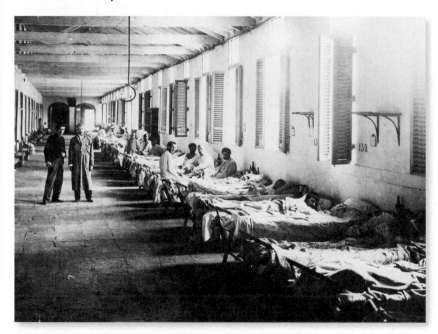

▲ Patients in a yellow fever hospital, Havana, Cuba

BUILD BACKGROUND

In this section, you will read a science article called **"The Great Fever."** It describes the struggle to find the cause of yellow fever. Discovering what caused this disease became a priority during the Spanish-American War in 1898. American troops were fighting in Cuba, and yellow fever was killing many U.S. soldiers.

Yellow fever was a mystery. It caused some people to become sick and even die. Others were not affected at all. Outbreaks occurred in some areas, but not in others. Finding the cause of this disease would be a slow, difficult, and life-threatening challenge.

► VOCABULARY

Listening and Speaking: Key Words

Read these sentences aloud with a partner. Use the context to figure out the meaning of the highlighted words. Use a dictionary to check your answers. Then write each word and its meaning in your notebook.

1. Yellow fever is a disease. People who have it often experience headaches and backaches.

2. The scientist conducted an experiment to find the cause of the illness.

3. The girl is sick. She feels warm and has a fever.

4. The scientist formed a hypothesis about how the disease spread. He believed that insects were to blame.

5. Some mosquitoes can spread disease by biting animals and people.

6. The virus spread throughout the school and caused many students to become sick.

Key Words
disease
experiment
fever
hypothesis
mosquitoes
virus

Practice

Workbook
Page 65

Write the sentences in your notebook. Choose a word from the box above to complete each sentence. Then take turns reading the sentences aloud with a partner.

1. An experiment proved that his _____ was incorrect.

2. Washing your hands can help stop a _____ from spreading.

3. I used bug spray to keep _____ from biting me.

4. The _____ was caused by a virus.

5. I used a thermometer to take my temperature. I have a _____.

6. We performed a chemistry _____ to test our hypothesis.

▲ Washing your hands can help keep you healthy.

Reading 4 **127**

Listening and Speaking: Academic Words

Study the **red** words and their meanings. You will find these words useful when talking and writing about informational texts. Write each word and its meaning in your notebook, then say the words aloud with a partner. After you read "The Great Fever," try to use these words to respond to the text.

objective = something that you are working hard to achieve	→	The scientist's **objective** was to find the cause of the illness.
theory = an idea that explains how something works or why something happens	→	He had to prove his **theory**—that a germ can cause disease.
transmit = send or pass something from one person to another	→	Some sick patients may **transmit** their illnesses to others nearby.
volunteers = people who offer to do something without expecting to be paid	→	The **volunteers** work at the hospital. They deliver flowers, clean rooms, and spend time with patients.

Audio

Practice

Workbook Page 66

Work with a partner to answer these questions. Try to include the **red** word in your answer. Write the sentences in your notebook.

1. What is one **objective** you hope to achieve in school?

2. Have you ever had to prove a scientific **theory**? If so, what was the theory and how did you prove it?

3. What is one way a person can **transmit** an illness to someone else?

4. Do you know any **volunteers**? What do they do?

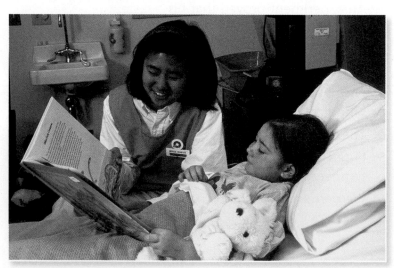

▲ A hospital volunteer reads to a child.

Word Study: Irregular Plurals

Most nouns in English are made plural by adding -s or -es to the end of the word. For some nouns, the spelling changes. Look at the examples below.

For a singular noun that ends in a consonant + *y*, change *y* to *i* and add -*es*.

Singular	Plural
enemy	enemies
laboratory	laboratories
priority	priorities

For a singular noun that ends in -*is*, change -*is* to -*es*.

Singular	Plural
crisis	crises
hypothesis	hypotheses
analysis	analyses

Practice  Workbook Page 67

Work with a partner. Take turns reading the words in the box below. Copy the words into your notebook. Change each singular noun to a plural noun. Use a dictionary if necessary.

army	colony	discovery	paralysis	theory
basis	diagnosis	emphasis	supply	thesis

READING STRATEGY | RECOGNIZE CAUSE AND EFFECT

Recognizing a cause-and-effect structure can help you better understand a text, especially informational texts. Most nonfiction and fiction texts tell about events that happen. Why an event happens is a cause. What happens as a result of a cause is an effect. To recognize causes and effects, follow these steps:

- As you read, look for events or actions in the text. These are the effects. Look for reasons for these events or actions. These are the causes.

- Look for words and phrases the author uses to talk about causes and effects, for example, *because, since, so that, therefore, as a result of, therefore.*

As you read "The Great Fever," look for causes and effects. Make sure you understand the relationship between each cause and its effect.

 Workbook Page 68

Set a purpose for reading As you read, think about the challenges scientists faced as they worked to find the cause of yellow fever.

The Great Fever

In 1801, a fierce **rebellion** broke out in Haiti. At the time, this small country belonged to France. Almost 30,000 soldiers were sent to battle the **rebels**. But the French forces lost. They were defeated by a deadly enemy—yellow fever. This terrible disease killed all but a few thousand French troops.

A Scientific Mystery

Yellow fever was among the most feared and mysterious of diseases. It first appeared in North America in the late 1600s. Yellow fever swept through both wealthy and poor areas. It appeared in some years, but not in others. No one understood what caused the disease, or how it spread.

Yellow fever was feared not only because of the thousands who died from it, but also because of the great suffering it caused. Victims would have symptoms such as headaches, backaches, and fever. When the symptoms briefly disappeared, patients would think they had gotten well. Then the disease would cause a condition

▲ Places in America that experienced major yellow fever outbreaks between 1793 and 1905

called jaundice. It would turn victims' skin and eyes a yellow **hue**. This is how yellow fever got its name.

In the last stages of the illness, patients' fevers would rise. Then, victims would begin to bleed **internally**. Some individuals would recover, but many others would not.

---

rebellion, act of fighting against a leader or government
rebels, people who fight against a leader or government

hue, color
internally, inside

A Doctor's Theory

Scientists began to discover clues about yellow fever after an **epidemic** that killed 20,000 people in 1878. However, scientists still did not know what caused and spread the disease. Did something in the water or the air create yellow fever epidemics? Did people spread the disease through human contact? How could epidemics be prevented?

Dr. Carlos Finlay had been interested in yellow fever for many years. He was from Cuba, a country with a warm, wet climate that experienced frequent epidemics. After reading scientists' theories and studying photographs of yellow fever victims, Finlay formed a hypothesis about how the disease spread. He believed that a biting insect—the mosquito—might transmit

epidemic, illness that spreads quickly to a lot of people

▲ An *Aedes aegypti* mosquito

yellow fever when it fed on animal and human blood. But since there are more than 2,000 types of mosquitoes, he wanted to find out which type might be responsible.

Finlay created a map that showed the locations of yellow fever epidemics and the **habitats** of different mosquitoes. He learned that the habitats of the *Aedes aegypti* mosquito and the locations of yellow fever epidemics were the same.

habitats, natural environments

▲ Dr. Carlos Finlay

BEFORE YOU GO ON

1 How did yellow fever get its name?

2 What did Finlay's map show? Why was this significant?

On Your Own
Do you think Finlay's hypothesis was a good one? Why or why not?

▲ Major Walter Reed

▲ Dr. James Carroll

▲ Dr. Jesse Lazear

Jesse Lazear

Finding out more about yellow fever became an even higher **priority** two decades later. In 1898, the United States declared war on Spain. President Theodore Roosevelt sent 40,000 troops to seize Cuba, which was then a Spanish **colony**. While in Cuba, 2,000 American troops **came down with** yellow fever!

The problem was so serious that the army sent a surgeon, Major Walter Reed, to Cuba in 1900. He was placed in charge of a special commission to find the cause of yellow fever. Others on the **commission** included Dr. James Carroll and a young doctor and scientist named Jesse Lazear.

Reed, Carroll, and Lazear had heard about Finlay's experiments. They decided to visit the scientist at his home in Cuba. There had been many scientific advances since Finlay first proposed his mosquito theory. By 1900, scientists had linked certain germs with specific diseases. They also discovered a relationship between mosquitoes and a disease called malaria. Lazear thought that if mosquitoes could cause malaria, they might also transmit yellow fever.

Finlay had continued to study the *Aedes aegypti* mosquito. He gave Lazear the mosquitoes from his **laboratory**. Lazear took them back to commission headquarters and experimented on human volunteers.

Lazear even experimented on himself. He allowed mosquitoes that fed on yellow fever patients to bite him. To everyone's horror, Lazear contracted yellow fever and died from it. He was only thirty-five years old.

---

priority, thing that is most important and that needs attention before anything else
colony, country controlled by another country
came down with, got sick with
commission, group of people who have been given the official job of finding out about something

---

laboratory, room in which a scientist works

The Experiment at Camp Lazear

Lazear's sacrifice seemed to show that the *Aedes aegypti* mosquito transmitted yellow fever. However, more **proof** was needed.

Reed set up a new experiment with other men and women. He offered to pay them $100. The volunteers would receive an additional $100 if they became ill. The experiment's location was called *Camp Lazear*, **in honor of** that brave scientist.

The healthy volunteers at Camp Lazear were separated into two groups. One group lived in a tent among clothes, sheets, and other items that had been used by yellow fever patients. This tent was screened and kept completely free of mosquitoes. No one in this tent became ill.

In the second tent, mosquitoes that fed on yellow fever patients were set loose and allowed to bite healthy volunteers. Items used by yellow fever patients were not allowed in this tent. Even so, all the volunteers in this tent came down with the disease.

The scientific evidence was clear. Proof had been found that mosquitoes passed

---

proof, facts or information that proves something is true
in honor of, to show respect for

◀ Camp Lazear

yellow fever from sick people to healthy ones. These insects transmitted the disease when they fed on human blood.

More Discoveries

Once scientists proved that mosquitoes caused yellow fever, epidemics could be prevented. Places where mosquitoes bred, such as backyard containers that held water, could be covered. People were encouraged to screen their windows. Chemicals were used to kill the eggs of the *Aedes aegypti* mosquito. As a result, many countries experienced fewer cases of yellow fever.

▲ Howler monkeys, like this one, are one source of the yellow fever virus.

More discoveries about yellow fever followed. It was found that monkeys in the African rain forest were the original source of the yellow fever virus. In addition to the *Aedes aegypti*, scientists also identified other types of mosquitoes that carry and transmit the virus. Finally, in the 1930s, a **vaccine** was created to prevent yellow fever.

---

vaccine, substance that is put into a person's body to protect him or her from a disease

BEFORE YOU GO ON

1 What happened to Jesse Lazear after his meeting with Dr. Finlay? Why?

2 Describe Major Reed's experiment. What was the conclusion?

On Your Own
Would you have volunteered to participate in the experiments at Camp Lazear? Explain.

Review and Practice

> ## COMPREHENSION

Workbook Page 69

Recall

1. What was discovered to be the source of yellow fever?
2. What was created to prevent yellow fever?

Comprehend

3. How did Dr. Finlay help find the cause of yellow fever?
4. How were Jesse Lazear's experiments similar to Major Walter Reed's experiments?

Analyze

5. Why do you think Dr. Finlay wanted to find the cause of yellow fever?
6. How does the author feel about Jesse Lazear? Explain.

Connect

7. Have you ever received a vaccine? What was it supposed to prevent?
8. What measures do you take to avoid mosquitoes?

▲ A flyswatter can be used to fight mosquitoes.

> ## IN YOUR OWN WORDS

Work with a partner. Copy the chart below into your notebook. Fill in the blank boxes. Use the chart to summarize the article.

Cause		Effect
	➡	The army sent Major Walter Reed to Cuba.
Jesse Lazear allowed mosquitoes to bite him.	➡	
	➡	*Aedes aegypti* mosquitoes transmit yellow fever.
Governments worked to control yellow fever epidemics.	➡	

▶ DISCUSSION

»)) Listening TIP

If you don't understand someone's answer, ask the speaker to repeat or explain it.

Discuss in pairs or small groups.

1. Do you think the United States government did enough to try to control the yellow fever epidemic in the late 1800s? Explain.

2. How were volunteers helpful in finding the cause of yellow fever?

Q What are the benefits of facing challenges? You read about doctors and scientists who worked to find the cause of yellow fever. What might motivate a person to accept such a challenge? In what ways could they benefit professionally?

▶ READ FOR FLUENCY

When we read aloud to communicate meaning, we group words into phrases, pause or slow down to make important points, and emphasize important words. Pause for a short time when you reach a comma and for a longer time when you reach a period. Pay attention to rising and falling intonation at the end of sentences.

Work with a partner. Choose a paragraph from the reading. Discuss which words seem important for communicating meaning. Practice pronouncing difficult words. Give each other feedback.

▶ EXTENSION
Workbook
Page 69

A yellow fever epidemic has not occurred in the United States for about 100 years. Still, yellow fever continues to be a problem in other countries.

Work with a partner. Go to the library or use the Internet to research areas around the world in which people continue to contract yellow fever. Then create a world map and flag these countries or regions. Share your map and findings with the class.

Grammar

Passive Voice: Simple Past; Regular and Irregular Past Participles

Form the passive voice with a form of the verb *be* + the past participle. Regular past participles are formed by adding *-d* or *-ed* to the base form of the verb. Irregular past participles, like the one below, must be memorized.

> **It was found** that monkeys in the African rain forest were the original source of the virus.

Here are a few more examples of irregular past participles.

Base Form of Verb	Simple Past	Past Participle
build	built	built
have	had	had
take	took	taken

Writers use the passive voice when the focus is on the receiver, not the performer, of an action. A *by*-phrase can be used to identify the performer. When the performer is unknown or not important, the *by*-phrase is left out.

> The experiment **was conducted by Jesse Lazear**.
>
> The healthy volunteers at Camp Lazear **were separated** into two groups.

Practice  **Workbook Page 70**

Work with a partner. Rewrite the sentences below in your notebook, changing them into passive voice. Use the correct verb tense. Use the *by*-phrase if necessary.

1. The pharmacist delivered the medicine to the doctor's office.
2. They sprayed chemicals on the plants.
3. The U.S. government took action to eliminate the disease.
4. They built a yellow fever hospital in Cuba.
5. Hospital workers retrieved the supplies.
6. Dr. Finlay completed the research.

Grammar SKILL

In passive voice, use a *by*-phrase to indicate the performer of the action:

The disease was spread **by** mosquitoes.

When the performer of the action is unimportant or unknown, omit the *by*-phrase.

✔ GRAMMAR CHECK

*How is the **passive voice** formed?*

Passive Voice: Review

You can use the passive voice with all verb forms. The passive voice is always formed with a form of *be* + the past participle. Look at the different forms of the passive voice below.

Simple Present	*is/am/are* + past participle	A vaccine **is created**.
Simple Past	*was/were* + past participle	A vaccine **was created**.
Present Progressive	*is/am/are being* + past participle	A vaccine **is being created**.
Present Perfect	*has/have been* + past participle	A vaccine **has been created**.
Past Perfect	*had been* + past participle	A vaccine **had been created**.
Simple Future	*will be* + past participle	A vaccine **will be created**.
Be going to	*is/am/are going to be* + past participle	A vaccine **is going to be created**.

Practice

Workbook
Page 71

Work with a partner. Rewrite the sentences below in your notebook, changing the active voice to passive voice. Use a *by*-phrase only when it is important to know the performer of the action.

Example: Tom opened the letter. *The letter was opened by Tom.*

1. The prince has kissed the princess.
2. Penelope will suggest a new idea.
3. People had signed the documents.
4. At the end of class, someone is going to collect the papers.
5. The horse will eat all the oats.

Apply

Work with a partner. Write seven active voice sentences with subjects and objects using the verb forms shown above. Then rewrite the sentences in passive voice.

Writing

Ongoing Writing Skills Practice

Write a Personal Narrative

In this lesson, you will write a personal narrative from your own point of view. When you write a personal narrative, you tell the reader about an event in your life that was memorable and meaningful to you. Most often, the event you choose to write about will involve other people, or characters. It is important to describe and develop these characters for the reader. One way to do so is through the use of dialogue, or what the characters say to each other.

> ### Writing Prompt
>
> Write a personal narrative. You might write a paragraph about a memorable experience you had with a friend or a classmate. Be sure to use the passive voice correctly.

1 **PREWRITE** Begin by choosing a memorable event.

- Think about the details of the time and place of your narrative.

- Who are the other characters in your narrative?

- What happened?

- What did the people in the story say?

- List your ideas in a graphic organizer like the one below.  **Workbook Page 72**

Here's a three-column chart created by a student named Ari.

Who was there	What happened	What was said
my mother and I	I had the flu.	"Oh my gosh! You're as pale as a ghost! What's wrong?!"

138 Unit 2

2 **DRAFT** Use your graphic organizer to help you write a first draft.

- Remember to establish the time and the setting.

- Use dialogue to make the characters seem real.

- As you write, think about your audience.

3 **REVISE** Read over your draft. Look for places where the writing is unclear or needs improvement. Use the Writing Checklist to help you identify problems. Then revise your draft, using the editing and proofreading marks listed on page 458.

4 **EDIT** Check your work for errors in grammar, usage, mechanics, and spelling. Trade papers with a partner to obtain feedback. Use the Peer Review Checklist on Workbook page 72. Edit your final draft in response to feedback from your partner and your teacher.

5 **PUBLISH** Prepare a clean copy of your final draft. Share your personal narrative with the class. Save your work. You'll need to refer to it in the Writing Workshop at the end of the unit.

Here is Ari's narrative. Notice how he included the passive voice in his writing.

Writing Checklist

IDEAS:
☑ I described a memorable event.

VOICE:
☑ I tried to sound like myself.

Ari Janoff

As Pale as a Ghost

When I woke up last Tuesday, I wasn't lying in my room, but on the living room couch. My mother did not make me sleep in my room because I had a heavy cough the night before. I felt "under the weather" and nauseous. I looked like a sloth, lying motionless. I called to my mom for help. She came running down the stairs and exclaimed, "Oh my gosh! You're as pale as a ghost! What's wrong?!" She brought me cough drops and juice. But I didn't feel any better. In fact, as the day wore on, I felt worse. Finally, I was taken by my mother to the doctor. He ran some tests and concluded that I had the flu. He told me I wasn't allowed to return to school until I was better—I might transmit the virus to my classmates. In all, I missed six days of school!

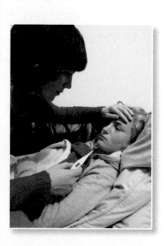

Link the Readings

Critical Thinking

Look back at the readings in this unit. Think about what they have in common. They all tell about challenges. Yet they do not all have the same purpose. The purpose of one reading might be to inform, while the purpose of another might be to entertain or persuade. In addition, the content of each reading relates to challenges differently. Now copy the chart below into your notebook and complete it.

Title of Reading	Purpose	Big Question Link
"The Train to Freedom"		It describes challenges slaves experienced as they traveled on the Underground Railroad.
"Five New Words at a Time"		
From *Hatchet*	to entertain	
"The Great Fever"		

Discussion

Discuss in pairs or small groups.

- Compare and contrast the challenges faced by Harriet Tubman and Brian Robeson. How were they the same? How were they different?

- **Q** **What are the benefits of facing challenges?** Think about the people in the readings. Does change always improve people's lives? Explain by evaluating information in the readings.

Media Literacy & Projects

Work in pairs or small groups. Choose one of these projects.

1 Research songs that are part of our African-American heritage, such as slave songs or spirituals. Learn to sing the songs, and play or perform them for your classmates.

2 You read about Harriet Tubman and her involvement in the Underground Railroad. Do research to learn about other people who took risks to help put an end to slavery. Choose one person and prepare an oral presentation about them. Use visuals. Tell the class why you chose that particular person.

3 Have you ever heard of survival skills courses? They are designed to teach people how to survive in the wilderness with little or no equipment. Use the Internet to research an organization that offers these courses. Use the information you find to make a brochure. Include the organization's address, contact information, course descriptions, and photographs. Then share your brochure with the class.

Further Reading

Choose from these reading suggestions. Practice reading silently with increased ease for longer and longer periods.

Extreme Sports, Michael Dean
This Penguin Reader® describes the challenging world of extreme sports for those with a sense of adventure.

Women in Business, David Evans
Here are the stories of five successful businesswomen: Paloma Picasso, Anita Roddick, Madonna, Oprah Winfrey, and Hanae Mori.

The World I Live In, Helen Keller
This is Helen Keller's most personal work—one that highlights her extraordinary achievements. In it, she describes what it is like to experience the world as a deaf and blind woman.

Put It All Together

LISTENING & SPEAKING WORKSHOP
Personal Narrative

As you have learned, a personal narrative is a story about events in your life. You will present a personal narrative about a challenge you have faced.

1 **THINK ABOUT IT** Look back at the readings in this unit. Talk in small groups about challenges. Describe some challenges you have faced in the past.

Work together to develop a list of challenges you could tell about in a personal narrative, for example:

- A difficult class or homework assignment
- Trying to defeat a fierce sports opponent
- Relationships you've had with friends
- Issues within your neighborhood

2 **GATHER AND ORGANIZE INFORMATION** Choose a challenging experience from your group's list. Think about the setting and plot of your personal narrative. List the characters involved in your story.

Reflect Think about what made the challenge difficult. How did you meet the challenge? Why was the experience memorable? How was facing this challenge beneficial? Write down the most important points you would like to communicate to your classmates. Include specific details.

Order Your Notes List the events you want to share in chronological order.

Use Visuals Make a poster that illustrates the events in your story. Point to the poster as you tell your story. Be ready to answer questions.

3 PRACTICE AND PRESENT Use your list of events as the written outline for your presentation. Keep your outline nearby, but practice talking to your audience without reading from it word-for-word. To make your narrative richer and more interesting, use a variety of grammatical structures, sentence lengths, sentence types, and connecting words. If possible, use a tape recorder to record your storytelling. Then play back the recording and listen to yourself. Keep practicing until you are relaxed and confident, and know your presentation well.

Deliver Your Personal Narrative Remember that presentations of this type are informal. Try to create that atmosphere during your presentation. Look at your audience as you speak. Emphasize key events with your voice and actions. For example, slow down when you come to the most important events in your narrative, and point to pictures of them on your poster. Give your classmates a chance to ask questions at the end.

4 EVALUATE THE PRESENTATION
You will improve your skills as a speaker and a listener by evaluating each presentation you give and hear. Use this checklist to help you judge your presentation and the presentations of your classmates.

- ☑ What was the speaker's topic?
- ☑ Was the setting clearly described?
- ☑ Did the speaker explain why the event was memorable?
- ☑ Did the speaker use formal or informal language? Was it appropriate?
- ☑ Did the speaker answer your questions?
- ☑ What suggestions do you have for improving the presentation?

Speaking SKILL

Learning Strategy: As you speak, employ non-verbal cues, such as facial expressions and gestures to show how you felt during this challenging experience.

Listening SKILLS

As you listen, identify the speaker's topic. Listen for the general meaning, main ideas, and important details. After each presentation, exchange this information with a partner to confirm that you have understood it correctly.

What else would you like to know about this challenging experience? Write down questions and ask them at the end of the presentation. When responding, provide your audience with as much information as possible.

STRENGTHEN YOUR SOCIAL LANGUAGE

Sharing stories with others helps to expand your English vocabulary. Go to www.LongmanKeystone.com and do the activity for this unit. This activity will help you to retell simple stories and basic information that is represented or supported by pictures.

WRITING WORKSHOP

Fictional Narrative

Write a Fictional Narrative

In this workshop, you will write a fictional narrative. A fictional narrative is a story created from the writer's imagination. A good fictional narrative has a clear setting and interesting characters. Dialogue helps bring the characters to life. The events in a fictional narrative are called the *plot*. Most plots take place in sequence and focus on a conflict that is resolved by the story's end. Another important element of a fictional narrative is the point of view, or who tells the story. Sometimes the writer tells what happens. Sometimes a character in the story tells what happens.

> **Writing Prompt**
>
> Write a fictional narrative about someone who faces a problem and successfully meets the challenge. Try to make your characters' actions believable and their dialogue realistic. Use sensory details to establish setting. Decide on the point of view you will use.

1 **PREWRITE** Review your previous work in this unit. Brainstorm a list of possible challenges to write about. Invent a situation that interests you. You might write about someone who wins a contest, overcomes an illness, or stands up against injustice. Then think about your main character. What are his or her traits? From whose point of view will you tell your story? In your notebook, answer these questions:

Ongoing Writing Skills Practice

- Where does the story take place?
- Who is the main character and what kind of person is he or she?
- What kind of problem does he or she face?
- How does the main character meet the challenge?  **Workbook Page 73**

List your ideas in a graphic organizer like the one below.
Here is a graphic organizer created by a student named Austin.

Characters	Setting	Problem	Solution
Julia Melissa	School auditorium Julia's house	Julia wins the part Has trouble learning the role	Melissa helps Julia practice Great performance!

2 **DRAFT** Use your graphic organizer and the model on page 148 to help you write a first draft.

- Remember to establish a setting for your story.
- Tell the story events in chronological order.
- Use transitions to keep the ideas flowing smoothly.
- Keep the point of view consistent and use correct pronoun agreement.
- Use dialogue to bring the characters to life.

3 **REVISE** Read over your draft. Think about how well you have addressed questions of purpose, audience, and genre. Your purpose is to entertain. Is your story entertaining? Is it appropriate in content and tone for the intended audience? Does your story include all the elements of the genre?

Keep these questions in mind as you revise your draft. Use the Writing Checklist below to help you identify additional issues that may need revision. Mark your changes on your draft using the editing and proofreading marks listed on page 458.

SIX TRAITS OF WRITING CHECKLIST

☑ **IDEAS:** Did I establish the setting? Did I present the events in chronological order?

☑ **ORGANIZATION:** Are my ideas organized logically so that my writing has internal and external coherence?

☑ **VOICE:** Does my writing have energy and personality? Did I use dialogue to bring the characters to life?

☑ **WORD CHOICE:** Did I choose precise words in order to create vivid images?

☑ **SENTENCE FLUENCY:** Did I use transitions in an effective way? Did I vary my use of simple, compound, and complex sentences?

☑ **CONVENTIONS:** Is my point of view consistent? Do my pronouns agree in gender and number?

Here are the revisions Austin plans to make to his first draft.

A Challenge and Success!

The New York streets were bustling with people as ~~I~~ ^Julia made ~~my~~ ^her way to the audition. Lucky charm in hand, ~~I~~ ^she entered the auditorium of the performing arts academy where ~~I~~ ^she attended school. The room was filled with other students rehearsing lines, dancing, and singing.

Julia tried her best. ^but She didn't think the director looked too impressed with her performance. ^In fact, She was shocked and thrilled a week later, when she learned that she had ^been awarded the leading role!

^The part was long and difficult. One day, after rehearsing alone in her room, Julia began to doubt she would ever learn her lines. "I don't even know a page, she exclaimed. She repeated her lines over and over.

"I think I've got it!" she shouted Then, a minute later, she cried, "Darn, I forgot them again." She threw her script ~~in~~ ^on the floor and wondered, "Should I just drop out? NO! It would upset Mom and Dad so much."

^The phone rang. "Hello?" Julia said tiredly.

"JULIA, JULIA, OH, MY GOSH! How are you?" said her friend melissa.

"Stressed!" Julia answered.

"Why?" Melissa demanded.

Julia confessed all her fears.

> Edited to change point of view and adjust pronoun agreement.

> Revised to create a compound sentence, add a transition word, and use the passive voice.

> Edited to include a descriptive detail.

> Revised to correct an error in use of preposition.

"Don't worry," Melissa said. "Why don't I come over everyday to help you."

Julia thought about it. Then she admitted, "That would be great!"

"DEAL!" Melissa said.

Had rehearsing with Melissa really helped? On opening night, Julia was so nervous she almost couldn't breathe. After two hours, the last line of the show was sayed. Julia had done it! As she stood up to a standing ovation, she made eye contact with Melissa at the crowd and smiled a big thank-you.

Melissa silently mouthed the words, "You're welcome." Julia felt a rush of happiness and gratitude as she took her bow.

Revised to improve narrative flow and to correct spelling and use of preposition.

4 EDIT Check your work for errors in grammar, usage, mechanics, and spelling. Then trade stories with a partner and use the Peer Review Checklist below to give each other constructive feedback. Edit your final draft in response to feedback from your partner and your teacher.

Workbook
Page 73

PEER REVIEW CHECKLIST

- ☑ Did the story sustain my interest?
- ☑ Is the story line engaging?
- ☑ Is the action well paced?
- ☑ Is the setting specific and believable?
- ☑ Are the characters interesting? Are they well developed?
- ☑ What changes could be made to improve the story?

Here are the changes Austin decided to make to his final draft.

Austin Saiz

A Challenge and Success!

The New York streets were bustling with people as Julia made her way to the audition. Lucky charm in hand, she entered the auditorium of the performing arts academy where she attended school. The room was filled with other students rehearsing lines, dancing, and singing.

Julia tried her best, but she didn't think the director looked too impressed with her performance. In fact, she was shocked and thrilled a week later, when she learned that she had been awarded the leading role!

Revised to correct errors in punctuation.

The part was long and difficult. One day, after rehearsing alone in her room, Julia began to doubt she would ever learn her lines. "I don't even know a page," she exclaimed. She repeated her lines over and over.

"I think I've got it!" she shouted. Then, a minute later, she cried, "Darn, I forgot them again." She threw her script on the floor and wondered, "Should I just drop out? NO! It would upset Mom and Dad so much."

The phone rang. "Hello?" Julia said tiredly.

"JULIA, JULIA, OH, MY GOSH! How are you?" said her friend melissa.

"Stressed!" Julia answered.

Revised to correct errors in punctuation.

"Why?" Melissa demanded.

Julia confessed all her fears.

"Don't worry," Melissa said. "Why don't I come over everyday to help you."

Julia thought about it. Then she admitted "That would be great!"

"DEAL!" Melissa said.

On opening night, Julia was so nervous she almost couldn't breathe. Had rehearsing with Melissa really helped? After two hours, the last line of the show was said. Julia had done it! As she stood up to a standing ovation, she made eye contact with Melissa in the crowd and smiled a big thank-you.

Melissa silently mouthed the words, "You're welcome." Julia felt a rush of happiness and gratitude as she took her bow.

5 **PUBLISH** Prepare a clean copy of your final draft. Share your story with the class.

Workbook Page 74

Test Preparation

PRACTICE

Read the following test questions. Study the tips in the boxes. Work with a partner to answer the questions.

1 Where is the sign found?

   A   In a car
   B   In a store
   C   By the road
   D   By the door

2 A square is a quadrilateral. It is a rhombus because it has four congruent _____. It is a rectangle because it has four 90° angles. All squares are rectangles and rhombi, but all rhombi and rectangles are not squares.

   F   geometry
   G   similar
   H   sides
   J   shapes

Taking Tests
You will often take tests that help show what you know. Study the tips below to help you improve your test-taking skills.

Tip
Pay attention to the time. You do not want to take a long time on one question if you must finish the test quickly.

Tip
Sometimes test questions give more information than is needed to answer the question. Reread the question to decide what information is needed and what is not.

Workbook
Pages 75–78

The Challenge of Illness

*M*ost people face illness at some point in their lives. Sometimes medicine alone cannot heal them. People need help from family and friends as well as their own personal strength to get well. American artists often celebrate the spirit that moves people to recover from disease or injury.

Alice Eugenia Ligon, *Embroidered Garment* (about 1949)

Alice Eugenia Ligon had to go to the hospital for a medical problem in 1949. Later, she turned the symbol of her illness—her hospital gown—into a holiday present and work of art for her children. She gives the viewer this information by sewing the story in green thread in the bottom left corner of the gown, under the second rainbow. Using every blank area, she also embroidered dozens of religious, patriotic, and personal phrases and images on the gown that held great meaning to her. This piece of folk art celebrates Ligon's ability to face the challenge of her illness and turn it into something positive. If she had to sit and heal, then she could also sit and create!

Alice Eugenia Ligon, *Embroidered Garment*, about 1949, muslin, cotton, 43¾ × 38½ in., Smithsonian American Art Museum ▶

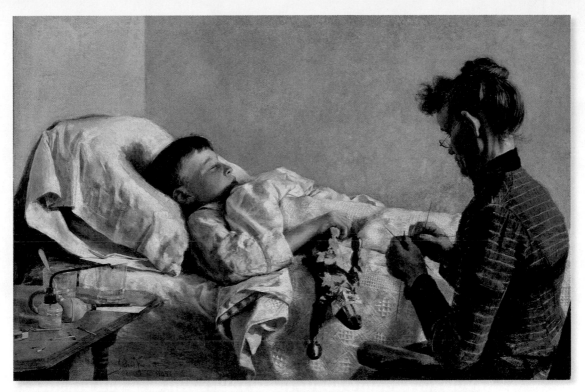

▲ J. Bond Francisco, *The Sick Child*, 1893, oil, 32 x 48 in., Smithsonian American Art Museum

J. Bond Francisco, *The Sick Child* (1893)

In J. Bond Francisco's *The Sick Child*, a mother sits nervously in her chair. She knits and stares through her glasses at a boy resting in bed. The boy holds a toy clown, which stands out in the center of the painting. It's uncertain if the boy will have enough strength to continue to hold on to the clown. It looks as if it might fall to the floor. Francisco leaves it unclear whether the boy will survive his illness. The mother faces the challenge the best way that she knows how: sitting by her son's side and keeping busy to pass the long hours.

Francisco painted *The Sick Child* at a time when medicine was still very limited. Unfortunately, many parents in the 1800s experienced the horror of watching a child die. This made it easy for them to understand the subject matter of Francisco's painting. Thousands of doctors' offices across the United States hung a copy of *The Sick Child* in their waiting rooms, which made Francisco's painting very well known.

Both artworks celebrate the human need to face challenges and to reach out to family during troubled times.

Discuss What You Learned

1 What creates an air of uncertainty in Francisco's painting?

2 How does each of these artworks celebrate the spirit that helps people to recover from illness? In what ways are they similar and different?

Q **Big Question**
What other kinds of challenges do people face besides illness, and how could they be shown in an artwork?

Workbook
Pages 79–80

THE BIG Q QUESTION How are relationships with others important?

This unit is about relationships. You will read informational texts and literature that describe different kinds of relationships and how they change the lives of the people involved. Reading about these topics will give you practice using academic language and will help you become a better student.

Reading

1 Novel

From *Salsa Stories,* "Aguinaldo" by Lulu Delacre

Reading Strategy: Analyze cultural context

2 Social Studies

- "Sowing the Seeds of Peace" by Mandy Terc
- "Seeds of Peace: Cultivating Friendships"

Reading Strategy: Compare and contrast

3 Legend

From *Blue Willow* by Pam Conrad

Reading Strategy: Identify with a character

4 **Science**

"The Ladybird and
the Wildflowers"

Reading Strategy:
Classify

Listening and Speaking—Expository

At the end of this unit, you will choose a topic
and deliver a **how-to demonstration** about it.

Writing—Expository

In this unit you will practice **expository writing**,
which presents factual information about a
topic. After each reading you will learn a skill to
help you write an expository paragraph. At the
end of the unit, you will use these skills to help
you write an expository essay.

Quick **Write**

List the different kinds of relationships that
you have with other people. Circle the three
relationships that are the most important
to you.

DVD **VIEW AND RESPOND**
Watch the DVD for Unit 3 and answer the
questions at
www.LongmanKeystone.com.

What You Will Learn

Reading
- Vocabulary building: *Literary terms, word study*
- Reading strategy: *Analyze cultural context*
- Text type: *Literature (novel excerpt)*

Grammar
Imperatives; Embedded questions

Writing
Write instructions

➤ ◉ THE BIG QUESTION

How are relationships with others important? There is an old saying that when you help someone, you are really helping yourself. What do you think that means? Do you think it is important to reach out to others? Discuss with a partner.

➤ BUILD BACKGROUND

In this section, you will read **"Aguinaldo,"** an excerpt from the novel *Salsa Stories*. It is about a young Puerto Rican girl named Marilia. Her class is going on a field trip to a nursing home where her classmates plan to deliver surprise Christmas gifts, or *aguinaldos*, to the elderly people who live there. However, Marilia is afraid to participate; her only grandmother died in a nursing home the year before, and the thought of returning to one makes her sad.

Currently, more than 1.5 million elderly Americans live in nursing homes, or places where elderly people live. Some of them cannot care for themselves. They receive medical care, healthy meals, opportunities to participate in organized activities, and companionship.

◀ A caregiver hugs an elderly nursing-home resident.

➤ VOCABULARY

Learn Literary Words

Foreshadowing is an author's use of clues to hint at what might happen later in a story. Writers use foreshadowing to build readers' expectations and to create suspense.

Irony is the difference between what the reader expects to happen and what actually happens in a story. Writers include ironic situations in stories to create surprise and amusement. Read the example of irony below.

> Jonathan didn't want to study in France, but his parents thought it would be beneficial for him to experience another culture. After saying good-bye to his parents at the airport, Jonathan made a mental list of all the reasons why he *should not* be flying to France: He didn't speak the language, none of his friends lived there, he didn't even like French food.
>
> * * *
>
> Three months later, Jonathan decided to call his parents—it wouldn't hurt to ask. He was nervous as he listened to the phone ring. His mother answered. "Hi, Mom. Do you think I could stay here for the rest of the school year?"

What is ironic about Jonathan's situation?

Practice    **Workbook** Page 81

In a small group, discuss a movie you have seen that contains an ironic situation. Describe the difference between what you thought would happen and what actually happened. Also, describe any foreshadowing that may have occurred.

Listening and Speaking: Academic Words

Study the **red** words and their meanings. You will find these words useful when talking and writing about literature. Write each word and its meaning in your notebook, then say the words aloud with a partner. After you read "Aguinaldo," the excerpt from *Salsa Stories*, try to use these words to respond to the text.

Academic Words

distributes
positive
rejected
residents

distributes = gives something to different people or places	→	Our class **distributes** gifts to needy people each year.
positive = good or useful	→	Simonese enjoyed her visit to the nursing home. It was a **positive** experience.
rejected = decided not to do something	→	Aaliyah **rejected** the opportunity to visit the nursing home.
residents = people who live in a place	→	The **residents** of the nursing home were happy to have visitors.

Practice

Workbook Page 82

Work with a partner to answer these questions. Try to include the **red** word in your answer. Write the sentences in your notebook.

1. Is there a shelter in your area that **distributes** food or clothing to the needy? Have you ever volunteered to work there?

2. Do you think volunteering is a **positive** use of your time? Why or why not?

3. Have you ever **rejected** the opportunity to volunteer somewhere? Explain.

4. Are there **residents** that volunteer to pick up trash in and around your neighborhood? How would the area be different if these people did not volunteer their time and energy?

These volunteers work to keep school grounds clean. ▶

156 Unit 3

Word Study: Spelling *s-* Blends

A consonant blend is the sound that two or three consonants make when they come together in a word. You can hear the sound of each consonant in the blend. Identifying *s-* blends can help you spell new and unfamiliar words. Read the *s-* blends and examples in the chart below.

sw- (/sw/)	sp- (/sp/)	st- (/st/)	str- (/str/)
swept	**sp**ecial	**st**ay	**str**anger
swim	**sp**ace	**st**omach	**str**ong

Practice

Work with a partner. Copy the sentences below into your notebook. Read the sentences aloud. Complete each sentence with the correct *s-* blend.

1. We are _____ending the day at the nursing home.
2. The building is across the _____eet.
3. The woman told me _____ories about her childhood.
4. She _____oke softly.
5. I _____allowed the juice.
6. She _____ared at the card.
7. The _____udents decorated the room with _____eamers.

READING STRATEGY **ANALYZE CULTURAL CONTEXT**

Analyzing the cultural context of a story or text helps you visualize and understand what's happening. Cultural context includes the beliefs, art, ideas, and values of a particular community. To analyze cultural context, follow these steps as you read:

- Think about the characters' native language and country.
- Think about what you already know about the place and the people.
- Notice how the author describes the houses, food, music, and clothing.
- Pay attention to the characters' ideas and beliefs.

As you read "Aguinaldo," think about the place where the story happens. Compare and contrast it with your own experience.

Set a purpose for reading As you read, notice how Marilia's views about the nursing home change. What are the reasons for this change?

from
Salsa Stories

Aguinaldo

Audio

Lulu Delacre

On New Year's Day, a neighbor gives Carmen Teresa a blank notebook. Although she is grateful for the gift, Carmen Teresa has no idea how to fill it. Her guests suggest she use it to record family stories. When she agrees, her family members eagerly share their childhood experiences. This excerpt is **Tía** *Marilia's tale.*

When I was growing up in Puerto Rico, I went to a small, Catholic girls' school. Every December, Sister Antonia, our religion teacher, insisted that students visit the nursing home in Santurce. Bringing Christmas cheer to the old and **infirm** was an experience she felt all students should have.

"I'm not going," I whispered to my friend Margarita.

"You have to, Marilia," she said. "Everyone has to go."

All of my classmates looked forward to the trip. But ever since my only grandma died in a nursing home, the thought of going back to one made me feel sad. I didn't want to go.

As I sat at my desk making the Christmas card that I would give to a resident, I tried to figure out how I could skip this **field trip**. Maybe they

---

Tía, aunt
infirm, weak or sick
field trip, trip students take with their classmates and teacher

would let me help at the library. Maybe I could write a special book report at school while they were out. Or better yet, I could wake up ill and stay home from school. As soon as the recess bell rang, I ran over to the library to try out my first plan.

"**Hola**, Marilia," **Señora** Collazo greeted me.

"Hola, Señora Collazo," I said, smiling sweetly. "I came to ask you if I could stay here tomorrow to help you paint posters for the book fair. I really don't mind spending the whole day at the library."

"Aren't you going on a field trip tomorrow?" Señora Collazo asked.

"My class is going. But I could be excused if you need my help." The librarian thanked me and said that if I wanted to help I could join the other students who had already volunteered to stay after school to do the posters. Biting my lip, I left the library in a hurry. It was time to try my second plan.

I marched right back to my classroom. Sister Antonia was grading papers at her desk as I went in.

"Sister Antonia," I said softly.

"Yes, Marilia," Sister Antonia answered.

I stared for a moment at the buckles of my shoes. Then without looking up, I took a deep breath, swept back my black curls, and asked, "May I stay in school tomorrow to do an extra book report?"

"I'm afraid not, Marilia," Sister Antonia said firmly. "Tomorrow is our trip to the nursing home. But if you want to do an extra book report, you can do it over the weekend."

---

hola, *hello*
Señora, *Mrs.*

»)) *Listening* SKILL

As you listen to the Audio CD, look at the illustrations on pages 158–165. Use these visuals to help explain new words or ideas. Discuss these words or concepts with a partner to gain understanding.

BEFORE YOU GO ON

1 What does Sister Antonia insist her students do every year? Why?

2 Explain why Marilia **rejected** Sister Antonia's idea.

On Your Own
Would you want to go on this field trip? Why or why not?

I glanced across the room to the trays of *besitos de coco*, the coconut sweets that my class had prepared to bring to the nursing-home residents as an *aguinaldo*. *Aguinaldos*, surprise Christmas gifts, were fun to receive. But still, I wasn't going, so it wasn't my concern. I whispered thank you to the sister, and left.

That evening at dinnertime, I put my third plan into action. To my parent's surprise, I had two big helpings of rice and kidney beans, two helpings of dessert, and three glasses of **mango** juice. I *never* ate so much. I figured that with all this food, I was sure to get **indigestion**. I went to bed and waited. I tossed and turned. I waited for several hours expecting a stomachache any second, but instead, the heavy meal made me tired and I fell sound asleep.

"Marilia, get dressed!" Mami called early the next morning. "We have to leave soon for school!"

How unlucky. I woke up feeling quite well. There was only one thing left to do, I ran to the bathroom, let the hot water run, and drank a full glass of it. Then I went back to bed.

"Marilia." Mami came in. "Get up! What is going on with you?"

"I feel warm, Mami," I **mumbled**.

Mami looked with **concern**. She touched my forehead and my neck. She left the room and in a few minutes came back with the **thermometer** in her hand. I opened my mouth and she slipped it under my tongue.

---

mango, sweet tropical fruit
indigestion, stomach pains from eating too much food
mumbled, spoke quietly and unclearly
concern, worry
thermometer, instrument that measures the temperature of your body

When the time was up, Mami pulled the thermometer out and read it.

"One hundred and six degrees?" she exclaimed. "That's impossible. You look perfectly fine to me."

After a little questioning, I confessed what I had done. I told Mami how much I didn't want to go on the field trip.

"You know, Marilia," she advised, "you might enjoy yourself after all. Besides, I've already promised Sister Antonia two trays of **tembleque** to bring as an *aguinaldo* to the residents of the home."

There was no way out. I had to go.

In the big lobby of the nursing home, paper streamers hung from the tall windows. The residents were **scattered** everywhere. Sister Antonia took out her guitar and at the sound of the first bar we began to sing a medley of carols. Meanwhile, the residents clapped and sang along while a student passed around our cards for us to give to them later. As I watched how happy our music made the residents, memories of my grandma rushed to me, making me **dizzy** with sadness. Suddenly, I saw that everybody was visiting with their residents. I was alone. I didn't feel like joining one of the groups. Maybe I could quietly slip away until the visit was over. I hoped it would be soon. Then I noticed a chair against the yellow wall. I sat there still holding the card I had made.

---

tembleque, dessert made from coconut milk
scattered, spread out
dizzy, unsteady

BEFORE YOU GO ON

1 What are *aguinaldos*? What *aguinaldos* does Marilia's class **distribute** to the residents of the nursing home?

2 How does Marilia feel when she goes to the nursing home? Why?

On Your Own
Have you ever known someone who lived in a nursing home?

Reading 1 **161**

Across the room there was a frail old lady in a wheelchair. She was alone, too. I looked at my card again. It was rather pretty. I had painted it with shades of blue and gold. Maybe I could just hand it to her and leave. It might brighten her day. So **gingerly**, I crossed the lobby and stood next to her.

"Who is there?" the old lady asked as she **coquettishly** fixed her silver bun with the light touch of her **manicured** hand.

"My name is Marilia," I said. "I brought you a card."

"*Dios te bendiga,*" the old woman said. "God bless you."

She reached for the card but her hand was nowhere near it. Her gaze was lost in the distance, and I knelt down to place the card in her hand. It was then that I saw the big clouds in her eyes. She was blind. *What was the use of a card if you couldn't see it?* I felt cheated. I stood up to go back to my chair.

"My name is Elenita," she said as I tried to slip away. "Tell me, Marilia, what does your card look like?"

I knelt down beside her and, in as **vivid** detail as I could, described the three **wise men** I had drawn. Then, Elenita's curious fingers **caressed** every inch of the card. She couldn't have enjoyed it more if she had seen it.

---

gingerly, cautiously
coquettishly, in a feminine way
manicured, professionally cared for
vivid, clear, specific
wise men, kings who came to see the baby Jesus
caressed, felt in a gentle way

162 Unit 3

When the coconut sweets were passed around, she **mischievously** asked for two.

"I bet you are not supposed to eat one of these," she giggled.

"No," I replied. "Sister Antonia told us that the sweets were just for residents."

"Well," she whispered. "Nobody said I couldn't give you one of *mine*."

I liked Elenita. I placed the *besito de coco* in my mouth and **relished** it even more. Especially since I wasn't supposed to have it. I enjoyed being her partner in mischief. After all, she asked me if I liked music and if I knew how to dance.

"Ay," I said, "I love to listen to music and dance."

Then she told me how, when she was young, she had been a great dancer.

"I used to dance so well that men would line up for a chance to dance with me. I had many, many **suitors** at one time," she said. "I had suitors that **serenaded** me in the evening and others that brought me flowers. But I didn't go out with all of them. You have to be selective, you know."

Too soon we were interrupted by Sister Antonia. It was time to get on the bus and return to school. I didn't want to leave.

---

mischievously, playfully
relished, enjoyed
suitors, men who want to marry a woman
serenaded, sang a romantic song to

✔ **LITERARY CHECK**

What is the irony of Marilia's trip to the nursing home?

BEFORE YOU GO ON

1 Why does Elenita ask Marilia to describe the card?

2 Why does Marilia have **positive** feelings when she leaves the nursing home?

On Your Own
Did you like Elenita? Why or why not?

Reading 1 **163**

"Thank you for the card, Marilia," Elenita said. She opened her hand and **gestured** for me to give her mine. "I'll keep this card to remember you by."

"I'm sorry you can't see it," I said as I squeezed her hand. For a moment it felt as warm and giving as my own grandma's. "I wish I had brought you a better *aguinaldo*."

"The best *aguinaldo*," Elenita said, "was your visit, Marilia."

As I left, I felt light and warm and peaceful. On the bus ride back, I told my friend Margarita all about our visit. I couldn't wait to come back next year. I already knew what I would bring Elenita. I would make her a **collage**. That way she would be able to feel the many textures of my picture, even if she couldn't see it. And maybe I could make a picture of her dancing. I knew she had been very pretty when she was young.

"Are you going to wait until next Christmas to give her your collage?" Margarita asked.

I thought for a moment. "Maybe Mami could bring me back sooner," I said.

As I looked out the window, I remembered how good Elenita's hand felt to touch. It's funny how sometimes things change unexpectedly. Just that morning I didn't want to go at all. But then, I couldn't wait to visit my new friend again. We had gone to the nursing home to give *aguinaldos*. And what a very special *aguinaldo* I had been given—Elenita's friendship.

✔ **LITERARY CHECK**
*Look back at the story. Identify one instance of **foreshadowing**.*

---

gestured, made a motion
collage, work of art made by sticking pictures, photographs, cloth, etc.
   onto a surface

Marilia's Besitos de Coco

(Coconut Kisses)

3¼ cups fresh frozen grated
    coconut, firmly packed
1 cup brown sugar, firmly packed
8 **tbs.** all-purpose flour
¼ **tsp.** salt
4 tbs. butter, at room temperature
3 **lg.** egg yolks
½ tsp. vanilla

Preheat oven to 350°F. Place grated coconut in a bowl. Add brown sugar, flour, salt, butter, yolks, and vanilla. Mix well. Grease a 9- by 13-inch glass baking dish. Take mixture by the tablespoon, shape into balls, and arrange in baking dish. Bake for about 35 minutes or until golden. Let cool in baking dish for 10 minutes. With a small spatula, remove *besitos* carefully and place upside down onto platter. Let cool completely and turn over.

Makes about 35.

---

tbs., short for tablespoon, which is a large spoon used for measuring food
tsp., short for teaspoon, which is a small spoon used for measuring food
lg., large

ABOUT THE **AUTHOR**

Lulu Delacre was born in Puerto Rico to Argentine parents. She showed an early interest in drawing and attended painting classes in Argentina when she was ten. Later she studied fine arts in Puerto Rico and France. The stories in her books, which she both writes and illustrates, come from her cultural heritage.

BEFORE YOU GO ON

1 What *aguinaldo* does Marilia receive during her trip to the nursing home?

2 What are *besitos de coco*? What are they made of?

On Your Own
Do you think it is important for young people to develop and maintain relationships with elderly individuals? Explain.

Reading 1 **165**

▶ **READER'S THEATER**

Act out the following scene between Marilia and her mother.

Mami: [*reading a thermometer*] One hundred and six degrees! You don't look that sick. Marilia, what's going on?

Marilia: Mami, I don't want to go on the field trip to the nursing home.

Mami: Why not?

Marilia: [*sounding sad*] It reminds me of Grandma. I miss her.

Mami: I know, I miss her, too. But Marilia, you might enjoy your trip to the nursing home more than you think.

Marilia: [*shaking her head no*] I don't think so, Mami.

Mami: Besides, we have to bring *aguinaldos* for the residents. Now, get ready. We have to leave soon.

Marilia: [*sounding defeated*] Okay, Mami, I'm coming.

▶ **COMPREHENSION**  **Workbook**
Page 85

Recall

1. Where does the story take place?

2. What will Marilia bring on her next visit to the nursing home? Why?

Comprehend

3. In what ways does Marilia try to skip the field trip?

4. What activities do the students participate in at the nursing home?

Analyze

5. Why does Sister Antonia think it is important for the students to bring Christmas cheer to the old and infirm? Support your answer by evaluating information in the story.

6. How does the students' visit affect the nursing home **residents**?

Connect

7. Do you have elderly friends? How are they important to you?

8. Describe a special recipe that you like to share with friends.

LEARNING STRATEGY

Speak using non-verbal cues, such as facial expressions and gestures, to show the character's feelings and actions.

Audio

➤ DISCUSSION

Discuss in pairs or small groups.

1. How are Marilia and Elenita similar?

2. How do you think Marilia's experience at the nursing home might affect her the next time she has to do something she's afraid to do?

Q **How are relationships with others important?** In what ways did Marilia help herself by reaching out to Elenita? Has someone ever reached out to you in this way when you needed a friend? Explain.

➤ RESPONSE TO LITERATURE  Workbook Page 85

Utilize Marilia dreads having to go on the school field trip to the nursing home. Prior to leaving, she discusses her fears with her mother.

Work with a partner. Write a dialogue that occurs between Marilia and her mother after the field trip. In it, include Marilia's description of events—what she saw at the nursing home, what she did there, and who she met. Include her plans to return to the nursing home. Ask your peers and teacher for their feedback about your dialogue. Then perform your dialogue for the class.

»)⁹ Listening SKILL

Respect each speaker. Listen politely, even if you disagree with the speaker's ideas.

LEARNING STRATEGY

Monitor your written language production. Ask a classmate for feedback. If necessary, use different words, place them in a different order, or reorganize your sentences to make your message clear.

Grammar

Imperatives

You can use an imperative to give a command or instructions. You can also make a request or an offer using an imperative with *please*. An imperative is always in the simple present. The subject is *you*, but it is not stated. Form a negative imperative by adding *do not* or *don't* before the verb.

| **Give a Command** |
| Marilia, **get** dressed! **Don't tell** me you're sick! |
| **Give Instructions** |
| **Place** grated coconut in a bowl. |
| Carefully **break** the eggs. |
| **Make a Request or Offer** |
| Please **take** a *besito de coco*. OR **Take** a *besito de coco*, please. |

Grammar SKILL

When an adverb is used in an imperative, it usually comes at the beginning of the imperative.

You can also use "let's" before the verb to make a suggestion if you are including yourself in the imperative.

| **Let's go** to the nursing home again. |

Practice  Workbook Page 86

Work with a partner. Copy the sentences below into your notebook. Then rewrite the sentences as imperatives.

Example: You must go to the nursing home. *Go to the nursing home.*

1. You should go to the zoo to see the panda.
2. You can't cross the street now!
3. We should order some pizza.
4. You shouldn't forget to study for the test.
5. You need to slow down—you're going too fast!

Apply

Work with a partner. Using imperatives, give your partner instructions to do something or directions to go somewhere.

Example: Take some bread. Put some butter on it . . .

Embedded Questions

An embedded question is a type of noun clause. It can be the subject or object of the sentence. Begin embedded information questions with a question word. Begin embedded *yes / no* questions with *if* or *whether*.

> **INFORMATION QUESTION:** What would I bring Elenita?
> **EMBEDDED QUESTION:** I already knew **what I would bring Elenita**. [object]
> **EMBEDDED QUESTION:** **What I would bring Elenita** would make her happy. [subject]
> **YES / NO QUESTION:** Could I stay here tomorrow?
> **EMBEDDED QUESTION:** I came to ask you **if I could stay here tomorrow.**

Use normal word order (subject + verb + object), not question order, for most embedded questions. Use question word order when the question word is both the subject of the question and the noun clause.

> What had I done?   I confessed **what I had done**.
> Who is there?   I don't know **who is there**.]

Practice

Workbook Page 87

Work with a partner. Copy the sentence starters into your notebook. Then change the questions in parentheses to noun clauses and complete the sentences.

Example: (Where do you live?) Please tell me *where you live*.

1. (Who are they?) Do you know _____?
2. (When did he leave?) I wonder _____.
3. (Who is coming?) I need to know _____.
4. (What are we doing in class?) _____ is easy.
5. (What did she say?) _____ made me angry.

Apply

Work with a partner. Find questions in the reading. Use the phrases in the Practice exercise to change them into embedded questions.

Writing

Ongoing Writing Skills Practice

Write Instructions

At the end of this unit you will write an expository essay. Expository writing explains or informs. Instructions are one kind of expository writing. They explain how to do or make something. For example, the recipe on page 165 teaches the reader how to make *besitos de coco*. First, the recipe lists the ingredients, such as coconut and brown sugar. Then a clear sequence of steps tells the reader how to mix the ingredients together. Finally, the recipe instructs the reader how to cook the treats. When describing a sequence of steps, writers use sequence words, such as *first, then, next,* and *finally*, to keep the order clear.

> ### Writing Prompt
>
> Write a set of instructions. Be sure to write about something you know how to do well, such as baking cookies or using an MP3 player. Be sure to use imperatives correctly.

1 **PREWRITE** Begin by choosing something you know how to do.

- Write the name of the activity at the top of the page in your notebook.

- Think about how to explain the activity. What equipment or tools do you need? What are the steps in the activity?

- List your ideas in a sequence chart.

- Decide which sequence words to use with each step.

Workbook Page 88

Here's a sequence chart created by a student named Haley. She is explaining how to find volunteer opportunities.

First: Do an Internet search with the key word <u>volunteer</u> and your zip code.

↓

Then: Collect information about each place that interests you.

↓

Next: Call your friends and ask them if they are interested in volunteering.

↓

Finally: Choose a place to volunteer and call or visit them to find out more.

2 **DRAFT** Use your sequence chart to help you write a draft.

- Keep in mind your purpose for writing.
- Remember to explain the steps in the correct order.
- Remember to use imperatives.
- Make sure to use sequence words.

3 **REVISE** Read over your draft. Look for places where the writing is unclear or needs improvement. Use the Writing Checklist to help you identify problems. Then revise your draft, using the editing and proofreading marks listed on page 458.

4 **EDIT** Check your work for errors in grammar, usage, mechanics, and spelling. Trade papers with a partner to obtain feedback. Use the Peer Review Checklist on Workbook page 88. Edit your final draft in response to feedback from your partner and your teacher.

5 **PUBLISH** Prepare a clean copy of your final draft. Share your instructions with the class. Save your work. You'll need to refer to it in the Writing Workshop at the end of the unit.

Writing Checklist

ORGANIZATION:
☑ I explained the steps in the correct order.

SENTENCE FLUENCY:
☑ My instructions are clear and easy to follow.

Here is Haley's paragraph about how to find volunteer opportunities.

Haley Coy

How to Find Volunteer Opportunities in Your Area
Volunteering is a great way to help your community. One way to find a volunteer opportunity is to look on the Internet. To do this you will need a computer with Internet access, a pen or a pencil, and a phone. First, do a search. Use the key word "volunteer" and your zip code to find nearby places in which to volunteer, such as nursing homes, hospitals, food banks, and homeless shelters. Next, collect information about each place that interests you. Be sure to find out what skills or experience you need in order to volunteer at these places. Then call your friends and ask them if they are interested in volunteering, too. It'll be fun to volunteer together. After you decide on a place to volunteer, write down the address, telephone number, and the name of a person to contact. Finally, call or visit the organization to find out more about it.

What You Will Learn

Reading

■ Vocabulary building: *Context, dictionary skills, word study*

■ Reading strategy: *Compare and contrast*

■ Text type: *Informational text (social studies)*

Grammar
Complex sentences; Agreement in complex sentences

Writing
Write a critique

➤ THE BIG QUESTION

How are relationships with others important? Think about one of your friends. What beliefs do you share with him or her? What beliefs don't you share? Sometimes a difference in beliefs can cause conflict between people. Was this ever true for you and your friend? How did you resolve the conflict? Discuss with a partner. Share your ideas with your peers and teacher. Ask for their feedback and support in order to develop background knowledge about this topic.

➤ BUILD BACKGROUND

In this section, you will read two informational articles: "**Sowing the Seeds of Peace**" and "**Seeds of Peace: Cultivating Friendships.**" The Seeds of Peace International Camp brings teenagers from the Middle East together to confront the conflict that has defined the region for more than fifty years. In doing so, the camp hopes to teach these future leaders the communication and leadership skills they will need to interact with each other, to work toward peace, and to develop lasting relationships with one another.

▲ Campers at the Seeds of Peace International Camp in Maine

► VOCABULARY

Listening and Speaking: Key Words

Read aloud and listen to these sentences. Use the context to figure out the meaning of the highlighted words. Use a dictionary to check your answers. Then write each word and its meaning in your notebook.

Key Words

barriers
confront
cultivate
enemies
political
violence

1. There were personal barriers that kept the girls from becoming friends.

2. If you confront your fears, they often go away.

3. Hassan and Anastasia cultivate their friendship by calling each other every day.

4. Rashad and Hassan do not speak to one another. They are enemies.

5. The students debate about political issues that relate to government and the rights of people.

6. The fighting between the countries has continued for more than fifty years. The violence in that region is frightening.

Practice  **Workbook Page 89**

Write the sentences in your notebook. Choose a key word from the box above to complete each sentence. Then take turns reading the sentences aloud with a partner.

1. The president works hard to _____ relationships with other world leaders.

2. The country's government has made great _____ progress in improving relations with its neighbors.

3. There are _____ that make it difficult to achieve world peace.

4. The leaders did not want to _____ each other about their differing beliefs.

5. _____ erupted when the citizens of one country attacked those of another.

6. Members of the warring nations are _____.

▲ Two students conduct a political debate.

Listening and Speaking: Academic Words

Study the **red** words and their meanings. You will find these words useful when talking and writing about informational texts. Write each word and its meaning in your notebook, then say the words aloud with a partner. After you read "Sowing the Seeds of Peace" and "Seeds of Peace: Cultivating Friendships," try to use these words to respond to the texts.

Academic Words

assumed
focus
individuals
similarities

assumed = thought that something was true without having proof	➡	I **assumed** the test would be easy to pass because I studied hard.
focus = pay special attention to a particular person or thing instead of others	➡	It was noisy in the library. I had to **focus** very hard on the textbook to study for the test.
individuals = people; not a whole group	➡	A few **individuals** passed the test easily, but for most students it was difficult.
similarities = the qualities of being similar, or the same	➡	There are **similarities** in all people. We are all alike in some ways.

Practice

Work with a partner to answer these questions. Try to include the **red** word in your answer. Write the sentences in your notebook.

1. Have you ever **assumed** that a class would be easier than it actually was? Explain.

2. What is your main **focus** at school?

3. Which **individuals** in your classroom do you work well with? Why?

4. What are three **similarities** that all people share?

▲ Only a few individuals passed the test.

Word Study: Suffixes -er, -or

A suffix is a letter or group of letters placed at the end of a base word. Adding a suffix changes the meaning of the base word.

The most common meaning of the suffixes -er and -or is "one who." For example, a learner is one who learns; a visitor is one who visits. The only way to know which of these two suffixes to use is to check the dictionary. Remember, if a base word ends with an e, drop the e before adding the suffix. Study the examples in the chart below.

Base Word	+ Suffix	= New Word
travel	-er	travel**er**
bake	-er	bak**er**
act	-or	act**or**
educate	-or	educat**or**

Practice
Workbook Page 91

Copy the sentences below into your notebook. Complete each sentence by adding -er or -or to the word in parentheses. Use a dictionary if necessary. Have a partner check your work.

1. The camp _____ led the students in a variety of activities. (counsel)
2. Each student was allowed to invite one _____ to the camp. (visit)
3. A _____ encouraged students to discuss political issues. (facilitate)
4. Each _____ presented a persuasive argument. (debate)
5. Andrea, a _____, performed during cultural night. She is a good _____. (camp, sing)

READING STRATEGY | COMPARE AND CONTRAST

Comparing and contrasting helps you to understand what you read more clearly. When you compare, you see how things are similar. When you contrast, you see how things are different. To compare and contrast, follow these steps as you read:

- How are the people, events, experiences, and settings in the stories similar? How are they different?
- Think about your own experiences. Do they help you better understand the text?

As you read "Sowing the Seeds of Peace," compare and contrast the teenagers and their beliefs.

Workbook Page 92

Set a purpose for reading As you read, look for examples of the conflicts between the two groups of teenagers. How has the politics of their countries affected their relationships with each other?

Sowing the Seeds of Peace

Mandy Terc

One rainy rest hour at a summer camp in Maine, fifteen-year-old Noor from the Palestinian West Bank was learning to write her name. She glanced back quickly at the example that sixteen-year-old Shirlee, a Jewish Israeli from a seaside town, had provided. After a few more seconds of intense writing, Noor triumphantly handed the piece of paper to me, her **bunk** counselor. Parading across the top of the paper in large, careful print were the Hebrew letters that spelled her Arabic name.

A spontaneous lesson on the Hebrew and Arabic alphabets probably does not happen at most summer camp bunks, but the Seeds of Peace International Camp challenges the traditional definition of what teenagers can learn and accomplish at a summer camp. Seeds of Peace brings Middle Eastern teenagers from Israel, Palestine, Jordan, Egypt, and other countries to Maine to help them confront

▲ Seeds of Peace campers

the conflict and violence that has defined their region for more than fifty years.

At this camp, things like table and bunk assignments, sports teams, and seating are never accidental. They are all part of encouraging **interaction**. Here, Israelis and Arabs not only meet for the first time but also sleep side by side, share a sink and participate in group games. In the

---

bunk, cabin

interaction, action or communication between or among people

close quarters of tiny cabins and bunk beds, bunk counselors encourage the campers to ignore national and ethnic **boundaries** as they make friends with their immediate neighbors.

The three weeks spent in Maine combine ordinary camp activities with a daily two-hour coexistence session, during which trained facilitators encourage discussion of political and personal issues. The remainder of the day is spent in **traditional summer camp activities**.

Teenagers are asked to analyze questions that have **perplexed** world leaders, and even bedtime can become a political **forum**. In my bunk, I asked the girls to summarize one positive and one negative aspect of their day before going to sleep.

---

boundaries, borders or barriers
traditional summer camp activities, typical, well-known games and sports
perplexed, confused
forum, meeting in which people have a chance to publicly discuss important subjects

Sometimes, the discussions were about quite ordinary and uncontroversial things.

At other times, our bedtime discussions reflected the complexity and difficulties of living with perceived enemies. On one occasion, Adar, a strongly nationalistic Israeli, began by expressing frustration with a Palestinian girl's comment that Israel unjustly occupied Jerusalem, which the Palestinian felt truly belonged to the Palestinian people.

Instantly, eight bodies snapped from snug sleeping positions to tense, upright postures. Jerusalem is the most **contentious** issue between the Arab and Israeli campers, and each girl in the bunk was poised to take this opportunity to talk about her opinion on the disputed city. Adar asked if all Palestinians refused to recognize Israelis as **legitimate** residents of the city.

---

contentious, likely to cause an argument
legitimate, lawful

▲ Campers participate in a traditional summer camp activity.

BEFORE YOU GO ON

1 What kinds of things do the campers at the Seeds of Peace International Camp **focus** on?

2 What issue caused a serious discussion at bedtime?

On Your Own
Would you like to go to a summer camp? If so, what kind?

Almost before Adar could finish her question, Aman was ready to answer. Aman is a strong, athletic Palestinian who does not waste her words. When she begins to speak, she is both **intimidating** and impressive as she defends her opinions.

Calm and **composed**, she explained to Adar that the presence of Muslim holy sites in Jerusalem meant that the Palestinians were the rightful **proprietors** of the city. With an equally rapid response, Adar reminded her that Jerusalem also contained Jewish holy sites.

Aman seemed prepared for this answer. "We would be very nice to you [the Jewish people]. We would always let you come visit your sites, just like all the other tourists," she replied.

Adar had no intention of allowing her people to become theoretical tourists in this debate: "Well, we have the city now," Adar said. "You can't just make us leave, because it's ours. We might decide to give some of it to the Palestinians, but it belongs to us now."

---

intimidating, aggressive
composed, thoughtful
proprietors, owners

I spent such times in the bunk listening. I only **sporadically** interjected my voice, reminding them not to hold each other, as individuals, responsible for the actions of their governments.

The conversation eventually wound down. As the girls drifted off to sleep, I felt relieved. As much as I want the girls in my bunk to express all their concerns and thoughts, any conversation about such a sensitive issue keeps me **tense**. The bunk must feel safe but issues of conflict can't be ignored or downplayed. As a bunk counselor, I must provide campers with the safety and security they need to continue the process of breaking down barriers.

---

sporadically, from time to time
tense, nervous and worried

▲ **Cultural Night activities**

ABOUT THE **AUTHOR**

Mandy Terc has worked at the Seeds of Peace International Camp in Maine and also in Seeds of Peace's New York development office. She is currently a doctoral candidate at the University of Michigan.

Seeds of Peace: Cultivating Friendships

Author John Wallach founded Seeds of Peace in an effort to bring understanding to the Middle East. In the summer of 1993, Wallach invited forty-six Israeli, Palestinian, and Egyptian teenagers to his camp in Maine. There, the teens lived alongside those they were previously taught to hate. They participated in activities designed to confront the fears, mistrust, and prejudices that continue to **fuel** the conflicts in their home countries. Through such interactions, Wallach and his staff worked to ensure that the leaders of tomorrow are friends, rather than enemies.

Since that first camp, Seeds of Peace has expanded its programming to include participants from twenty-five different nations. To date, over 3,000 teens have graduated from Seeds of Peace.

Following graduation, many teenagers continue to participate in follow-up conferences and workshops. Below, two campers speak of their experiences, the lessons they learned, and the friendships they continue to cultivate.

Eitan Paul (New Jersey)

We arrived as separate delegations, debaters of our country's positions; we would leave as friends, aware that coexistence is possible.

Every day teenagers wearing the green Seeds of Peace T-shirts accomplish something that world leaders struggle to achieve. They listen to each other, **suspending** personal agendas, cultivating meaningful friendships.

John Wallach always used to say, "Make one friend." I made many.

Marisa Gorovitz (Florida)

Camp was more amazing than I ever imagined. I learned an incredible amount about Arabic culture, Israel, the Palestinians, Islam, and the history of the Middle East.

Leaving camp and my new friends was the hardest thing I've ever done. We shared unforgettable moments, from debating, to climbing, to dancing. I keep in touch with my friends through e-mail, the phone, and the mail. I hope to visit them in their various countries!

fuel, make worse
suspending, stopping for a short time

BEFORE YOU GO ON

1 What was the author's advice to the campers during the discussion?

2 How did the campers change during Eitan Paul's stay at camp?

On Your Own
Do you have political discussions with others? What do you discuss?

► COMPREHENSION

Workbook
Page 93

Recall

1. Who founded the Seeds of Peace International Camp? Why?
2. What two groups of people meet for the first time at the camp?

Comprehend

3. In what ways does the camp encourage interaction among campers?
4. In what kinds of daily activities do campers participate?

Analyze

5. Why do you think the camp is called Seeds of Peace?
6. Why does the author feel tense about some of the political discussions that occur in the bunk?

Connect

7. Do you think a camp is a good place to bring **individuals** with opposing views together? Explain.
8. Have you ever been to a summer camp? If so, what kind of camp was it? What did you do there?

► IN YOUR OWN WORDS

Work with a partner. Copy the chart below into your notebook. Write the missing information in the chart. Try to use as many new vocabulary words as possible. Using this information, demonstrate your comprehension of the article by summarizing it for your partner.

▲ Seeds of Peace campers learn how to sail.

Seeds of Peace International Camp	
Location	Maine
Campers	
Activities	
Goals	

➤ DISCUSSION

Discuss in pairs or small groups.

1. Compare and contrast Adar's and Aman's views of Jerusalem. What **similarities** and differences do you see?

2. Do you think Seeds of Peace can make a difference in the world? Why or why not?

Q **How are relationships with others important?** Describe a time when you met someone whose views were different from your own. Did you try to understand that person's way of thinking? Were you able to get along?

➤ READ FOR FLUENCY

It is often easier to read a text if you understand the difficult words and phrases. Work with a partner. Choose a paragraph from the reading. Identify the words and phrases you do not know or have trouble pronouncing. Look up the difficult words in a dictionary.

Take turns pronouncing the words and phrases with your partner. If necessary, ask your teacher to model the correct pronunciation. Then take turns reading the paragraph aloud. Give each other feedback on your reading.

➤ EXTENSION  Workbook Page 93

Utilize The relationship between Arabs and Israelis is constantly in the news. Work with a partner. Find two articles about current events happening in this region. Use newspapers, news magazines, or the Internet. Summarize each article, and present the information to your classmates. Use as many academic words as possible.

Grammar

Complex Sentences

A complex sentence is a sentence that contains a main, or independent, clause and one or more subordinate, or dependent, clauses. A subordinate clause is not a complete sentence; it "depends" on the independent clause. A subordinate clause often begins with a subordinating conjunction. When a clause with a subordinating conjunction begins the sentence, use a comma.

Grammar SKILL

Remember that a conjunction is a connecting word.

main clause	subordinate clause
You can't just make us leave **because** it's ours.	

subordinate clause	main clause
Before Adar could finish her question,	Aman was ready to answer.

main clause	subordinate clause
Bunk counselors encourage the campers to ignore boundaries **as**	they make friends with their neighbors.

Here are some common subordinating conjunctions used in complex sentences.

after	although	as	because	before	if	once
since	that	though	until	when	whether	while

Practice

Workbook Page 94

Work with a partner. Combine the main clauses on the left with the appropriate subordinate clauses on the right to make complex sentences. Write the sentences in your notebook.

Example: Yolanda eats a lot of yogurt because it's healthy.

Yolanda eats a lot of yogurt	although it was raining.
1. My father stepped on the paint	while I was driving.
2. Randy went swimming	after she cleared the table.
3. Aimee washed the dishes	because it's healthy.
4. A cat ran in front of me	once we were all standing together.
5. Adam took a picture	before it was dry.

Apply

Work with a partner. Switch the clauses in the Practice exercise so that the subordinate clause comes first.

Example: Because yogurt is healthy, Yolanda eats a lot of it.

Agreement in Complex Sentences

Make sure that you use verb forms consistently in complex sentences. Both the main and the subordinate clauses should usually refer to the same time (such as past, present). For example, if the main clause is in the past, the subordinate clause should also be in the past.

Antecedents, the nouns that come before the pronouns they refer to, should be consistent in number and gender with those pronouns.

Past	Before **Adar could finish** her question, Aman **was** ready to answer. [verbs in both clauses are in the past; *her* refers to *Adar*]
Present	You **can't** just **make us** leave because it**'s ours**. [verbs in both clauses are in the present; *ours* refers to *us*] Bunk counselors **encourage the campers** to ignore boundaries as **they make** friends with **their** neighbors. [verbs in both clauses are in the present; *they* and *their* refer to the *campers*]

Practice  **Workbook Page 95**

Work with a partner. Copy the sentences below into your notebook. Then circle the correct word or phrase to complete each sentence

Example: He **assumed** they agreed because (he was /(they were))
Israelis.

1. The food was delicious even though (it was / they were) fattening.
2. We worked quickly since a storm (is / was) coming.
3. His parents sent him to a private school until (he / they) ran out of money.
4. Since it was snowing so hard, all the cars (are / were) covered.
5. Before she called her parents, (they / she) finished her homework.

Apply

Write five simple sentences. Then add a subordinating conjunction from the box on page 182. With a partner, finish the complex sentences.

✔ **GRAMMAR CHECK**

What is an antecedent?

Writing

Write a Critique

A critique is a type of expository writing in which you judge a work or an experience based on standards, or a level of quality that is acceptable to you. You tell what the standards are and then explain why the work or experience did or did not meet them. For example, imagine that you and your friends like video games that include a lot of action. If a friend asked you about two games you played yesterday, you could judge the games based on this standard.

> **Writing Prompt**
>
> Write a critique of a story, movie, video game, or place you have visited. It may be an experience that you enjoyed, or one that disappointed you. Be sure to use main and subordinate clauses correctly.

1 **PREWRITE** Begin by choosing a topic.

- Think of a story or movie you saw recently, or a place that you visited, such as a restaurant or an amusement park.
- Ask yourself what you liked or did not like about this experience.
- Make a list of the standards that you would use to evaluate it.
- List your ideas in a graphic organizer.  **Workbook Page 96**

Here's a graphic organizer created by a student named Nicole for a critique of an after-school program:

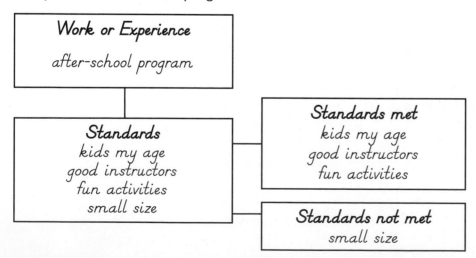

2 DRAFT Use your graphic organizer to help you write a first draft.

- Remember to identify your standards for evaluation.
- Explain why your experience did or did not meet the standards.
- As you write, think about your audience. What opinion will the reader have after reading your work?

3 REVISE Read over your draft. Look for places where the writing is unclear or needs improvement. Use the Writing Checklist to help you identify problems. Then revise your draft, using the editing and proofreading marks listed on page 458.

4 EDIT Check your work for errors in grammar, usage, mechanics, and spelling. Trade papers with a partner to obtain feedback. Use the Peer Review Checklist on Workbook page 96. Edit your final draft in response to feedback from your partner and your teacher.

5 PUBLISH Prepare a clean copy of your final draft. Share your critique with your class. Save your work. You'll need to refer to it in the Writing Workshop at the end of the unit.

Here is Nicole's critique of an after-school program. Notice how Nicole clearly identifies her standards for evaluating the program.

Writing Checklist

IDEAS:
☑ I clearly identified the standards I used to judge a work or an experience.

CONVENTIONS:
☑ I made sure that pronouns and verbs agreed in complex sentences.

Nicole Siley

    The Community Arts Center After-School Program
    Last year, I attended an after-school program at the Community Arts Center in my town. It had many of the qualities I was hoping it would have: kids my age, good instructors, and fun activities. Many of my classmates attended. Because many students from other schools also came, I was able to make new friends, and we still keep in touch with one another. Unfortunately, a lot of kids—more than 100—signed up for the program. Our instructors, however, kept things moving and made the program fun. There were many activities to choose from, such as painting, drawing, dancing, and acting. I took a painting class. I learned how to paint and took a trip to the art museum. Even though it was crowded, I'm going to sign up for the after-school program again this year.

What You Will Learn

Reading
- Vocabulary building: *Literary terms, word study*
- Reading strategy: *Identify with a character*
- Text type: *Literature (legend)*

Grammar
Transitions to show contrast and cause-and-effect; Transitions to show similarity and add information

Writing
Write to compare and contrast

THE BIG QUESTION

How are relationships with others important? As you know, people can be involved in different kinds of relationships. Work with a partner. Use your prior experiences to discuss the relationships you have had with others. Answer the following questions: How and when did each relationship begin? What makes you value each relationship? How would you feel if you could not experience these relationships?

BUILD BACKGROUND

In this section, you will read an excerpt from a legend called *Blue Willow*. A legend is a story that is often based on fact. However, over time, details in legends move further away from factual events to describe people and actions that are more fictional than real.

The *Blue Willow* legend explains the Blue Willow china pattern, which always includes a willow tree, a bridge, and a moon pavilion, or a decorative building. Plates with this pattern were produced in England during the eighteenth century—a time when the English were inspired by Chinese culture.

Set in ancient China, the legend describes the relationship between Kung Shi Fair, the daughter of a wealthy merchant, and a village fisherman named Chang the Good. The couple wants to marry, but the merchant will not grant his permission. This causes a series of events that no one could have anticipated.

◀ A plate with a
Blue Willow pattern

➤ VOCABULARY

Learn Literary Words

Long before there were books, there were stories. Storytelling was a form of entertainment in ancient cultures. Stories were passed along by word of mouth from one generation to the next. This is called the **oral tradition**.

A **legend** is one kind of story that was originally shared by oral tradition. Because legends were told orally and were not written down, they moved away from factual events to describe more fictional events and characters.

Character motive is the reason for a character's thoughts, feelings, actions, or speech. Characters are often motivated by needs, such as food and shelter. They are also motivated by feelings, such as fear, love, and pride. Knowing characters' motives helps the reader understand the characters and the story better. Read the passage below. What is Lisa's motivation?

Literary Words

oral tradition
legend
character motive

Audio

Lisa longingly looked out the window. This was the fourth day in a row that she had stayed after school to work on her science project. "I'd rather be with my friends," Lisa thought to herself as she sighed loudly. She turned her head from the window. Out of the corner of her eye, she caught a glimpse of the science fair poster. She focused on the words printed in bright red letters: *Grand Prize Winner—$200*. All thoughts of her friends faded as Lisa got back to work.

Practice

Workbook
Page 97

Work with a partner. Narrate, or tell, a story that has been passed down in your family from generation to generation in the oral tradition. Is the story a legend? Try to identify the main characters' motivations.

Listening and Speaking: Academic Words

Study the **red** words and their meanings. You will find these words useful when talking and writing about literature. Write each word and its meaning in your notebook, then say the words aloud with a partner. After you read the excerpt from *Blue Willow*, try to use these words to respond to the text.

Academic Words

authoritative
consent
encounter
reaction

authoritative = respected and trusted as being true, or making people respect or obey you	→	My mother makes the rules in our home. She is the most **authoritative** member of our family.
consent = permission to do something	→	We have to get her **consent** before we can leave the house with friends.
encounter = an occasion when you meet someone without planning to	→	I had an unexpected **encounter** with my friend at the mall.
reaction = the way you behave in response to someone or something	→	My friend and I had the same **reaction**. We were both surprised and happy to see each other.

Audio

Practice

Workbook
Page 98

Work with a partner to answer the questions. Try to include the **red** word in your answer. Write the sentences in your notebook.

1. In your opinion, who is the most **authoritative** person in your school?

2. Do you have to receive your teacher's **consent** before leaving the classroom?

3. Who did you have an **encounter** with at school today?

4. What was your **reaction** to this encounter?

▲ This teacher is the authoritative figure in her classroom.

Word Study: Synonyms

Synonyms are words that have the same or nearly the same meaning. The words *clever* and *intelligent*, *glisten* and *shine*, and *toss* and *throw* are synonyms. Writers often choose one synonym over another to express a specific idea or emotion. Look at the chart below for examples.

Synonym	Meaning	Sentence
claim (verb)	to say something without proof or evidence	They **claimed** to have heard the leopard cries.
state (verb)	to say something in a strong and formal way	Her father **stated** that she could not marry him.

Practice

Work with a partner. Copy the chart above into your notebook, leaving the columns blank. Fill in the first column with the pairs of synonyms in the box below. Use a dictionary or thesaurus to find the meaning of each synonym. Then write the meaning and a sentence for each one.

drift/float	look/gaze	shriek/yell
special/unusual	startle/surprise	love/adore

READING STRATEGY IDENTIFY WITH A CHARACTER

Identifying with a character helps you better understand and enjoy a story. When you identify with a character, you understand his or her actions and feelings. To identify with a character, follow these steps as you read:

- Think about the character's actions. What does he or she do?
- How do you think the character feels?
- Think about your own experiences. How would you feel? Would you act in the same way as the character?

As you read the excerpt from the legend *Blue Willow*, imagine how you would feel if you were the main character. Think about the things you would do differently.

Set a purpose for reading As you read, notice how Kung Shi Fair's relationship with Chang the Good affects her father. How does his reaction affect the young couple's relationship?

from

Blue Willow

Pam Conrad

Many years ago, there was a river called Wen that flowed past a small and peaceful village.

On one side of the Wen River, in a large mansion, lived a wealthy **merchant**. Everyone knew that he had one daughter, Kung Shi Fair. She was a beautiful girl with hands as small as starfish, feet as swift as **sandpipers**, and hair as black as the ink on her father's **scrolls**. As she grew, the people of the village wondered who she would marry, because they all knew that the merchant always gave her whatever she asked for.

One day Kung Shi Fair was sitting in her **moon pavilion** when she saw something **glistening** on the bank of the river. She made her way to the water. When she got there, she saw it was only a broken shell. She picked it up, then looked up and saw for the first time a boat and a young man pulling his dripping nets out of the water.

This was Chang the Good who lived across the river. He was a young fisherman.

---

merchant, person who makes money by selling things
sandpipers, wading birds
scrolls, books written on long sheets of papers that roll up
moon pavilion, decorative building
glistening, shining

Now Kung Shi Fair and Chang the Good were both startled to see each other. The fish spilled out of his nets. The shell dropped from Kung Shi Fair's hand. Tossing the nets on the floor of his boat, Chang the Good picked up his oars, and he rowed across the river to her.

When he reached the shore, Kung Shi Fair watched as he pulled the boat onto the land. She came close and touched his nets. "How beautiful," she said.

"I made them myself," he told her, thinking he, as well, had never seen something so beautiful this close.

"And what a wonderful bird!" she exclaimed as the cormorant held out its wings to dry in the breeze.

"I fish with her. She dives for fish and—because I have trained her so well—she brings the fish to me."

"You are very clever," she said, turning her gaze full on him.

"Can I tell you something?" he asked her softly.

She nodded, silent.

"One morning I came down to the river, thinking my boat would be **anchored** where I had left it, but the **currents** had taken it away. All day long I searched along the river for my boat. Then, when I had given up hope, I came upon a **cove**, and there it was, drifting toward me. My heart swelled with love."

Kung Shi Fair tilted her head. "And so?"

"And so, this is how I felt just now, seeing you here on the bank of the river."

---

anchored, kept in place by a heavy weight that is connected to the boat and dropped into the water.
currents, moving waters
cove, small area of water that is surrounded by land

)) Listening SKILL

Follow along in your book as you listen to the Audio CD. Notice the words in bold type. To understand them, read the definitions at the bottom of the page. Knowing the meanings of these words will help you to confirm and enhance your comprehension of the story.

BEFORE YOU GO ON

1 Who is Kung Shi Fair? Who is Chang the Good?

2 How do Kung Shi Fair and Chang the Good meet?

On Your Own
Chang the Good talks about loving Kung Shi Fair within moments of their first **encounter**. Do you think love at first sight is possible? Explain.

Reading 3 **191**

Kung Shi Fair frowned. "My boat has never been in the river," she said. "So I have never lost a boat, or found one." Then she smiled at him. "But I came to the river just now thinking I saw something glistening on its bank, and now I know I came for you."

But it so happened that Kung Shi Fair's father was watching from the window of his mansion. He watched as his daughter led the fisherman across the stone footbridge, and he watched her lead Chang the Good to her moon pavilion.

That night he said nothing to his daughter about what he had seen. They were drinking their tea, sitting quietly, when one of the **servants** came **panting** onto the **veranda**.

"There is terrible news, Master. It seems there is a wild **leopard on a rampage**."

"This is frightening," the merchant said. "You must tell me if you hear news of the leopard coming in this direction."

The merchant looked at his daughter. "Perhaps, until the leopard is caught, you should not go down into your moon pavilion."

Kung Shi Fair laughed, "Don't be silly, silly father. My pavilion is perfectly safe."

* * *

The next day and every day after that, when the work of the fishing was through, Kung Shi Fair and Chang the Good would meet on the shore. First they would go to the pavilion. Then they would trail peony petals down the path to the bridge, where they would sit and talk, and eat mulberries beneath the cool willow tree.

Finally, after many days of this, Chang the Good came with a bundle.

"I have something to show you," he said.

Very carefully, he unfastened the knot and opened his bundle on the floor before her. There were **brooches** and necklaces, bracelets, and pendants hung not on gold chains as she was used to, but on rough silk cords dull with wear.

He told her, "These belonged to my mother, who died when I was very young."

---

servants, people who are paid to clean someone's house, cook food, etc.
panting, breathing quickly with short noisy breaths
veranda, porch with a roof
leopard, large wild cat with black spots
on a rampage, behaving wildly or violently
brooches, pieces of jewelry

BEFORE YOU GO ON

1 What news does the servant have for the merchant?

2 What is in the bundle Chang the Good brings to Kung Shi Fair? Why are its contents special?

On Your Own
Do you own a special piece of jewelry? If so, describe it and explain why it is important to you.

Reading 3 **193**

"And this was her own ring," Chang the Good was saying, and he slipped a small **jade** ring onto her thumb.

"Beautiful," Kung Shi Fair told him.

"I want you to have them," he told her. "I want you to be my wife."

Kung Shi Fair held very still.

"Yes, I would like this, too," she said. "But I must tell my father."

* * *

That night Kung Shi Fair went to her father. She said to him, "I would marry now, Father."

And he answered, "Not yet, my daughter, not yet."

"But, Father, you have always been so good to me. And this is what I want more than anything. If not now, then when?"

"When I find a copper coin in my path," he said.

Kung Shi Fair ran from the room to hide her tears, past the servant who was coming to tell the merchant that the leopard was terribly close.

Chang the Good could not be **discouraged**. Sitting in Kung Shi Fair's moon pavilion, he thought of a plan. He did not stay that day for he had special work to do, and he told Kung Shi Fair to sit by her window at dawn.

The next morning, Kung Shi Fair leaned on the window. Her father was preparing to go to a meeting concerning the rampaging leopard.

She saw the servants bring the carriage around to him, and just as her father was about to climb on, he looked down and saw coins **strewn** at his feet— hundreds of little copper coins. He looked up at his daughter in the window.

She saw no anger in his face, just sadness. She smiled kindly at him. "Now, Father? Can I now?"

He shook his head. "Not yet, my daughter, not yet."

Her smile turned to tears. "Then when, Father? Oh, then when?"

"When there's a rainbow over the stone bridge that leads to your moon pavilion," he told her, and he drove away.

Later the servants claimed to have heard Kung Shi Fair's sad crying that morning, even above winds that whistled over the river's surface. They decided she had gone to find Chang the Good, to tell him his plan had failed.

The village women later whispered about how she went down to the bank of the tumbling Wen River, to her boat. She had watched many times as Chang the Good had sailed away, and now—hoping she could remember how—she awkwardly pushed her boat into the **surging** river.

✔ LITERARY CHECK
*What is the merchant's **motive** in refusing to let the couple marry?*

---

jade, green stone
discouraged, persuaded to lose the confidence needed to do something
strewn, lying
surging, quickly moving

Turning her face into the wind, she steered bravely through the river's foam and **rapids**. When she was halfway across the river, the wind ripped the fig leaf sails from their mast, and the cassia bark **hull** snapped apart, tipping the merchant's beautiful daughter into the **torrential** river. For a few moments her silken robe could be seen floating near the surface, and then it was gone.

In the village, Chang the Good had gone to the meeting to hear the news about the rampaging leopard. Everyone was frightened that the leopard would come and kill their families. Then the merchant spoke to them.

"While the storm is raging," he said, "we must go out, seek the leopard, and **slay** him before he comes to our village again."

"Yes!" "Yes!" the villagers cried. "Kill the leopard now!"

Chang the Good had thoughts only for Kung Shi Fair. He had no heart for a hunt. Without being seen, he stepped out into the rain. He thought to himself how once the winds calmed, he would sail over and see her and ask her how things had gone with her father and the coins.

Meanwhile the swords were brought out and the bows and arrows, the spears and the clubs, and everyone received a weapon. The villagers poured out of the hall, and they took to the rain-slick road, in search of the leopard.

---

rapids, fast-moving waters
hull, body of the boat
torrential, quickly flowing
slay, kill

BEFORE YOU GO ON

1. What is Kung Shi Fair's **reaction** to her father's refusal to let her marry? What is the result of her actions?

2. What do the villagers determine they have to do? Why?

On Your Own
Are you able to relate to Kung Shi Fair's feelings? Explain.

Reading 3 **195**

It was dark when the winds finally calmed and the river slowed its fury. The cormorant perched on the back of Chang the Good's boat, as he eased it into the river. Chang the Good gave it a final push and jumped in. Slowly and carefully, he made his way across, peering into the darkness of the pavilion to see if Kung Shi Fair waited for him. But there was no sign of her.

He pulled his boat ashore and called, "Kung Shi!" There was silence.

He ran to the pavilion and threw back the rain-soaked silks, "Kung Shi!"

Frightened, he turned towards her father's house that was dark and lifeless. His feet barely touched the ground. He ran from room to room, calling her name and hearing the silence answer. He knew something terrible had happened.

Slowly he left the house. The song of small green frogs carried him to the stone bridge and he decided to sit there and wait for her.

Suddenly the cormorant flapped her wings, **shrieked**, and dived into the water and disappeared. Then she flew straight up and landed beside Chang the Good. She dropped what she was carrying into her master's hand.

It was a small, jade thumb ring.

---

shrieked, yelled in a high-pitched voice

Chang the Good saw it and at that moment, he knew. He jumped up, and his eyes searched the shore for the cassia boat and he knew. He saw the whole story before him and threw back his head. He knew it was too late.

Just as the moon began to slip into sight, the **weary** villagers were returning home empty-handed. As they came back toward the village, they heard a sound coming from across the water near the merchant's house. "The leopard!" they whispered. At that, three of them jumped into a boat and sailed silently across the river to the place where the sound came from.

Now for many years after, the villagers tried to describe to each other what the sound was like. Most thought it sounded like the ragings of a leopard before it **strikes**. Later they all knew it was the sound of Chang the Good, crying his heart into the night.

Silently the boat slipped onto the riverbank, and the three men crept up the shore. In the moonlight they saw their enemy. In one thrust they all shot arrows, threw spears, and sent clubs sailing through the wailing air. Their mark was made, and Chang the Good **toppled** into the river beneath the bridge.

If this was the end of the story, it would probably have been forgotten by now, it was so long ago. But because the merchant was so heartbroken, he cried his **sorrows** to whomever would listen to him, and the entire village soon knew he had kept his daughter away from the man she loved.

It was some time later, while the last leaves were still on the willow, that there was a cloudburst in the late afternoon. The merchant heard the villagers cry out, and he went to the window.

His heart leapt at the sight, for just above the footbridge that led to his daughter's pavilion, there appeared a most wondrous rainbow of every color. While the villagers and the merchant watched, two **swallows** fluttered above the willow tree and kissed.

---

weary, very tired
strikes, attacks
toppled, fell
sorrows, feelings of grief and sadness
swallows, small birds

ABOUT THE **AUTHOR**

Pam Conrad (1948–1996) wrote stories for both children and adults. Before her death, she authored twenty-nine books. Often she used her own experiences as inspiration for many of her award-winning tales.

✔ **LITERARY CHECK**

*This **legend** was originally shared with others as part of the **oral tradition**. Retell the story to a partner. How does your oral version differ from the written story?*

BEFORE YOU GO ON

1 How does Chang the Good find out what happened to Kung Shi Fair?

2 What happens to Chang the Good at the end of the story?

On Your Own
Did the story end as you thought it would? Why or why not?

Reading 3   **197**

► READER'S THEATER

Act out the following scene between Kung Shi Fair and Chang the Good.

Kung Shi Fair: These nets are beautiful.

Chang the Good: I made them myself. I use them to catch fish.

Kung Shi Fair: And this lovely bird! What kind of bird is it?

Chang the Good: It's a cormorant. She's very smart! I have taught her how to catch fish and bring them to me.

Kung Shi Fair: Then it is you who is smart!

Chang the Good: Can I tell you something? One morning the currents took away my boat during the night. I searched for my boat all day long. Finally, I found it in a small cove. My heart was filled with joy.

Kung Shi Fair: Why are you telling me this?

Chang the Good: Because that is how I felt when I saw you.

> **♪)) Speaking SKILL**
>
> Read the lines in a way that reflects your character's personality. This will help to make your character seem real.

► COMPREHENSION

Workbook Page 101

Recall

1. Why do the people of the village wonder who Kung Shi Fair will marry?

2. What do the villagers mistake Chang the Good's crying for?

Comprehend

3. What is the significance of the willow tree, the bridge, and the moon pavilion in the story?

4. What does the merchant say has to happen before Kung Shi Fair and Chang the Good can marry?

Analyze

5. Who places the copper coins in the merchant's path?

6. Why do you think the author chooses to share the *Blue Willow* legend with others in the form of a written story?

▲ A copper coin

Connect

7. Do you think it is important to be able to choose your own friends? Explain.

8. What kinds of relationships would your parents object to you having?

▶ DISCUSSION

Discuss in pairs or small groups. Ask your peers and teacher for their feedback about your ideas.

1. Could the merchant have prevented his daughter's death? If so, how?

2. In your opinion, was the merchant right to refuse to give his **consent** to his daughter's marriage? Why or why not?

Q **How are relationships with others important?** Do you think parents have the right to put an end to certain relationships between their children and other people? Explain.

»⌇ Listening SKILL

Think about what you are hearing. Does it make sense? If not, seek clarification. Ask the speaker to repeat or further explain his or her answer.

▶ RESPONSE TO LITERATURE
Workbook Page 101

Utilize Because legends were often shared orally, many versions of the *Blue Willow* legend exist. Work with a partner. First, find an account that is different from the one you read in class. Use library resources or the Internet. Then compare both stories. Copy the chart below into your notebook. Add information about the characters, settings, story events, and conclusions. Finally, share this information with your classmates. How many different versions were presented?

Reading Skill

Make sure you understand sequence words commonly found in instructions, such as *first, next, then,* and *finally.* These words help you to understand how to complete a task.

Blue Willow				
Version	**Setting**	**Characters**	**Story Events**	**Conclusion**
Pam Conrad's				
Internet				

Grammar

Transitions to Show Contrast and Cause-and-Effect

Transitions help your reader follow your line of thought. A one-word transition is a type of conjunctive adverb; a transitional phrase is a type of conjunctive adverbial phrase. When a transition connects two sentences, use a period. When it connects two independent clauses, use a semicolon (;).

Use a comma when a transition begins a sentence or clause. Don't use a comma with most one-word transitions when they appear midsentence. When a transitional phrase appears midsentence, offset it with commas.

Contrast ideas	Kung Shi Fair loved Chang. **However,** she didn't want to hurt her father. She respected her father; **on the other hand,** she loved Chang. He thought his boat would be there. The currents had **instead** taken it away.
Show cause-and-effect	Her father disapproved of Chang; Chang, **as a result,** decided on a plan. Chang saw the jade ring. **Therefore, / Thus,** he knew it was too late. She wanted to be with Chang. **Consequently,** she sailed after him.

Practice

Workbook Page 102

Work with a partner. Copy the sentences below into your notebook. Then complete each sentence with a transition from above, using each only once. Remember to add proper punctuation. More than one answer may be possible.

Example: He's not studying English. *Instead,* he's studying French.

1. She works hard during the week. _____ she takes weekends off.
2. Marta's father is very **authoritative**. _____ he's also very loving.
3. Sandra doesn't eat well; _____ she is often sick.
4. Children are very curious. _____ they get in a lot of trouble.
5. It snowed all weekend. _____ school was cancelled on Monday.

Apply

Work with a partner. Copy the sentence starters and transitions into your notebook. Take turns finishing the sentences with your own ideas.

Example: I like watching movies. However, I don't have much free time.

1. I like . . . . However, . . .
2. I don't like . . . . Instead, . . .
3. I want to . . . . On the other hand, . . .
4. I don't want to . . . . Therefore, . . .

200 Unit 3

Transitions to Show Similarity and Add Information

Transitions can also show similarity or add information. Remember that transitions can begin a sentence or can be used after a semicolon. Use a comma when a transition begins a sentence or clause. Don't use a comma with one-word transitions when used midsentence, except for *furthermore*. When using *furthermore* and transitional phrases, use commas before and after.

Show similarities	She dropped the shell. **Similarly,** Chang spilled the fish from his net. She loved him as soon as she saw him. Chang, **as well,** loved her. She was startled to see him; **likewise,** he wasn't expecting to see her.
Add information	The gold chain was his mother's. The jade ring was hers **also**. Kung Shi Fair respected her father. **Besides,** she loved him. Kung Shi Fair was gentle; she was, **furthermore,** kind. The storm was raging; **in addition,** the leopard was on a rampage. Chang would not give up. **In fact,** he was determined to marry her. The servants heard her crying. **Indeed,** they thought she was with Chang.

Practice  **Workbook** Page 103

Work with a partner. Copy the sentences below into your notebook. Then rewrite the two sentences connecting them with the transition in parentheses.

Example: He's good at languages. He's good at art. (similarly)
He's good at languages; similarly, he' good at art.

1. Sidney runs every day. He swims twice a week. (in addition)
2. Joe loves cheeseburgers. His brother loves cheeseburgers. (likewise)
3. Bill can't come. He doesn't like parties. (besides)
4. She looked great. I've never seen her look better. (indeed)
5. We really enjoyed the restaurant. We're going there again tonight. (in fact)

Apply

Work with a partner. Look at the reading. Find sentences that you can combine with transitional words and phrases.

Writing

Ongoing Writing Skills Practice

Write to Compare and Contrast

A compare-and-contrast paragraph looks at the similarities and differences between two people, places, or things. For example, you can compare and contrast two friends. First, write down the ways your friends are similar and different. Then write your paragraph. In your introduction, tell your reader about the friends you are comparing and contrasting. Next, tell how your friends are the same. Then write about how they are different. Include specific examples that emphasize their similarities and differences.

> **Writing Prompt**
>
> Write a paragraph that compares and contrasts two people, places, or things that you know well. Be sure to use transitions to show contrast or similarity or to add information correctly in your writing.

1 **PREWRITE** Begin by choosing the people, places, or things you want to write about.

- Think of all the ways in which they are similar or different.

- Which ideas go together? Are some ideas about physical appearance, for example, and others about personality?

- List your ideas in a Venn diagram like this one.  **Workbook Page 104**

Here's a Venn diagram created by a student named Austin.

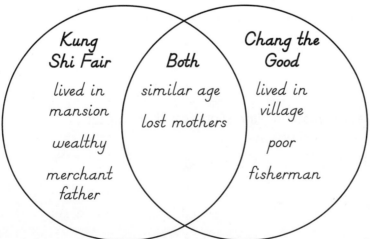

2 **DRAFT** Use your Venn diagram to help you write a first draft.

- First, explain who or what you are comparing.
- Then describe the similarities and differences.
- Make sure to include specific examples.
- Use transitions to show contrast and add information.

3 **REVISE** Read over your draft. Look for places where the writing is unclear or needs improvement. Use the Writing Checklist to help you identify problems. Then revise your draft, using the editing and proofreading marks listed on page 458.

4 **EDIT** Check your work for errors in grammar, usage, mechanics, and spelling. Trade papers with a partner to obtain feedback. Use the Peer Review Checklist on Workbook page 104. Edit your final draft in response to feedback from your partner and your teacher.

5 **PUBLISH** Prepare a clean copy of your final draft. Share your compare-and-contrast paragraph with the class. Save your work. You'll need to refer to it in the Writing Workshop at the end of the unit.

Writing Checklist

ORGANIZATION:
☑ I used a compare-and-contrast organization.

WORD CHOICE:
☑ I used transitions to show contrast, similarity, cause-and-effect, or to add information.

Here is Austin's paragraph. Notice how he used transitions to show similarity, contrast, cause-and-effect, and to add information in his paragraph.

Austin Saiz

Blue Willow

Kung Shi Fair and Chang the Good are the two main characters in <u>Blue Willow</u>. They are similar in some ways, but they are also very different. First, both characters are similar in age. Also, at the time they meet, both Kung Shi Fair and Chang the Good have lost their mothers. Kung Shi Fair lives with her wealthy father in a mansion near the Wen River. Chang the Good also lives near the Wen River. However, Chang the Good lives in the village. His family isn't wealthy at all. In fact, he's a poor fisherman. Despite the differences in their backgrounds and lifestyles, Kung Shi Fair and Chang the Good see something good in each other and fall in love. Kung Shi Fair's father is against the marriage. As a result, both lovers die tragically. They meet again and are happy after death.

READING 4

Prepare to Read

What You Will Learn

Reading

- Vocabulary building: *Context, dictionary skills, word study*
- Reading strategy: *Classify*
- Text type: *Informational text (social studies)*

Grammar

More about antecedent / pronoun agreement; Parallel structure

Writing

Write a classifying paragraph

▶ 🔍 THE BIG QUESTION

How are relationships with others important? The relationships you have with people in your family, with your friends, and with your neighbors have a real impact on your everyday life. They have an effect on your overall health and are important to your well-being. In the same way, the relationships between the plants and animals around you affect the health of our environment. Plants allow life to exist. They are a source of food for many living things. Plants also provide the oxygen that all animals and humans need in order to breathe.

▶ BUILD BACKGROUND

"The Ladybird and the Wildflowers" is a social studies article about Lady Bird Johnson and her relationship with nature. It may be hard to believe that wildflowers could have an impact on a community, but they can. Wildflowers play an important role in the environment. They provide food and shelter for wildlife. They take carbon dioxide out of the air and release oxygen. However, without care they will not survive. This article describes the efforts being made to protect and save them.

▼ Wildflowers

➤ VOCABULARY

Listening and Speaking: Key Words

Read aloud and listen to the sentences. Use the context to figure out the meaning of the highlighted words. Use a dictionary to check your answers. Then write each word and its meaning in your notebook.

Key Words

carbon dioxide
conservation
native
nature
oxygen
symbiotic

Audio

1. Experts argue that automobiles release too much carbon dioxide into the air.
2. Lady Bird worked for the conservation of wildflowers. She wanted to protect them.
3. Bluebonnets are flowers that are native to Texas.
4. A walk in the forest is a good place to observe nature.
5. All plants need oxygen to live.
6. Bees and flowers need each other to live. They have a symbiotic relationship.

Audio

Practice

Workbook Page 105

Write the sentences in your notebook. Choose a key word from the box above to complete each sentence. Then take turns reading the sentences aloud with a partner.

1. When you breathe in, you fill your lungs with _____.
2. Friends that always help each other have a _____ relationship.
3. The gardener said these flowers were not _____ to the area.
4. Rocks, trees, animals, and even weather are all part of _____.
5. Too much _____ is bad for the environment.
6. Protecting land is an important step in the _____ of wildflowers.

Bees and flowers have a symbiotic relationship. ▶

Listening and Speaking: Academic Words

Study the **red** words and their meanings. You will find these words useful when talking and writing about informational texts. Write each word and its meaning in your notebook, then say the words aloud with a partner. After you read "The Ladybird and the Wildflowers," try to use these words to respond to the text.

beneficial = good or useful	⟹	Plants have a **beneficial** function in the environment. They supply oxygen.
interact = talk to other people and work together with them	⟹	The partners **interact** with one another as they work together.
partnership = a relationship in which two or more people, organizations, etc., work together to achieve something	⟹	The bee and the flower depend on each other. They have a **partnership**.
role = the position or job that something or someone has in a particular situation or activity	⟹	The bee's **role** is to carry the pollen from one flower to another

Practice  **Workbook** Page 106

Work with a partner to answer the questions. Try to include the **red** word in your answer. Write the sentences in your notebook.

1. How can working with a partner in the classroom be **beneficial**?
2. Can you think of a time when you worked with a classmate to complete a project? How did you **interact** with one another?
3. What did or did not make this **partnership** successful?
4. What was your **role** within the partnership?

▲ Students interact with one another to complete a project.

Word Study: Sound-Letter Relationships

In English, the letters *th* are pronounced together to make one sound. There are two ways to pronounce these two letters. The first way is the soft sound, as in the word *with*. The other *th* sound is hard, as in the word *the*. Practice with a partner reading these common *th* words. Listen carefully to the sound the *th* makes.

Soft Sound	Hard Sound
three	whether
think	they
without	there

Practice

Work with a partner. Copy the chart below into your notebook. Look in the article or in the dictionary to find words containing the soft and hard *th* sounds. Write these words in the chart.

Soft Sound of *th* as in *with*	Hard Sound of *th* as in *the*

READING STRATEGY   CLASSIFY

Classifying information helps you organize new ideas and facts. It also makes it easier for you to understand the text. To classify, follow these steps:

- As you read, make a list of new information that you learn.
- When you finish, review your list. Decide which facts are most important. Think about how the ideas or facts are similar and different. Think about how they are related.
- Group the facts and ideas together under different headings, according to their subject.

As you read "The Ladybird and the Wildflowers," you can practice classifying some of the native plants you have read about in the story. Copy the chart below into your notebooks. When you come across the name of a plant, put it in the correct column.

Native Trees	Native Grasses	Wildflowers

Set a purpose for reading As you read, identify the importance of plants in nature. Why are native plants beneficial to an area? What are the important relationships described in this article?

The *Ladybird* and the *Wildflowers*

Once known as buffalo clover, the Texas bluebonnet is a **hardy** plant that has **adapted** perfectly to its environment. Every April, the roadways and hillsides across the state are in bloom. These beautiful spring scenes are a **tribute** to the former First Lady who made it happen. Lady Bird Johnson had all the beauty and grace of the wildflowers she loved. She also had the strength to endure hard times.

> **Reading Skill**
>
> To help you understand the reading, study the title and headings. This will help you identify the most important ideas.

The Ladybird Becomes Lady Bird

Mrs. Johnson was born Claudia Alta Taylor near Karnack, Texas. Her caregiver described her as "pretty as a ladybird." Ladybirds, also called ladybugs, are beautiful black and red insects prized by farmers. Claudia's description stuck. Growing up, she was called either "Lady" or "Bird" by her family and friends.

Claudia grew up listening to the wind in the pine trees near her home. She found great joy in the variety of wildflowers she saw there. She studied the arts and journalism at the University of Texas, and learned about business from her father. She was a good student and studied hard. Her marriage to Lyndon Baines Johnson proved to be a beneficial partnership. She helped him with his political career but had her own dreams and ideas as well.

▼ **Lady Bird Johnson**

---

hardy, strong and healthy
adapted, changed to survive
tribute, honor or compliment

A First Lady's Project

Every First Lady has her own special role in history. First Ladies interact with so many people; they have a great chance to make a difference in the world.

As wife of the president of the United States, Lady Bird had an opportunity to focus on a project of her own. She knew this would be an opportunity to do something good for her country. She decided to beautify the country by preserving its wildflowers, native plants, and grasses. Native plants are those that have existed in an area for a long time without having ever been planted. Each area of the country has its own native plants. Unfortunately, these plants, such as switch grass, are disappearing quickly because of human activities. Some of these activities are part of **urban development.** Farmers are using some of the land as well. And sometimes people bring in non-native plants that take over an area and push the native plants out.

Some people may question why Lady Bird decided on wildflower conservation as her **mission.** With so many other problems in the world, small plants like the beautiful red Indian blanket may not seem important. Lady Bird realized long ago what many people are now beginning to see. "For the **bounty** of nature is also one of the deep needs of man," she said. Restoring a landscape and allowing the native plants to grow is an important step in conservation.

---

urban development, the expansion of people and buildings into rural areas
mission, important job
bounty, things occurring in large amounts

▲ Native plants in Big Bend National Park

BEFORE YOU GO ON

1 Where does the name "Lady Bird" come from?

2 Why are some native plants disappearing?

On Your Own
What parts of your state are threatened by urban development?

Conservation

In 1982, Lady Bird founded an organization to protect and preserve two of America's valuable resources—native plants and natural landscapes. The National Wildlife Research Center displays the flowers and plants it helps to preserve, and it supports programs to protect our **ecological** heritage.

While native grasses, plants, and wildflowers add beauty to the land, they are also extremely important to wildlife and the environment. A sudden heavy rainfall can cause the soil to wash away. Native plants protect the soil from **eroding.** These plants anchor, or hold down, the soil and keep it in place. Wildflowers and native plants also hold water in the soil.

There is another important reason that plants are important to us. Plants release oxygen into the air. When you inhale, or breathe in, you breathe in oxygen, which is a gas. When you exhale, or breathe out, you release carbon dioxide. Plants are the opposite. They use carbon dioxide from the air to make food. In that process, they release oxygen. Many animals also use plants for food, including humans. Humans have important relationships with plants.

Some insects also have important relationships with plants. For example, ladybirds, or ladybugs, have a symbiotic relationship with some **crops.** Each depends on the other to survive. Ladybugs eat insects called aphids. Farmers keep ladybugs to eat aphids, which can damage their crops. The crops benefit because they are protected, and the ladybugs benefit because they get food.

---

ecological, having to do with living things
eroding, slowly wearing away
crops, plants that farmers grow and sell

▲ Ladybug, or Ladybird beetle

Fields come alive with color in the spring. ▼

Lady Bird's Legacy

Inspired by Lady Bird's hard work, the federal government has passed laws to help states with conservation efforts. One example is the 2007 **Endangered Species** Recovery Act. The government gives tax credits to citizens who conserve and protect the endangered plants and animals on their land.

Protecting native grasses, plants, and wildflowers means much more than simply making America beautiful. It means clean air, clean water, and preservation of **wilderness areas.** Of course, it also has an impact on beauty. The highways are cleaner and more beautiful with stretches of bluebonnets, yuccas, and honey daisy. The prairies have stretches of native grasses that horses and cows eat. Big bluestem is a prairie grass that some call "ice cream for cows" because cows love it so much. Native grasses, plants, and wildflowers also provide homes for birds and insects.

▲ Wildflowers next to a highway

Lady Bird Johnson died in 2007, but people will always remember her as the "Environmental First Lady." As she once said, "I'm **optimistic** that the world of native plants will not only survive, but will **thrive** for environmental and economic reasons, and for reasons of the heart. Beauty in nature nourishes us and brings joy to the human spirit. It also is one of the deep needs of people everywhere."

---

endangered species, plant or animal population that is nearly extinct
wilderness area, land that has never been farmed or built on
optimistic, confident that good things will happen
thrive, be successful, strong, and healthy

BEFORE YOU GO ON

1 In what ways do people depend on plants?

2 In what way do ladybugs and crops have a **partnership**?

On Your Own
What native plants grow in the area where you live?

► **COMPREHENSION**  Workbook Page 109

Recall

1. Why are plants important to the soil?
2. Why did Lady Bird select wildflowers for her project?

Comprehend

3. Why are plants **beneficial** for people?
4. Why do people remember Lady Bird as the "Environmental First Lady?"

Analyze

5. Why do you think that people questioned Lady Bird's **role** in preserving wildflowers?
6. What do you think Lady Bird meant by "Beauty in nature nourishes us"?

Connect

7. What endangered species do you know about? Explain.
8. Do you think it is important to protect native plants? Why or why not?

▲ Cactuses are native plants in many states.

► **IN YOUR OWN WORDS**

Copy the chart below into your notebook. Find the information from the article. **Interact** with a partner. Use the chart to summarize the important points the article tells about the topic in each column.

Human activities that destroy native plants	Benefits of using native plants	Why plant conservation is important

► DISCUSSION

Discuss in pairs or small groups.

1. What role did Lady Bird play in beautifying America?
2. What could happen if plants are not protected
Q **Why are relationships with others important?**
   How do conservation efforts help people understand
   our relationships with nature?

»)) *Listening* SKILL

Listen for Key Words
and important details.
Take notes to help
you remember this
information.

► READ FOR FLUENCY

When we read aloud to communicate meaning, we group words
into phrases, pause or slow down to make important points, and
emphasize important words. Pause for a short time when you reach a
comma and for a longer time when you reach a period. Pay attention
to rising and falling intonation at the end of sentences.

Work with a partner. Choose a paragraph from the reading. Discuss
which words seem important for communicating meaning. Practice
pronouncing difficult words. Take turns reading the paragraph aloud
and give each other feedback.

► EXTENSION  Workbook Page 109

Utilize Work with a partner. Think about the relationship between
plants, animals, and people described in the article. Go to the
library or use the Internet to learn more about these relationships
or partnerships. Pair this information with pictures to create your
own science article. As you write, try to use as much new academic
language as possible.
Then share your
completed article with
your classmates.

LEARNING STRATEGY

To better acquire
and understand new
academic language, use
and reuse these words
in meaningful ways in
your writing.

A honeybee
collects pollen
from a flower. ►

Grammar

More about Antecedent / Pronoun Agreement

An antecedent is the word, phrase, or clause that determines what a pronoun refers to. All pronouns must agree in number (singular or plural) and gender (masculine, feminine, or neutral) with their antecedents.

> If we do not protect **native plants, they** will disappear.
> **Sally** loves animals. **She** wants to adopt a cat.

When the gender of a noun is not known, it is called a "generic noun." A generic noun does not refer to any person or thing in particular, but rather a whole group. With a singular generic noun, a singular pronoun (masculine, feminine, or neutral) should be used. With a plural generic noun, use a plural pronoun.

> **A pet** depends on **its** owner for all **its** needs.
> Without dogs, **sight-impaired people** would not be able to navigate **their** environment.

Grammar **SKILL**

When a singular generic noun refers to a person, you may use a phrase such as *he* or *she* when referring to the antecedent.

Practice
Workbook Page 110

Work with a partner. Copy the sentences into your notebook. Circle the antecedent in each and underline all pronouns that refer to it.

Example: (The boys) left their coats at my house.

1. When my brother got home, he went straight to his bed.
2. Manny discussed his ideas about his paper with us.
3. Pat doesn't know what time she'll be finished with her appointment.
4. The young girl made her parents very upset with her.
5. My friend gave me her phone number and her address.

Apply
Write four sentences describing a relative. Then tell a partner about him or her.

Example: My cousin Alexandra lives in Germany. She . . .

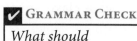

GRAMMAR CHECK

What should **pronouns** *always agree with?*

Parallel Structure

Parallel structure means using a similar pattern of words in a sentence or series of sentences so that your writing flows and makes sense.

Your word choice must be parallel. Try to use the same form of nouns when possible. When listing nouns, make sure all nouns are either singular or plural. When listing adjectives or adverbs, make sure they are all the same form.

> **Parallel:** The owner must provide **food and care** for the animal to survive.
> **Not parallel:** The owner must provide food and caring for the animal to survive.

> **Parallel:** One special relationship is between **owners and support animals**.
> **Not parallel:** One special relationship is between an owner and support animals.

> **Parallel:** A support animal can be **loving**, **helpful**, and **committed**.
> **Not parallel:** A support animal can be loving, helpful, and show commitment

Use the same verb form and voice in compound and complex sentences.

> **Parallel:** The bird **is helping** the rhino and the rhino **is helping** the bird.
> **Not parallel:** The bird helps the rhino and the rhino is helping the bird.

> **Parallel:** The horses **were adopted** and they **were given** land.
> **Not parallel:** The horses were adopted and she gave them land.

Practice

Workbook Page 111

Work with a partner. Rewrite the sentences so they have parallel structure.

Example: She loves to cook, read, and go shopping.
She loves to cook, read, and shop.

1. It is easier to tell the truth than lying to people you love.
2. Jim scared us by telling us a ghost story and showed us a horror movie.
3. Brian liked playing baseball but also to run long distances.
4. He was tall, thin, and had blond hair.
5. This plan is creative but a risk.

Apply

Write five sentences about the things you like to do. Make sure you use parallel structure. Then tell a partner about yourself.

Example: I really like to listen to music. I also enjoy . . .

Writing

Write a Classifying Paragraph

You have already learned about three types of expository writing: instructions, critiques, and compare-and-contrast paragraphs. Classifying objects and writing about them is another kind of expository writing. Classification is the process of putting people or things into groups, called categories, according to the qualities they share.

> **Writing Prompt**
>
> Write a paragraph in which you classify something. For example, you could write about movies and classify them into three categories: comedy, drama, and action. Be sure to make pronouns agree with antecedents and use parallel structure.

1 PREWRITE Begin by choosing a topic that you want to classify.

- Think of three different categories within the topic.

- List the characteristics that make each group different from the others.

- Think of an example for each type of classification.

- List your ideas in a graphic organizer like the one below.

Workbook Page 112

Here's a three-column chart created by a student named Katie. She is explaining three different ways that animals care for their young.

Bald eagles	Bottlenose dolphins	Meerkats
Males and females share the duty of sitting on their eggs.	Male dolphins are not involved in raising their young.	Young meerkats are not cared for by their parents.
One sits while the other looks for food.	Dolphins have a baby calf about every 3 years.	They are cared for by surrounding females.
Eaglets stay with their parents for 8 to 14 weeks.	The calf lives with its mother for up to 6 years	These females protect them from predators.

2 DRAFT Use your three-column chart to help you write a first draft.

- Remember to introduce the main topic first.
- Present each category by describing it and giving an example.
- As you write, think about your audience. Are the three different categories clear to the reader?

3 REVISE Read over your draft. Look for places where the writing is unclear or needs improvement. Use the Writing Checklist to help you identify problems. Then revise your draft, using the editing and proofreading marks listed on page 458.

4 EDIT Check your work for errors in grammar, usage, mechanics, and spelling. Trade papers with a partner to obtain feedback. Use the Peer Review Checklist on Workbook page 112. Edit your final draft in response to feedback from your partner and your teacher.

5 PUBLISH Prepare a clean copy of your final draft. Share your classifying paragraph with the class. Save your work. You'll need to refer to it in the Writing Workshop at the end of the unit.

Here is Katie's paragraph. Notice how she clearly explains and presents each category.

Writing Checklist

ORGANIZATION:
☑ I organized my ideas in a way that makes my categories clear.

WORD CHOICE:
☑ I used pronouns that agree with their antecedents.

Katie Veneziano

Parenting Styles in Nature

Many animals care for their young until their offspring can survive on their own. The bald eagle, the bottlenose dolphin, and the meerkat all care for their young in different ways. Male and female bald eagles share the duty of sitting on their eggs. One parent watches the eggs while the other looks for food. After the eaglets hatch, they live with their parents for eight to fourteen weeks. Bottlenose dolphins live mostly in tropical waters, and the female dolphins usually have a baby about every three years. The baby, or calf, will live with its mother for up to six years. Unlike bald eagles, male dolphins are not involved in raising their young. Young meerkats are not cared for by their parents, but by surrounding female meerkats. When the young meerkats leave the burrow, these females protect them from predators.

Link the Readings

Critical Thinking

Look back at the readings in this unit. Think about what they have in common. They all tell about relationships. Yet they do not all have the same purpose. The purpose of one reading might be to inform, while the purpose of another might be to entertain or persuade. In addition, the content of each reading relates to relationships differently. Now copy the chart below into your notebook and complete it.

Title of Reading	Purpose	Big Question Link
"Aguinaldo," from *Salsa Stories*		*A young girl makes a new friend.*
"Sowing the Seeds of Peace"		
From *Blue Willow*		
"The Ladybird and the Wildflowers"	*to inform*	

Discussion

Discuss in pairs or small groups.

- How are the relationships between the campers in "Sowing the Seeds of Peace" similar to the relationship between Marilia and Elenita in "Aguinaldo"?

- **Q How are relationships with others important?** What do you think is important about each relationship within the readings? What are the most important relationships in your life? What makes them important to you?

Media Literacy & Projects

Work in pairs or small groups. Choose one of these projects.

1 Think about foods that are part of your family's tradition. Write two or three of your favorite family recipes on note cards. Include a list of the necessary materials and instructions for what to do with those materials. Share the recipes with your classmates. Describe why your recipes are special. Then combine your recipes to make a class cookbook. Use the Internet to find photographs to put in your cookbook.

2 You read about the Seeds of Peace International Camp. Write an informational brochure that describes the camp's mission, location, and programs. The brochure should make people understand what makes this camp special. Then share it with the class.

3 In the legend *Blue Willow*, both Kung Shi Fair and Chang the Good die tragically. Rewrite the final scenes of the legend to include a description of their lives together had they lived. Illustrate your new ending. Then share it with the class.

Further Reading

Choose from these reading suggestions. Practice reading silently with increased ease for longer and longer periods.

The Scarlet Letter, Nathaniel Hawthorne
In this Penguin Reader® adaptation of the classic story, a young woman in seventeenth-century New England is scorned by her community. She and her baby face a harsh punishment.

Under the Royal Palms: A Childhood in Cuba, Alma Flor Ada
The author recollects growing up in a small Cuban town and the many people who touched her life, including her grandmother, a mysterious uncle, and a dance teacher who helped her through a difficult year at school.

Shabanu: Daughter of the Wind, Suzanne Fisher Staples
Life is both sweet and cruel to strong-willed Shabanu, whose home is a windswept desert of Pakistan. When a tragic encounter with a wealthy landowner ruins the marriage plans of her older sister, Shabanu is asked to sacrifice everything she's dreamed of.

Put It All Together

How-To Demonstration

You will give a presentation that explains a process.

1 **THINK ABOUT IT** Have you ever shown a friend or family member how to do something? Think about everyday tasks you know how to do well, such as washing dishes or making a bed. How would you tell someone else to do these tasks? Review the use of imperative verbs to give commands and instructions.

Work in a team to develop a list of processes that you know something about. Think of interesting activities that you could demonstrate in class. For example:

- How to make a sandwich
- How to organize your CDs and DVDs
- How to use a digital camera
- How to ride a skateboard

2 **GATHER AND ORGANIZE INFORMATION** Choose a process from your team's list. Begin by thinking about how you learned to do this activity. Then make a list of the steps involved. Remember to include small steps that are obvious to you but that someone else might not think about. Write down any remaining questions you may have about this process.

Research Go to the library, talk to an adult, or search the Internet for more information. Look for answers to your questions. Take notes on what you find.

Order Your Notes Revise your list of steps based on your research. Then write each step on a separate note card. Think about the best order in which to present the steps. Arrange your note cards in this order, and then number them.

Use Visuals Find or make props you can use to show key steps in your demonstration. You can also create posters, models, or other visuals to help you.

3 PRACTICE AND PRESENT Practice your demonstration until you know it well. Begin by telling your audience what you will demonstrate for them. Glance at your note cards while you speak, but don't read from them. Use your visuals and props to help you explain or act out each step. If possible, ask friends or family members to listen and give you feedback. Can they hear and understand what you are saying? Keep practicing until you feel relaxed and confident.

Deliver Your How-To Demonstration Make sure your note cards are in order and your visuals are ready before you begin. Look at your audience as you speak. Think about each step as you explain it. Emphasize imperative verbs by changing the tone of your voice. Slow down when you come to the most important points. At the end of the demonstration, give your audience a chance to ask questions.

4 EVALUATE THE PRESENTATION
You will improve your skills as a speaker and a listener by evaluating each demonstration you give and hear. Use this checklist to help you judge your demonstration and the demonstrations of your classmates.

- ✔ Did the speaker present the process in a clear sequence?
- ✔ Do you feel that you were given enough information to complete the activity on your own?
- ✔ Did the speaker use props and other visuals effectively?
- ✔ Did the speaker answer your questions?
- ✔ What suggestions do you have for improving the demonstration?

 Speaking SKILLS

Highlight the most important words on your note cards so that you can see them easily.

Use ordinal numbers (*first, second, third . . .*) and sequence words (*before, next, then, finally*) to clearly explain the order of your steps.

 Listening SKILLS

Watch and listen carefully. Give the speaker your full attention.

Monitor what you are hearing. Does it make sense? Would you be able to explain the steps to someone else? If not, seek clarification. Write down questions and ask them at the end of the demonstration. When responding, give as much information as possible.

 STRENGTHEN YOUR SOCIAL LANGUAGE

In social contexts as well as in some of your content-area classes, you will need to ask for and give information. Go to www.LongmanKeystone.com and do the activity for this unit. This activity will help you acquire key structures, expressions, and words needed during extended speaking assignments and in everyday academic and social contexts.

WRITING WORKSHOP

Expository Essay

Write an Expository Essay

In this workshop, you will write an expository essay. An expository essay is a group of paragraphs that gives information about a topic. A good expository essay begins with a paragraph that introduces the writer's topic and purpose. The writer develops the topic in two or more body paragraphs. Each body paragraph presents a main idea supported by facts and details. A concluding paragraph sums up the important information in the essay.

> **Writing Prompt**
>
> Choose one of the paragraphs you wrote for this unit and expand it into a five-paragraph essay.

Ongoing Writing Skills Practice

1 **PREWRITE** Review your previous work in this unit. Choose one of your paragraphs. Now brainstorm ideas for your essay. How can you develop the ideas in your paragraph? In your notebook, answer these questions:

- What is the main topic?

- What kind of information am I going to add?

- How can I organize the information into paragraphs?

Workbook Page 113

- What kind of research do I need to do on the topic and where will I find the information?

List your ideas in a graphic organizer such as a Venn diagram, T-chart, or three-column chart. A student named Katie decided to write about how three different animal species relate to their offspring. Here is her three-column chart:

Bald Eagle	Bottlenose Dolphin	Meerkat
bird species	mammal species	mammal species
both father and mother sit on and guard eggs	mother raises offspring	young raised communally by females in colony
eggs hatch after about 35 days	young stay with mother for up to 6 years	young leave burrow at 21 days old
young stay with parents until able to care for selves—about 14 weeks		group continues to protect young

2 **DRAFT** Use your graphic organizer and the model on pages 225–226 to help you write a first draft.

- Remember to introduce your topic in the first paragraph.

- Support your information with facts and specific details.

- Sum up the important information in your concluding paragraph.

3 **REVISE** Read over your draft. Think about how well you have addressed questions of purpose, audience, and genre. Your purpose is to inform. Is your essay clearly organized? Is it appropriate in content and tone for the intended audience?

Keep these questions in mind as you revise your draft. Use the Writing Checklist below to help you identify additional issues that may need revision. Mark your changes on your draft using the editing and proofreading marks listed on page 458.

SIX TRAITS OF WRITING CHECKLIST

☑ **IDEAS:** Does my essay present interesting information about the topic?

☑ **ORGANIZATION:** Do I present information in an order that makes sense?

☑ **VOICE:** Does my writing show my knowledge of the topic?

☑ **WORD CHOICE:** Do I use linking words and comparison/contrast structures to connect ideas?

☑ **SENTENCE FLUENCY:** Did I vary my use of simple, compound, and complex sentences in order to achieve sentence fluency?

☑ **CONVENTIONS:** Does my writing follow the rules of grammar, usage, mechanics and spelling?

LEARNING STRATEGY

Monitor your written language production. Using a writing checklist will help you assess your work. Evaluate your essay to make sure that your message is clear and easy to understand.

Here are the revisions Katie plans to make to her first draft.

Animal Parents and Their Young

Many animals in the wild care for their young~~Then~~ *until* their offspring can survive on their own. *However,* Animals have different ways of raising

Revised to use a complex sentence and a transition word.

their young. The bald eagle, the bottlenose dolphin, and the meerkat are examples of animals that care for their young in different ways.

The bald eagle is the national bird of the united States. The male and female of this species share the duty of incubating the eggs. While one parent watches the eggs the other looks for nesting material or food. Incubation lasts about thirty-five days. Once The eaglets are hatched, They continue to live with their parents for eight to fourteen weeks. By then, the eaglets can fend for themselves.

Revised to create a complex sentence.

The bottlenose dolphin is a marine mammal that lives mostly in tropical waters. Usually, a female dolphin will have a baby, called a calf, about every three years. A calf lives with its mother for up to six years. Male bottlenose dolphins are not involved in raising their offspring. During this time, a calf is taught how to find food and survive.

Revised to improve logical sequence of ideas.

A meerkat is a small African mongoose that lives in communal burrows. The male meerkat like the male bottlenose dolphin does not get involved in raising its young. Instead, the young are communally raised with the assistance of other females. After about twenty-one days, the young leave the burrow, but They are still cared for by the group In fact, female "babysitter" meerkats act as lookouts near the burrow to protect the young from predators.

Edited to introduce a comparison and to create a compound sentence.

All three of these animal species brood their young. However, different animals live with their parents for different periods of time.

In addition ∧

∧The young of some species are raised by both parents. ∧ and ∧The young of

other species are raised by one parent or by the group. The examples

of the bald eagle the bottlenose dolphin, and the meerkat show

in how animal species care for their offspring

similarities and differences∧.

Revised to introduce a transition, create a compound sentence, and reinforce the main idea of the essay.

4 **EDIT** Check your work for errors in grammar, usage, mechanics, and spelling. Then trade essays with a partner and use the Peer Review Checklist below to give each other constructive feedback. Edit your final draft in response to feedback from your partner and your teacher.

Workbook
Page 113

PEER REVIEW CHECKLIST

☑ Was the essay clearly organized?

☑ Was the information interesting?

☑ Did I understand the topic better after reading it?

☑ Did the first paragraph introduce the topic?

☑ Did the concluding paragraph sum up the main points?

☑ What changes could be made to improve the essay?

Here are the changes Katie decided to make to her final draft as a result of her peer review.

Katie Veneziano

Animal Parents and Their Young

Many animals in the wild care for their young until their offspring can survive on their own. However, animals have different ways of raising their young. The bald eagle, the bottlenose dolphin, and the meerkat are examples of animals that care for their young in different ways.

The bald eagle is the national bird of the <u>u</u>nited States. The male and female of this species share the duty of incubating the eggs. While one parent watches the eggs⌄the other looks for nesting material or food. Incubation lasts about thirty-five days. Once the eaglets are hatched, they continue to live with their parents for eight to fourteen weeks. By then, the eaglets can fend for themselves.

The bottlenose dolphin is a marine mammal that lives mostly in temperate and ⌄tropical waters. Usually, a female dolphin will have a baby, called a calf, about every three years. A calf lives with its mother for up to six years. During this time, a calf is taught how to find food and survive. Male bottlenose dolphins are not involved in raising their offspring.

A meerkat is a small African mongoose that lives in communal burrows. The male meerkat, like the male bottlenose dolphin, does not get involved in raising its young. Instead, the young are communally raised with the assistance of other females. After about twenty-one days, the young leave the burrow, but they are still cared for by the group⌄In fact, female "babysitter" meerkats act as lookouts near the burrow to protect the young from predators.

All three of these animal species brood their young. However, different animals live with their parents for different periods of time. In addition, the young of some species are raised by both parents, and the young of other species are raised by one parent or by the group. The examples of the bald eagle⌄the bottlenose dolphin, and the meerkat show similarities and differences in how animal species care for their offspring.

Revised to correct errors in mechanics and punctuation.

Revised to improve factual accuracy.

Revised to correct an error in punctuation.

5 **PUBLISH** Prepare a clean copy of your final draft. Share your essay with the class.

Workbook
Page 114

Test Preparation

PRACTICE

Read the following test sample. Study the tips in the boxes. Work with a partner to answer the questions.

The Red River War

1   In the mid-1800s, the United States <u>expanded</u> west. Native Americans living on land that belonged to the United States were forced to leave their homes. The tribes were moved to reservations. The reservations were not like the homes the Native Americans left behind. The government gave them food. They trained to be farmers. But this was not the life that many of the Native Americans wanted.

2   In 1874, some of the Native Americans were not on reservations. A few attacked a group of buffalo hunters in Texas. The army then declared war on all Native Americans who were not on reservations. Leaders of the tribes were sent to Florida. The Native Americans did not have leaders on the reservations. Soldiers hunted any Native American in the area. Native Americans were forced onto the reservations or killed.

3   In 1875, the army negotiated with the last group of Native Americans outside of the reservations. Their leader, Quanah Parker, led his people to Fort Sill, ending the war.

1   What is the purpose of the selection?
   A   To inform the reader about an important event
   B   To persuade the reader to visit Fort Sill
   C   To explain to the reader how to live in peace
   D   To describe to the reader life on the reservations

2   In the selection, what does <u>expanded</u> mean?
   F   lived
   G   hunted
   H   spread
   J   traveled

Taking Tests
You will often take tests that help show what you know. Study the tips below to help you improve your test-taking skills.

Tip
Do not skip around when taking a test. Skipping around makes it very easy to mark an answer on the wrong line or to forget to return to answer a question.

Tip
Do not think the test has a trick question. Reread the question to be sure you understand it correctly.

Workbook Pages 115–118

Smithsonian American Art Museum

Embracing Family, Friends, and Neighbors

*A*ll *people have relationships in their lives. The way you act with a parent may be different from the way you act with a friend. But both relationships may offer something important to your life. American artists have used all sorts of media to capture this idea.*

Franz Kline, *Merce C* (1961)

In this large oil painting, Franz Kline painted bold black brushstrokes against a white background. Kline wanted the painting to celebrate the talent of his friend Merce Cunningham, a dancer and choreographer. Kline uses only two colors, black and white, in *Merce C*, but the viewer feels motion and excitement anyway. Kline probably used his whole body to create the wide brushstrokes, which push against the border of the canvas. He even lets spatters and drops of black paint show on the canvas. Kline did this to celebrate the unexpected movements Cunningham made in his dances. Although this may not look like a traditional portrait of his friend, Kline's painting captures a very physical grace. Some people think it looks like dancers moving.

Franz Kline, *Merce C*, ▶
1961, oil, 93 x 74⅝ in.,
Smithsonian American Art Museum

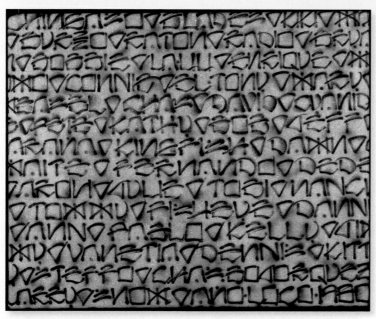

▲ Charles "Chaz" Bojórquez, *Placa/Rollcall*, 1980, acrylic, 68¼ × 83⅛ in., Smithsonian American Art Museum

Charles "Chaz" Bojórquez, *Placa/Rollcall* (1980)

In *Placa/Rollcall*, artist Charles "Chaz" Bojórquez uses stylized letters to create a painting. His painting is a wall of words that celebrates the names of his family, friends, and mentors, or teachers.

Bojórquez grew up in East Los Angeles, California. Gangs there often wrote graffiti on public places to list their members' names. Bojórquez turns this practice around. He celebrates people who have made a positive contribution to his life. He created his own secret alphabet to do it. For example, Bojórquez's *Y* is a triangle with a dot underneath it. He starts in the upper-left corner with his girlfriend's name and ends in the lower-right corner with the date. Once you adjust to the patterns in the lettering, you can find many names you'll recognize, including Tony, Tommy, Fernando, and Connie. Bojórquez sprayed the names against a huge 7-foot-wide gray-colored canvas so the painting would look like a wall or *placa* (Spanish for "plaque") of honor.

These two artists show how important caring relationships are, either in their own lives or in the lives of the people around them.

Discuss What You Learned

1 In what way does a wall of words honor people's lives? Do you know about other walls of words that do this?

2 In what way are these artworks different from those you might expect to see about friends and family relationships? Explain.

Big Question
What kind of artwork would you create to celebrate the relationships in your life?

THE BIG QUESTION

What does home mean?

This unit is about home. You will read texts about the homes immigrants lived in long ago, the cranes that migrate from Wisconsin to Florida each year, and the feelings people experience when they are far from home. Reading, writing, and talking about these topics will give you practice using academic language and will help you become a better student.

Reading

1 Social Studies	2 Short Story	3 Poetry

• "97 Orchard Street" • "The Pros and Cons of Tenement Life"	"Somebody's Son" by Richard Pindell	"The Lotus Seed" by Sherry Garland
Reading Strategy: Use visuals	**Reading Strategy:** Summarize	**Reading Strategy:** Analyze text structure 1

Listening and Speaking—Expository

At the end of this unit, you will choose a topic and deliver a **TV news show** about it.

Writing—Expository

In this unit you will practice **expository writing**, which tells factual information about a topic. After each reading, you will learn a skill to help you write an expository paragraph. At the end of the unit, you will use these skills to help you write an expository essay.

Quick Write

In your notebook, write a few sentences that describe your home. Share them with a partner.

4 | Science

"Operation Migration"
by Joyce Styron Madsen

Reading Strategy:
Monitor comprehension

VIEW AND RESPOND
Watch the DVD for Unit 4 and answer the questions at
www.LongmanKeystone.com.

What You Will Learn

Reading

- Vocabulary building: *Context, dictionary skills, word study*

- Reading strategy: *Use visuals*

- Text type: *Informational texts (social studies)*

Grammar

Adjectival clauses: subject and object relative pronouns

Writing

Write a magazine article

 THE BIG QUESTION

What does home mean? Why might someone leave their home country? What do you know about immigrants that came to the United States in the mid-1800s to early 1900s? Use your prior knowledge to take the quiz below. Then share your answers with a partner.

1. All immigrants came from Europe.   True / False

2. Immigrants came to America for different reasons.   True / False

3. Most immigrants found high-paying jobs.   True / False

4. Immigrants in large cities often lived in large houses with lots of space.   True / False

▶ **BUILD BACKGROUND**

"97 Orchard Street" is an informational article. It provides factual information about a tenement museum located in New York City. The article is followed by **"The Pros and Cons of Tenement Life."** It lists both the advantages and disadvantages of living in tenements.

A tenement is a large building that is divided into many apartments. At the turn of the twentieth century, many immigrants from around the world left their homelands to come to the United States. They came to find jobs, to escape violence and discrimination, to get an education, or to own property.

After they arrived, many poor immigrants lived in tenements. Often as many as eight to ten people lived in one small apartment, many of which did not have running water or indoor plumbing. This led to unsanitary conditions. In addition, the tenements themselves were often in disrepair and unsafe.

◀ Immigrants on Ellis Island, near New York City, in 1907

► VOCABULARY

Listening and Speaking: Key Words

Read and listen to these sentences. Use the context to figure out the meaning of the highlighted words. Use a dictionary to check your answers. Then write each word and its meaning in your notebook.

1. The museum exhibit displays children's toys from the 1800s.
2. The fire inspectors decided it was safe for people to live in the building.
3. The museum's mission is to provide its visitors with historical information about immigrants and how they lived.
4. There are many people who live in that area, or neighborhood.
5. The museum preserved the old buildings, or kept them from being destroyed.
6. Eight people lived together in one small apartment within the tenement.

Practice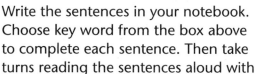

Workbook Page 121

Write the sentences in your notebook. Choose key word from the box above to complete each sentence. Then take turns reading the sentences aloud with a partner.

1. That family just moved into the apartment building across the street. They are new to the _____.
2. Early tools and inventions are displayed in the science _____.
3. The old wedding dress looks new. It has been carefully _____.
4. The _____ forced the building's owner to install lights in the stairways.
5. The crowded _____ was home to many families.
6. The school's _____ was to help immigrants learn English quickly.

▲ An immigrant family of seven in their one-room tenement apartment

Listening and Speaking: Academic Words

Study the **red** words and their meanings. You will find these words useful when talking and writing about informational texts. Write each word and its meaning in your notebook. After you read "97 Orchard Street" and "The Pros and Cons of Tenement Life," try to use these words to respond to the texts.

Academic Words

benefit
community
cultural
immigrants
items

Audio

benefit = something that helps you or gives you an advantage	⇒	One **benefit** of living in a small town is that you know your neighbors.
community = all the people living in one place	⇒	New York City's SoHo district is known as a **community** of artists.
cultural = relating to a particular society and its way of life	⇒	The Jewish Museum offers many **cultural** programs. They teach art, music, and crafts.
immigrants = people who enter another country in order to live there	⇒	In the early 1900s, many **immigrants** left their homelands and came to America.
items = things in a set, group, or list	⇒	The museum displays **items** that immigrants brought from their home countries.

Audio

Practice

Workbook Page 122

Work with a partner to answer these questions. Try to include the **red** word in your answer. Write the sentences in your notebook.

1. What is one **benefit** of living in your town?
2. How would you describe your **community**?
3. What kinds of **cultural** events take place at your school or in your neighborhood?
4. Do you know any **immigrants**? Where are they from?
5. If you had to move to a new country, what **items** would you bring with you?

Immigrant artifacts ▶

Word Study: Silent Letters

In English there are certain letter combinations in which one letter is "silent." It is important to know these combinations when spelling many words. Some common combinations are listed in the chart below. Try to pronounce each word aloud.

Words with Silent Letters	Letter Combination	Sound	Silent Letter
campai**gn**	gn	/n/	g
de**bt**	bt	/t/	b
cli**mb**	mb	/m/	b
knock	kn	/n/	k

Practice

Work with a partner. Take turns pronouncing and spelling the words in the box below. Copy the words into your notebook. Then underline the letter combinations *gn*, *bt*, *mb*, and *kn* and circle the silent letter in each word.

align	doubtful	knife	lamb
comb	foreign	know	subtle

READING STRATEGY | USE VISUALS

Using visuals helps you understand the text better. Visuals are art, photographs, diagrams, charts, maps, etc. Many informational texts include visuals. To use visuals, follow these steps:

- Look at the visual. Ask yourself, "What does the visual show? How does it help me understand the reading?"
- Read the titles, headings, labels, or captions carefully.
- Think about how the visual helps you understand what is in the text. Does the visual give you extra information? In what way?

As you read "97 Orchard Street," pay close attention to the visuals. What do they show? How do they help you understand the text better?

Set a purpose for reading As you read, think about what it was like for **immigrants** to live in tenements. How do you think immigrants made the tenements feel like home?

97 Orchard Street

Audio

Have you ever visited New York City and seen the Statue of Liberty? Have you ever walked through Ellis Island and strolled around Castle Clinton? These **landmarks symbolize** the welcoming of immigrants to a new life. But did you ever wonder what happened *after* immigrants arrived in the United States? We suggest you make one more stop on the Immigrant Heritage Trail— 97 Orchard Street.

At this address, you will find a tenement building. It is located in the most famous immigrant neighborhood in America. Built in 1863, this structure is the first home of urban poor and immigrant people to be preserved in the United States. **Restored** and run by the Lower East Side Tenement Museum, the building allows us to travel back in time. Visitors can see firsthand the immigrant experience at the turn of the twentieth century.

---

landmarks, buildings or important, historical places
symbolize, represent
restored, made to look like it used to

The Lower East Side Tenement Museum ▶

▲ An unrestored tenement apartment

▲ The same tenement apartment after its restoration

The only way to explore the museum is through a guided tour. Carefully restored apartments reflect the lives of residents from different historical periods and cultures. You will hear the stories of immigrant families who struggled to make a life in America.

Learn about the impact of **economic depressions** on the Gumpertz family in the 1870s. Discover the imaginative ways this family made their way through hard times. A visit to the Levines' apartment illustrates the Lower East Side's connection to the nation's **garment industry**. It also shows the impact this type of work had on immigrant families.

In one museum exhibit, a costumed woman portrays immigrant Victoria Confino. This is a hands-on experience. You can touch any items in the apartment and try on **period clothing**. Victoria will answer any questions about life in 1916.

An unrestored apartment in the building drives home the nineteenth-century **reform movement**'s **campaign** for improved housing. Here you can participate in a program that lets you role-play. You can pretend to be a housing inspector: Determine what is acceptable housing at different times, and learn how people fought for better housing. Visitors also learn about housing rights today and how to report housing problems.

---

economic depressions, times when many people are out of work
garment industry, businesses that make clothes

period clothing, clothes that were worn long ago
reform movement, movement intended to bring about change
campaign, series of actions intended to achieve a particular result

BEFORE YOU GO ON

1 What is located at 97 Orchard Street?

2 What are some of the **items** that visitors can see there?

On Your Own
Would you want to visit the tenement museum? Why or why not?

▲ A Lower East Side street scene in early 1900s

The museum offers public tours and school tours. More than 25,000 schoolchildren each year participate in the site's original programs, which use history to teach **tolerance**. You can also take part in discussions of current issues such as immigration, labor, and **social welfare**. And walking tours of the Lower East Side describe the neighborhood's role as the nation's most famous gateway for immigrants.

An important part of the museum's mission is addressing current social issues by looking back at history. For example, immigrant students who visit the museum today use the diaries and letters of past immigrants to learn English.

To help unite the diverse community surrounding it, the museum has organized the Lower East Side Community Preservation Project. The project helps community leaders identify and restore local historic places. It is working currently to create historical markers at sites around the neighborhood. The sites represent the different groups who have lived in the neighborhood since the 1800s.

---

tolerance, the acceptance of other people and cultures as they are

social welfare, a government program that gives assistance to the poor

The Pros and Cons of Tenement Life

Audio

Pros (+):

Closeness to work: Tenement residents had a difficult time finding transportation to bring them to work. Living and working close together made life easier.

Fraternity: Immigrants sharing the same backgrounds often lived in the same neighborhoods. In this way, they found support in **fraternal organizations**. These groups offered help in finding jobs and places to live.

Assimilation: Living among people of the same background helped immigrants cope with the American way of life.

Amusements: Coney Island, **nickelodeons**, and dance halls offered nearby, inexpensive ways to have fun and relax. Taking strolls to see store windows and riding the trolley provided entertainment, too.

Cons (–):

Disease and poor sanitation: There was a high death rate among immigrants who lived in tenements. Health officials blamed this on overflowing garbage and lack of proper **sanitary facilities**.

Lack of outside air and ventilation: Prior to 1879, rooms in tenements were not required by law to have access to outside air. That meant that residents had to endure **sweltering** heat during the summer.

Darkness: One social worker nearly tripped over children sleeping in a tenement's dark hallway. Eventually, building owners were forced to install lights near the stairs.

Fire hazards: Wooden staircases, few windows, and overcrowding turned many tenements into death traps when a fire started.

---

fraternal organizations, groups of people, usually men, who consider each other brothers and support and help one another
nickelodeons, early movie theaters where a ticket cost five cents
sanitary facilities, services and equipment that keep buildings and streets clean
sweltering, extremely hot

BEFORE YOU GO ON

1 What is the Lower East Side Community Preservation Project? What is its goal? How does it help the **community**?

2 In what ways were some tenements dangerous to live in?

On Your Own
Would you want to live in a tenement? Why or why not?

Reading 1 **239**

Review and Practice

► COMPREHENSION

Workbook
Page 125

Recall

1. When was the tenement at 97 Orchard Street built?

2. What can visitors to the museum's unrestored apartment learn about it?

Comprehend

3. Describe some of the **benefits** of living in a tenement for a new immigrant.

4. What were some of the struggles immigrants faced in the United States?

Analyze

5. Why did so many immigrants choose to live in tenements?

6. What do you think was the author's purpose for writing this text?

Connect

7. Do you think the immigration experience is easier or harder today than it was 100 years ago? Explain.

8. People from all over the world continue to immigrate to the United States. Why?

▲ Nearby places like Coney Island in New York offered tenement residents inexpensive ways to have fun.

► IN YOUR OWN WORDS

Copy the chart below into your notebook. Complete the chart with information from the article "97 Orchard Street." Then, using the chart, demonstrate your comprehension of the article by summarizing it for your partner.

"97 Orchard Street"	
Subject	**Details**
Location	97 Orchard Street, New York City
Exhibits	
Cultural programs	

► DISCUSSION

Discuss in pairs or small groups.

1. What are the missions of the tenement museum?

2. In your opinion, which mission do you think is the most important and why?

Q **What does home mean?** Do you think it is difficult to create a new home in a new country? Why or why not?

»)⤷ Listening SKILL

Summarize what the speaker says in your own mind. Do you agree or disagree?

► READ FOR FLUENCY

It is often easier to read a text if you understand the difficult words and phrases. Work with a partner. Choose a paragraph from the reading. Identify the words and phrases you do not know or have trouble pronouncing. Look up the difficult words in a dictionary.

Take turns pronouncing the words and phrases with your partner. If necessary, ask your teacher to model the correct pronunciation. Then take turns reading the paragraph aloud. Give each other feedback on your reading.

► EXTENSION   Workbook Page 125

Utilize You have learned about immigrants who came to this country at the turn of the twentieth century. In particular, you learned about their reasons for coming, where they lived, their way of life, and how they worked.

What about immigrants today? How are they the same? How are they different? Work with a partner to find the answers to these questions on the Internet or in the library. Then organize your information in a Venn diagram like the one below. Write facts about each individual group in the corresponding circles. Write facts that are true about both groups in the middle of the diagram. Then share this information with the class. Use as much academic language as possible.

LEARNING STRATEGY

To better acquire and understand new academic language, use and reuse these words in meaningful ways in your writing.

Immigrants past   Immigrants present

Grammar

Adjectival Clauses: Subject Relative Pronouns

An adjectival clause describes a noun or noun phrase and can begin with a relative pronoun. A relative pronoun can be the subject of the adjectival clause. Use the subject relative pronoun *who* to describe people; use *that* with nonrestrictive clauses and *which* with restrictive clauses to describe things. A restrictive clause is essential to the meaning of the sentence and commas are not used. A nonrestrictive clause gives additional information and commas are used. A relative pronoun does not change form, whether its antecedent is singular or plural, masculine or feminine.

> Victoria, **who answered all my questions about life in 1916**, was in costume
> [The antecedent of *who* is *Victoria*; *who* is the subject of the clause.]
> Here you can participate in a program **that lets you role-play**.
> [The antecedent of *that* is a *program*; *that* is the subject of the clause.]
> You can see restored apartment buildings, **which reflect tenement life**.
> [The antecedent of *which* is *apartment buildings*; *which* is the subject of the clause.]

Practice  Workbook Page 126

Work with a partner. Copy the sentences into your notebook, connecting them with the correct relative pronoun.

Example: The cup is on the table. It is mine.
   The cup which is on the table is mine.

1. I read his latest book. It was a best seller.

2. Jenny met a woman. The woman helped her.

3. We visited our neighbors. They were so helpful to us when we moved in.

4. I liked your friend. She came to the party.

5. Our classroom was cold. It had no heat.

Apply

In your notebook, write three sentences about a vacation you have taken, using the relative pronouns *who, that,* and *which.* Then tell a partner about the place.

Example: I've been to Staunton, which is a small historic city in Virginia.

Adjectival Clauses: Object Relative Pronouns

A relative pronoun can also be the object of an adjectival clause. Use the object relative pronoun *whom* to describe people; use *that* and *which* to describe things; use *where* to describe a place; use *when* to describe a time; and use *whose* to show possession.

> The tour guide, **whom I learned a lot from,** told us stories about immigrant families.
> They had an interesting program **that I participated in**.
> I participated in a program, **which I thought was very interesting**.
> I visited an unrestored apartment **where I role-played a housing inspector**.
> I went to the museum on Thursday, **when it wasn't so crowded**.
> We learned about the Levines, **whose house we visited**.

Although objects follow verbs or prepositions, object relative pronouns come at the beginning of the clause.

> People fought for housing rights. We have **housing rights** today. →
> People fought for housing rights, **which** we have today.

Practice  Workbook Page 127

Work with a partner. Copy the sentences into your notebook. Complete each sentence with an appropriate object relative pronoun.

Example: They made us lunch, *which* we enjoyed.

1. The talk _____ I went to was interesting.
2. The man _____ I was telling you about is over there.
3. Sandy went to the beach _____ there are a lot of sharks.
4. His new movie, _____ we saw last night, wasn't very good.
5. I played chess with Jane, _____ sister I study with.

Apply

Copy the sentence starters below into your notebook. Complete them with your own ideas. Then use the sentences to tell a partner about yourself.

Example: I just read a book that I . . . I just read a book that I really liked.

1. I know a place where you can . . .
2. I saw a great movie which you . . .
3. I have a friend whose . . .
4. My favorite food is . . . , which I . . .

Writing

Ongoing Writing Skills Practice

Write a Magazine Article

Expository writing tells factual information about a topic. A magazine article is one type of expository writing. When you write a magazine article, you try to grab the reader's attention quickly with interesting information. Your article should answer as many of the 5Ws as possible. The 5Ws are *Who? What? Where? When?* and *Why?* The article "97 Orchard Street" answered the following questions: *Who created the tenement museum? What is displayed there? Where is it located? When was it built? Why was it created?*

> ### Writing Prompt
>
> Write a magazine article about an event in your town such as the opening of a museum exhibit, a sporting event, or a concert. Be sure to use adjective clauses correctly in your writing.

1 **PREWRITE** Begin by choosing a recent event in your town.

- Write the name of the event at the top of the page in your notebook.

- Ask yourself the 5W questions about the event.

- List your answers in a graphic organizer such as a chart.

Workbook Page 128

Here's a chart created by a student named Blaise. She is writing an article about an exhibit at the Museum of Science in Boston, Massachusetts.

Who?	anyone who is curious about the way things work
What?	the lightning exhibit
Where?	Museum of Science in Boston, Massachusetts
When?	whenever the museum is open to visitors
Why?	Staff members describe how lightning is made. Then they replicate the process right in front of you!

2 **DRAFT** Use your chart to help you write a first draft.

- Remember to answer the 5W questions.
- Remember to use adjectival clauses to combine sentences.
- Try to grab the reader's attention with interesting information.

Writing Checklist

IDEAS:
☑ I answered the 5Ws in my article.

SENTENCE FLUENCY:
☑ I combined sentences using adjectival clauses.

3 **REVISE** Read over your draft. Look for places where the writing is unclear or needs improvement. Use the Writing Checklist to help you identify problems. Then revise your draft, using the editing and proofreading marks listed on page 458.

4 **EDIT** Check your work for errors in grammar, usage, mechanics, and spelling. Trade papers with a partner to obtain feedback. Use the Peer Review Checklist on Workbook page 128. Edit your final draft in response to feedback from your partner and your teacher.

5 **PUBLISH** Prepare a clean copy of your final draft. Share your magazine article with the class. Save your work. You'll need to refer to it in the Writing Workshop at the end of the unit.

Here is Blaise's paragraph about a museum exhibit. Notice how she answers the 5W questions and uses content-based vocabulary.

Blaise Yafcak

A Museum Worth Visiting

Anyone who is curious about the way things work in nature should visit the lightning exhibit at the Museum of Science in Boston, Massachusetts. The Museum of Science is one of the most exciting science museums in the country, and the lightning exhibit, which is on permanent display, is a highlight of any tour. Visitors to Boston, residents of the city, kids, teenagers, and adults will all find the exhibit fascinating. It is located in a large amphitheater, which is where museum staff members describe how lightning is made. They explain how positive charges in the ground can be attracted to and collide with negative charges in a rain cloud. These collisions are what you see during a lightning storm. After the lesson, the museum staff actually replicates the process of colliding charges right in front of you! This thrilling exhibit can be seen whenever the museum is open to visitors. Check the museum's website for hours of admission.

What You Will Learn

Reading

- Vocabulary building: *Literary terms, word study*

- Reading strategy: *Summarize*

- Text type: *Literature (short story)*

Grammar
Adjectives and adjectival phrases; Adverbs and adverbial phrases

Writing
Write a plot summary

► **THE BIG QUESTION**

What does home mean? We have all had arguments, or disagreements, with members of our family. Can you imagine ever being so angry that you would leave your family and home? Do you think it would be difficult to return home afterwards? Discuss with a partner.

► **BUILD BACKGROUND**

In this section, you will read a fictional short story called **"Somebody's Son."** Like a novel, a short story consists of characters and a fully developed theme, or main idea. However, it is much shorter than a novel.

"Somebody's Son" is the story of a young man, named David, who ran away from home after arguing with his father. During his time away from home, David traveled by train and car to the West Coast, Mexico, and Canada. You will read about how David wanted to return home, how he wanted to repair the relationship with his father, and the journey that he took to get there.

➤ VOCABULARY

Learn Literary Words

Authors create **suspense** to keep readers interested. Suspense is a feeling of uncertainty about the outcome of a story. Suspense makes readers ask, "What will happen next?" Read the passage below to see how one author has created suspense.

> Jillian walked into the room. She had to find the missing letter. Surely, the letter would reveal who had stolen the diamond necklace. She could smell a faint, flowery perfume. Someone had just been there before her. But who? All of a sudden, she heard a rustling sound coming from the closet in the corner.

What questions does the passage leave you with? Are you curious to find out what happens next?

Most stories have a buildup of suspense that usually leads to a **climax**, or the moment of highest intensity. It is usually the most exciting part of the story. The passage below is an example.

> She whirled around and saw the closet door opening slowly. Jillian stepped back. Old Mrs. Wentworth came out of the closet. She was holding a piece of paper in her hand.
>
> "Mrs. Wentworth! What is that piece of paper?" Jillian asked.
>
> "It's the letter you're looking for, my dear. It tells who stole the diamond necklace," said Mrs. Wentworth.
>
> "Who stole it?" Jillian asked excitedly.
>
> Mrs. Wentworth walked toward the fireplace. She threw the paper into the burning flames and turned back to face Jillian.
>
> "I did, of course," she said. "And now, you have no way to prove it."

Practice  Workbook Page 129

In a small group, reread the passages above. Talk about how each passage made you feel. How was your response to the first passage different from your response to the second passage?

Listening and Speaking: Academic Words

Study the **red** words and their meanings. You will find these words useful when talking and writing about literature. Write each word and its meaning in your notebook, then say the words aloud with a partner. After you read "Somebody's Son," try to use these words to respond to the text.

correspond = write to someone and receive letters from him or her	→	Even though my cousin lives far away, we **correspond** by e-mail every day.
indicate = say or do something that shows what you want or intend to do	→	Students are supposed to **indicate** that they finished a test by laying their pencils on top of their papers.
occurs = happens	→	The reunion **occurs** every ten years.
transportation = the process or business of moving people or goods from one place to another	→	The only **transportation** available is a bus that leaves at 6:30 in the morning.

Audio

Practice

Workbook
Page 130

Work with a partner to answer these questions. Try to include the **red** word in your answer. Write the sentences in your notebook.

1. How do you **correspond** with friends who live far away?

2. In what ways do you **indicate** to others how you feel about them?

3. Can you name an event that **occurs** in your town year after year?

4. What kinds of **transportation** do you use to get from place to place?

Using the computer is one way for friends to correspond with each other. ▶

Word Study: Homophones

Homophones are words that sound the same but are spelled differently and have different meanings. For example, compare and contrast the words *see* and *sea*. *Sea* is a noun. *See* is a verb. Both words sound the same, but have different spellings and meanings.

| **sea** = a large area of salty water | The stormy *sea* has huge waves. |
| **see** = to perceive something with your eyes | The boy was sad to *see* the sun go down. |

Practice
Workbook Page 131

Work with a partner. Read the sentences aloud. Copy them into your notebook. Then use one of the homophones in parentheses to complete each sentence. You can use a dictionary to help you.

1. (mail / male)
   a. The dog is not a female, it's a _____.
   b. They get their _____ at the post office.

2. (sun / son)
   a. Robert is Maria's _____.
   b. The _____ is shining brightly today.

3. (plane / plain)
   a. I like _____ yogurt, not the kind with fruit.
   b. The _____ is flying to California.

Now write sentences using these homophones: *cent* / *sent* / *scent*.

READING STRATEGY   SUMMARIZE

Summarizing is a basic reading skill that helps you to understand and remember the most important points in the text. When you summarize, you find the main ideas and state them in a few short sentences. To summarize, follow these steps:

- Read the text. Then reread each paragraph or section.
- Decide what the main idea is in each paragraph or section. Make notes. Leave out details. Just focus on the most important points.
- Write a few sentences that summarize the main ideas. Use your own words.

As you read "Somebody's Son," stop from time to time to note the main ideas. Demonstrate your comprehension of the text by summarizing it in two or three sentences.

Workbook Page 132

Set a purpose for reading As you read, think about why David wants to return home. What about his home is important to him?

Somebody's Son

Richard Pindell

He sat, washed up on the side of the highway, a slim, sun-beaten driftwood of a youth. He was hunched on his strapped-together suitcase, chin on hands, elbows on knees, staring down the road. Not a car was in sight.

Now he was eager to write that letter he had kept putting off. Somehow, writing it would be almost like having company.

He unstrapped his suitcase and fished out of the pocket on the underside of the lid a small, unopened package of **stationery**. Sitting down in the **gravel** of the roadside, he closed the suitcase and used it as a desk.

Reading Skill

Identify the words you don't understand *as you read* and ask your teachers or peers for help with those words.

---

stationery, paper used for writing letters
gravel, small stones used to pave roads

Dear Mom,

*If Dad will permit it, I would like to come home. I know there's little chance he will. I'm not going to **kid** myself. I remember he said once, if I ever ran off, I might as well keep on going.*

*All I can say is that I felt leaving home was something I had to do. Before even considering college, I wanted to find out more about life and about me. Please tell Dad—and I guess this'll make him **sore** all over again—I'm still not certain that college is the answer for me. I think I'd like to work for a time and think it over.*

You won't be able to reach me by mail, because I'm not sure where I'll be next. But in a few days I hope to be passing by our place. If there's any chance Dad will have me back, please ask him to tie a white cloth to the apple tree in the south pasture—you know the one, beside the tracks. I'll be going by on the train. If there's no cloth on the tree I'll just quietly, and without any hard feelings toward Dad—I mean that—keep on going.

Love,
David

A series of headlights made a domino of the highway. **High beams** flickered over him curiously. He put out his thumb almost hesitantly, wishing he didn't have to emerge so suddenly, so **menacingly**. One by one, the cars passed him, their **back draft** slapping him softly, **insultingly**, on the cheek.

---

kid, fool
sore, angry
high beams, bright headlights from cars
menacingly, threateningly or in an angry way
back draft, wind that comes from passing by very fast
insultingly, offensively or in an impolite way

BEFORE YOU GO ON

1 Why did David leave home?

2 In his letter, what does David ask his mother to do?

On Your Own
Describe what you hope to do after high school.

Much later, turning woodenly to gaze after a car, he saw the glow of taillights **intensify**. Brakes squealed. The car **careened** wildly to a stop, and he was running down the road to capture it, his breath rushing against his upturned collar and the taillights glowing nearer as in a dream.

A door was flung open like a friendly arm reaching out to a tired swimmer. "Hop in, boy."

It was a gruff, outdoors voice. "I pret' near missed you. You ain't easy to see out there."

"Thanks, mister."

"Forget it. Used the thumb a lot myself when I was a kid."

"How far are you going?" asked David.

The man named a small place in Iowa about two hundred miles away.

"Where you headin'?" the man asked him.

David glanced at him. His nose was big; his mouth, wide and gentle.

The boy looked out on the highway with affection. It would be a good ride with a good companion. "Home," he said with a grin. "I'm heading home."

The man heard the smile in the boy's voice and **chuckled**. "That's a good feelin', ain't it? Where 'bouts?"

"Maryland. We have a farm about thirty miles outside of Baltimore."

"Where you been?"

"West Coast, Canada, a little of Mexico."

"And now you're **hightailin'** for home, huh?" There was a note in the man's voice as if this were a pattern he understood **intimately**.

---

intensify, get stronger
careened, moved from side to side
chuckled, laughed quietly
hightailin', traveling quickly
intimately, very well

"Yes, sir."

"Yeah," the driver was saying now, "I know how it is." The corners of his eyes crinkled as if he were going to smile, but he didn't. "I was out on that same old road when I was a kid. **Bummin' around**. Lettin' no grass grow under me. Sometimes wishin' it would."

"And then, afterward," David asked, "did you go back home?"

"Nope. I didn't have no home to go back to, like you do. The road was my only home. Lost my ma and pa when I was a little **shaver**. Killed in a car wreck."

"That's rough," David said with such feeling the man glanced at him sharply.

The boy was staring into the night. The man shifted his grip on the wheel. He spoke softly to the boy as if he were aware he was interrupting important thoughts. "Bet you could do with some sleep."

"You sure you won't be needing me later to help you keep awake?" David asked.

"Don't worry 'bout me none. I like drivin' at night. You just lean back there and help yourself."

"Well, okay," David said. "Thanks."

Sometime later, he was awakened by a sharp decrease in speed. They were entering a town. He sat up and jerked the letter out of his jacket pocket. He had almost forgotten.

---

bummin' around, wandering around without any particular place to go
shaver, young male child

BEFORE YOU GO ON

1 How does David **indicate** that he is looking for a ride?

2 What do David and the driver have in common?

On Your Own
Would you like to travel to new places? If so, where do you want to go and why?

Reading 2 **253**

"Excuse me, sir, but would you mind stopping at a mailbox so I can mail this? I want to make sure that it gets home before I do."

"Course not," the man said. "Here's one comin' up now." He pulled over to the curb and stopped.

When the boy got back in, the man smiled kindly. "Bet your folks'll be **tickled** to hear from you."

"I hope so, sir." David tilted his head back and closed his eyes.

The next day, rides were slow. They were what David called "farmer rides," a few miles here, a couple of miles there, with long waits in between.

Toward nightfall, he swung onto a panting, slow-moving freight aimed stolidly east. The train was hammering along beside a highway. He stared at the houses on the other side. How would it be at home? Would his house be like that one, the one with the porch light burning? Or would it be like that one, where the porch was dark and where over each of the lighted windows a yellow shade was pulled down firmly to the sill?

A couple of days later, in the middle of Maryland, maddeningly close to home, the flow of rides **narrowed to a trickle** and then **ceased** altogether. When cars weren't in sight, he walked. After a while, he didn't even bother to stop and hold out his thumb. Furiously, he walked.

Later, seated on the passenger train he wished with slow, frightened heartbeats that he were back on the road, headed the other way.

---

tickled, pleased
narrowed to a trickle, got fewer and fewer
ceased, stopped

Three inches from his nose was the dust-stained window through which in a few minutes he would look out across his father's fields. Two different pictures tortured him—the tree with the white cloth and the tree without it. His throat closed and he could hardly breathe.

He tried to fortify himself with the idea that whether or not he still was welcome, at least he would see the place again.

The field was sliding closer, one familiar landmark at a time. He couldn't stop the train. Nothing could **postpone** the **denouement** now. The tree was around the next bend.

He couldn't look. He was too afraid the cloth would not be there—too afraid he would find, staring back at him, just another tree, just another field, just another somebody else's strange place, the way it always is on the long, long road, the nameless staring back at the nameless. He jerked away from the window.

Desperately, he **nudged** the passenger beside him. "Mister, will you do me a favor? Around this bend on the right, you'll see an apple tree. I wonder if you'll tell me if you see a white cloth tied to one of its branches?"

As they passed the field, the boy stared straight ahead. "Is it there?" he asked with an uncontrollable **quaver**.

"Son," the man said in a voice slow with **wonder**, "I see a white cloth tied on almost every twig.

---

postpone, delay
denouement, conclusion or ending
nudged, gently poked
quaver, trembling voice
wonder, amazement or surprise

ABOUT THE **AUTHOR**

Richard Pindell received his doctorate from Yale University in 1971. He is now a popular and award-winning professor of English at the University of Binghamton in New York, where he specializes in teaching Southern and Civil War literature.

✔ **LITERARY CHECK**
What was the climax of the story?

BEFORE YOU GO ON

1 What kept David from looking at the apple tree?

2 What did the stranger see when he looked out the window?

On Your Own
Were you surprised by the story's ending? Explain.

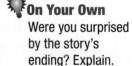

Reading 2 **255**

Review and Practice

► READER'S THEATER

Act out the following scene between David and the driver.

Driver: Hi, get in. I almost missed you—it's so dark out there.

David: Thanks for stopping.

Driver: No problem. Where you headed?

David: Home. [*reaches into his pocket and feels the letter*] Oh! I almost forgot! Sir, would you mind stopping at a mailbox? I have a letter—I'd like it to get home before I do.

Driver: Not at all. In fact, here's a mailbox now.

[*pause while David mails the letter and gets back in the car*]

Driver: It'll be good to be back home, huh? I bet your parents will be happy to hear from you.

David: [*uncertainly*] I hope so. We'll see.

Speaking **SKILL**

As you speak, be sure to make eye contact with your partner.

► COMPREHENSION

Workbook
Page 133

Recall

1. Where is David's home?

2. Why couldn't the driver return to his childhood home?

Comprehend

3. What forms of **transportation** does David use on his journey?

4. Where has David been?

Analyze

5. Why do you think David wrote the letter to his mother instead of his father?

6. Why did David's father tie more than one white cloth to the apple tree?

Connect

7. Have you ever felt angry towards a parent or another relative? Explain.

8. What do you think is the best way to resolve a conflict?

➤ DISCUSSION

Discuss in pairs or small groups.

1. How does David feel about college after his travels?

2. Is this a present-day story? Explain.

Q What does home mean? Some people say that young adults need to leave home and explore the world around them in order to discover more about themselves and what they want to do with their lives. Do you agree? Why or why not?

Workbook
Page 133

➤ RESPONSE TO LITERATURE

Utilize Work in groups of three. Use your imagination as you discuss the following: What do you think **occurs** when David returns home? How do his parents react? What does David say to his parents? Write a dialogue that answers these questions. Be sure to include parts for David, his mother, and his father. Then act out your dialogue in front of the class.

Listening SKILL

Listen carefully to your classmates. Identify the most important ideas. Retell or summarize these ideas in your own words. Use complete sentences.

Grammar

Adjectives and Adjectival Phrases

An adjective is a type of modifier used to describe nouns or pronouns. An adjectival phrase is a phrase that functions as an adjective. It can consist of a series of adjectives or it can consist of any other elements that modify that adjective. A single adjective or a series of adjectives appear before the noun they modify; adjectival phrases always occur inside noun phrases but may come after the noun.

> He fished out a **small, unopened** package of stationery. [modifies *package*]
> He saw a tree **full of white ribbons**. [modifies *tree*]

A prepositional phrase, called a prepositional adjective, can also act as an adjective.

> Sitting down in the gravel **of the roadside**, he closed the suitcase. [modifies *gravel*]

An adjective or adjectival phrase can also follow a linking verb, acting as a subject complement.

> The next day, rides were **slow with long waits in between**. [modifies *rides*]

Practice  Workbook Page 134

Work with a partner. Copy the dialogue below into your notebook, putting the adjectives in parentheses in the correct order. Then take turns role-playing the following conversation.

Example: Julia has a *white cotton* (cotton, white) cloth.

Patrick: What are you doing with that _____ _____ (white, large) cloth?

Julia: I'm going to embroider an egg and worm with _____ _____ (cotton, regular) thread, and use _____ _____ (beautiful, silk) thread for the cocoon.

Patrick: Great. Maybe I can bring my mom's _____ _____ _____ (silk, red, fancy) scarf, too.

Julia: Nice idea. Silk is amazing. It's hard to believe it comes from these _____ _____ _____ (white, little, odd) cocoons.

Apply

Write five sentences using adjectival phrases about objects you see in your classroom. Then read your sentences to a partner.

Adverbs and Adverbial Phrases

An adverb describes a verb, but it can also describe an adjective or another adverb. These types of adverbs are called qualifiers. An adverbial phrase is a group of words that collectively modifies a verb, adjective, or another adverb.

Grammar SKILL

A *phrase* is a group of words that go together, but do not make a complete sentence.

Adverbs take many forms. Look at the following sentence.

> He put out his thumb **almost hesitantly, wishing he didn't have to emerge so suddenly, so menacingly**.

- *Almost* is a qualifier modifying the adverb *hesitantly*.
- *Hesitantly* is an adverb of manner modifying the verb *put*.
- *So*, in both instances, modifies the adverbs *suddenly* and *menacingly*.
- *Suddenly* and *menacingly* are adverbs of manner modifying the verb *emerge*.
- The entire adverbial phrase w*ishing he didn't have to emerge so suddenly,* so *menacingly* modifies the main clause *He put out his thumb*.

Adverbs are also extremely flexible in placement. Look at how the sentence above might also be written.

> Wishing he didn't have to so suddenly, so menacingly emerge, he, almost hesitantly, put out his thumb.

Practice

Workbook Page 135

Work with a partner. Copy the sentences. Circle the adverbs. Then rewrite each sentence moving the adverb to a different place.

Example: (Quietly,) he opened the door.
He quietly opened the door.

1. Lilly joyfully opened her presents.
2. The wind blew gently.
3. We walked quickly to the shop.
4. Sally probably will go to Egypt.
5. Gene tapped his fingers nervously.

Apply

Work with a partner. Write three sentences with adverbs. Take turns moving the adverbs in each other's sentences to different places.

Writing

Ongoing
Writing
Skills
Practice

Write a Plot Summary

You have learned that a magazine article is one kind of expository writing. A plot summary is another kind of expository writing. A plot is what happens in a story. The events in most plots focus on a conflict or problem. Usually, it is resolved by the story's end. When you summarize a plot, describe, in a shortened form and in your own words, what happens. Introduce the main characters and the setting. Then describe the conflict or problem the character(s) face. Include the most important story events, and explain how the conflict is resolved.

Writing Prompt

Think about a story you know well. It may be a story presented in a book, film, or television show. Write a summary of the plot. Be sure to use adjectives and adverbs correctly.

1 **PREWRITE** Begin by choosing a story.

- Think of a book, film, or television show.

- Who were the main characters? What was the setting? What was the conflict at the center of the story? What were the main events? What was the resolution?

- Write your ideas in a graphic organizer.

Workbook
Page 136

Here's a graphic organizer created by a student named Andrew for the story "Somebody's Son."

Characters: David, his father and mother, strangers, a passenger
Setting: journey back to David's home in Maryland
Conflict: David ran away from home and wants to return.
Main events: David ran away but wants to return. He writes a letter asking his parents to tie a white cloth to a tree if he can come back.
Resolution: He goes home and there are pieces of cloth tied to almost every one of the tree's branches!

2 DRAFT Use your graphic organizer to help you write a first draft.

- Remember to include only the main points of the story.
- Include adjectives and adverbs.
- Make sure that the main conflict and the resolution of the story are clear to the reader.

3 REVISE Read over your draft. Look for places where the writing is unclear or needs improvement. Use the Writing Checklist to help you identify problems. Then revise your draft, using the editing and proofreading marks listed on page 458.

4 EDIT Check your work for errors in grammar, usage, mechanics, and spelling. Trade papers with a partner to obtain feedback. Use the Peer Review Checklist on Workbook page 136. Edit your final draft in response to feedback from your partner and your teacher.

5 PUBLISH Prepare a clean copy of your final draft. Share your plot summary with your class. Save your work. You'll need to refer to it in the Writing Workshop at the end of the unit.

Here is Andrew's summary of the story "Somebody's Son." Notice how he describes the main character, the setting, and the most important events. He also presents the conflict and tells how it is resolved.

Writing Checklist

ORGANIZATION:
☑ I included only the most important events in my summary.

WORD CHOICE:
☑ I included adjectives and adverbs in my summary.

Andrew Denkus

"Somebody's Son": A Summary

   "Somebody's Son" is a short story about a teenager named David, who ran away from home after arguing with his father. Now David wants to return home to Maryland, but he is not sure his parents will welcome him. Sitting in the hot sun by the side of a road, he writes a letter to his mother. In it, he asks his father to signal permission for David to return by tying a white cloth to an apple tree in the family's pastures. After mailing the letter, David still has a long journey ahead of him. He hitches rides from various strangers and eventually boards a train headed for Maryland. As it nears his parents' land, David nervously asks the passenger beside him to look out the window for the white cloth. The surprised passenger tells him that pieces of white cloth are tied to almost every one of the tree's branches!

What You Will Learn

Reading

■ Vocabulary building:
*Literary terms,
word study*

■ Reading strategy:
*Analyze text
structure 1*

■ Text type: *Literature
(poetry)*

Grammar
Adverbial clauses of
time; Adverbial clauses
of purpose, reason, and
contrast

Writing
Write a response to
literature

▶ 🔍 THE BIG QUESTION

What does home mean? Imagine that you have to leave
your home in a hurry. If you could take one possession with you,
what would it be? Why is this item important to you? Discuss
with a partner.

▶ BUILD BACKGROUND

In this section, you will read a narrative poem called ***The Lotus
Seed***. A narrative poem, like a short story, has a plot and characters.
However, the structure of a narrative poem looks different. It tells a
story in verse.

   The Lotus Seed is about a woman who was forced to leave her
home country, Vietnam. For hundreds of years, emperors ruled
Vietnam. The Vietnamese believed the emperor was wise about
all things. The emperors lived in a magnificent palace that had
beautiful gardens filled with lotus plants.

   The last emperor was Nguyen Vinh Thuy, who became emperor
at the age of twelve in 1926. He took the name Bao Dai, meaning
"Keeper of Greatness." Because the French had conquered Vietnam
in the late 1800s, he had little power, but was a symbol of
Vietnam's heritage.

   By 1945, many Vietnamese wanted to be
independent from France. Bao Dai resigned
as emperor in support of Ho Chi Minh, the
leader of the independence movement.
After a long war, the Vietnamese defeated
the French in 1954.

   Soon after, a civil war began between the
northern and southern parts of the country.
The United States helped the southerners.
The war ended in 1975, when the south
was defeated. As the northern armies began
to move south, many Vietnamese left the
country by boat. Most of them came to live
in the United States.

◀ Refugees flee Vietnam in 1975.

► VOCABULARY

Learn Literary Words

Literary Words

speaker Audio
symbol

The **speaker** of a poem is the imaginary character, or voice, a poet uses when writing a poem. This voice is the one you "hear" when you read the poem. This speaker is often not identified by name. Read the excerpt from the poem below for an example.

> I years had been from home,
> And now, before the door,
> I dared not open, lest a face
> I never saw before
>
> Stare vacant into mine
> And ask my business there.
> My business,—just a life I left,
> Was such still dwelling there?
>
> —*Emily Dickinson*

A **symbol** is anything that stands for or represents something else. In addition to having its own meaning, a symbol stands for something other than itself, often an idea or a feeling. For example, a flag is a piece of cloth with a design on it that represents both a country and people's feelings of patriotism toward that country.

Practice

Workbook Page 137

Work with a partner. Copy the chart below into your notebook. Create a symbol for each idea. Then explain to your partner why you chose each symbol.

Idea	Symbol
happiness	
sadness	
Earth-friendly	
freedom	
victory	

◄ The American flag

Listening and Speaking: Academic Words

Study the **red** words and their meanings. You will find these words useful when talking and writing about literature. Write each word and its meaning in your notebook, then say the words aloud with a partner. After you read *The Lotus Seed*, try to use these words to respond to the text.

attached = emotionally connected to	⇒	I am very **attached** to that vase. It belonged to my grandmother.
removed = took something away from where it was	⇒	When it was time to eat, I **removed** the vase from the table.
source = where something comes from	⇒	Rose hips, or the fruit of roses, are a good **source** of vitamin C.
symbolize = represent a quality or a feeling	⇒	To many people, yellow roses **symbolize** friendship.

Practice

Work with a partner to answer these questions. Try to include the **red** word in your answer. Write the sentences in your notebook.

1. What is one family item that you are **attached** to?

2. How would you feel if someone **removed** this item from its current location without your permission?

3. Who or what is the **source** of this item?

4. What does the item **symbolize** to you?

A Chinese vase ▶

Word Study: Spelling Long *o*

Learning to identify sound-spelling relationships will help you read more fluently. The story you are going to read contains words with the long *o* sound. Here are a few different spellings: *o, oa, o_e,* and *ow.*

o	oa	o_e	ow
so	boat	home	own
lotus	soak	throne	show

Practice
Workbook
Page 139

Work with a partner. First, copy the headings from the chart above into your notebook. Next, take turns spelling the words in the box. Then write each word in the correct column. Finally, write a sentence using each word.

alone	below	close	coast	golden	old	road	window

READING STRATEGY | ANALYZE TEXT STRUCTURE 1

Analyzing text structure can help you understand what kind of text you're reading. It can also help you set a purpose for reading. Different kinds of writing, or genres, have different kinds of text structures. Read these descriptions to help you understand the various types of text structures:

- Stories and novels are written in sentences and paragraphs. Dialogue is enclosed within quotation marks.

- Narrative poems are written in verse. Look at the way the lines are grouped together in the narrative poems you read.

- Plays are mainly written in dialogue. The characters' names are given, followed by colons (:) and the words the speakers say. Stage directions are usually in brackets ([]) and set in italics. Many plays are divided into numbered scenes.

Preview the text structure of *The Lotus Seed.* Discuss it with a partner.

Workbook
Page 140

READING 3

LITERATURE

POETRY

Set a purpose for reading As you read, think about why Bà chose the lotus seed as a memory of home. What aspect(s) of home does the seed represent?

The Lotus Seed

Audio

Sherry Garland

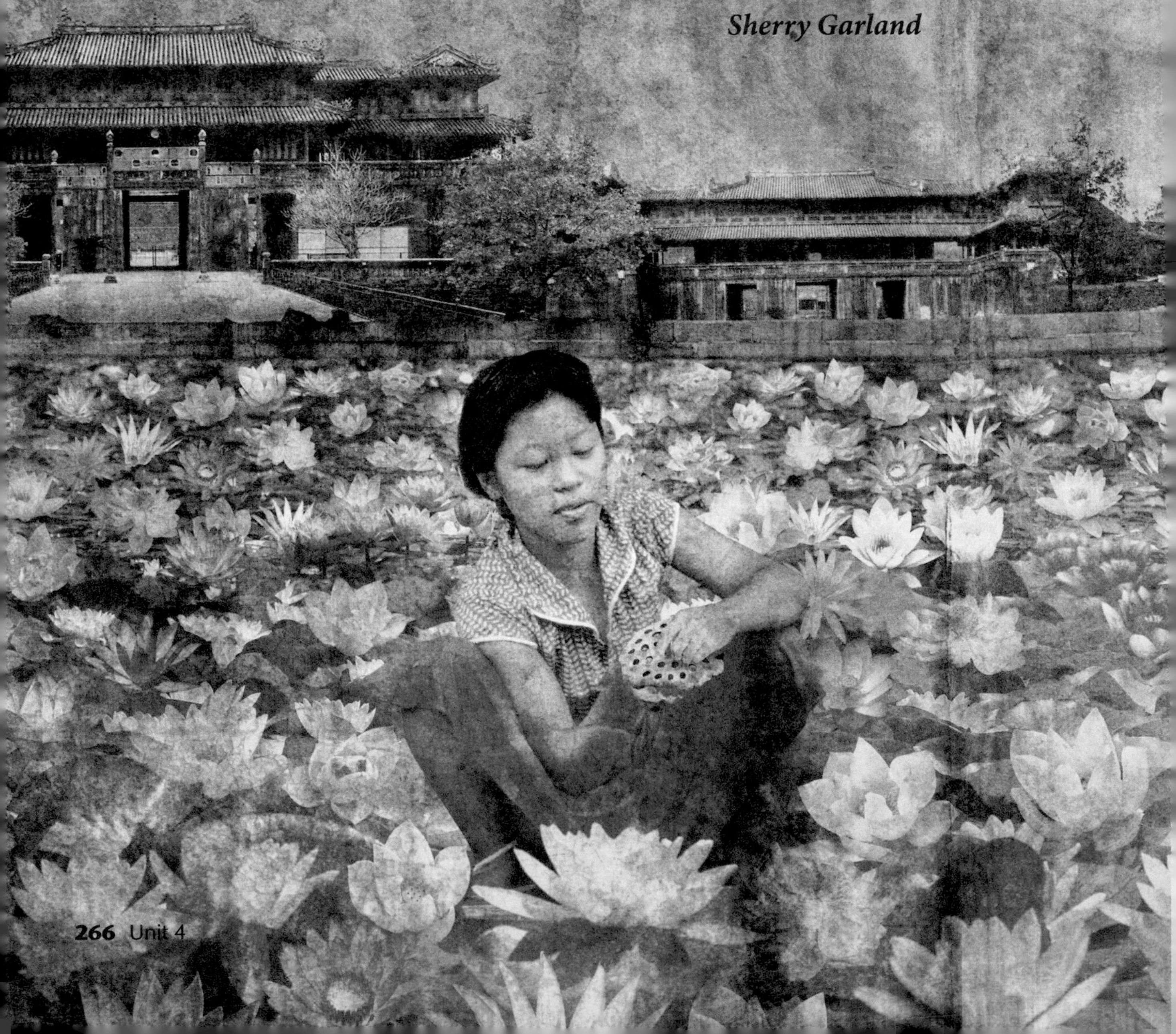

My grandmother saw
the emperor cry
the day he lost
his golden dragon throne.

She wanted something
to remember him by,
so she snuck down
to the silent palace,
near the River of Perfumes,
and plucked a seed
from a **lotus pod**
that rattled
in the Imperial garden.

She hid the seed
in a special place
under the family altar,
wrapped in a piece of **silk**
from the **ao dai**
she wore that day.
Whenever she felt sad
or lonely,
she took out the seed
and thought of the
brave young emperor.

And when she married
a young man
chosen by her parents,
she carried the seed
inside her pocket
for good luck, long life,
and many children.
When her husband
marched off to war,
she raised her
children alone.

---

lotus pod, hard, natural pouch that
   holds the seeds of the lotus plant
silk, soft, delicate material
ao dai, long dress

One day bombs fell
all around,
and soldiers
clamored door to door.
She took the time
to grab the seed,
but left her **mother-of-pearl**
hair combs lying
on the floor.

✔ **LITERARY CHECK**
*What is the symbol
in this poem?*

One terrible day
her family scrambled
into a crowded boat
and set out
on a stormy sea.
Bà watched the mountains
and the waving **palms**
slowly fade away.
She held the seed
in her shaking fingers
and silently said good-bye.
She arrived in a
strange new land
with blinking lights
and speeding cars
and towering buildings
that scraped the sky
and a language
she didn't understand.

---

clamored, shouted loudly
mother-of-pearl, shiny substance
   found inside some seashells
palms, trees with broad, flat leaves
   that grow only at the top

Reading Skill

Take turns reading each
stanza of the poem. Listen to
the way your partner reads. If
you don't understand an idea
or word, ask your partner to
clarify or explain. This will
help you understand the
poem.

BEFORE YOU GO ON

1 What caused the
emperor to cry?

2 How can you tell that
Bà is **attached** to
the young emperor?

On Your Own
Name a person that
has had a strong
impact on your
life. Explain.

She worked many years,
day and night,
and so did her children
and her sisters
and her cousins, too,
living together
in one big house.

Last summer
my little brother
found the special seed
and asked questions
again and again.
He'd never seen a lotus **bloom**
or an emperor
on a golden dragon throne.

So one night
he stole the seed
from beneath the family altar
and planted it
in a pool of mud
somewhere near Bà's
onion patch.

Bà cried and cried
when she found out
the seed was gone.
She didn't eat,
she didn't sleep,
and my silly brother
forgot what spot of earth
held the seed.

bloom, open up its flowers

Then one day in spring
my grandmother shouted,
and we all ran
to the garden
and saw
a beautiful pink lotus
unfurling its petals,
so creamy and soft.

"It is the flower
of life and hope,"
my grandmother said.
"No matter how ugly the mud
or how long the seed lies **dormant**,
the bloom will be beautiful.
It is the flower
of my country."

When the lotus blossom
faded and turned
into a pod,
Bà gave each of
her grandchildren
a seed
to remember her by,
and she kept one
for herself
to remember the emperor by.

I wrapped my seed
in a piece of silk
and hid it
in a secret place.
Someday I will plant it
and give the seeds
to my own children
and tell them about the day
my grandmother saw
the emperor cry.

✔ **LITERARY CHECK**
What can you tell about the speaker by reading the poem?

unfurling, unrolling and opening
dormant, inactive

ABOUT THE **POET**

Sherry Garland is the award-winning author of over twenty-five books for children and teenagers. Seven of her books focus on Vietnam and came about because of her close association with Vietnamese families in the Houston, Texas, area. She also traveled to Vietnam for research purposes. As a fifth-generation Texan, she sets many of her books in the Lone Star State. Ms. Garland currently lives in Central Texas.

BEFORE YOU GO ON

1 Why did Bà get so upset when she "lost" her lotus seed?

2 What does the speaker plan to do with the seed Bà gave her?

On Your Own
Why do you think Bà thought it was important to give a lotus seed to each of her grandchildren? Explain.

Review and Practice

▶ DRAMATIC READING

One of the best ways to understand the pace and flow of a poem is to recite it aloud. Work with a partner. Take turns reading *The Lotus Seed* aloud. Work together to interpret any difficult words or phrases. After you have examined the poem carefully, memorize your favorite section and act it out for the class. Comment on one another's oral reading and make helpful suggestions for improvement.

> **LEARNING STRATEGY**
>
> Use non-verbal cues, such as facial expressions and gestures, to show the characters' feelings and actions.

▶ COMPREHENSION

Workbook
Page 141

Demonstrate your comprehension of the poem by responding to the questions.

Recall

1. What was the **source** of the lotus seed?
2. Why did the speaker's grandmother pluck a seed from the Imperial garden?

Comprehend

3. Why did looking at the lotus seed help Bà when she felt sad or lonely?
4. The lotus seed represented many things to Bà. What were they?

Analyze

5. How did Bà feel when she left her homeland of Vietnam?
6. What country do you think Bà moved to? Explain.

Connect

7. How would you feel if you had to flee your homeland?
8. Name some items that **symbolize** your homeland.

▲ Mekong Delta, Vietnam

▶ DISCUSSION

Discuss in pairs or small groups.

1. Do you think the lotus flower was more important to Bà before she left her country or after she left her country? Explain.

2. Do you think the lotus seed will ever mean as much to the speaker as it did to Bà?

Q **What does home mean?** The speaker says she plans to tell her children about the day her grandmother saw the emperor cry. Is there a story that is told over and over again in your family? How does passing stories along to family members keep a sense of home alive?

Workbook
Page 141

▶ RESPONSE TO LITERATURE

Utilize Think about an item that is important to your family. Write a poem that describes this item and why it has so much meaning to you. Your poem can be short, or you can write a longer narrative poem like *The Lotus Seed*. Share the poem with your classmates.

Speaking **SKILL**

Learning Strategy:
Use formal language in class. Use informal language with your family and friends. Know when to use formal and informal language.

Grammar

Adverbial Clauses of Time

An adverbial clause of time answers the question *When?* An adverbial clause is a subordinate clause. It must be used with a main clause. Sentences with main and subordinate clauses are called complex sentences. Adverbial clauses begin with subordinate conjunctions. An adverbial clause can come at the beginning or end of a sentence. When it comes at the beginning, use a comma after the clause.

After Bà arrived in a new land, she lived in one big house with her family.
Bà took the seed **before she left**.
When her husband marched off to war, she raised her children alone.
My brother stole the seed **while we weren't looking**.
As soon as Bà found out the seed was gone, she cried and cried.
By the time the lotus bloom faded, it was the end of summer.
I will hide the seed **until I have children of my own**.
Whenever* she felt sad or lonely, she took out the seed and thought of the emperor.

*Use *whenever* to talk about something that happens many times.

Practice  Workbook Page 142

Work with a partner. Copy the clauses below into your notebook, combining them to make complex sentences.

Example: *Whenever I eat shellfish, I get sick.*

Whenever I eat shellfish,	I eat breakfast.
After she washed the car,	until she's finished studying.
Before I brush my teeth,	after I get up.
She isn't coming	the store was closed.
I always make my bed	it rained.
By the time we got there,	I get sick.

Apply

Write five sentences about what you usually do on the weekend. Use adverbial clauses of time. Then tell a partner about your habits.

Example: As soon as I get up, I eat breakfast.

Grammar SKILL

Remember that an adverbial clause is not a complete sentence since it begins with a subordinating conjunction.

✔ GRAMMAR CHECK

*What question does an **adverbial clause of time** answer?*

Adverbial Clauses of Purpose, Reason, and Contrast

Some adverbial clauses answer the questions *How?* and *Why?* Adverbial clauses can also contrast two ideas. Use the following subordinating conjunctions to show purpose, reason, and contrast. Remember that when an adverbial clause begins a sentence, it is followed by a comma.

Purpose	**In order that she would have good luck,** she carried a seed. She carried the seed **so that she would have good luck**.
Reason	I'll hide my seeds **because I want to give some to my children.** **Since I want to give my children seeds,** I'll hide mine in a secret place. **As I want to give my children seeds,** I'll hide mine in a secret place.
Contrast	**Although Bà was angry,** she gave each of her grandchildren a seed. Bà gave each of her grandchildren a seed **even though she was angry**. **Though Bà was angry,** she gave each of her grandchildren a seed.

Practice  **Workbook Page 143**

Work with a partner. Copy the sentences below into your notebook. Choose the best subordinating conjunction in parentheses to complete each sentence.

Example: ((Although,) Since, So that) I was tired, I stayed up late.

1. Sara didn't want to see him (because, so that, in order that) she was upset.

2. He **removed** his bag (so that, because, even though) she could sit down.

3. (As, So that, Although) I hate shopping, I love new clothes.

4. (Since, In order that, Though) she's a flight attendant, she travels a lot.

5. We got up early (since, in order that, because) we could catch our train.

Apply

Work with a partner. Take turns switching the order of the clauses in the sentences in the chart above.

Grammar SKILL

The subordinating conjunction *as* can also show time: *As the soldiers came, she grabbed the seed.* Don't confuse this meaning with its meaning here.

Writing

Write a Response to Literature

You have learned that expository works provide the reader with factual information.

A response to literature is a type of expository writing in which you explain, interpret, or respond to some aspect of a piece of literature. You should organize your response around a clear idea and support the idea with details and examples from the text.

> **Writing Prompt**
>
> Write a response to a story or another piece of literature. Be sure to use adverbial clauses of time, purpose, reason, or contrast in your writing.

1 **PREWRITE** Begin by choosing a story or a poem to write about.

- Think about the main idea.

- How was the main idea developed through the details of the story or poem?

- List your ideas in a graphic organizer like the one below.  **Workbook Page 144**

Here's a word web created by a student named Madeline in response to the poem "The Lotus Seed."

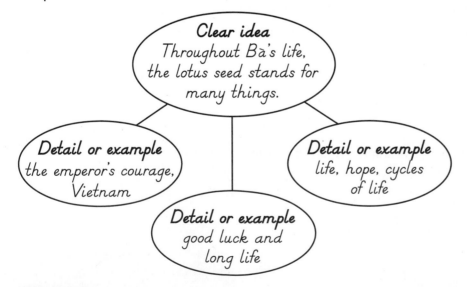

Clear idea
Throughout Bà's life, the lotus seed stands for many things.

Detail or example
the emperor's courage, Vietnam

Detail or example
good luck and long life

Detail or example
life, hope, cycles of life

2 DRAFT Use your word web to help you write a first draft.

- Be sure to explain the main idea.
- Support your ideas with evidence from the text.
- Use adverbial clauses of time, purpose, reason, or contrast.

3 REVISE Read over your draft. Look for places where the writing is unclear or needs improvement. Use the Writing Checklist to help you identify problems. Then revise your draft, using the editing and proofreading marks listed on page 458.

4 EDIT Check your work for errors in grammar, usage, mechanics, and spelling. Trade papers with a partner to obtain feedback. Use the Peer Review Checklist on Workbook page 144. Edit your final draft in response to feedback from your partner and your teacher.

5 PUBLISH Prepare a clean copy of your final draft. Share your response to literature with the class. Save your work. You'll need to refer to it in the Writing Workshop at the end of the unit.

Writing Checklist

ORGANIZATION:
☑ I organized my response around a clear idea.

IDEAS:
☑ I supported my ideas with evidence from the text.

SENTENCE FLUENCY:
☑ I used adverbial clauses of time, purpose, reason, or contrast.

Here is Madeline's paragraph. Notice how she uses adverbial clauses of time to describe the symbolic significance of the lotus seed.

Madeline Shaw

The Lotus Seed

"The Lotus Seed" tells the story of Bà, a woman who flees her home in Vietnam to go to the U.S. Bà takes only one thing with her: a lotus seed. She had taken the lotus seed from the emperor's garden on the day he lost his throne. It reminded her of his bravery and gave her courage. She carried the seed for luck when she got married. And she clutched it in her hand as she sailed away from home. One night her grandson steals the seed and plants it, breaking her heart. But in the spring Bà discovers that her seed has grown into a beautiful lotus blossom. She calls it "the flower of life and hope." Throughout Bà's life, the seed stands for many things. First it reminds her of the emperor's courage. When she weds, it represents good luck and long life. When she first comes to the U.S., it represents Vietnam. When the lotus flower blooms, it represents life and hope. Finally, when the lotus flower produces seeds, it represents the continuing cycles of life.

What You Will Learn

Reading

■ Vocabulary building: *Context, dictionary skills, word study*

■ Reading strategy: *Monitor comprehension*

■ Text type: *Informational text (science)*

Grammar

Factual conditional in the present and future; Present and past unreal conditional

Writing

Write a problem-and-solution paragraph

▶ 🔍 THE BIG QUESTION

What does home mean? Do you know what an endangered species is? Animals that are endangered are at risk of extinction, or of dying out. Work with your classmates to make a list of endangered animals that you know of. Then discuss the following with a partner: Did any of these animals become endangered as the result of losing their homes? Why would the loss of a home cause animals to become endangered?

▶ BUILD BACKGROUND

In this section, you will read an informational science article called **"Operation Migration."** Migration occurs when a group of animals or birds move from one place to another year after year.

Whooping cranes are birds that migrate. Because humans took over much of their habitat, the whooping crane population decreased. By 1941, there were only fifteen whooping cranes left, and they were declared an endangered species. In an effort to raise the population, scientists conducted an experiment called Operation Migration.

▲ A whooping crane

► VOCABULARY

Listening and Speaking: Key Words

Read these sentences. Use the context to figure out the meaning of the highlighted words. Use a dictionary to check your answers. Then write each word and its meaning in your notebook.

1. Polar bears are an endangered species. There are only a few of these animals left on Earth.

2. The migration of monarch butterflies occurs both in the fall and spring. In the fall, the butterflies fly from north to south. In the spring, they return to their habitats in the north.

3. Scientists monitor the progress of the injured birds each day.

4. There are more bald eagles now than there were ten years ago. Their population has risen.

5. The giant panda is a rare animal. It is found only in China.

6. The birds live in a safe place—they live in a wildlife refuge.

Key Words

endangered species
migration
monitor
population
rare
refuge

Audio

Audio

Practice Workbook Page 145

Write the sentences in your notebook. Choose a word from the box above to complete each sentence. Then take turns reading the sentences aloud with a partner.

1. Because they were hunted by whalers, the _____ of blue whales dropped.

2. Salmon can travel hundreds of miles during their _____.

3. The whooping crane only exists in North America. It is a _____ bird.

4. You cannot hunt animals that live in a wildlife _____.

5. There are very few gray wolves left in the United States. They are an _____.

6. Bird-watchers _____ the migration of birds each year.

Polar bears ►

Listening and Speaking: Academic Words

Study the **red** words and their meanings. You will find these words useful when talking and writing about informational texts. Write each word and its meaning in your notebook. After you read "Operation Migration," try to use these words to respond to the text.

interaction = the activity of talking with other people and working together with them	→	There was constant **interaction** between the scientists as they performed the experiment.
outcome = the final result of a meeting, process, etc.	→	The experiment's **outcome** was successful— the birds completed their migration.
route = the way from one place to another	→	Migrating animals follow the same **route** home year after year.
substitute = someone who does someone else's job	→	The scientist fed the chicks. He acted as a **substitute** for the chicks' mother.

Practice

**Workbook
Page 146**

Work with a partner to answer these questions. Try to include the **red** word in your answer. Write the sentences in your notebook.

1. What kinds of daily **interaction** do you have with your classmates?
2. What was the **outcome** of the last test you took in this class?
3. What **route** do you take to school each morning?
4. Have you ever had a **substitute** teacher? What does a substitute teacher do?

▼ **Migrating reindeer**

Word Study: Suffix *-ion*

Learning about suffixes, or word parts, is a good way to build your vocabulary. The suffix *-ion* means "an act or a process." Adding *-ion* to the end of a base word changes its meaning. It also changes a verb into a noun.

Word	Definition	Example
subtract	**v.** to take one number from another	To find the answer, **subtract** 3 from 5.
subtraction	**n.** the process of taking one number from another	We learned **subtraction** in math class.

For words that end in a silent *-e*, drop the *-e* before adding *-ion*.

Word	Definition	Example
migrate	**v.** to travel at the same time each year from one part of the world to another	The birds **migrate** in the fall.
migration	**n.** the act of moving from one place to another	We studied the **migration** of birds.

Practice  Workbook Page 147

Work with a partner. Change these verbs to nouns: *populate, select, extinct, separate.* Write the words in sentences using nouns and then verbs. Use a dictionary to check your work.

READING STRATEGY | MONITOR COMPREHENSION

Monitoring comprehension helps you to understand difficult texts. To monitor comprehension, follow these steps:

- Reread the text.
- Make a list of words that are difficult. Try to figure out their meanings from the context. If you can't, look them up in a dictionary.
- Try to put the information you read into your own words.

As you read "Operation Migration," stop from time to time. Ask yourself whether you understood each section.

 Workbook Page 148

Set a purpose for reading As you read, think about how human behavior impacts wildlife. In particular, what effect did human behavior have on the whooping cranes' habitat?

Operation Migration

Joyce Styron Madsen

Have you ever seen a pilot fly an "**ultralight**" plane? How about a bright yellow ultralight with the pilot dressed in a bird costume—and leading a formation of thirteen young sandhill cranes?

While this may sound like a wild **publicity stunt**, it's actually part of a long-term, well-researched plan to save the endangered whooping crane from extinction. The graceful whooping crane has always been a rare bird, found only in North America. In the late 1800s and early 1900s, American cities expanded rapidly. New buildings and roads took over much of the cranes' wetland habitat. The whooping crane population shrank year by year. By 1941, there were only fifteen left.

Fortunately, **naturalists**, **biologists**, and the government took action before it was too late. The whooping crane was declared an endangered species. It became protected by international law. The crane's wintering and breeding grounds became protected refuges. As a result of this careful study and care, the number of whooping cranes began to increase.

---

ultralight, airplane with a single seat that weighs less than 115 kilograms (254 lbs.)
publicity stunt, action performed to get attention
naturalists, people who study nature, or who work to preserve nature
biologists, scientists who study living things

Some cities are situated close to an animal's habitat. ▼

◀ A human caretaker
dressed as a sandhill crane

By the 1990s, the whooping crane population had grown to more than 180. All of the cranes were part of one single, migratory **flock**. What would happen if a dangerous disease were to spread through the flock? To prevent such a **disaster**, government agencies joined together with such groups as the International Crane Foundation in Baraboo, Wisconsin. Together, they created a ten-year plan to encourage a second migratory flock. It would nest in Wisconsin and winter in Florida. They called the plan Operation Migration.

The plan was to be tested, using plentiful sandhill cranes instead of the rare whooping cranes. In the spring of 2000, sandhill crane eggs were removed shortly before **hatching** from their nests. The eggs were kept at the Necedah National Wildlife Refuge in Wisconsin and Patuxent Wildlife Center in Maryland. When the eggs hatched, both refuges were careful to let the chicks "stay wild."

For their own protection, the hatchlings needed to **stay shy of** humans. They also needed to become used to the sounds of the ultralight. Their human caretakers wore gray overalls and covered their hands with sandhill crane puppets. Loudspeakers played recorded sounds of ultralight engines and the calls of adult sandhills.

Soon the chicks were ready to be let out into the exercise yard. There they were met by the ultralight pilot. He was dressed in his crane costume and seated in the plane. Caretakers trained the chicks to run behind the very slow-moving ultralight. They followed it as they would follow a mama crane.

---

flock, group of birds
disaster, sudden, terrible event
hatching, breaking through an egg in order to be born
stay shy of, avoid

BEFORE YOU GO ON

1 What took over much of the cranes' wetland habitat?

2 What was the goal of Operation Migration?

💡**On Your Own**
Would you be interested in participating in an experiment like Operation Migration? Why or why not?

Reading 4 **281**

Ordinarily when cranes migrate, they take off on a clear morning with a steady wind. A soaring **breeze** helps the cranes to **glide** a long distance with little effort. But when following the ultralight, a very calm day was needed. The cranes had to continually flap their wings to stay **aloft**. Without the winds to help them, the ultralight flight was much longer and more tiring for the cranes. A flight that usually would take about five days of gliding might take six or seven weeks of flapping.

After years of planning and months of training, Operation Migration took to the air on October 3, 2000, from the Necedah refuge. The route from Wisconsin to Florida was 1,250 miles. It was the longest bird migration ever led by a human. Following along by road was a team of support vehicles: a mobile **veterinary** van, a night pen for the cranes, and four mobile homes for the support crew. The team also included a larger, faster scouting plane to follow the ultralight and the cranes. The pilot of this plane would keep an eye on the entire formation.

The flight was carefully watched and tracked at every stage. The cranes were able to fly no more than a total of two hours and twenty minutes a day, depending on the weather. When it was time for a rest stop, the scouting plane would speed ahead and clear the landing site of any people or other animals.

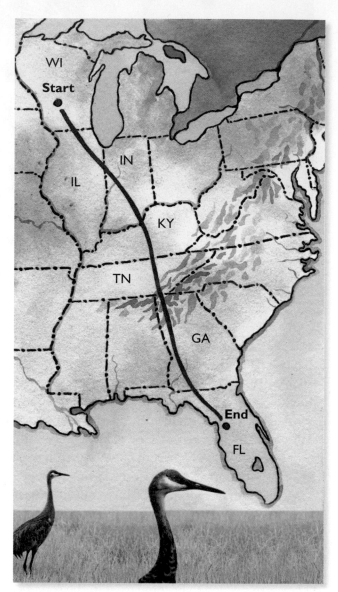

▲ Cranes' migration route

---

breeze, gentle wind
glide, easily move through the air
aloft, high up in the air
veterinary, relating to health care for animals

▲ An ultralight pilot leads a flock of six cranes as they fly south.

On Saturday, November 11, the sandhill cranes circled the St. Martin's Marsh Aquatic Preserve in Florida. After flying 1,250 miles in forty days, the cranes and their human companions touched down in their winter home. Of the thirteen sandhills that began the journey, eleven actually landed in the Florida refuge. Along the way, one crane left the flock and joined a different wild group. Unfortunately, another crane died in the overnight holding pen.

After the sandhill cranes' **trailblazing** migration and successful landing, Operation Migration moved into the next phase of its plan. The crew will continue to monitor the cranes because several questions remain: Will the cranes be able to find food and survive through the winter? Will they stay wild? In spring, will they migrate back to Wisconsin on their own? Once these questions are answered, Operation Migration will be one step closer to its goal—a second migratory flock of whooping cranes.

---

trailblazing, first ever

Reading 4 **283**

Review and Practice

► COMPREHENSION

Workbook
Page 149

Recall

1. What was the whooping crane population in 1941?
2. What are whooping cranes named for?

Comprehend

3. Why did the ultralight pilot dress in a crane costume?
4. How was Operation Migration monitored by scientists?

Analyze

5. The cranes' habitat was overrun by America's expanding cities. In what other ways does expansion threaten birds and animals?
6. Do you think the author believes in saving whooping cranes? Why or why not?

Connect

7. Do you think it's important to protect endangered species? Explain.
8. In what other ways can humans help prevent animals from becoming endangered?

▲ Litter can cause animal endangerment.

► IN YOUR OWN WORDS

Work with a partner. Read the topics in the chart below. Then recall as many facts about those topics as you can from "Operation Migration." List these facts in the chart. Use this information to summarize the article for your partner.

Topics	Facts
Actions taken by scientists and government to save whooping cranes	
How Operation Migration worked	
Outcome	

► DISCUSSION

Discuss in pairs or small groups.

1. What actions did the government take to increase the whooping crane population?

2. Have you ever been to a wildlife refuge? Where was it? What did you see?

Q What does home mean? The whooping crane population became endangered because humans disturbed their habitat. Do you think humans have a responsibility to preserve animal habitats? Why or why not?

▲ Bird-watchers observe birds at a wildlife refuge.

Listening TIP

Be a careful listener so that you don't repeat what someone else has already contributed to the discussion.

► READ FOR FLUENCY

When we read aloud to communicate meaning, we group words into phrases, pause or slow down to make important points, and emphasize important words. Pause for a short time when you reach a comma and for a longer time when you reach a period. Pay attention to rising and falling intonation at the end of sentences.

Work with a partner. Choose a paragraph from the reading. Discuss which words seem important for communicating meaning. Practice pronouncing difficult words. Take turns reading the paragraph aloud and give each other feedback.

► EXTENSION

Scientists were successful in teaching sandhill cranes to migrate. However, were they successful in boosting the whooping crane population? Were they able to create a second migratory flock of whooping cranes as they had planned? Are whooping cranes still on the endangered species list? What is their population like today? Work with a partner. Use the Internet to find the answers to these questions. Then present your findings to the class. You may want to include visuals, such as a population graph, as you do so.

Grammar

Factual Conditional in the Present and Future

A conditional sentence consists of an *if*-clause that presents a condition and a result clause that tells what may or may not happen if the condition is met.

A factual conditional can tell about a condition that is true in the present. Use the simple present in both the *if*-clause and the result clause. You can also use *when* instead of *if* with present factual conditionals.

> **If** a disease spreads, birds die. **When** a disease spreads, birds die.

A factual conditional can also tell about a condition that will be true in the future. Use the simple present in the *if*-clause clause and the simple future with *will* or *be going to* in the result clause.

> If your house **floods**, where **will** you **go**?
> If your house **floods**, where **are** you **going to go**?

Practice

Work with a partner. Copy the sentences into your notebook. Complete each future factual conditional with the correct form of the verb in parentheses.

Example: If it _rains_ (rain) tomorrow, I _'ll stay_ (stay) home.

1. If we _____ (eat) out, I _____ (pay) the check.
2. If you _____ (study) hard, you _____ (pass) the test.
3. My parents _____ (say) no if I _____ (ask) them.
4. If we _____ (not leave) early, we _____ (be) late.
5. Sharon _____ (come) if Paul _____ (not be) there.

Apply

Work with a partner. Rewrite the sentences in the Practice exercise as present factual conditionals using *when* in the *if*-clause.

Example: When it rains, I stay home.

Present and Past Unreal Conditional

A present unreal conditional tells about a condition that is untrue in the present. Use the simple past in the *if*-clause and *would, could, should,* or *might* + the base form of the verb in the result clause.

> What **would** happen if a disease were to **spread** through the flock?
> **If** a disease **spread**, the flock **could die**.
> [UNREAL CONDITION: The disease hasn't spread, so the flock hasn't died.

A past unreal conditional tells about a condition that is untrue in the past. Use the past perfect (*had* + the past participle) in the *if*-clause and *would, could, should,* or *might have* + the past participle in the result clause. Use the contraction *'d* for *had* with pronouns only.

> If they**'d known** about the storm, the residents **might not have lost** so much.
> [UNREAL CONDITION: They didn't know about the storm, so the residents lost a lot.]

Practice  Workbook Page 151

Work with a partner. Copy the sentences into your notebook. Decide whether each is a present or past unreal conditional.

Example: If I didn't come home, my parents would worry.
present unreal conditional

1. If you got a haircut, you would look a lot better. _____
2. If I were you, I would tell the truth. _____
3. If we had gotten an invitation to the party, we would have gone.
   _____
4. She wouldn't have eaten it if she'd known it had fish in it. _____
5. You should leave early if it snows. _____

Apply
Work with a partner. Discuss your answers to the following questions.

What would you do if . . .
   you found someone's wallet?
   you learned your friend had cheated on a test?
   you were caught lying to your parents?

Grammar SKILL

You can also use *were* when talking about yourself in the present unreal conditional. *If I were older, I would go to New York.*

✔ **GRAMMAR CHECK**

*Which **conditional** tells about a condition that is untrue in the past?*

Writing

Write a Problem-and-Solution Paragraph

You have learned that expository writing presents factual information about a topic. One way to organize your facts is by problem and solution. To write a problem-and-solution paragraph, begin by clearly stating the problem. Then tell the process that was used, or the steps that were taken, to solve the problem. If you write about this information in chronological order, include words such as *first, then, next,* and *after* to make the sequence of events clear. Also include supporting facts and details to help your readers understand how your solution worked.

Writing Prompt

Write a paragraph in which you describe a problem in your school. As you write your sentences, be sure that the subjects and verbs agree in number.

---

1 **PREWRITE** Begin by choosing a problem.

- Write the problem at the top of the page.
- Think of a solution to the problem.
- Think of the steps that are part of the solution.
- Write your ideas in a graphic organizer like the one below.

Workbook Page 152

Here's a problem-and-solution chart created by a student named Pablo. He is explaining how scientists helped to protect the endangered whooping crane.

Problem
The whooping crane is threatened with extinction.

↓

Solution
1. Put the bird on the endangered species list and protect its breeding grounds.

2. Create a second migratory flock by training chicks to follow a new migration route.

---

2 **DRAFT** Use your chart to help you write a first draft.

- Remember to explain the problem first.
- Present your solution to the problem.
- If your solution has several steps, use sequence words.
- Use factual and unreal conditional sentences.

3 **REVISE** Read over your draft. Look for places where the writing is unclear or needs improvement. Use the Writing Checklist to help you identify problems. Then revise your draft, using the editing and proofreading marks listed on page 458.

4 **EDIT** Check your work for errors in grammar, usage, mechanics, and spelling. Trade papers with a partner to obtain feedback. Use the Peer Review Checklist on Workbook page 152. Edit your final draft in response to feedback from your partner and your teacher.

5 **PUBLISH** Prepare a clean copy of your final draft. Share your problem-and-solution paragraph with the class. Save your work. You'll need to refer to it in the Writing Workshop at the end of the unit.

Writing Checklist

ORGANIZATION:
☑ I used a problem-and-solution organization to guide my writing.

SENTENCE FLUENCY:
☑ I used factual and unreal conditional sentences.

Here is Pablo's paragraph. Notice how he clearly states the problem and includes facts that describe the solution.

Pablo Espínola

Future Looks Bright for Whooping Cranes

When the whooping crane was threatened with extinction, government officials quickly declared it an endangered species. Its breeding grounds became protected refuges. However, scientists still faced a serious challenge. All of the cranes belonged to the same migratory flock. If a disease spread through this flock, the whooping cranes would again be in danger of extinction. So scientists launched an experiment, called Operation Migration, to create a second migratory flock. First, scientists removed whooping cranes' eggs from their nests. After the chicks hatched, scientists trained the chicks to fly behind an ultralight plane. Eventually, the cranes followed the ultralight plane along their migration route to their winter home. As a result of all of these efforts, the whooping crane population has once again increased.

Link the Readings

Critical Thinking

Look back at the readings in this unit. Think about what they have in common. They all tell about home. Yet they do not all have the same purpose. The purpose of one reading might be to inform, while the purpose of another might be to entertain or persuade. In addition, the content of each reading relates to home differently. Now copy the chart below into your notebook and complete it.

Title of Reading	Purpose	Big Question Link
"97 Orchard Street" "The Pros and Cons of Tenement Life"		
"Somebody's Son"	*to entertain*	
The Lotus Seed		*A young woman must leave her home country.*
"Operation Migration"		

Discussion

Discuss in pairs or small groups.

- "97 Orchard Street" and *The Lotus Seed* are both about immigrants who left their home countries. What other similar experiences did the people in each reading share?
- **What does home mean?** What ideas do the readings in this unit share? Which reading do you relate to the most? Why?

Media Literacy & Projects

Work in pairs or small groups. Choose one of these projects.

1 Create a brochure or poster that describes the Lower East Side Tenement Museum, its exhibits, and its tours. You may want to visit the library for additional information or use the Internet to find images to include in your brochure or on your poster. Remember to include the museum's location, operating hours, and telephone number. Share your brochure or poster with the class.

2 Use the Internet to learn more about Hurricane Katrina. In your opinion, did the federal government do a good job taking care of the victims? Why or why not? What should they have done differently? Share your ideas with the class.

3 The lotus plant is important in many cultures and religions. Research a legend or myth about a lotus flower and narrate, or tell, it to a partner.

Further Reading

Choose from these reading suggestions. Practice reading silently for longer periods with increased comprehension.

Grey Owl, Vicky Shipton
This Penguin Reader® tells the amazing story of Grey Owl, a Native American who wanted to save his land and its forests and animals.

Homesick: My Own Story, Jean Fritz
In this blend of fact and fiction, the author describes the many things she loved about her childhood in China during the 1920s. But her parents' stories of home in America made her feel homesick for a place she had never seen.

Making It Home: Real Life Stories from Children Forced to Flee, Beverly Naidoo
Displaced from their homes by war, children, ages six to seventeen, from Kosovo, Bosnia, Afghanistan, Iraq, the Congo, Liberia, Sudan, and Burundi talk about their experiences as refugees. They describe the horror, the family separation, and the other struggles they face as asylum seekers adjusting to new places.

Put It All Together

LISTENING & SPEAKING WORKSHOP

TV News Show

With a team, you will present a TV news show about events in your community.

1 **THINK ABOUT IT** You have probably watched the news on TV—but do you know what reporters do before the cameras roll? They interview people, conduct research, and write a script. Their reports focus on the 5Ws of a story: *who*, *what*, *where*, *when*, and *why*.

Work in small groups. Make a list of recent or upcoming events in your community. For example:
- An election for mayor or city council
- The school board's decision to build a new school
- A concert by a local band
- The opening of a new skate park

Have each group member choose a different story idea from the list.

2 **GATHER AND ORGANIZE INFORMATION** Discuss and plan the overall structure of your show. If possible, watch a TV news show to get ideas. Choose one person to be your news anchor (the main person who presents the news on TV). The anchor will introduce each story and its reporter.

Research Check local newspapers or interview community members to find information for your story. Take notes and get answers to the 5Ws.

Order Your Notes Think about the best order in which to tell your story. Then make an outline showing your main points in this order.

Use Visuals Look for photos, maps, and other visuals to use during your news show. Think about how and when you will show each visual.

Prepare a Script As a group, write a short opening and closing for your news show. For example, the anchor might say: "Welcome to the Channel 6 Evening News. I'm Stanley Stevens. Tonight's top story will be of special interest to young people. Here's Julia Jenkins reporting live from Springfield's new skate park." Then use your outline and notes to write a script for your individual report. Start your story in a way that will catch people's interest. Remember to focus on the 5Ws.

3 PRACTICE AND PRESENT Read your script over and over again until you know it well. To make your script richer and more interesting, use a variety of grammatical structures, sentence lengths, sentence types, and connecting words. Be sure to look "into the camera." Make smooth transitions between stories. Help each other with visuals as needed. Listen to your team members as they provide you with directions about how to better your performance. Be sure to follow these directions as they are given to you.

Deliver Your TV News Show Although this is a formal presentation, you should appear relaxed and comfortable as you present it. Be sure your scripts and visuals are ready before you begin. Do not rush or mumble! Speak clearly, and pronounce names and numbers carefully. Emphasize key ideas by pausing, slowing down, speaking more loudly, or repeating them at the end of your story.

4 EVALUATE THE PRESENTATION

You will improve your skills as a speaker and a listener by evaluating each presentation you give and hear. Use this checklist to help you judge your team's TV news show and the news shows of your classmates.

- ☑ Was the news show presented in a professional and interesting way?
- ☑ Did the speakers look "into the camera" most of the time?
- ☑ Was each story about an event in your community?
- ☑ Did the speaker use formal or informal language? Was it appropriate?
- ☑ What suggestions do you have for improving the show?

 Speaking SKILLS

Always face the audience (or imaginary TV camera) when you speak. Don't hide behind your script or visuals!

Use action verbs and descriptive adjectives to help the audience visualize the event.

 Listening SKILLS

Listen carefully to your fellow team members, and learn your *cues*— words or actions that signal it is your turn to speak.

Listen for answers to the 5Ws. Does each story include these important details? If not, request more information. When responding, provide your audience with as many details as possible.

 STRENGTHEN YOUR SOCIAL LANGUAGE

In social contexts as well as in some of your content-area classes, you will need to ask for and give information. Go to www.LongmanKeystone.com and do the activity for this unit. This activity will help you acquire key structures, expressions, and words needed during extended speaking assignments and in everyday academic and social contexts.

WRITING WORKSHOP
Expository Essay

Write an Expository Essay

In this workshop, you will use your skills to write an expository essay. As you have learned, an expository essay gives information about a topic. An expository essay may be written to report news about someone or something, to respond to a work of literature, to describe solutions to a problem, or for other reasons. A good expository essay begins with a paragraph that tells what the essay is about. Two or more body paragraphs develop the topic by adding ideas, details, and examples. This information is presented in a logical order. A concluding paragraph sums up the writer's main points in a lively and interesting way.

> **Writing Prompt**
> Choose one of the paragraphs you wrote for this unit and expand it into a five-paragraph essay.

1 **PREWRITE** Review your previous work in this unit. Choose the paragraph you want to expand. Then think about your readers. In your notebook, answer these questions:

Ongoing Writing Skills Practice

- What do your readers already know about your topic?

- What questions do you think they will have?  **Workbook** Page 153

List your questions and answers in a graphic organizer such as a question-and-answer outline. Also think about interesting details you want to add when you expand your paragraph into an essay.

A student named Blaise decided to expand her paragraph about a Boston museum. Here is the outline she prepared:

> I. What is the Museum of Science?
>   A. An exciting science museum
>   B. Located in Boston
> II. What is its mission?
>   A. Stimulate interest in science
>   B. Show importance of science
> III. What can a visitor do there?
>   A. Planetarium and movie theater
>   B. Courses and exhibits
> IV. What is my favorite exhibit?
>   A. Lecture on lightning
>   B. Demonstration of lightning
> V. What makes the museum special?
>   A. One of the foremost science museums
>   B. Educational, interactive, and fun

2 **DRAFT** Use your graphic organizer and the model on page 298 to help you write a first draft.

- Remember to introduce your topic in the first paragraph.

- Develop the topic by adding ideas, details, and examples.

- Sum up the important information in your concluding paragraph.

3 **REVISE** Read over your draft. Think about how well you have addressed questions of purpose, audience, and genre. Your purpose is to inform. Is your essay clearly organized? Is it appropriate in content and tone for the intended audience?

Keep these questions in mind as you revise your draft. Use the Writing Checklist below to help you identify additional issues that may need revision. Mark your changes on your draft using the editing and proofreading marks listed on page 458.

SIX TRAITS OF WRITING CHECKLIST

- ☑ **IDEAS:** Does my essay present interesting information about the topic?
- ☑ **ORGANIZATION:** Do I present ideas, details, and examples in an order that makes sense?
- ☑ **VOICE:** Does my writing show my interest in the topic?
- ☑ **WORD CHOICE:** Do I use transitions accurately?
- ☑ **SENTENCE FLUENCY:** Do my sentences begin in different ways? Do subjects and verbs agree in number?
- ☑ **CONVENTIONS:** Does my writing follow the rules of grammar, usage, mechanics, and spelling?

LEARNING STRATEGY

Monitor your written language production. Using a writing checklist will help you assess your work. Evaluate your essay to make sure that your message is clear and easy to understand.

Here are the revisions Blaise plans to make to her first draft.

A Great Place to Visit

The Museum of Science in Boston, Massachusetts, is an exciting
museum. ~~It~~ ^that^ can be visited many times without losing its appeal. The
museum was founded in the 1830s but opened at its present ~~sight~~ ^site^
along the Charles River in 1951. It offer exhibits and activities. ~~They~~ ^that^
are both educational and fun.

The museum's mission is "to stimulat^e^ interest in and further
understanding of science and technology and their importance for
individuals and for society." ^In fact,^ The Museum of Science was the first
all-inclusive science museum in the United States. It has also been
~~important~~ ^a pioneer^ in introducing interactive exhibits.

The museum has a planetarium where laser light shows are set to
popular music. The museum also has a theater. ~~It~~ ^that^ presents movies
about dinosaurs, sea life, the Grand Canyon, and other topics. One
series of classes for high school kids are called "Mini Med-School."
Each class focus on a different health issue and is taught by a doctor.
~~They~~ ^who^ specialize^s^ in that field. Courses for kids and adults are held at
the museum throughout the year. Examples of the museum's many
exhibits include *Beyond the X-ray*, *Butterfly Garden*, *Making Models*,
Natural Mysteries, and *New England Habitats*.

Edited to introduce adjective clauses and to correct an error in the spelling of a homophone.

Revised to correct use of the possessive case, correct spelling, add a transition word, and improve word choice.

Edited to improve logical sequence of ideas and to introduce adjective clauses.

My favorite exhibit at the museum is about lightning. After visitors are seated, one of the staff members talk about how lightning is made. The lecture is fascinating, but the demonstration that follows is even better! A machine actually produces bolts of lightning. Lightning right there in front of you! This exhibit is both dramatic and informative.

boston's Museum of Science is one of the foremost science museums in the nation. If you visit this museum, you will learn about science and technology, while at the same time have fun. It is a wonderful museum to explore, whether you are a resident of Boston or a tourist from far away.

4 **EDIT** Check your work for errors in grammar, usage, mechanics, and spelling. Then trade essays with a partner and use the Peer Review Checklist below to give each other constructive feedback. Edit your final draft in response to feedback from your partner and your teacher.

Workbook
Page 153

PEER REVIEW CHECKLIST

- ✔ Was the essay clearly organized?
- ✔ Was the information interesting?
- ✔ Did I understand the topic better after reading it?
- ✔ Did the first paragraph introduce the topic?
- ✔ Did the concluding paragraph sum up the main points?
- ✔ What changes could be made to improve the essay?

Look at the next page to see the changes Blaise decided to make to her final draft as a result of her peer review.

Blaise Yafcak

A Great Place to Visit

The Museum of Science in Boston, Massachusetts, is an exciting museum that can be visited many times without losing its appeal. The museum was founded in the 1830s but opened at its present site along the Charles River in 1951. It offer^s exhibits and activities that are both educational and fun.

Revised to correct an error in subject-verb agreement.

The museum's mission is "to stimulate interest in and further understanding of science and technology and their importance for individuals and for society." In fact, the Museum of Science was the first all-inclusive science museum in the United States. It has also been a pioneer in introducing interactive exhibits.

The museum has a planetarium where laser light shows are set to popular music. The museum also has a theater that presents movies about dinosaurs, sea life, the Grand Canyon, and other topics. Courses for kids and adults are held at the museum throughout the year. One series of classes for high school kids are^is called "Mini Med-School." Each class focus^es on a different health issue and is taught by a doctor who specializes in that field. Examples of the museum's many exhibits include *Beyond the X-ray*, *Butterfly Garden*, *Making Models*, *Natural Mysteries*, and *New England Habitats*.

Revised to correct errors in subject-verb agreement.

My favorite exhibit at the museum is about lightning. After visitors are seated, one of the staff members talk^s about how lightning is made. The lecture is fascinating, but the demonstration that follows is even better! A machine actually produces bolts of lightning. Lightning right there in front of you! This exhibit is both dramatic and informative.

Revised to correct an error in subject-verb agreement.

boston's Museum of Science is one of the foremost science museums in the nation. If you visit this museum, you will learn about science and technology, while at the same time have fun. It is a wonderful museum to explore, whether you are a resident of Boston or a tourist from far away.

Revised to correct an error in spelling.

5 **PUBLISH** Prepare a clean copy of your final draft. Share your essay with the class.

Workbook
Page 154

Test Preparation

PRACTICE

Read the following test sample. Study the tips in the boxes. Work with a partner to answer the questions.

Coming Home

1   Natalia and her family had a terrific vacation. Visiting family in Colombia is always fun. Natalia played with cousins she had not seen in years.

2   The long plane ride home made Natalia tired. Her little sister Anna whined and cried. Mother tried to quiet her. Father gave Anna candy. Nothing worked.

3   Anna curled up against Natalia's shoulder. Natalia talked softly to the girl. She told Anna that she should fall asleep. If she did, she could dream about home. Anna could play with her friends. She could play with her toys. Anna could dream of lying in bed with Natalia in their own bedroom.

4   All the talking made Natalia very sleepy. She <u>drifted off</u>, still holding Anna's hand. She had sweet dreams. Soon she heard Anna calling her name. They were finally home.

1 According to the passage, Natalia visited—.
- **A** her parents and sister
- **B** cousins at the airport
- **C** family in Colombia
- **D** friends back home

2 In the selection, what does <u>drifted off</u> mean?
- **F** floated away
- **G** landed softly
- **H** flew away
- **J** fell asleep

Workbook Pages 155–158

Smithsonian American Art Museum

Acknowledging the Past, Reaching for the Future

*T*he United States is a country made up of millions of people who are far away from their homelands. American artists often explore the emotions that this situation can bring about. Sometimes they show hope and excitement, other times loneliness and grief.

Carmen Lomas Garza, *Camas para Sueños* (1985)

In *Camas para Sueños* (Spanish for "Beds for Dreams"), two girls sit on the roof of their home looking at the full moon. Inside the house their mother stretches out a bright pink blanket to make the bed. Mexican-American artist Carmen Lomas Garza painted this scene of herself and her sister as young girls. They wear almost matching outfits—spotted shirts, pants, and similar shoes—which highlight their closeness. Below, their mother works hard to make their home a clean, safe place to have pleasant dreams. This painting celebrates Garza's sense of place as a girl within her family. As a Mexican American she sometimes felt less than welcomed by the locals in her town in south Texas, but in her own home she felt safe.

▲ Carmen Lomas Garza, *Camas para Sueños*, 1985, gouache, 28⅛ x 20½ in., Smithsonian American Art Museum

Hung Liu,
The Ocean Is the Dragon's World,
1995, mixed media, 96 × 82½ in.,
Smithsonian American Art Museum ▶

Hung Liu, *The Ocean Is the Dragon's World* (1995)

Artist Hung Liu grew up in China in the 1950s when there was great political unrest. Liu did her artwork in the United States, but she uses her art to recreate a world that was lost in China. In *The Ocean Is the Dragon's World*, she painted a portrait of the great aunt of the last Emperor of China, who sits in the center of the canvas looking out at the viewer.

The decorated robes of the Empress fill the painting. You can also see peacock feathers (upper left) and flowers. Liu hung an actual empty metal birdcage onto the canvas! She also added a piece of bamboo painted with Chinese letters on the far right border. This added touch makes the painting look like the cover of a bound book (the Chinese read from right to left). Who knows what stories this grand courtly woman might have to tell?

Both of these artists either came from another country or were the first generation in their family to live in the United States. They use their art to explore the distance between the world their families left behind and the world they discovered in the United States.

Discuss What You Learned

1 Why do you think Carmen Lomas Garza called her painting "Beds for Dreams"?

2 In what way is the subject matter of *The Ocean Is the Dragon's World* different from *Camas para Sueños*?

Q Big Question
If you were an artist creating an artwork that explored the idea of "home," would you concentrate on the past or would you look toward the future? Explain your answer.

Workbook
Pages 159–160

301

THE BIG QUESTION What is the human spirit ?

This unit is about the human spirit. You will read informational texts that describe people who conquer life's obstacles with determination. You will also read literature that describes individuals who stand up for what they believe in. Reading, writing, and talking about these topics will help you practice using academic language and will help you become a better student.

Reading

1 Social Studies

From *César Chávez: We Can Do It!* by Sunita Apte

Reading Strategy:
Distinguish fact from opinion

2 Short Story

"The Scholarship Jacket" by Marta Salinas

Reading Strategy:
Draw inferences

3 Play

From *The Diary of Anne Frank: The Play* by Frances Goodrich and Albert Hackett, adapted by Wendy Kesselman

Reading Strategy:
Read aloud

ANNE FRANK · 2.6.1929 · 31.3.1945
1979

CESAR E. CHÁVEZ
2003

Listening and Speaking—Persuasive

At the end of this unit, you will create and present a **radio commercial**.

Writing—Persuasive

In this unit you will practice **persuasive writing**, which tries to influence the reader to change his or her opinion about a topic. After each reading, you will learn a skill to help you write a persuasive paragraph. At the end of the unit, you will use these skills to help you write a persuasive speech.

Quick **Write**

Write a few sentences about a time when you fought for what you believed in. Read them to a partner.

4 **Social Studies**

"Listen Up" by Phil Taylor

Reading Strategy:
Identify main idea and details

VIEW AND RESPOND
Watch the DVD for Unit 5 and answer the questions at <u>*www.LongmanKeystone.com*</u>*.*

Prepare to Read

What You Will Learn

Reading

- Vocabulary building: *Context, dictionary skills, word study*

- Reading strategy: *Distinguish fact from opinion*

- Text type: *Informational text (social studies)*

Grammar

Inseparable phrasal verbs; Separable phrasal verbs

Writing

Write an advertisement

▶ 🔍 THE BIG QUESTION

What is the human spirit? The United States is proud of its Declaration of Independence, the document that proclaimed the United States to be free of British rule. In this document, there is a line that reads, *We hold these truths to be self-evident: that all men are created equal.* This means that all people should be treated fairly.

Do you think that all people are treated fairly in the United States? How does a person feel when he or she is treated unfairly? How can this affect the human spirit? Share your ideas with your peers and teacher. Ask for their feedback and support in order to develop background knowledge about this topic.

▶ BUILD BACKGROUND

You will read an excerpt from a biography called ***César Chávez: We Can Do It!*** A biography is a form of nonfiction. The writer tells the life story of another person. Most biographies are about famous or admirable people.

Chávez was a Mexican-American farm worker. For decades, Mexican-American farm workers were poorly paid and discriminated against. Chávez decided to do something about it. He organized protests and fought for better pay and treatment. Chávez did not believe in using violence to advance the workers' cause. His life and work inspired many people to regard him as a hero.

▲ César Chávez

➤ VOCABULARY

Listening and Speaking: Key Words

Read and listen to these sentences. Use the context to figure out the meaning of the highlighted words. Use a dictionary to check your answers. Then write each word and its meaning in your notebook.

Key Words

chemicals
crops
demand
migrant workers
strike
union

1. Farmers should not spray their fields with chemicals that can harm farm workers.

2. The farmer grows two crops, grapes and oranges.

3. The farm workers marched to demand fair pay for their hard work.

4. The migrant workers traveled from Mexico to the United States to find work.

5. The auto workers went on strike. They refused to work until the factory owners made conditions safer.

6. The teachers joined together to form a union. Working together gave them more power to protect their rights.

Practice 📖 **Workbook Page 161**

Write the sentences in your notebook. Choose a key word from the box above to complete each sentence. Then take turns reading the sentences aloud with a partner.

1. The _____ never had steady jobs. They moved from place to place looking for work.

2. The union leader told the workers to _____ better treatment from the grape growers.

3. The farmer said that his corn and wheat _____ are growing well.

4. The workers are going on _____ because they want to be paid more money.

▲ Union workers meet in a vineyard.

5. Some _____ used on farms are so dangerous that farm workers must wear masks and rubber gloves to handle them.

6. The group of workers belong to the _____. They meet to discuss problems and find solutions in the workplace.

Listening and Speaking: Academic Words

Study the **red** words and their meanings. You will find these words useful when talking and writing about informational texts. Write each word and its meaning in your notebook. After you read the excerpt from *César Chávez: We Can Do It!*, try to use these words to respond to the text.

Academic Words

founded
impact
labor
persistence

Audio

founded = established a business, organization, school, etc.	→	Carlos **founded** the union. He started it last year.
impact = effect that an event or situation has on someone or something	→	The union's efforts had a great **impact** on the factory's owners.
labor = work that requires a lot of physical effort	→	The farm owners relied on the **labor** of the migrant workers.
persistence = determination to do something even though it is difficult or other people oppose it	→	The workers showed great **persistence**. They continued to strike until their pay was increased.

Audio

Practice  Workbook Page 162

Work with a partner to answer these questions. Try to include the **red** word in your answer. Write the sentences in your notebook.

1. Who **founded** the United States of America?

2. What one event has had the greatest **impact** on your life? Why?

3. Have you ever had to do hard **labor**? If so, what was it?

4. Has there ever been a time when you showed great **persistence**? Explain.

Migrant workers' lives are filled with hard labor. ▼

Word Study: Capitalization

There are rules for using capital letters. Some of these rules are listed below.

Use Capital Letters for . . .	Examples
The word *I*	Sometimes **I** work at night.
The first letter of the first word in every sentence	**T**he farm workers had come to see one man.
All proper nouns: • The names/titles of people • Geographical terms • Historical events, eras, calendar items • Streets, cities, states, countries, continents • Ethnic groups, national groups, languages	**F**red **R**oss, **S**eñor **C**hávez, **D**r. **B**ouchard **L**ake **T**ahoe **C**ésar **C**hávez **D**ay **B**eacon **S**treet, **S**acramento, **C**alifornia **M**exican **A**merican, **S**panish

Practice
Workbook Page 163

Work with a partner. Copy the sentences below into your notebook. Capitalize each proper noun.

1. luis is from bogota, colombia.

2. We don't have to go to school on memorial day.

3. In the summer, we like to spend time near the pacific ocean.

4. My aunt, lisa velarde, speaks both spanish and italian.

READING STRATEGY   DISTINGUISH FACT FROM OPINION

Distinguishing a fact from an opinion will help you form ideas about what you read. A fact is something that can be proven. An opinion is what someone believes or thinks. To distinguish between facts and opinions, follow these steps:

- As you read, ask yourself whether you can check what you are reading in an encyclopedia, a history book, or with some other research. If you can, it's probably a fact.

- Look for phrases the author uses to give opinions, for example, *I think, I believe, I suppose, personally.*

- Look for adjectives that go with opinions, for example, *best, wonderful, luckiest, horrible, bad.*

As you read about César Chávez, look for facts and opinions within the text. How can you tell the difference between them?

Workbook Page 164

Set a purpose for reading As you read, think about the difficulties César Chávez faced. How did they strengthen his spirit? How did this help him accomplish his goals?

César Chávez:
We Can Do It!

Audio

Sunita Apte

It was April 10, 1966. More than 10,000 people were gathered in Sacramento, the capital city of California. Most of them were Mexican-American farm workers. These workers **toiled** in fields all day, picking grapes, cotton, or other crops. The work was hard. Their lives were hard.

The farm workers had come to see one man. He was a Mexican American who gave them hope. His name was César Chávez. César had walked 547 kilometers (340 mi.) to Sacramento. It took him almost a month. He had walked to draw attention to the lives of farm workers. Now, the entire nation was paying attention.

A Hard Life

César Chávez knew about the farm worker's life. He had been a migrant farm worker for many years. He had moved from place to place to find work, picking crops. He had spent long hours in the hot sun. He had bent down all day, working in the fields.

---

toiled, worked hard

▲ Chávez as a young boy, watching a family member pick crops

▲ Many migrant families drove to California to look for work during the Great Depression.

»🎧 Listening SKILL

Follow along in your book as you listen to the Audio CD. Notice the words in bold type. To understand them, read the definitions at the bottom of the page. Knowing the meanings of these words will help to enhance and confirm your comprehension of the story.

Farm workers weren't paid much for all their hard work. Often, the growers they worked for cheated them. Most farm workers made barely enough to live. To survive, the whole family had to work in the fields, including the children. César had been working in the fields since he was eleven years old.

Yuma

César's life hadn't always been so hard. He was born near Yuma, Arizona, in 1927. His family owned a small store and a farm. They were not rich, but life was good.

Then the **Great Depression** hit. People lost their jobs and had no money. No one could afford to shop at the store. César's parents had to sell it. During the Great Depression a terrible **drought** struck many states. It lasted for years. The river that watered the Chávez family farm eventually dried up.

The family struggled to survive. Soon, however, they lost the farm. At that point, they decided to leave Arizona and drive to California to look for work.

Great Depression, a period of economic troubles in the 1930s that left many people poor and without jobs
drought, period of time when there is no, or very little, rain

BEFORE YOU GO ON

1 Why were farm workers' families forced to work in the fields?

2 What **impact** did the Great Depression have on the Chávez family?

💡**On Your Own**
What do you think would be the most challenging aspect of the migrant-worker lifestyle?

Reading 1 **309**

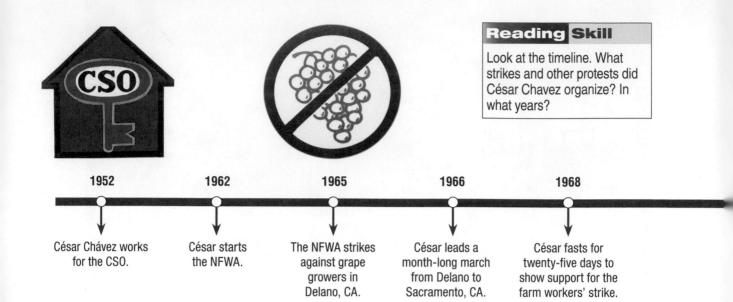

Reading Skill

Look at the timeline. What strikes and other protests did César Chavez organize? In what years?

1952	1962	1965	1966	1968
César Chávez works for the CSO.	César starts the NFWA.	The NFWA strikes against grape growers in Delano, CA.	César leads a month-long march from Delano to Sacramento, CA.	César fasts for twenty-five days to show support for the farm workers' strike.

César's father often had trouble finding work in California. Sometimes, he would hear about a farm job. The family would drive long hours to get to the farm. When they arrived, there would be no job, or the job paid much less than the family had hoped.

The Chávez family also faced discrimination. Many Californians looked down on Mexican Americans. Some restaurants had signs that read, "No Dogs or Mexicans Allowed." Mexican Americans were even supposed to sit in a special section at the movie theatre.

From School to the Fields

César's family finally settled in a poor neighborhood near San Jose, California. The neighborhood was called Sal Si Puedes, or "Get Out If You Can."

When César was fifteen years old, his father was hurt in a car accident. Instead of going to high school, César had to work in the fields. It was the only way his family could survive.

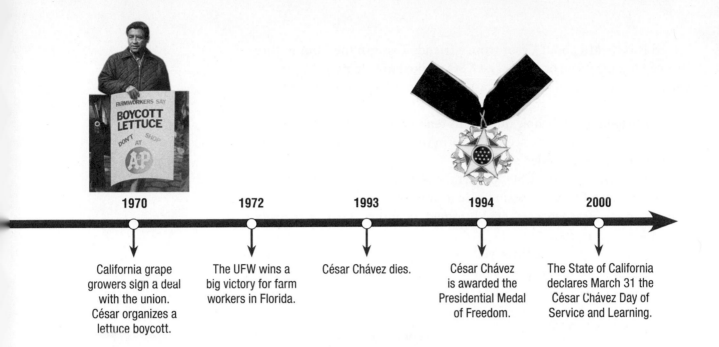

1970	1972	1993	1994	2000
California grape growers sign a deal with the union. César organizes a lettuce boycott.	The UFW wins a big victory for farm workers in Florida.	César Chávez dies.	César Chávez is awarded the Presidential Medal of Freedom.	The State of California declares March 31 the César Chávez Day of Service and Learning.

Farm work was **grueling**. César's back ached from bending down all day. His eyes stung from the chemicals sprayed in the fields to kill insects. His skin tore from yanking out beets. He had no rest breaks, no bathrooms, and no clean water to drink.

César wanted to go back to school. Instead, however, he joined the U.S. Navy. César hated the discrimination he experienced in the Navy. He felt that people did not treat Mexican Americans fairly.

The Chance to Change Things

When César got out of the Navy, he married Helen Fabela. Together, they worked in the fields. César's time in the Navy had convinced him that Mexican-American farm workers needed to demand better treatment.

César talked to other farm workers about fighting for change. He listened to their problems. He became known around his neighborhood as someone worth talking to.

---

grueling, very difficult and painful

BEFORE YOU GO ON

1 What happened to the Chávez family when César was fifteen years old? What did this mean for César?

2 What made farm **labor** grueling?

On Your Own
Have you ever felt a need to make a demand? Describe.

Reading 1 **311**

Fred Ross heard about César from a friend. Ross ran the Community Service Organization, or CSO. The CSO worked to help poor Mexican Americans. Ross hired César. At last, César would have a chance to change things.

César helped many people during his ten years at the CSO. Still, he thought that farm workers needed to form their own group to demand fair treatment. They needed a union.

In 1962, César quit the CSO to start the National Farm Workers Association, or NFWA. He wasn't sure it would be a success. To his surprise, many farm workers quickly joined the union. They were ready to fight for their **rights**.

The first big fight came three years later. In 1965, the union went on strike against some grape growers in Delano, California. Union members stopped work and demanded better pay.

"Don't Buy Grapes!"

Day after day, workers picketed grape farms. They marched up and down, shouting "¡Huelga!" or "Strike!"

The growers didn't **give in**. They thought the farm workers would run out of money. Then the workers would have to come back to their jobs.

César wanted to **put pressure** on the growers.

He needed the rest of America to support the strike. He sent union workers to cities across the United States. They went to supermarkets and told people, "Don't buy grapes."

The growers lost a lot of money because of the **boycott**. Still, they didn't give in.

▲ A National Farm Workers Association poster

---

rights, freedoms that are or should be allowed by law
give in, admit defeat
put pressure, attempt to make someone do something by using influence, arguments, or threats
boycott, act of refusing to buy the products or services of a company

César decided that something more was needed to grab the public's attention. So, he organized a march with sixty-seven other protestors. He began walking the 547 kilometers (340 mi.) from Delano to Sacramento on March 17, 1966. The marchers carried banners reading, "¡Viva la Causa!" Each day, more people joined the march.

Reporters and film crews followed the marchers. They learned how farm workers lived. They saw the migrant **shacks**. They shared the truth with people everywhere.

The growers didn't like the **publicity**. Finally, they agreed to the union's demands. On the steps of Sacramento's capitol building, César joyously announced the victory.

César continued the fight. It took four more years. Finally, in 1970, the rest of Delano's grape growers signed **contracts** with the union.

Then César turned his attention to California's lettuce growers. He organized strikes and boycotts against them. He was sent to jail for his work. In the end, however, his union won.

In 1975, California passed the Agricultural Labor Relations Act. This law promised basic rights for all farm workers.

▲ César and Helen Chávez march from Delano to Sacramento.

A True Friend of Farm Workers

César Chávez died in 1993, at the age of sixty-six. Fifty-thousand people came to his funeral.

For over thirty years, César had fought for a better life for farm workers. He had starved himself, marched hundreds of miles, spent time in jail, and even received death threats.

Through it all, César never lost hope. He never stopped believing that change was possible. "¡Sí, se puede!" he said. "Yes, it can be done." César proved that poor people could fight and win. He had done it.

---

shacks, buildings made of cheap materials
publicity, attention someone or something gets from newspapers, television, or other media sources
contracts, legal written agreements between two or more people or companies, which say what each side will do

BEFORE YOU GO ON

1 What was the CSO? What was its purpose?

2 When was the NFWA **founded**? What were the results of the grape strike?

On Your Own
Would you join a union? Why or why not?

Review and Practice

► **COMPREHENSION**  **Workbook** Page 165

Utilize

1. How old was Chávez when he began working in the fields?

2. What did the Agricultural Labor Relations Act promise to do?

Comprehend

3. What kinds of things did the workers demand?

4. What kinds of growers did Chávez protest against?

Analyze

5. Why did Chávez focus his attention on farm workers?

6. Why do you think Chávez chose Sacramento as the final destination for his march against grape growers?

Connect

7. Do you think forming a union is an effective way for workers to communicate their wants and needs? Explain.

8. How important is the media's coverage of events such as union strikes? Explain.

▲ A union flag

► **IN YOUR OWN WORDS**

Use the vocabulary below to summarize the reading for a partner.

A Hard Life	⇒	migrant workers, growers, children
Yuma	⇒	farm, drought
From School to the Fields	⇒	hard labor, Navy
The Chance to Change Things	⇒	CSO, NFWA
"Don't Buy Grapes!"	⇒	Delano, strike, march, contracts
A True Friend of Farm Workers	⇒	funeral, fought for a better life, never lost hope

► DISCUSSION

Discuss in pairs or small groups.

1. In what ways did the NFWA protest against growers? Which way do you think was the most effective and why?

2. Why is it important to be persistent? Can you give other examples of **persistence**, either your own or those of people you've read or heard about?

Q **What is the human spirit?** Do you think that obstacles, such as those faced by César Chávez, make a person stronger? Explain.

🔊 Speaking SKILL

Learning Strategy:
When you speak, decide if you will use formal or informal language. Use formal language in class. Use informal language with family and friends.

► READ FOR FLUENCY

It is often easier to read a text if you understand the difficult words and phrases. Work with a partner. Choose a paragraph from the reading. Identify the words and phrases you do not know or have trouble pronouncing. Look up the difficult words in a dictionary.

Take turns pronouncing the words and phrases with your partner. If necessary, ask your teacher to model the correct pronunciation. Then take turns reading the paragraph aloud. Give each other feedback on your reading.

► EXTENSION  Workbook Page 165

▲ A woman holds a sign at an event honoring César Chávez.

Utilize In 2000, California declared March 31 the César Chávez Day of Service and Learning. Work with a partner to find out which other states recognize this day. Use the library or Internet to learn about the activities that occur and the opportunities for people to get involved. When your research is complete, share your information with the class. Explain where and how people honor this American hero.

Grammar

Inseparable Phrasal Verbs

A phrasal verb is created by combining a verb and one or more preposition(s). A phrasal verb has its own special meaning, different from the meaning of the original verb.

Many phrasal verbs are inseparable, which means that the object always follows, and never comes before, the preposition(s). A negative phrasal verb is formed the same as a one-word verb, with a form of *do + not* or a form of *be + not*.

> César wanted to **go back to** school. [means *return to a place*]
> The growers **didn't count on** the determination of the workers. [means *not expect*]
> You **can count on** me.

Grammar **SKILL**

A phrasal verb can be in any form (past, present, future, etc.) that a one-word verb can be in. It can also be used with modals.

Practice

Workbook Page 166

Work with a partner. Copy the sentences below into your notebook. Choose the correct meaning of each underlined phrasal verb from the box.

Example: The teacher <u>called on</u> me to give an answer. <u>*ask to speak*</u>

ask to speak	enter	meet by chance	leave	originate	help

1. Where do those grapes <u>come from</u>? _____
2. I <u>ran into</u> Philip the other day. _____
3. <u>Get in</u> the taxi! We'll be late for the concert. _____
4. We should <u>get off</u> the bus here. _____
5. My mom expects me to <u>chip in</u> with the housework. _____

✔ **GRAMMAR CHECK**
What makes up a phrasal verb?

Apply

Work with a partner. Find the following phrasal verbs in the reading. Use the context of the reading to figure out their meanings.

run out of	come back to	look down on

Separable Phrasal Verbs

Many phrasal verbs are separable. The object can either follow the preposition or can come between the verb and preposition.

> César **thought over** the problem.
> César **thought** the problem **over**. [means *considered*]

Here is a list of some common separable phrasal verbs and their meanings.

bring back [means *return*]	cheer up [means *make happier*]	find out [means *discover*]
work out [means *solve*]	look over [means *examine*]	make up [means *invent*]
help out [means *assist*]	talk over [means *discuss*]	

Practice  Workbook Page 167

Work with a partner. Copy the sentences into your notebook. Then complete each sentence with one of the phrasal verbs from above.

Example: When I'm sad, my friends always ___cheer___ me ___up___.

1. After many hours, she _____ the crossword puzzle.
2. Let's _____ this situation _____. I don't want us to be angry with each other.
3. I _____ my book _____ to the library yesterday.
4. My two-year-old daughter loves to _____ stories.
5. If I have any problems, my brother always _____ me _____.

Apply

Work with a partner. Restate each sentence in the Practice exercise, changing the position of the object. If it's not possible, say why.

Example: It's not possible with the example because the object is a pronoun.

Writing

Write an Advertisement

An advertisement is an example of persuasive writing. It is a message that encourages the reader to buy a product or service. When you write a print advertisement, it is important to identify your intended audience. Tailor your message to this audience. Begin with an attention-grabbing phrase or question. Then include facts and details that describe the product, its function, and how it will benefit the buyer.

> **Writing Prompt**
>
> Write a print advertisement for a product, such as a computer, or a service, such as babysitting. Be sure to include phrasal verbs in your paragraph.

1 **PREWRITE** Begin by choosing a product or service that you want to advertise.

- Write the name of the product or service in your notebook.
- Ask yourself what the benefits of this product or service are.
- Think of some facts to support your claims.
- Write your ideas in a graphic organizer.  **Workbook Page 168**

Here's a word web created by a student named Andrew. He is writing an advertisement to persuade people to eat grapes.

```
┌─────────────────────────┐
│ Product: grapes         │
└─────────────────────────┘
       │            │
┌──────────────────┐  ┌──────────────────┐
│ Benefits: good   │  │ Benefits: great  │
│ health           │  │ snack            │
│                  │  │                  │
│ potassium        │  │ high energy      │
│ vitamins A and C │  │ bite-sized       │
│ antioxidants     │  │ refreshing       │
│ prevent chronic  │  │ can be frozen    │
│ illnesses        │  │                  │
│ lower cholesterol│  │                  │
└──────────────────┘  └──────────────────┘
```

2 DRAFT Use your word web to help you write a first draft.

- Keep in mind your purpose for writing.
- Begin with an attention-grabbing phrase or question.
- Present facts and details that will appeal to your audience.
- Remember to use phrasal verbs.

3 REVISE Read over your draft. Look for places where the writing is unclear or needs improvement. Use the Writing Checklist to help you identify problems. Then revise your draft, using the editing and proofreading marks listed on page 458.

4 EDIT Check your work for errors in grammar, usage, mechanics, and spelling. Trade papers with a partner to obtain feedback. Use the Peer Review Checklist on Workbook page 176. Edit your final draft in response to feedback from your partner and your teacher.

5 PUBLISH Prepare a clean copy of your final draft. Share your advertisement with the class. Save your work. You'll need to refer to it in the Writing Workshop at the end of the unit.

Writing Checklist

IDEAS:
☑ I began with an interesting phrase or question.
☑ I included facts and details to try and persuade the audience.

CONVENTIONS:
☑ I included phrasal verbs in my paragraph.

Here is Andrew's advertisement for grapes. Notice how he uses facts and specific details and content-related vocabulary to explain why grapes are good for you.

Andrew Denkus

Grapes Are Great!

Grapes are known as nature's candy. But did you know that they have been celebrated for years because of their health benefits? Grapes are a great source of potassium and vitamins A and C, and they also contain powerful antioxidants. Researchers agree that by adding grapes to your diet, you can help prevent chronic illnesses, including heart disease, cancer, and age-associated diseases such as Alzheimer's. They also lower your cholesterol! Plus, they are a great high-energy, bite-sized snack, perfect for busy people on the go. They are very refreshing and can even be frozen for a cool after-school treat. So whether you enjoy red, white, or seedless, show your strength in numbers, don't delay—buy your grapes today!

Prepare to Read

What You Will Learn

Reading

- Vocabulary building: *Literary terms, word study*

- Reading strategy: *Draw Inferences*

- Text type: *Literature (short story)*

Grammar

Punctuation in quotations; Reported speech: reporting verbs *said, asked, told*

Writing

Write a review

► ◉ THE BIG QUESTION

What is the human spirit? Teenagers in the United States are required to attend school. There they learn about academic subjects and develop skills that will help them in the future. Think about a time when you studied hard for a test and received a good grade on it. Did you feel that the result was worth the effort? What if you hadn't received a good grade? Would the experience have broken your spirit? Use your prior experiences to answer these questions with a partner.

► BUILD BACKGROUND

In this section, you will read a short story called **"The Scholarship Jacket."** The word *scholarship* has several meanings; in this story, *scholarship* means *academic award*.

"The Scholarship Jacket" is a story about a Mexican girl named Marta. She is the class valedictorian, or the student with the highest grades. Different schools have different ways of recognizing a valedictorian's academic achievement. Some schools invite the valedictorian to present a speech at their graduation ceremony. The valedictorian at Marta's school is rewarded with a special scholarship jacket. Marta expects to receive the jacket, but she is surprised when the school considers giving it to someone else.

A class valedictorian gives a speech at her graduation ceremony. ►

► VOCABULARY

Learn Literary Words

A **dialogue** is a conversation between characters. In poems, novels, and short stories, dialogue is usually shown by quotation marks (" ") to indicate a speaker's exact words. Punctuation marks (! . , ?) let the reader know how the conversation should be read. Read the dialogue from "The Scholarship Jacket" below.

> He turned to me and asked quietly, "What does a scholarship jacket mean?"
> I answered quickly; maybe there was a chance. "It means you've earned it by having the highest grades for eight years and that's why they're giving it to you."

The **theme** is a central message in a story. Sometimes a theme is directly stated in the text. More often, it is presented indirectly. The reader must decide what the theme is based on and what the text reveals about people and life. Some themes in literature include friendship, celebration, forgiveness, and bravery.

Practice  Workbook Page 169

Work with a partner. Read the excerpt from "The Scholarship Jacket" below. Then answer the questions.

> "I refuse to do it! I don't care who her father is, her grades don't even begin to compare to Marta's. I won't lie or falsify records. Marta has a straight A plus average and you know it." That was Mr. Schmidt and he sounded very angry. Mr. Boone's voice sounded calm and quiet.
> "Look, Joann's father is not only on the Board, he owns the only store in town; we could say it was a close tie and—"
> The pounding in my ears drowned out the rest of the words, only a word here and there filtered through. ". . . Marta is Mexican . . . resign . . . won't do it. . . ."

1. What are the spoken words, or the quotations, in the story excerpt?
2. Who is the speaker of each quotation?

Listening and Speaking: Academic Words

Study the **red** words and their meanings. You will find these words useful when talking and writing about literature. Write each word and its meaning in your notebook, then say the words aloud with a partner. After you read "The Scholarship Jacket," try to use these words to respond to the text.

academic = relating to work done in schools, colleges, or universities	→	Elena earned the highest grades in her class. She is proud of her **academic** achievement.
policy = a plan that is agreed to by a political party, government, or organization	→	It was the school's **policy** to give a special jacket to the class valedictorian.
principal = someone who is in charge of a school	→	The **principal** called me into her office to talk about my grades.
tradition = a belief or custom that has existed for a long time	→	Every year, the students at my school hold a bake sale to help raise money for charity. It is a **tradition**.

Practice

Workbook Page 170

Work with a partner to answer these questions. Try to include the **red** word in your answer. Write the sentences in your notebook.

1. What is your greatest **academic** achievement?

2. What is your school's **policy** regarding cell phones in the classroom?

3. Who is the **principal** of your school? Have you or someone you know ever been called to the principal's office? Why?

4. What is one **tradition** that your school celebrates every year?

Word Study: Words Ending with Consonant + *-le, -al, -el*

Words that end with a *consonant* + *-le, -al,* or *-el* can be difficult to spell because they share the sound, /əl/. Specific rules for when to use *-le, -al,* or *-el* do not exist. Therefore, it is best to memorize the spelling of each new word you learn. Read the examples below.

Word Ending	Example	Sentence
-le	litt**le**	My grandfather tended to his **little** bean plants.
-al	princip**al**	The **principal** called me into his office.
-el	caram**el**	I took the **caramel** from my grandmother.

Practice
Workbook Page 171

Work with a partner. Copy the words from the box below into your notebook. Circle each word ending. Then say one of the words. Ask your partner to spell it aloud. Check your partner's spelling. Then have your partner say the next word. Continue until you can spell all of the words correctly.

bagel	crumple	dental	handle	jewel	unable

READING STRATEGY | DRAW INFERENCES

Drawing inferences helps you figure out the information that authors do not always give directly. When you draw inferences (or infer), you are figuring out what the author means. To draw inferences, follow these steps:

- As you read, think about the characters and setting. Pay attention to the events and situations described. What can you guess about the characters and setting?

- Think about your own experiences. Do they help you understand the events and situations that you are reading about?

- Now use the information in the story and your own experiences to draw inferences.

As you read "The Scholarship Jacket," think about what the author means, but does not say directly. What inferences can you draw from what the author wrote?

Workbook Page 172

Set a purpose for reading As you read, notice Marta's reactions to the discrimination she encounters. How is she able to retain her spirit in the face of such negativity?

THE SCHOLARSHIP JACKET

Audio

Marta Salinas

The small Texas school that I attended carried out a tradition every year during the eighth grade graduation; a beautiful gold and green jacket, the school colors, was awarded to the class valedictorian, the student who had maintained the highest grades for eight years. The scholarship jacket had a big gold S on the left front side and the winner's name was written in gold letters on the pocket.

My oldest sister Rosie had won the jacket a few years back and I fully expected to win also. I was fourteen and in the eighth grade. I had been a straight A student since the first grade, and the last year I had looked forward to owning that jacket. My father was a farm laborer who couldn't earn enough money to feed eight children, so when I was six I was given to my grandparents to raise. We couldn't participate in sports at school because there were **registration fees**, **uniform** costs, and trips out of town; so even though we were quite **agile** and athletic, there would never be a sports school jacket for us. This one, the scholarship jacket, was our only chance.

In May, close to graduation, spring fever struck, and no one paid any attention in class; instead we stared out the windows and at each other, wanting to speed up the last few weeks of school. I **despaired** every time I looked in the mirror.

---

registration fees, monies paid when signing up for something
uniform, clothing that members of an organization, such as a sports team, wear
agile, able to move quickly and easily
despaired, felt very sad

Pencil thin, not a curve anywhere, I was called "Beanpole" and "String Bean" and I knew that's what I looked like. A flat chest, no hips, and a brain, that's what I had. That really isn't much fun for a fourteen-year-old to work with, I thought, as I absentmindedly wandered from my history class to the gym.

Another hour of sweating in basketball and displaying my toothpick legs was coming up. Then I remembered my **P.E.** shorts were still in a bag under my desk where I'd forgotten them. I had to walk all the way back and get them. Coach Thompson was a real bear if anyone wasn't dressed for P.E. She had said I was a good **forward** and once she even tried to talk Grandma into letting me join the team. Grandma, of course, said no.

I was almost back at my classroom's door when I heard angry voices and arguing. I stopped. I didn't mean to **eavesdrop**; I just hesitated, not knowing what to do. I needed those shorts and I was going to be late, but I didn't want to interrupt an argument between my teachers. I recognized the voices: Mr. Schmidt, my history teacher, and Mr. Boone, my math teacher. They seemed to be arguing about me. I couldn't believe it. I still remember the shock that **rooted** me flat against the wall as if I were trying to blend in with the **graffiti** written there.

P.E., Physical Education, or gym class
forward, basketball player whose main job is to shoot the ball at the basket
eavesdrop, listen secretly to other people's conversations
rooted, made it so someone or something cannot move
graffiti, rude or humorous writing and pictures on the walls of buildings

Reading Skill

Take turns rereading paragraphs aloud with a partner. As you read along in the text, listen closely to the way your partner reads. Listen for pauses, stressed words, and rhythm. This will help you understand the story.

BEFORE YOU GO ON

1 Why couldn't Marta and her siblings participate in school sports?

2 What happened when Marta returned to her classroom?

On Your Own
Do you think students should be rewarded for their **academic** achievements? If so, in what ways?

Reading 2 **325**

"I refuse to do it! I don't care who her father is, her grades don't even begin to compare to Marta's. I won't lie or falsify records. Marta has a straight A plus average and you know it." That was Mr. Schmidt and he sounded very angry. Mr. Boone's voice sounded calm and quiet.

"Look, Joann's father is not only on the **Board**, he owns the only store in town; we could say it was a close **tie** and—"

The pounding in my ears drowned out the rest of the words, only a word here and there filtered through. " . . . Marta is Mexican . . . **resign** . . . won't do it. . . . " Mr. Schmidt came rushing out, and luckily for me went down the opposite way toward the auditorium, so he didn't see me. Shaking, I waited a few minutes and then went in and grabbed my bag and fled from the room. Mr. Boone looked up when I came in but didn't say anything. To this day I don't remember if I got in trouble in P.E. for being late or how I made it through the rest of the afternoon. I went home very sad and cried into my pillow that night so Grandmother wouldn't hear me. It seemed a cruel coincidence that I had overheard that conversation.

The next day when the principal called me into his office, I knew what it would be about. He looked uncomfortable and unhappy. I decided I wasn't going to make it any easier for him so I looked him straight in the eye. He looked away and fidgeted with the papers on his desk.

"Marta," he said, "there's been a change in policy this year regarding the scholarship jacket. As you know, it has always been free." He cleared his throat and continued. "This year the Board decided to charge fifteen dollars—which still won't cover the complete cost of the jacket."

I stared at him in shock and a small sound of **dismay** escaped my throat. I hadn't expected this. He still avoided looking in my eyes.

"So if you are unable to pay the fifteen dollars for the jacket, it will be given to the next one in line."

Standing with all the **dignity** I could **muster**, I said, "I'll speak to my grandfather about it, sir, and let you know tomorrow." I cried on the walk home from the bus stop. The first road was a quarter of a mile from the highway, so by the time I got home, my eyes were red and puffy.

"Where's Grandpa?" I asked Grandma, looking down at the floor so she wouldn't ask me why I'd been crying. She was sewing on a quilt and didn't look up.

✔ LITERARY CHECK

*Which lines in this **dialogue** are Marta's? Which are the principal's?*

Board, committee that controls how schools in an area are run
tie, situation in which two people in a competition have the same result or finish
resign, officially quit a job
dismay, disappointment and unhappiness
dignity, self-respect
muster, collect

BEFORE YOU GO ON

1 Who did Mr. Boone want to give the jacket to? Why?

2 How do you think the **principal** felt about having to give the jacket to Joann? Why?

On Your Own
What would you do if you were in Marta's situation?

Reading 2 **327**

"I think he's out back working in the bean field."

I went outside and looked out at the fields. There he was. I could see him walking between the rows, his body bent over the little plants, **hoe** in hand. I walked slowly out to him, trying to think how I could best ask him for the money.

There was a cool breeze blowing and a sweet smell of **mesquite** in the air, but I didn't appreciate it. I kicked at a dirt clod. I wanted that jacket so much. It was more than just being a valedictorian and giving a little thank you speech for the jacket on graduation night. It represented eight years of hard work and **expectation**. I knew I had to be honest with Grandpa; it was my only chance. He saw me and looked up.

He waited for me to speak. I cleared my throat nervously and clasped my hands behind my back so he wouldn't see them shaking. "Grandpa, I have a big **favor** to ask you," I said in Spanish, the only language he knew. He still waited silently. I tried again. "Grandpa, this year the principal said the scholarship jacket is not going to be free. It's going to cost fifteen dollars and I have to take the money in tomorrow, otherwise it'll be given to someone else." The last words came out in an eager rush. Grandpa

---

hoe, garden tool with a long handle, used to loosen soil
mesquite, tree bark used to cook food
expectation, the belief that one will get something
favor, thing one does for someone else out of kindness

straightened up tiredly and leaned his chin on the hoe handle.
He looked out over the field that was filled with the tiny green bean plants.
I waited **desperately** hoping he'd say I could have the money.

He turned to me and asked quietly, "What does a scholarship jacket mean?"

I answered quickly; maybe there was a chance. "It means you've earned it by having the highest grades for eight years and that's why they're giving it to you."

Too late I realized the **significance** of my words. Grandpa knew that I understood it was not a matter of money. It wasn't that. He went back to hoeing the weeds that sprang up between the delicate little bean plants. It was a time consuming job; sometimes the small shoots were right next to each other. Finally he spoke again.

"Then if you pay for it, Marta, it's not a scholarship jacket, is it? Tell your principal I will not pay the fifteen dollars."

I walked back to the house and locked myself in the bathroom for a long time. I was angry with Grandfather even though I knew he was right, and I was angry with the Board, whoever they were. Why did they have to change the rules just when it was my turn to win the jacket?

---

desperately, in an anxious manner
significance, importance or meaning

BEFORE YOU GO ON

1. What did Marta ask her grandfather?

2. Why was the scholarship jacket important to Marta?

On Your Own
Make a prediction: Do you think the principal will give the jacket to Joann if Marta does not have the money to buy it?

Reading 2 **329**

It was a very sad and **withdrawn** girl who dragged into the principal's office the next day. This time he did look me in the eyes.

"What did your grandfather say?"

I sat very straight in my chair.

"He said to tell you he won't pay the fifteen dollars."

The principal **muttered** something I couldn't understand under his breath, and walked over to the window. He stood looking out at something outside. He looked bigger than usual when he stood up; he was a tall gaunt man with gray hair, and I watched the back of his head while I waited for him to speak.

"Why?" he finally asked. "Your grandfather has the money. Doesn't he own a small bean farm?"

I looked at him, forcing my eyes to stay dry. "He said if I had to pay for it, then it wouldn't be a scholarship jacket," I said and stood up to leave. "I guess you'll just have to give it to Joann." I hadn't meant to say that; it just slipped out. I was almost to the door when he stopped me.

"Marta—wait."

I turned to him, waiting. What did he want now?

I could feel my heart pounding. Something **bitter** and vile tasting was coming up in my mouth; I was afraid I was going to be sick. I didn't need any **sympathy** speeches. He sighed loudly and went back to his big desk. He looked at me, biting his lip, as if thinking.

---

withdrawn, quiet and not wanting to be with people
muttered, spoke in a quiet voice
bitter, having a strong, bad taste
sympathy, concern for someone

"Okay, damn it. We'll make an exception in your case. I'll tell the Board, you'll get your jacket."

I could hardly believe it. I spoke in a trembling rush. "Oh, thank you, sir!" Suddenly I felt great. I didn't know about **adrenaline** in those days, but I knew something was pumping through me, making me feel as tall as the sky. I wanted to yell, jump, run the mile, do something. I ran out so I could cry in the hall where there was no one to see me. At the end of the day, Mr. Schmidt **winked** at me and said, "I hear you're getting a scholarship jacket this year."

His face looked as happy and **innocent** as a baby's, but I knew better. Without answering I gave him a quick hug and ran to the bus.

I cried on the walk home again, but this time because I was so happy. I couldn't wait to tell Grandpa and ran straight to the field.

I joined him in the row where he was working and without saying anything I crouched down and started pulling up the weeds with my hands. Grandpa worked alongside me for a few minutes, but he didn't ask what had happened. After I had a little pile of weeds between the rows, I stood up and faced him.

"The principal said he's making an **exception** for me, Grandpa, and I'm getting the jacket after all. That's after I told him what you said."

Grandpa didn't say anything, he just gave me a pat on the shoulder and a smile. He pulled out the crumpled red handkerchief that he always carried in his back pocket and wiped the sweat off his forehead.

"Better go see if your grandmother needs any help with supper."

I gave him a big grin. He didn't fool me. I skipped and ran back to the house whistling some silly tune.

---

adrenaline, a chemical produced by your body that makes your heart beat faster
winked, closed and opened one eye quickly
innocent, inexperienced
exception, exclusion from a rule

ABOUT THE **AUTHOR**

Marta Salinas was born in California. She attended college at the University of California, Irvine, where she studied writing. Today she is a writer and an environmental advocate.

✔ **LITERARY CHECK**
What is the theme of this story?

BEFORE YOU GO ON

1 How do you think Marta's grandfather felt after Marta won the jacket?

2 What do you think Marta learned from her experience with the principal?

💡 **On Your Own**
Do you feel Mr. Boone and the principal should have been disciplined for their behavior? If so, how?

Review and Practice

▶ READER'S THEATER

Act out the following scene with a partner.

Marta: Grandpa, can you please give me fifteen dollars?

Grandpa: Why? What do you need it for?

Marta: My scholarship jacket.

Grandpa: You have to pay for the jacket? Your sister didn't have to pay for hers.

Marta: I know, but the school changed its policy.

Grandpa: Why do you want this jacket so badly?

Marta: Because I've earned it.

Grandpa: If you've earned it, Marta, you shouldn't have to pay for it. Tell your principal that I will not give you the money.

> **Speaking SKILL**
>
> As you speak, use expressions and movements that match the lines you are reading.

▶ COMPREHENSION  Workbook Page 173

Recall

1. What **tradition** does the school that Marta attends carry out every year?

2. Why did Marta live with her grandparents?

Comprehend

3. Which two people in the story wanted Joann to receive the scholarship jacket?

4. How and why is Marta's behavior different each time she meets with the principal?

Analyze

5. How are the actions of Marta's grandfather an example of the human spirit?

6. What do you think the author's purpose was in writing this text?

Connect

7. Have you ever overheard a conversation you were not supposed to hear? What was it about?

8. Does your school have a **policy** to reward students for their academic achievements?

➤ **DISCUSSION**

Discuss in pairs or small groups.

1. Why do you think the principal gave Marta the scholarship jacket after all?

2. What other kinds of achievements can people earn besides academic achievements?

Q **What is the human spirit?** How does performing a task well and being recognized for it affect a person's spirit?

Listening SKILL

Learning Strategy: Think about what you are hearing. Try to relate what you hear to what you already know.

◀ A champion swimmer holds a trophy.

➤ **RESPONSE TO LITERATURE** 📖 Workbook Page 173

Utilize At the end of the story, the principal promises to give the scholarship jacket to Marta. How would the story be different if the principal had given Joann the jacket? Work with a partner. Write a new ending to the story. Include the reactions of Marta, Grandpa, and Mr. Schmidt.

Grammar

Punctuation in Quotations

Proper use of punctuation is important so that your reader knows when you are using a speaker's exact words. Use quotation marks (" ") and a comma (,) to separate direct, or quoted, speech from the phrase that identifies the speaker.

> "I think he's out back working in the bean field," Grandma said.
> He said, "I hear you're getting a scholarship jacket this year."

If the phrase that identifies the speaker interrupts the direct speech, use a comma after the first part of the direct speech and after the phrase. If the phrase connects two complete sentences, use a comma after the first part and a period after the phrase.

> "Marta," he said, "there's been a change in policy regarding the scholarship jacket."
> "No," he firmly replied. "I will not give the jacket to someone else."

If the direct speech is a question, use a question mark (?) instead of a comma at the end of the direct speech. If it is an exclamation, use an exclamation mark (!).

> "What does a scholarship jacket mean?" he asked.
> He said, "I refuse to do it!"

Grammar SKILL

Be sure to capitalize the first word within a quotation unless the phrase identifying the speaker interrupts the quotation.

Practice
Workbook Page 174

Work with a partner. Copy the sentences below into your notebook. Correctly punctuate and add capitalization to each sentence.

Example: "Sharon," he asked, "where are you going?"

1. The manager said the store is closing in five minutes
2. Why did they change their policy Grandpa asked
3. Dinner's ready my mom yelled from upstairs
4. Yes she said we can leave now
5. Grandpa said I will not give you the fifteen dollars

Apply

Work with a partner. Ask and answer questions about one of the readings in the book. Write five direct quotations from your discussion.

✔ GRAMMAR CHECK

What are the different kinds of punctuation you can use with quotations?

Reported Speech: Reporting Verbs *said*, *asked*, *told*

Reported speech does not use quotation marks and may be a paraphrase of the person's exact words. The verb form usually changes. Use the reporting verb *said* when reporting statements. *That* often follows *said*.

Direct Quotation	I **said**, "I'**ll speak** to my grandfather about it."
Reported Speech	I **said** (that) I **would speak** to my grandfather about it.

To report *Wh-* questions, use statement word order, not question word order. For *Yes-No* questions, use *if* or *whether* and statement word order. Use the reporting verb *asked* when reporting questions.

Direct Quotation	"What **does** a scholarship jacket **mean**?" he **asked**.
Reported Speech	He **asked** what a scholarship jacket **meant**.
Direct Quotation	"**Is** Grandpa here?" I **asked**.
Reported Speech	I **asked** if Grandpa **was** here.

Grammar SKILL

In reported speech, the phrase identifying the speaker comes at the beginning of the sentence.

When you mention the listener, you can use *told*. An object always follows the reporting verb *told*. *That* often follows the object.

Direct Quotation	The principal **told** Marta, "You'**ll** get your jacket."
Reported Speech	The principal **told** Marta (that) she **would** get her jacket.

Practice
Workbook Page 175

Work with a partner. Change the direct quotations into reported speech using *said*, *asked*, or *told*. Write the sentences in your notebook.

Example: She said, "I'm going to the park."
She said that she was going to the park.

1. "I'm not hungry," Maya said.
2. The salesman asked, "Is there anything else?"
3. She told him, "I love you."
4. His mother told him, "We are leaving soon."
5. Sheila asked, "Are you coming?"

Apply
Work with a partner. Find a dialogue (an exchange of direct speech) in the reading. Tell your partner what was said using reported speech.

Writing

Write a Review

A review, or a writer's opinion about a book, movie, or other work, is a kind of persuasive writing. The purpose of a review is to persuade the reader to experience the work or to avoid it.

When you write a review, begin with a brief summary or description of the work. Then state your opinion of it—whether you liked it or did not like it and why. Provide reasons for your opinion, and support it with examples, such as direct quotations or descriptions.

> ### Writing Prompt
>
> Choose a book, CD, film, or play to review. State your opinion clearly and support it with examples from the work. Be sure to use reported speech correctly.

1 PREWRITE Begin by choosing a story.

- Think of a book, CD, film, or play that you want to review.

- What was your opinion of it? Why did you like or dislike it? Think of some examples and details to support your reasons.

- Write your ideas in a graphic organizer.

Workbook Page 176

Here's an idea web created by a student named Blaise for the story "The Scholarship Jacket."

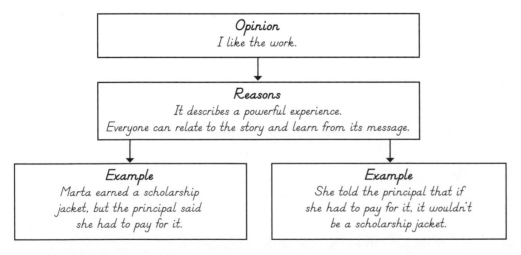

Opinion
I like the work.

↓

Reasons
It describes a powerful experience.
Everyone can relate to the story and learn from its message.

↓   ↓

Example
Marta earned a scholarship jacket, but the principal said she had to pay for it.

Example
She told the principal that if she had to pay for it, it wouldn't be a scholarship jacket.

2 **DRAFT** Use your idea web to help you write a first draft.

- Remember to include a summary of the main points.
- State your opinion, say why, and support it with examples.
- Be sure to check your punctuation.

3 **REVISE** Read over your draft. Look for places where the writing is unclear or needs improvement. Use the Writing Checklist to help you identify problems. Then revise your draft, using the editing and proofreading marks listed on page 458.

4 **EDIT** Check your work for errors in grammar, usage, mechanics, and spelling. Trade papers with a partner to obtain feedback. Use the Peer Review Checklist on Workbook page 176. Edit your final draft in response to feedback from your partner and your teacher.

5 **PUBLISH** Prepare a clean copy of your final draft. Share your review with your class. Save your work. You'll need to refer to it in the Writing Workshop at the end of the unit.

Writing Checklist

IDEAS:
☑ I stated my opinion clearly

WORD CHOICE:
☑ I used examples from the work to state my opinion clearly.

Here is Blaise's review of the story "The Scholarship Jacket." Notice how she includes her opinion and uses examples to support it.

Blaise Yafcak

"The Scholarship Jacket"

"The Scholarship Jacket" is about a girl named Marta who earns her school's top prize, a scholarship jacket. The principal tries to prevent Marta, whose family is poor, from receiving the jacket by telling her she will have to pay for it. Marta asks her grandfather for the money, but he refuses to give it to her. I liked this story because I think both Marta and her grandfather are admirable. Marta showed a lot of strength when she looked the principal in the eye as he told her she would have to pay for the jacket. In addition, Marta's grandfather could simply have ignored the school's discriminatory ways and paid for the jacket. Instead he said, "Tell your principal I will not pay the fifteen dollars." These characters are strong and realistic. As a result, I recommend "The Scholarship Jacket" to anyone who has had to fight for what he or she believes in.

Prepare to Read

What You Will Learn

Reading
- Vocabulary building: *Literary terms, word study*
- Reading strategy: *Read aloud*
- Text type: *Literature (play excerpt)*

Grammar
Present perfect; Present perfect progressive

Writing
Write a persuasive paragraph

➤ 🔍 THE BIG QUESTION

What is the human spirit? Imagine that you have to escape from an enemy. You move into a secret, cramped apartment, like the one shown below. You have to share it with seven other people. You cannot make any noise or go outside. How would you feel? What would you do all day? What would you miss most about the outside world? Would this experience break your spirit? Discuss with a partner.

➤ BUILD BACKGROUND

You will read an excerpt from ***The Diary of Anne Frank: The Play***. It is based on the book *Anne Frank: The Diary of a Young Girl*. Anne Frank wrote her diary in Amsterdam, Holland, between 1943 and 1945 while hiding from the Nazis during World War II.

Anne Frank and her family hid in a secret annex, a small hidden apartment, for over two years. They had to be very quiet during the day so no one would hear them. They could not leave the annex. They depended on Mr. Frank's work colleagues to bring them food and other necessities. These people heroically risked their lives to help the family.

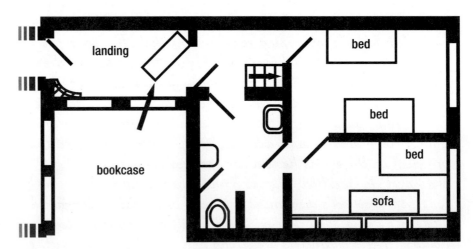

▲ A floor plan of the secret annex

► VOCABULARY

Learn Literary Words

A **diary** is a book in which you write about your own life. Each day you write about your personal thoughts, opinions, and/or the events in which you participated.

You will read a **drama** that is based on Anne Frank's diary. A drama is a play that is written and performed by actors. The written version of a drama is called a script. It is made up of dialogue and stage directions. Characters' names appear next to the dialogue they speak. **Stage directions** tell the actors how to speak and act; they can also describe the setting, sound effects, and lighting. Stage directions are often printed in italics and set within brackets [ ]. The actors do not read them aloud. For example, read the script excerpt below from *The Diary of Anne Frank: The Play*.

> **Mr. Frank:** [*quickly coming forward*] Peter. The first to arrive. [*Shaking his hand.*] Welcome, Peter. Peter van Daan, children.
> **Anne:** [*rushing toward him*] Welcome to the Annex!

Practice

Workbook Page 177

Read the script excerpt below with a partner. Then answer these questions: Who are the characters? What are the stage directions? Which lines are spoken?

Anne: [*looking down at the basket*] A cat! [*turning to Margot*] He has a cat!

Peter: [*self-conscious*] A black one.

Anne: We have a cat too. I wanted to bring her but. . . . [*glancing at her mother*] I know our neighbors will take care of her till we come back. I don't know what I'll do without her. But it'll be great having a cat here. . . .

Mrs. Frank: Anne dear, don't get so excited. Peter doesn't know you yet.

Anne: [*laughing*] He'll get to know me soon though. It's going to be so much fun having people around. A whole other family.

Listening and Speaking: Academic Words

Study the **red** words and their meanings. You will find these words useful when talking and writing about literature. Write each word and its meaning in your notebook, then say the words aloud with a partner. After you read the excerpt from *The Diary of Anne Frank: The Play*, try to use these words to respond to the text.

Academic Words

assisted
occupants
published
regulations

 Audio

assisted = helped someone	→	Angela's friends **assisted** her by carrying the heavy furniture into her apartment.
occupants = people who live in a building, room, etc.	→	Eight **occupants** lived in the apartment.
published = printed and distributed	→	Anne Frank's diary has been **published** in many different countries around the world.
regulations = official rules or orders	→	The soldier arrested the woman because she did not obey the **regulations**.

 Audio

Practice  **Workbook Page 178**

Write the sentences in your notebook. Choose a **red** word from the box above to complete each sentence. Then take turns reading the sentences aloud with a partner.

1. Over three hundred _____ lived in the building last year.

2. A theater employee _____ the elderly woman in finding a seat.

3. If you don't follow the theater's _____, you will be asked to leave.

4. After the success of their play, the writers _____ their script so that people around the world could read it.

▲ Anne Frank's diary has been published in multiple languages.

Word Study: Spelling the Sound /j/

In the excerpt from *The Diary of Anne Frank: The Play*, there are many words with the /j/ sound. There are different ways to spell this sound: *j* as in *jolly*, *g* as in *gem*, or *dge* as in *edge*. The letter *j* is usually used if the sound precedes an *a, o,* or *u*. The letter *g* is usually used when the sound is followed by an *e, i,* or *y*. The letters *dge* are often used when the sound comes at the end of a syllable or a word.

Sound of /j/		
j	**g**	**dge**
job	gentle	dodge
jury	original	ledge

Practice  Workbook Page 179

Work with a partner. Copy the chart above into your notebook. Add the words in the box below to the chart under the correct headings. Then say a word from the chart. Ask your partner to spell it aloud. Have your partner say the next word. Continue until you can spell all of the words correctly.

badge	dangerous	enjoy	June	large	object

READING STRATEGY   READ ALOUD

Reading aloud brings a story and characters to life. It can make reading more fun, especially when you're reading a play, a poem, or a story. To read a play aloud, follow these steps:

- Read the list of characters and choose one person to be each character.
- Read your lines to yourself. Read the stage directions.
- Read the play aloud as a group. Listen carefully to the other actors so that you know when to say your lines.

As you read the excerpt from *The Diary of Anne Frank: The Play*, pay attention to your lines and stage directions. When you perform the play in a group, speak clearly and listen carefully to the other actors.

 Workbook Page 180

Set a purpose for reading As you read, think about the responsibilities Miep and Mr. Kraler shared in hiding the families. Would you have done the same?

from

The Diary of Anne Frank:
The Play 🎵 Audio

▲ Anne Frank

Frances Goodrich and Albert Hackett, with Wendy Kesselman

On June 12, 1942, Anne Frank received a diary for her thirteenth birthday. A few weeks later, on July 6, the family was forced to move into the "Secret Annex." They lived there for two years with the van Pels family (Anne calls them the van Daans in her diary) and another Jewish man. Mr. Frank's former work colleagues, Mr. Kraler and Miep Gies, helped the families survive.

ANNE: [*voiceover*] July sixth, 1942. A few days ago, Father began to talk about going into hiding. He said it would be very hard for us to live **cut off** from the rest of the world. He sounded so serious I felt scared. "Don't worry, Anneke. We'll take care of everything. Just enjoy your **carefree** life while you can." [*She pauses.*]

Carefree? I was born in Frankfurt on June twelfth, 1929. Because we're Jewish, my father **emigrated** to Holland in 1933. He started a business, manufacturing products used to make jam. But Hitler **invaded** Holland

---

cut off, separated
carefree, problem-free
emigrated, left one country to live in another
invaded, entered a place using military force

✔ LITERARY CHECK

*Who did Anne Frank write about in her **diary**?*

Reading Skill

Identify the words you don't understand *as you read* and ask your teachers or peers for help with those words.

on May tenth, 1940, a month before my eleventh birthday. Five days later the Dutch surrendered, the Germans arrived—and the trouble started for the Jews. [*a pause*]

Father was forced to give up his business. We couldn't use streetcars, couldn't go to the theater or movies anymore, couldn't be out on the street after 9 P.M., couldn't even sit in our own gardens! We had to turn in our bicycles; no beaches, no swimming pools, no libraries—we couldn't even walk on the sunny side of the streets! My sister Margot and I had to go to a Jewish school. Our identity cards were stamped with a big black "J." And . . . we had to wear the **yellow star**. But somehow life went on. Until yesterday, when a call-up notice came from the **SS**. Margot was ordered to report for work in Germany, to the **Westerbork transit camp**. A call-up: Everyone knows what that means! [*She pauses.*]

At five-thirty this morning, we closed the door of our apartment behind us—ten days earlier than my parents had planned. My cat was the only living creature I said goodbye to. The unmade beds, the breakfast things on the table all created the **impression** we'd left in a hurry. [*a pause*]

And our destination? We walked two and a half miles in the pouring rain all the way to . . . Father's office building! Our hiding place, the "Secret Annex," is right behind it upstairs. Even though the Germans forced Father out, he still runs the office with Mr. Kraler and Miep, who've agreed to help us while we're in hiding. [*As Mr. Frank pulls a large **tarpaulin** off the kitchen table, he sees a rat move across the floor. Mrs. Frank shrieks.*]

MRS. FRANK: A rat!

MR. FRANK: Shhh! [*Quickly he motions her to be quiet, as Miep comes up the steps.*]

MR. FRANK: Ah, Miep!

MIEP: Mr. Frank. Thank God you arrived safely.

ANNE: Miep!

▲ Anne Frank's diary

✔ **LITERARY CHECK**
*What do the **stage directions** in this paragraph describe?*

---

yellow star, badge that Jews were required to wear
SS, high-ranking members of the Nazi Party
Westerbork transit camp, place in Holland where people were put on trains that took them to the concentration camps
impression, idea
tarpaulin, piece of material used to cover and protect an object

BEFORE YOU GO ON

1 Why do the Franks go into hiding?

2 Who helps them?

On Your Own
Imagine you have to go into hiding. What would you take with you?

▲ Anne's bedroom in the annex

▲ The secret annex was at the back of Mr. Frank's office building.

▲ The entrance to the annex was hidden by a swinging bookcase.

MIEP: Anne. Margot. [*as Margot and Mrs. Frank slowly sit up*] Mrs. Frank, you must be exhausted. If only we'd known we would have had it all ready for you.

MR. FRANK: You've done too much already, Miep. Besides, it's good for us to keep busy. As you see, Anne's my little helper.

MIEP: I can see that. [*She looks down the steps where Peter van Daan, a shy, awkward boy of sixteen, wearing a heavy coat with the **conspicuous** yellow star, waits nervously. He is carrying a cat in a basket.*] Peter— come in!

MR. FRANK: [*quickly coming forward*] Peter. The first to arrive. [*shaking his hand*] Welcome, Peter. Peter van Daan, children.

ANNE: [*Rushing toward him*] Welcome to the Annex!

MR. FRANK: Peter—Margot, Anne. You already know Mrs. Frank.

PETER: [***solemnly** shaking hands with Mrs. Frank*] Mrs. Frank.

MRS. FRANK: Forgive me, Peter. I'm not quite myself. But I'm so glad you'll be with us.

MARGOT: I am too.

ANNE: [*looking down at the basket*] A cat! [*turning to Margot*] He has a cat!

PETER: [***self-conscious***] A black one.

ANNE: We have a cat too. I wanted to bring her but . . . [*glancing at her mother*] I know our neighbors will take care of her till we come back. I don't know what I'll do without her. But it'll be great having a cat here. Won't it, **Pim**? Won't it be fantastic?

MRS. FRANK: Anne dear, don't get so excited. Peter doesn't know you yet.

ANNE: [*laughing*] He'll get to know me soon though. It's going to be so much fun having people around. A whole other family. Won't it, Margot?

MARGOT: Yes.

ANNE: [*skipping around the room*] Like being on vacation in some strange **pension** or something. An adventure—**romantic** and dangerous at the same time!

---

conspicuous, very easy to notice
solemnly, seriously or sadly
self-conscious, shy; awkward
Pim, Anne's nickname for her father
pension, hotel or boarding house
romantic, emotional or dream-like

BEFORE YOU GO ON

1 How does Anne feel about hiding in the annex?

2 What do Anne and Peter have in common?

On Your Own
Is Anne like you in any way? If so, how?

Reading 3 **345**

▲ Anne sitting at her school desk

▲ Peter van Daan

◄ (from left to right) Margot, Otto, Anne, and Edith Frank

MR. FRANK: [*watching Peter's* **anxious** *face*] What is it, Peter?

PETER: My parents. They were right behind me, one street away.

MR. FRANK: [*laying his hand on Peter's shoulder*] They'll be here.

PETER: You don't think they were. . . .

MRS. FRANK: Don't worry, Peter. [*smiling*] You're just like me.

ANNE: Mother's always jumping at every little thing. [*peeking into Peter's basket*] What's its name?

PETER: [*self-conscious*] Mouschi.

ANNE: [*to the cat*] Mouschi! Mouschi. I love cats. [*to Peter*] Where'd you go to school?

PETER: They set up a **technical school** in someone's house, once we were forbidden—

ANNE: [*breaking in*] I had to switch from my Montessori school to the Jewish Lyceum.

PETER: I know. I saw you there.

ANNE: You did? [*Mr. Kraler hurries up the stairs with Mr. and Mrs. van Daan. Mrs. van Daan is wearing a fur coat and carrying an umbrella and a large hat box. Mr. van Daan carries a* **satchel** *and his briefcase. All three are out of breath.*]

MR. FRANK: [*to Peter, smiling*] See—what did I tell you? Now we're all here.

MR. KRALER: [*obviously shaken*] Just in time. We had to take the long way around—there were too many **Green Police** on the streets. [*Mr. van Daan breaks open a package of cigarettes, nervously starts smoking*]

MR. FRANK: [*shaking hands with the van Daans*] Welcome, Mrs. van Daan. Mr. van Daan. You know my wife, of course, and the children. [*Mrs. Frank, Margot, and Anne shake hands with the van Daans.*]

MR. KRALER: We must hurry. The workmen will be here in half an hour.

MR. FRANK: Such trouble we're causing you, Mr. Kraler, after all you and Miep have done. And now we arrive early!

MR. KRALER: You couldn't let your daughter be taken away, Mr. Frank.

---

anxious, worried
technical school, school that teaches auto mechanics, machine repair, and other skills
satchel, small bag for carrying clothing, books, etc.
Green Police, Dutch police who supported the Nazis

BEFORE YOU GO ON

1 Why are Mr. and Mrs. van Daan the last to arrive?

2 Why is Mr. Kraler in a hurry to get the families settled in the annex?

On Your Own
What words would you use to describe Mr. Kraler and Miep?

Reading 3 **347**

◄ Miep and Mr. Frank

MIEP: Please don't worry. We will do everything we can to help you. Now I must run and get your **ration books**.

MRS. VAN DAAN: Wait—if they see our names on ration books, they'll know we're here, won't they?

MIEP: Trust me—your names won't be on them. I'll be up later. If you make a list every day, I'll try to get what you want. And every Saturday I can bring five library books. [*She hurries out.*]

MR. FRANK: Thank you, Miep.

ANNE: Five! I know what my five are going to be.

MRS. FRANK: Anne, remember, there are seven of us.

ANNE: I know, Mother.

MARGOT: [*troubled*] It's **illegal**, then, the ration books? We've never done anything illegal.

MR. VAN DAAN: I don't think we'll be living exactly according to regulations here. [*The* **carillon** *is heard playing the quarter hour before eight.*]

ANNE: Listen. The Westertoren!

MRS. FRANK: How will I ever get used to that clock?

ANNE: Oh, I love it!

MR. KRALER: Miep or I will be here every day to see you. I've hidden a **buzzer** to signal you when we come up, and tomorrow I'll have that bookcase placed in front of your door. Oh, and one last thing . . . the radio. . . . [*He points to a small radio hidden beneath a sheet.*]

---

ration books, booklets of coupons that allow people to buy food during wartime
illegal, not allowed by law
carillon, set of bells on a clock tower
buzzer, small device that makes a buzzing sound when you press it

ANNE: [***bounding*** *over to the radio*] A radio! Fantastic!

MRS. VAN DAAN: A radio. Thank God.

MR. VAN DAAN: How did you get it? We had to turn ours in months ago.

MR. FRANK: Thank you, Mr. Kraler. For everything. (Mr. Kraler turns to go, as Anne drops a batch of silverware.)

MR. KRALER: [*to Mr. Frank*] Oh . . . you'll tell them about the noise?

MR. FRANK: I'll tell them.

MRS. FRANK: [*following Mr. Kraler to the top of the stairs*] How can we thank you really? How can we ever—

MR. KRALER: I never thought I'd live to see the day a man like Mr. Frank would have to go into hiding. [*He hurries out, as she stands still, watching him.*]

* * *

On August 4, 1944, the secret annex was raided by the Security Police. Anne and the seven others in hiding were arrested. They were transported to Auschwitz concentration camp. After a month there, Anne and Margot were sent to Bergen-Belsen concentration camp, where they both got typhus, a deadly disease. They died within a short time of each other in March 1945, only a few weeks before the camp was liberated by the British. Only Anne's father, Otto Frank, survived. In 1947, he published Anne's diary.

---

bounding, running with a lot of energy

✔ **LITERARY CHECK**
*What character in this **drama** would you like to play?*

ABOUT THE PLAYWRIGHTS

Frances Goodrich and Albert Hackett wrote the screenplays for some of Hollywood's most famous movies. *The Diary of Anne Frank: The Play,* written in 1955, was perhaps their greatest achievement. Wendy Kesselman's adaptation, based on an expanded and unedited version of the original diary, portrays a more realistic Anne.

BEFORE YOU GO ON

1 In what ways does Miep offer to help the families?

2 How will Miep and Mr. Kraler signal that they are coming up to the annex?

💡**On Your Own**
Do you like Anne? Why or why not?

► DRAMATIC READING

One of the best ways to understand and appreciate a play is to perform it. Work in small groups to act out the scene from *The Diary of Anne Frank: The Play*. Each group should choose a director. The director will assign parts to other group members. He or she will also direct the actors using the description of the scene and the stage directions. As a team, discuss each character in the play and how he or she should be portrayed.

Evaluate your progress as you practice the scene. How can you improve your presentation? Can you add props, costumes, or music? Keep practicing until you feel comfortable. Then act out your scene for the rest of the class.

♪)) Speaking SKILL

Face the audience when you speak to the other actors. If you turn away from the audience too much, people may not be able to hear or understand you.

► COMPREHENSION  Workbook Page 181

Demonstrate your comprehension of the play by responding to the questions.

Recall

1. Where is the annex located? How are its **occupants** hidden from the outside world?

2. What did the Franks do to create the impression that they left their apartment in a hurry?

Comprehend

3. What kinds of items did the families bring with them to the annex?

4. In what ways do the families disregard Nazi **regulations**?

Analyze

5. Why do you think Anne calls the van Pels the "van Daans" in her diary?

6. Why do you think the playwrights created a play based on Anne's diary?

Connect

7. Do you keep a diary? If so, what do you write about?

8. Have you or someone you know ever been discriminated against due to your race, culture, or religion? What happened? How did you feel?

Reading Skill

Make sure you recognize the difference between information questions and *yes/no* questions so you can answer questions appropriately. *Yes/no* questions often begin with words *does/do, is/are, was/were,* or *has/have.*

▶ DISCUSSION

Discuss in pairs or small groups.

1. When the Germans invaded Holland, how did life change for Anne and her family?

2. What dangers did Miep and Mr. Kraler have to face as they **assisted** the families?

Q **What is the human spirit?** Would you be willing to help others in need even if it was dangerous for you to do so? Why or why not? Do you think we have a responsibility to help others? Explain.

Listening SKILL

Listen for implicit ideas, or ideas that are not stated directly. Pay attention to the speaker's tone of voice, gestures, and expressions. They are clues to the speaker's implicit ideas.

▶ RESPONSE TO LITERATURE

Workbook Page 181

Utilize You have learned about Anne Frank's diary. Now create a diary entry of your own. Write the date at the top of the page. Include your own personal thoughts and opinions, as well as things that happened to you. Use descriptive language. Then share your entry with a partner.

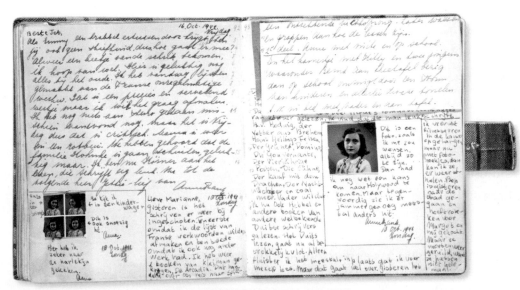

▲ Text and photos from Anne Frank's diary

Grammar

Present Perfect

You can use the present perfect to show that an action began at a specific time in the past and continues into the present. Form the present perfect with *has* or *have* and the past participle. Form questions by switching *has* or *have* and the subject. Form the negative with *hasn't* or *haven't*. Use the preposition *for* to describe the period of time that the action has been going on; use the preposition *since* to show the time or date in the past when the action began.

Grammar SKILL

For regular past participles, add *-d* or *-ed* to the base form of the verb. Other past participles are irregular and must be memorized.

> We **have lived** in the Secret Annex **for over two years**. We've lived here **since 1942**.

You can also use adverbs with the present perfect. Notice that *just, ever,* and *never* appear midsentence; *yet* and *before* appear at the end; *already* can come either place.

> The Dutch have **just** surrendered. [shows recently finished action]
> Have the Dutch surrendered **yet**? [asks about recent action]
> They've **already** surrendered. [responds in the affirmative]
> They haven't surrendered **yet**. [responds in the negative]
> Have you **ever** done anything illegal? [asks about your life up until now]
> Yes, I've done something illegal **before**. [responds in the affirmative]
> No, I've **never** done anything illegal. [responds in the negative]

Practice
Workbook Page 182

Work with a partner. Use the words below and the prepositions and adverbs above to write sentences in the present perfect.

Example: she / finish / the book? *Has she finished the book yet?*

1. The snow / start
2. you / see / this movie?
3. The cat / not eat / his dinner.
4. We / be / to the museum.
5. Rachel / live / there / 2002.

 GRAMMAR CHECK

How do you form the negative of the present perfect?

Apply

In your notebook, write five statements about something you have or haven't done in the past. Share your statements with a partner. Take turns asking each other questions about your past.

352 Unit 5

Present Perfect Progressive

The present perfect progressive is used to show the duration of an action that began in the past and continues into the present. You can use the prepositions *for* and *since* or the adverb phrases *all morning, all day long*, etc., to show this. Form the present perfect progressive with *has* or *have* + the past participle *been* + the present participle (*-ing* form of the verb).

> How long **have** you **been living** in the Secret Annex?
> We**'ve been living** here **for two years**. / We**'ve been living** here **since 1942**.

You can also use the present perfect progressive without a specific mention of time to show a general activity in progress recently or lately.

> Father **has been talking** about going into hiding.
> I**'ve been writing** in my diary a lot lately.

When using verbs like *teach*, *work*, *study*, and *live* with *for* or *since*, you can use either the present perfect progressive or the present perfect. The meaning is the same.

> We**'ve been living** here for two years. / We**'ve lived** here for two years.

Practice

Workbook
Page 183

Work with a partner. Copy the sentences into your notebook. Complete the sentences with the present perfect or present perfect progressive.

Example: *It's been snowing* (snow) all day, and it is still coming down.

1. I _____ (study) all night, and I'm still not finished.
2. He _____ (write) to them three times and they haven't responded yet.
3. I've _____ (study) English for two years.
4. Pam _____ (not be) to Europe before.
5. I _____ (consider) getting a dog, but I'm not sure it's a good idea.

Apply

Work with a partner. Interview your partner about his or her English studies.

Example: How long have you been studying English?

Writing

Write a Persuasive Paragraph

You have learned about different forms of persuasive writing. Now you will write a persuasive paragraph. Begin your paragraph by introducing a topic you feel strongly about. Clearly state your opinion on the issue. Support your opinion with facts and details. Anticipate opposing opinions and tell why they are incorrect. Conclude your paragraph by restating your opinion in a new way. Use strong words that will appeal to your readers' emotions.

> **Writing Prompt**
>
> Write a paragraph about an issue you feel strongly about. Be sure to use the simple past and the present perfect correctly.

1 PREWRITE Begin by choosing an issue that you feel strongly about.

- Think about why you feel strongly about this topic.

- What reasons can you give to support your opinion?

- Why might others disagree with your opinion?

- List your ideas in a graphic organizer like the one below.

Here's a pros-and-cons chart created by a student named George telling his opinion about whether it was right to publish Anne Frank's Diary.

Pros	Cons
Publishing helps millions of readers to better understand the tragedy of war. Editing personal passages respects Anne's privacy	Publishing private thoughts disrespects Anne's privacy. Editing any personal passages is wrong.

2 **DRAFT** Use your pros-and-cons chart to help you write a first draft.

- First, explain the issue.
- State your opinion and give supporting reasons.
- Include reasons why other people might disagree with you and say why you think they are wrong.

3 **REVISE** Read over your draft. Look for places where the writing is unclear or needs improvement. Use the Writing Checklist to help you identify problems. Then revise your draft, using the editing and proofreading marks listed on page 458.

4 **EDIT** Check your work for errors in grammar, usage, mechanics, and spelling. Trade papers with a partner to obtain feedback. Use the Peer Review Checklist on Workbook page 184. Edit your final draft in response to feedback from your partner and your teacher.

5 **PUBLISH** Prepare a clean copy of your final draft. Share your persuasive paragraph with the class. Save your work. You'll need to refer to it in the Writing Workshop at the end of the unit.

Writing Checklist

ORGANIZATION:
☑ I presented both sides of the argument.

VOICE:
☑ I clearly stated my opinion and gave supporting reasons for it.

Here is George's paragraph. Notice how he clearly states his opinion, supports it, and presents both sides of the argument.

George Delgrosso

The Diary of Anne Frank

I think Anne Frank's father, Otto Frank, was right to publish his daughter's diary. It is an important personal description of events as they happened during World War II. The diary reminds us about the awful effects of war and serves as an educational tool in schools around the world. However, not all people share these views. Some people believe Mr. Frank was disrespectful in publishing Anne's private thoughts. But many people do not know that Mr. Frank edited Anne's diary before it was published. He did not include pages that he thought were too personal and private. He respected his daughter and, in publishing her story, has inspired millions of people around the world.

Prepare to Read

What You Will Learn

Reading
- Vocabulary building: *Context, dictionary skills, word study*
- Reading strategy: *Identify main idea and details*
- Text type: *Informational text (social studies)*

Grammar
Present perfect and past perfect

Writing
Write a letter to the editor

 THE BIG QUESTION

What is the human spirit? Each of the five senses—sight, hearing, taste, smell, and touch—provides information about the world around us. Work with a partner. Copy the chart below into your notebook. Write three more items under each heading that you perceive with that sense. What is the importance of each sense? How would you react to the world differently if you lost one or more of these senses? What effect would this have on your spirit? Discuss with a partner.

Sight	Hearing	Taste	Smell	Touch
car	CD	lemon	flower	cotton ball

 BUILD BACKGROUND

You will read a nonfiction magazine article called **"Listen Up"** about the football team from the California School for the Deaf-Riverside (CSDR).

CSDR gives hearing-impaired students a chance to succeed in academics and athletics. Over 500 students attend CSDR. They range in age from eighteen months to twenty-two years old.

One of the school's goals is to teach their students that being hearing-impaired does not have to limit what they can do. The school's football team is a perfect example of this. Although they are not able to hear each other, the players have learned how to work as a team and how to believe in themselves—even in the face of opposition.

► VOCABULARY

Listening and Speaking: Key Words

Read these sentences. Use the context to figure out the meaning of the highlighted words. Use a dictionary to check your answers. Then write each word and its meaning in your notebook.

Key Words

accomplish
hearing impaired
mission
obstacle
opponent
sign language

1. We worked hard to accomplish our goal, and we were successful.

2. The team members are hearing impaired. They either cannot hear at all or are unable to hear well.

3. Our school's mission is to support students in academics and in sports.

4. The other team plays well. It is our only obstacle to winning the state title.

5. If we defeat our opponent, we will be the new champions.

6. The coaches use sign language to converse with their players. Each hand movement they use has a special meaning.

Practice

Write the sentences in your notebook. Choose a word from the box above to complete each sentence. Then take turns reading the sentences aloud with a partner.

1. Members of the debate team set goals and then work hard to _____ them.

2. Two team members were unable to participate. This was an _____ the team had not planned for.

3. The debate team lost to its _____ .

4. The team's _____ is to give all students a chance to play.

5. Because he is _____, Andrew didn't hear the teacher call his name.

6. People who cannot hear often use _____ to communicate with each other.

▲ Two women converse using sign language.

Listening and Speaking: Academic Words

Study the **red** words and their meanings. You will find these words useful when talking and writing about informational texts. Write each word and its meaning in your notebook. After you read "Listen Up," try to use these words to respond to the text.

participate = take part in an activity or event	→	Many students **participate** in after-school clubs and activities.
perceive = understand or think about something in a particular way	→	We use our senses to **perceive** the world around us.
prior = before	→	The team had a poor record **prior** to the coach's arrival. Then their performance improved.
team = a group of people who compete against another group in a sport, game, etc.	→	There are many players on Andrea's basketball **team**.

Practice

Workbook Page 186

Work with a partner to answer these questions. Try to include the **red** word in your answer. Write the sentences in your notebook.

1. In what kinds of school sports or clubs do you **participate**?

2. Which senses would you use to **perceive** a bouncing basketball?

3. Are there any special exercises you perform **prior** to playing a sport?

4. Have you ever been part of a **team**? If so, what kind?

Word Study: Antonyms

Antonyms are words that have the opposite or nearly opposite meanings from each other. For example, the antonym for the word *above* is *below*, and the antonym for *fast* is *slow*. Knowing antonyms can help build your vocabulary, and it also helps you to figure out the meanings of unfamiliar words.

> At first all they did was **lose** games, then they learned how to **win**.
> The crowd made a lot of **noise**, but all the players heard was **silence**.

Practice

Copy the chart below in your notebook and complete it by yourself. Then share your answers with a partner. Did you find the same antonyms? Check a thesaurus to see if there are other antonyms for each word.

Word	Antonym
forward	
doubt	
failure	
divide	
beginning	
strength	

READING STRATEGY | **IDENTIFY MAIN IDEA AND DETAILS**

Identifying the main idea and details in a reading helps you see key points the author is making. The main idea is the most important idea in the text. The details are small pieces of information that support the main idea. To identify the main idea and details, follow these steps:

- Read the first paragraph. What do you think is the most important idea?

- Read the whole text. Look for examples, facts, dates, and sentences that tell more about the main idea. These are the details.

- Remember that the main idea may be at the beginning, in the middle, or at the end of a paragraph.

As you read "Listen Up," identify the main idea of each paragraph and of the whole article. Then find details that support those main ideas.

READING 4

INFORMATIONAL TEXT

SOCIAL STUDIES

Set a purpose for reading In what ways can others help to strengthen our sense of self and lift our spirits? As you read, identify the people who made a difference to the CSDR team and how they did so.

Audio

LISTEN UP

Phil Taylor

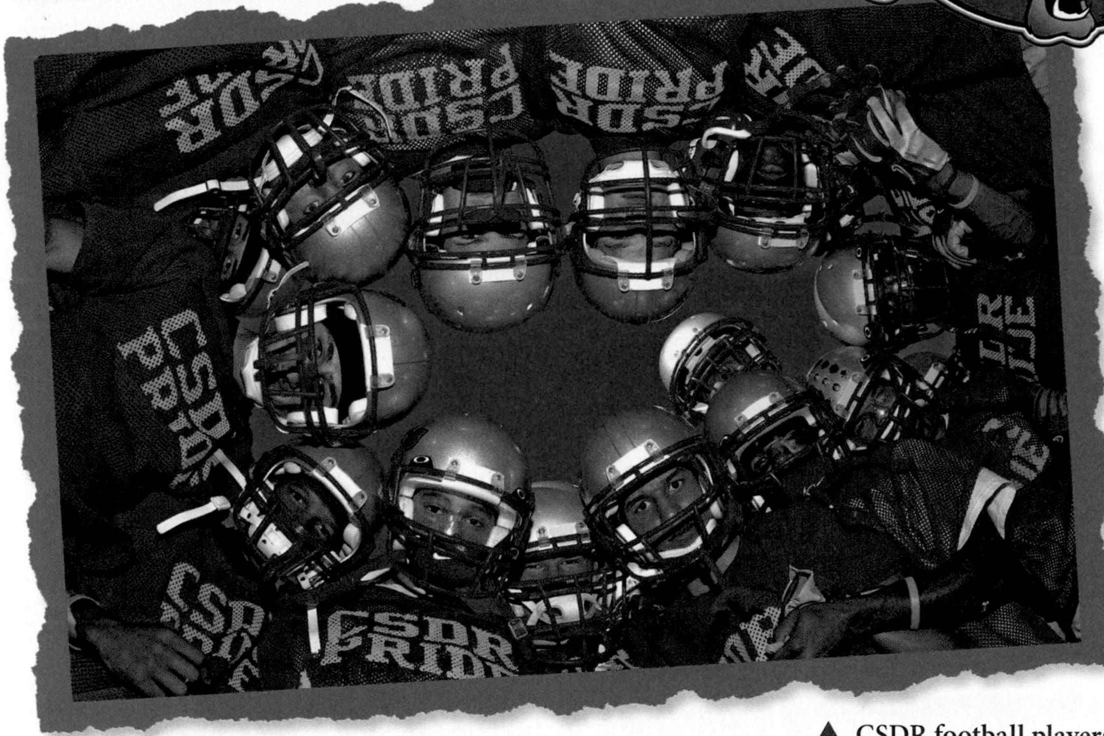

▲ CSDR football players

The sounds of high school football surrounded player Selwyn Abrahamson as he grabbed the football and ran upfield. There was the crash of **pads** as he **tackled** an opponent. There were the cheers of **fans**. There was the referee's whistle when he scored a **touchdown**. But Abrahamson heard only one thing:

Silence.

Abrahamson plays football for the California School for the Deaf-Riverside (CSDR). He and his teammates live in a quiet world. They cannot hear the words and noises that most of us **take for granted**.

---

pads, thick pieces of material players wear to protect their bodies
tackled, forced to the ground
fans, people who support a sports team

touchdown, play in football during which a team scores six points
take for granted, accept without question

But part of the school's mission is to teach students that being hearing impaired doesn't have to limit what they can accomplish in life. The **varsity** football team is proof of that.

The CSDR Cubs play against hearing and hearing-impaired schools. CSDR's entire team and all of its **coaches** are hearing impaired. Their comments for this story were made through a **sign-language interpreter**.

"We want to be known as a great team," says head coach Keith Adams. "Not a great deaf team; just a great team."

The Program

The Cubs are well on their way to becoming a great team. They finished with nine wins and one loss in 2004.

---

varsity, main team that represents a school in sports
coaches, people who give special lessons to a team
sign-language interpreter, person whose job is to put the words of sign language into spoken language

"I think we proved to other teams that they can't expect to beat us just because we have a hearing impairment," says senior player Gary Sidansky. "We proved some things to ourselves, too. If we can be this good at football, we can be just as good at anything else."

Losers to Winners

A lack of hearing isn't the only obstacle CSDR's football program has had to overcome. From 1998 through 2000, the Cubs won a total of two games. Players skipped practice whenever they felt like it. Those who did attend often went through **drills** at half-speed.

"The players didn't have any **pride** in themselves," said defensive coach Kaveh Angoorani. "I think their attitude was, 'We're not going to win anyway, so why should I show up on time? Why should I practice hard?'"

---

drills, activities repeated often for practice
pride, feeling of satisfaction

◀ A player runs from his opponents.

BEFORE YOU GO ON

1. What makes the CSDR football team unique?
2. What is the mission of CSDR?

On Your Own
Do you like American football? Why or why not?

Reading 4 **361**

▲ A coach uses hand signals to communicate with a player.

That all changed when a new coach, Len Gonzales, took over in 2001. Gonzales played football at CSDR in the 1980s and 1990s. He went on to play at Gallaudet, a college for the hearing impaired in Washington, D.C.

Gonzales and his coaching staff brought more **structure** to the program. They insisted on off-season weight-lifting sessions. They also took the players to summer football camps. The extra work helped the players develop their skills and **bond** as a team.

The results weren't obvious overnight. CSDR didn't win any games during Gonzales's first season. But the Cubs began to show signs of improvement. They won five out of ten games in 2002.

In 2003, they won four games. Gonzales left before the winning 2004 season for family reasons. But Adams has continued to build on the **foundation** that Gonzales established.

Special Communication

Opponents used to count on an easy victory when they played CSDR. Not anymore. Now coaches from opposing teams try to learn the Cubs' signals.

Figuring out the team's system of communication isn't easy. CSDR uses a combination of American Sign Language and its own code, designed by the coaches, to call **plays**. The coaches signal the play to sophomore Mark Korn with

structure, organization or discipline
bond, understand and trust one another

foundation, basic idea
plays, actions of someone in a game or sport

hand gestures from the **sidelines**. Korn then **relays** the play to the team in the **huddle**. During the play, Korn taps the **center** when it's time to pass the ball. The other players go when they see the center make the pass.

The Cubs ask for no special treatment from their opponents. They request only that the referees wave their arms as well as blow their whistles to signal the end of a play. "There's really not that much difference between the way one of our games operates and the way a game between two hearing teams would operate," says Adams.

---

sidelines, parts of the football field where coaches and players who are not in the game stand
relays, shares information about
huddle, gathering of players to talk briefly about what they are going to do next
center, player who tosses the ball to his teammate at the beginning of every play

▼ Fans cheer for the team.

Loud and Clear

Even though the Cubs can't hear noise, they can make it. The players and coaches **whoop** and **holler** during the games—as do their cheerleaders, who are also students at CSDR. But even some of the cheering is done through sign language. It's not unusual to look in the **stands** at a game and see fans holding both arms straight up in the air and wiggling their fingers—the sign language gesture for **applause**.

"You don't have to be able to hear to know when you've done a good job," says senior player Bobby Neil.

You also don't have to hear to feel like a winner. At California School for the Deaf-Riverside, that message comes through loud and clear.

---

whoop, shout supportively
holler, yell or shout
stands, sections where fans sit to watch a game
applause, clapping to show support

BEFORE YOU GO ON

1 How do the team members communicate with each other and with their coaches?

2 What request does the CSDR team make before each game? Why?

On Your Own
Do you think you would be able to participate in a sport without your sense of hearing? Explain.

➤ COMPREHENSION

Workbook
Page 189

Recall

1. What kinds of teams does CSDR play against?
2. What obstacles has the football program had to overcome?

Comprehend

3. What was the team's record from 1998 through 2000? What was it from 2000 through 2004?
4. How did the team change after Len Gonzales was hired?

Analyze

5. Why did the CSDR coaches design their own codes to call plays?
6. How do you think the author feels about the CSDR football team?

Connect

7. Name one goal you have had to work hard to achieve.
8. Did your attitude influence the outcome of that goal? Explain.

➤ IN YOUR OWN WORDS

Work with a partner. Copy the chart below into your notebook. Complete the chart with main ideas and details from the article "Listen Up." Then use this information to summarize the article for your partner.

Head	Main Idea	Detail(s)
The Program		
Losers to Winners		
Special Communication		
Loud and Clear	Even though the Cubs can't hear noise, they can make it.	Players, coaches, and cheerleaders yell during the games.

▶ DISCUSSION

Listening TIP

Be patient. Give the speaker enough time to express his or her ideas clearly.

Discuss in pairs or small groups.

1. Why do you think opponents used to count on an easy victory when they played against CSDR?

2. Would you want to attend a CSDR football game? Why or why not?

Q **What is the human spirit?** What did Coach Adams mean when he said, "We want to be known as a great team. Not a great deaf team; just a great team." How is this an example of the human spirit?

▶ READ FOR FLUENCY

Reading with feeling helps make what you read more interesting. Work with a partner. Choose a paragraph from the reading. Read the paragraph. Ask each other how you felt after reading the paragraph. Did you feel happy or sad?

Take turns reading the paragraph aloud to each other with a tone of voice that represents how you felt when you read it the first time. Give each other feedback.

▶ EXTENSION

Work with a partner. Use the Internet or library to learn more about people, like the CSDR football players and those listed below, who have overcome disabilities to accomplish great things. Present your findings to the class.

- Ray Charles
- Itzhak Perlman
- Stephen Hawking
- Marlee Matlin
- Heather Whitestone

Ray Charles ▶

Grammar

Present Perfect with *for* and *since*

The present perfect is formed with *have/has* + past participle. Writers use the present perfect with *for* or *since* to talk about an action that started in the past and continues into the present.

Use *for* to tell about a period of time in the past. Use *since* to tell about a specific period of time in the past.

> The Cubs have been a winning team **for** three years.
> The Cubs have been a winning team **since** last year.

You can also use the present perfect with adverbs to talk about when or how often something has happened in the past. Look at the examples below.

> I have **always** been a fan of the Cubs.
> He has **often** gone to the games.
> Have you **ever** seen them play? No, I **never** have.
> They've **recently** played against that team.
> They've won 3 out of 6 games **so far**.

Practice

Workbook
Page 190

Copy the sentences below into your notebook. Choose the correct word to complete each sentence. Share your work with a partner. Take turns reading the sentences to each other.

1. We have been big fans (for / always) the last three years.

2. Tim Carson has kicked twelve field goals (for / since) the season began.

3. Mrs. Carson has seen every game (still / so far).

4. Has the team (ever / always) lost a game?

5. The team has (never / for) played well.

6. The players have (so far / never) missed a practice.

Past Perfect

You can use the past perfect to tell about events that happened in the past.

> Between 1998 and 2000, the Cubs **had won** a total of two games.

You can use the past perfect with the simple past to tell about two events. The clause in the past perfect tells about an earlier event. The clause in the simple past tells about the event that came later.

They **had lost** many games   before they **got** a new coach.   **NOW**
|—————————————————|———————————————————|

Form the past perfect with *had* + the past participle. For regular past participles, add *-d* or *-ed* to the base form of the verb. Other past participles are irregular and must be memorized. Form the negative of the past perfect with *had not* or *hadn't* + the past participle. For questions, switch *had* and the subject.

> The crowd **had cheered** as they **watched** the game.
> **Had** they **won** many games before 2002? No, they **hadn't**.

Practice  Workbook Page 191

Work with a partner. Copy the sentences into your notebook. Complete each sentence with the simple past or the past perfect of the verbs in parentheses.

Example: Susan _threw_ (threw) away the letter after she _had read_ (read) it.

1. By the time she _____ (be) twenty, she (live) _____ in four countries.

2. Before her sixth birthday, Jane _____ (not be) to the zoo.

3. Pat _____ (live) in Seattle before he _____ (move) to Austin.

4. The game _____ already _____ (start) when we _____ (arrive).

5. I _____ (remember) later that I _____ (forgot) to lock the door.

Apply

Work with a partner. Complete the sentence starters with your own ideas.

1. I had never . . . before I . . .
2. Before this year, I
3. By the time . . . , I . . . .
4. Before I spoke English, I . . .

Reading 4 **367**

Grammar SKILL

The contraction *'d* is used only with pronouns.
He'd already gone.
NOT *His father'd already gone.*

✔ **GRAMMAR CHECK**

*When do you use the **past perfect** and when do you use the **simple past**?*

Writing

Ongoing Writing Skills Practice

Write a Letter to the Editor

People write letters to editors of newspapers or magazines to express their opinions about a topic. Sometimes a letter to the editor includes an idea for solving a problem or improving something within the community. Now you will write a letter to the editor. Begin your letter by stating the issue that concerns you. Then give your opinion on the issue. Provide facts and/or examples to support your opinion. Conclude by restating your opinion in a strong and persuasive way.

> ### Writing Prompt
>
> Write a letter to the editor of your school or local newspaper about an issue you feel strongly about in your school or community. Express your opinion clearly. Support your point of view with facts and/or examples. Be sure to use the present perfect correctly.

1 **PREWRITE** Begin by choosing an issue in your school or local community. Why are you writing to the editor?

- Write the issue at the top of the page in your notebook.

- Think about why you feel strongly about it. Why do you want change?

- Think of reasons to support your opinion.

- Write your ideas in a graphic organizer like the one here.

Here's a word web created by a student named Ari. He is writing about why he thinks girls should be allowed to play football in school.

Fact
Only boys are allowed to play on the football team.

Opinion
Girls should be allowed to play on the football team.

Fact: Girls should be given a chance to prove themselves

Fact: Not allowing girls on the team sends the wrong message about gender equality

Workbook Page 192

2 **DRAFT** Use your word web to help you write a first draft.

- Explain the issue and then present your opinion of it.
- Provide facts and examples to support your opinion.
- Use the past perfect.

3 **REVISE** Read over your draft. Look for places where the writing is unclear or needs improvement. Use the Writing Checklist to help you identify problems. Then revise your draft, using the editing and proofreading marks listed on page 458.

4 **EDIT** Check your work for errors in grammar, usage, mechanics, and spelling. Trade papers with a partner to obtain feedback. Use the Peer Review Checklist on Workbook page 192. Edit your final draft in response to feedback from your partner and your teacher.

5 **PUBLISH** Prepare a clean copy of your final draft. Share your letter to the editor with the class. Save your work. You'll need to refer to it in the Writing Workshop at the end of the unit.

Writing Checklist

IDEAS:
- ☑ I stated the issues clearly.

ORGANIZATION:
- ☑ I supported each statement with facts and/or examples.

Here is Ari's letter. Notice how he clearly states his opinion and supports it with facts and examples.

October 8, 2010

To the Editor,

    I am writing about our school's football program. Currently, only boys are allowed to play. I believe that girls should be able to try out for positions on the team. Since the early 1970s, girls have earned spots on school football teams. These athletes proved that females are just as capable of running, kicking, catching, and passing as their male teammates. And although these girls faced many challenges—coaches and other players had often teased them and treated them unfairly before they succeeded in proving their ability—this hasn't prevented future generations of girls from wanting to play. I think the girls in our school should be given a similar chance to prove themselves. By not allowing girls to try out, our school is sending the wrong message about gender equality.

          Sincerely,
          Ari Janoff

Link the Readings

Critical Thinking

Look back at the readings in this unit. Think about what they have in common. They all tell about the human spirit. Yet they do not all have the same purpose. The purpose of one reading might be to inform, while the purpose of another might be to entertain or persuade. In addition, the content of each reading relates to the human spirit differently. Now copy the chart below into your notebook and complete it.

Title of Reading	Purpose	Big Question Link
From *César Chávez: We Can Do It!*		*One man works to make the lives of others better.*
"The Scholarship Jacket"	*to entertain*	
From *The Diary of Anne Frank: The Play*		
"Listen Up"		

Discussion

Discuss in pairs or small groups.

- How is Mr. Schmidt in "The Scholarship Jacket" similar to Miep and Mr. Kraler in the excerpt from *The Diary of Anne Frank: The Play*?

- **Q** **What is the human spirit?** What character traits did the people in the stories share? How do these character traits reflect the strength of the human spirit?

Media Literacy & Projects

Work in pairs or small groups. Choose one of these projects.

1 Create a large "human spirit timeline" in your classroom. Use the Internet to do research. Draw pictures of people or groups whose lives and work have reflected the human spirit throughout history. Write a short paragraph that tells why each person or group belongs on the timeline.

2 Present a "Human Spirit Award" to someone in your school. Write a persuasive argument telling why the person you chose deserves the award. Read your argument to the class and take a vote. Invite the winner to your classroom and present that person with the award.

3 Interview someone in your community or in your school who has worked hard to help others. Before conducting your interview, prepare a list of questions to ask. If possible, invite the person to your school so that your class can ask questions. If this is not possible, use a tape recorder to be sure you do not miss anything. Share your interview with the class.

Further Reading

Choose from these reading suggestions. Practice reading silently for longer periods with increased comprehension.

The Last of the Mohicans, James Fenimore Cooper
This Penguin Reader® is an adaptation of the classic tale of adventure and struggle on the North American frontier.

The River, Gary Paulsen
Two years before this story begins, teenager Brian Robeson survived in the wilderness for fifty-four days with only a hatchet. Now he agrees to go back into the wilderness to teach a government worker how to survive.

Who Was Harriet Tubman? Yona Zeldis McDonough
Born a slave in Maryland, Harriet Tubman knew first-hand what it meant to be someone's property. After the Civil War brought an end to slavery, this amazing woman's long, rich life was proof of what just one person can do.

Put It All Together

LISTENING & SPEAKING WORKSHOP

Radio Commercial

You and a partner will create and present a radio commercial.

1 THINK ABOUT IT When you listen to the radio, you hear commercials. The purpose of a commercial is to persuade listeners to buy a product, attend an event, or support a cause. Radio commercials are very short: They typically last just thirty seconds or a minute.

Work in pairs to develop a list of products, events, or causes you could advertise in a radio commercial. These may be real or imaginary. For example:
- A new type of cell phone
- A community theater production
- A local fundraiser

2 GATHER AND ORGANIZE INFORMATION With a partner, choose a topic from your list. Then make notes about what to include in your radio commercial. What persuasive words could you use? What details should you use to describe the product, event, or cause? What sound effects or music would make your commercial interesting and memorable?

Research / Reflect If your topic is a real product, event, or cause, go to the library, talk to an adult, or conduct research on the Internet to get more information about it. Take notes on what you find. If your product, cause, or event is imaginary, make up the details that you will need to describe it. Use a dictionary or thesaurus to find persuasive language you can use.

Order Your Notes Study your notes. Decide which arguments, examples, and supporting details you will include in your commercial. Write each one on a separate note card. Choose the best order for presenting your ideas, and number your cards in that order.

Prepare a Script Use your note cards to write a script for your radio commercial. To make your script richer and more interesting, use a variety of grammatical structures, sentence lengths, sentence types, and connecting words. Also, be sure to start your commercial in a way that will catch the audience's attention.

3 **PRACTICE AND PRESENT** With your partner, choose which parts of the script each of you will each present. Remember, a radio audience can't see gestures or visuals, so you must convey your message with your words and tone of voice. Practice in front of a friend or family member, or record yourself and listen to the recording. If you are using recorded sound effects, check that your equipment works and that you can use it easily.

Deliver Your Radio Commercial Give your presentation from the back of the room so your classmates can hear but not see you—as if you were actual radio announcers. Emphasize persuasive words by changing the volume or tone of your voice. Slow down when you come to the most important points.

4 **EVALUATE THE PRESENTATION** You will improve your skills as a speaker and a listener by evaluating each presentation you give and hear. Use this checklist to help you judge your commercial and those of your classmates.

- ☑ Was the purpose of the commercial clear?
- ☑ Did the speakers persuade you to buy the product, attend the event, or support the cause? Why or why not?
- ☑ Could you hear and understand the speakers easily?
- ☑ Did the speakers make effective use of tone of voice, music, and sound effects?
- ☑ What suggestions do you have for improving the radio commercial?

 Speaking SKILLS

Learning Strategy: If you can't remember a specific word, try to define it, use other words to describe it, or use a synonym.

Use sound effects, music, and your tone of voice to catch the listeners' attention.

 Listening SKILLS

What is the speaker trying to persuade you to do? If you don't understand, seek clarification. Ask questions at the end of the presentation.

Listen for information that would make you want to buy the product, attend the event, or support the cause. Try to remember the important details.

 STRENGTHEN YOUR SOCIAL LANGUAGE

Writing a script helps you learn basic vocabulary and language structures. Go to www.LongmanKeystone.com and do the activity for this unit. This activity will require you to use and reuse basic language in other meaningful writing activities.

WRITING WORKSHOP

Persuasive Speech

Write a Persuasive Speech

In persuasive writing, the writer expresses an opinion and tries to convince others to agree with it. A speech is one form of persuasive writing. Speechwriters aim to persuade listeners to think or act a certain way. A strong persuasive speech begins with a paragraph that clearly states the writer's opinion. The speech gives reasons, facts, and examples that support the writer's position. Speechwriters also present both sides of an issue. Then they explain why they think opposing arguments are incorrect. A persuasive speech concludes with a paragraph that restates the writer's opinion in a new and memorable way. Speechwriters often use strong, persuasive words to appeal to their listeners' feelings.

> ### Writing Prompt
> Write a five-paragraph speech that tries to persuade your audience to agree with your opinion on an issue that concerns you.

1 **PREWRITE** Review your previous work in this unit. Brainstorm a list of possible topics for your speech in your notebook. Choose the issue that most interests you. In your notebook, answer these questions:

- What do you think is an important issue in your school or community?

- What is your opinion and how can you convince others to agree with you?

- What action would you like your listeners to take after hearing your speech?

Use a pros-and-cons chart to organize your ideas. In the *Pros* column, give arguments that support your opinion. In the *Cons* column, give arguments that oppose your opinion, so that you can respond to them in your speech.

A student named George decided to write a persuasive speech about the importance of volunteering. Here is the pros-and-cons chart he created:

Pros	Cons
Important to volunteer A way to help other individuals and the community Can meet new people and learn a lot	Not enough time to volunteer No local places to volunteer

2 **DRAFT** Use your pros-and-cons chart and the model on page 378 to help you write a first draft.

- Remember to introduce your topic in the first paragraph. Say why it is important.
- State your opinion and give supporting details.
- Explain why others might disagree with you and say why you think they are wrong.
- Write a concluding paragraph that restates your opinion in a memorable way.

3 **REVISE** Read over your draft. Think about how well you have addressed questions of purpose, audience, and genre. Your purpose is to persuade. Is your speech clearly organized? Is it appropriate in content and tone for the intended audience? Did you include details that will persuade your audience to agree with you? Read your speech aloud to hear how it sounds.

Keep these questions in mind as you revise your draft. Use the Writing Checklist below to help you identify additional issues that may need revision. Mark your changes on your draft using the editing and proofreading marks listed on page 458.

SIX TRAITS OF WRITING CHECKLIST

☑ **IDEAS:** Do I present both sides of the issue?

☑ **ORGANIZATION:** Do I support my opinion with reasons, facts, and examples in an order that makes sense?

☑ **VOICE:** Does my writing show my feelings about the issue?

☑ **WORD CHOICE:** Do I use persuasive words that will appeal to listeners?

☑ **SENTENCE FLUENCY:** Do my sentences flow well when read aloud?

☑ **CONVENTIONS:** Does my writing follow the rules of grammar, usage, and mechanics?

Here are the revisions George plans to make to his first draft.

The Importance of Volunteering

After disasters such as major hurricanes, people often join together
to assist the victims_{who have suffered losses}. Whether through food drives, clothing drives, or
soup kitchens, the efforts of volunteers have helped individuals and
communities recover from times of darkness. By volunteering and
taking time out of <u>your</u> day to do something beneficial for others, <u>you</u>
can be that one person who changes someone's life_{for the better}.

Many people I know volunteer out of "the goodness of their
hearts. Some also volunteer at more than one place. A few of the
organizations that welcome volunteers to work _{for} them include the
Salvation Army, People to People, and meals on Wheels, as well as
some hospitals, libraries, soup kitchens, and thrift shops
For example You might choose to visit the elderly or to assist at a daycare
center. As a volunteer you might find yourself aiding families who are
coping with everyday problems. Volunteers can also be called upon
to provide support to a community in a time of crisis. For example,
emergency situations can require immediate action by a large number
of volunteers to assist in running shelters or delivering food.

Revised to make the tone more persuasive.

Revised to add a missing preposition.

Edited to improve logical sequence of ideas and to introduce a transition word.

Many people don't volunteer because they "can't find the time," or because they "~~do not~~ don't have any local organizations to contact".I believe that if they really wanted to help out, they could probably make the time in their schedules or travel a small distance out of their way. Volunteering is important! It not only helps others but also benefits the person who volunteers! As a volunteer, <u>you</u> can meet new people and learn new things. I been a volunteer for several years, and it is a very rewarding experience.

¶ *Why don't you explore volunteer opportunities in your community today?* Volunteering is a way to show the good inside of you. When you harness this good, it can be used to change your life and the life of another.

Edited to correct an error in mechanics, add a missing preposition, and to use contraction appropriate to spoken language.

Revised to make the ending more dynamic and memorable.

4 **EDIT** Check your work for errors in grammar, usage, mechanics, and spelling. Then trade papers with a partner and use the Peer Review Checklist below to give each other constructive feedback. Edit your final draft in response to feedback from your partner and your teacher.

Workbook Page 193

PEER REVIEW CHECKLIST

- ☑ Was the writer's opinion clearly presented?
- ☑ Was the opinion supported with details and facts?
- ☑ Did the writer present both sides of the argument?
- ☑ Did the writer give reasons for not agreeing with the opposing opinion?
- ☑ Did the concluding paragraph sum up the main points in a memorable way?
- ☑ What changes could be made to improve the essay?

Look at the next page to see the additional changes George plans to make when he prepares his final draft.

George Delgrosso

The Importance of Volunteering

After disasters such as major hurricanes, people often join together to assist the victims who have suffered losses. Whether through food drives, clothing drives, or soup kitchens, the efforts of volunteers have helped individuals and communities recover from times of darkness. By volunteering and taking time out of <u>your</u> day to do something beneficial for others, <u>you</u> can be that one person who changes someone's life for the better.

Many people I know volunteer out of "the goodness of their hearts." Some also volunteer at more than one place. A few of the organizations that welcome volunteers to work for them include the Salvation Army, People to People, and meals on Wheels, as well as some hospitals, libraries, soup kitchens, and thrift shops.

As a volunteer, you might find yourself aiding families who are coping with everyday problems. For example, you might choose to visit the elderly or to assist at a daycare center. Volunteers can also be called upon to provide support to a community in a time of crisis. For example, emergency situations can require immediate action by a large number of volunteers to assist in running shelters or delivering food.

Many people don't volunteer because they "can't find the time," or because they "don't have any local organizations to contact." I believe that if they really wanted to help out, they could probably make the time in their schedules or travel a small distance out of their way. Volunteering is important! It not only helps others but also benefits the person who volunteers! As a volunteer, <u>you</u> can meet new people and learn new things. I have been a volunteer for several years, and it is a very rewarding experience.

Why don't you explore volunteer opportunities in your community today? Volunteering is a way to show the good inside of you. When you harness this good, it can be used to change your life and the life of another.

Revised to correct errors in mechanics.

Revised to correct an error in punctuation.

Revised to use the present perfect correctly.

5 PUBLISH Prepare a clean copy of your final draft. Share your speech with the class.

Workbook
Page 194

Test Preparation

PRACTICE

Read the following test sample. Study the tips in the boxes. Work with a partner to choose the best words to complete the sentences.

History Report

Today students are reading about what they will need to do to complete a report for a history class. The selection below is about preparing to present the report.

1   After you have finished your research, you are ready to create note cards. You will use the note cards to remind you of the information you found. This lets you talk about your ___1___, instead of reading the entire report. This makes your presentation more interesting to listen to.

2   The note cards should each give an important fact about this ___2___ in history. Add details about the fact on the card. Do not write in complete sentences. Just write phrases that will remind you of what to say.

3   After you write all of your note cards, put them in order. You can group your cards by ___3___ ideas, or you can put them in time order. Make sure that the grouping of the ideas will make sense to your audience.

4   Practice giving your report more than once. You should speak for five minutes. If you cannot speak that long, you need more information in your report. If you do not know what to say about a fact, add more details to your note cards. Ask friends or adults to listen to your presentation. Then let them tell you if anything was ___4___.

1	A	person		3	A	similar
	B	project			B	interesting
	C	present			C	faithful
	D	public			D	concerned

2	F	group		4	F	undone
	G	alarm			G	unclear
	H	watch			H	unopened
	J	period			J	untied

Workbook Pages 195–198

Everyday Obstacles, Everyday Courage

The media often shows dramatic images that celebrate the human spirit, for example, a photograph of a space shuttle blasting off. But the power of the human spirit plays out in everyday actions as well. Many American artists have celebrated these less obvious examples of courage.

Residents of Bourbon County, Kentucky, *Fan Quilt, Mt. Carmel* (1893)

Splendid fans of many colors parade across this quilt. A group of women from Paris, Kentucky, made it more than 100 years ago. They pieced together different types of brightly colored fabric into forty-two separate squares. Then they sewed in the names of 110 men and women who lived in their county. The fan shapes are certainly fun, but not unusual for a quilt from this time period. The fact that so many people worked together to create this one quilt is wonderful proof of the community spirit they shared.

Residents of Bourbon County, Kentucky, *Fan Quilt, Mt. Carmel*, 1893, mixed media, 85 x 72¼ in., Smithsonian American Art Museum ▶

Daniel Chester French, *Spirit of Life* (1914)

In *Spirit of Life*, a young woman with wings raises a basin in her left hand and a pine branch in her right. Daniel Chester French, one of America's most famous sculptors, made this small sculpture in bronze as a model for a larger work. He planned to have water flow from the basin. French made the sculpture as a memorial for a businessman who had built health resorts in Saratoga Springs, New York. *Spirit of Life* marks a death by celebrating life.

Michael Olszewski, *Speaking to Hear* (1989)

In *Speaking to Hear*, artist Michael Olszewski places two small panels side by side. He wants to show how difficult it can be to tell two sides of a story from two different points of view. The panels are made from silk, a delicate fabric. Olszewski then used complicated stitching and embroidery to represent the words of a conversation.

In the left panel, Olszewski painted alternating orange and black stripes like a flag across the center of the silk. Then he added a solid red band down the middle. He reverses these images in the panel on the right. The two pieces seem to represent people coming from two different directions. But there's a feeling that the two "sides" are working toward some kind of understanding.

▲ Daniel Chester French, *Spirit of Life*, 1914, bronze, 30 x 34⅞ in., Smithsonian American Art Museum

▲ Michael Olszewski, *Speaking to Hear*, 1989, silk, parts A and B: both 22½ x 21¼ in., Smithsonian American Art Museum

These artworks offer wonderful examples of artists working in all sorts of ways to capture and honor the spirit and courage that people show in their everyday lives.

Discuss What You Learned

1 How does each artwork relate to the idea of courage?

2 What kind of artwork would you create to illustrate how people face everyday obstacles with courage?

Big Question

Why do you think an artist might be interested in courage and the human spirit?

Workbook Pages 199–200

UNIT 6

THE BIG Q QUESTION

How does the sky influence us?

This unit is about the sky. In it, you will read both literary and informational texts about space. Reading about this topic will give you practice using academic language and will help you become a better student.

Reading

1 Letter and Poems

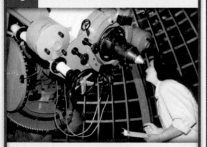

- "Starry Nights"
- "Stars" by Sara Teasdale
- "Escape at Bedtime" by Robert Louis Stevenson

Reading Strategy:
Analyze text structure 2

2 Myth

"The Girl Who Married the Moon" retold by Joseph Bruchac and Gayle Ross

Reading Strategy:
Read for enjoyment

3 Science

- "Return to the Moon" by Christy Brownlee
- "No Need to Establish a Moon Base" by Matt Kachur

Reading Strategy:
Take notes

Listening and Speaking—Expository

At the end of this unit, you will choose a topic and deliver an **oral report** about it.

Writing—Expository

In this unit you will learn about the elements of a **research report,** a kind of expository writing in which you present information that you have studied in depth.

Quick Write

In your notebook, write a few sentences about the ways in which you think the sky influences us.

4 | **Science**

"Solar Energy—Help from the Sky"

Reading Strategy:
Connect ideas

DVD **VIEW AND RESPOND**
Watch the DVD for Unit 6 and answer the questions at
www.LongmanKeystone.com.

Prepare to Read

What You Will Learn

Reading
- Vocabulary building: *Literary terms, word study*
- Reading strategy: *Analyze text structure 2*
- Text type: *Literature (letter and poetry)*

Grammar
Punctuation: semicolons; Punctuation: colons

Writing
Write an introductory paragraph

THE BIG QUESTION

How does the sky influence us? For centuries, the night sky has been a subject explored in both science and art. Why do you think people are so fascinated by the night sky? Work with a partner to answer this question. Then use your prior knowledge to make a list of objects that you can see in the night sky. Share your list with the class. Combine your answers to create a class list.

LEARNING STRATEGY

Use your prior knowledge. Relating what you already know to a new topic will make it easier to understand new meanings in English.

► BUILD BACKGROUND

In this section, you will read an article called **"Starry Nights."** It is about Vincent van Gogh, a troubled artist who lived from 1853–1890. Van Gogh was fond of writing letters. You will read an excerpt from one of the letters that he wrote to his sister, Wilhelmina. In it, van Gogh describes how his painting of a starry night differs from those of other painters.

You will also read two poems: **"Stars"** by Sarah Teasdale and **"Escape at Bedtime"** by Robert Louis Stevenson. Both poems describe the stars in the night sky, but do so in different ways.

▲ A self-portrait by Vincent van Gogh

► VOCABULARY

Learn Literary Words

A **stanza** is a group of lines in a poem that are usually similar in length and pattern. Stanzas are separated by spaces. A stanza is like a paragraph of poetry. It states and develops a single main idea. For example, read the stanza below from the poem "Stars."

> And a heaven full of stars
> Over my head.
> White and topaz
> and misty red.

Sometimes the words in a stanza rhyme. **Rhyme** is the repetition of sounds at the ends of words. Poets use rhyme to create a song-like quality to their verses and to emphasize certain words and ideas. Many poems contain end rhymes, or rhyming words at the ends of lines. Reread the poem above. Notice how *head* and *red* is an example of an end rhyme.

LEARNING STRATEGY

Use words that you already know to learn new and essential language, or words that you must know in order to understand your schoolwork.

Practice
Workbook
Page 201

Read the poem "Canis Major" about the constellation of the same name. How many stanzas are there? What is the main idea of each stanza? Circle the rhyming words.

> The great Overdog
> That heavenly beast
> With a star in one eye
> Gives a leap in the east.
>
> He dances upright
> All the way to the west
> And never once drops
> On his forefeet to rest.
>
> I'm a poor underdog,
> But to-night I will bark
> With the great Overdog
> That romps through the dark.
> —*Robert Frost*

Listening and Speaking: Academic Words

Study the **red** words and their meanings. You will find these words useful when talking and writing about literature. Write each word and its meaning in your notebook, then say the words aloud with a partner. After you read "Starry Nights," "Stars," and "Escape at Bedtime," try to use these words to respond to the texts.

analyze = examine or think about something carefully in order to understand it	➡	Most artists **analyze** their subjects before painting them.
image = a picture that you can see through a camera, on a television, in a mirror, etc.	➡	The **image** of the child in the painting is very lifelike.
interpretation = an explanation of the meaning or significance of something	➡	My **interpretation** of the painting is different from yours. You think the painting looks realistic; I disagree.
visible = something that can be seen	➡	The stars in the painting are barely **visible**.

Practice

Work with a partner to answer these questions. Try to include the **red** word in your answer. Write the sentences in your notebook.

1. **Analyze** the painting on the right.
2. What does the **image** represent?
3. What is your **interpretation** of the painting?
4. Are any objects **visible** in the painting? If so, what are they?

City in Shards of Light by
Carolyn Hubbard-Ford ▶

Word Study: Lexical Sets

Lexical sets are sets of words that describe a central idea. For example, a lexical set for the word *light* includes the following words: *bright, brilliant, dazzling, illuminated, radiant, sparkling,* and *starry*. Read the lexical sets below.

dark	dim, gloomy, murky, shadowy
fast	fleeting, quick, rapid, speedy, swift
loud	deafening, ear-splitting, harsh, noisy, shrill, strident

Practice

Workbook
Page 203

Work with a partner. Copy the chart below into your notebook. Take turns reading the words in the chart. Create a lexical set for each word. Include at least three words in each set.

beautiful	
slow	
strong	
sweet	

READING STRATEGY | ANALYZE TEXT STRUCTURE 2

Analyzing text structure can help you understand what kind of text you're reading. It can also help you to set a purpose for reading. To analyze the text structure of a poem, follow these steps:

- Look for lines and groups of lines, called stanzas.

- Be aware that punctuation doesn't always follow the same rules in poetry as it does in other types of text.

- Notice how the poet uses commas, dashes, periods, or line breaks to show you where to pause.

Review the text structures of "Stars" and "Escape at Bedtime." Discuss them with a partner.

Workbook
Page 204

Set a purpose for reading As you read the letter and study the painting, think about how van Gogh's thoughts influenced his art. Then read the poems. How do the poets' descriptions of the stars differ?

Starry Nights

Audio

Vincent van Gogh was born in 1853 in Holland. He became a painter when he was in his twenties and moved to France in 1886. Van Gogh spent the last years of his life in the south of France, painting landscapes and people. He suffered from **mental illness** and was confined at various times to mental hospitals, where he continued to paint until his death in 1890. Van Gogh sold only one painting during his lifetime. Today a van Gogh painting is worth millions of dollars. One of van Gogh's most famous paintings is called *Starry Night*.

Vincent van Gogh often wrote letters to his siblings. Some of these letters have been preserved in museums and are available for viewing. Following is an excerpt of a letter Vincent sent to his sister, Wilhelmina. In it, he describes painting the picture *Café Terrace on the Place du Forum, Arles, at Night*.

---

mental illness, a sickness relating to the mind

▼ *Starry Night* by Vincent van Gogh

Arles, 9 and 16 September 1888

My dear sister,

Your letter gave me a great deal of pleasure, and today I have the leisure to calmly reply. . . .

*At present I absolutely want to paint a starry sky. It often seems to me that night is still more richly colored than the day; having **hues** of the most intense violets, blues, and greens. If only you pay attention to it you will see that certain stars are lemon-yellow, others pink or a green, blue and forget-me-not brilliance. And without my **expatiating** on this theme it is obvious that putting little white dots on the blue-black is not enough to paint a starry sky. . . .*

*In point of fact I was interrupted these days by my **toiling** on a new picture representing the outside of a café at night. On the **terrace** there are the tiny figures of drinkers. An immense yellow lantern illuminates the terrace, the **façade** and the sidewalk, and even casts its light on the pavement of the streets, which takes a pinkish violet tone. The **gables** of the houses in the street stretching away under a blue sky spangled with stars are dark blue or violet with a green tree. Here you have a night picture without black in it, done with nothing but beautiful blue and violet and green, and lemon-yellow. It amuses me enormously to paint the night right on the spot. They used to draw and paint the picture in the daytime after the **sketch**. But I find satisfaction in painting the thing immediately. . . .*

▲ *Café Terrace on the Place du Forum, Arles, at Night* by Vincent van Gogh

hues, colors
expatiating, speaking or writing in detail about a particular subject
toiling, working hard
terrace, patio
façade, front or outside of a building
gables, top, triangular parts of walls
sketch, drawing

BEFORE YOU GO ON

1 How many paintings did van Gogh sell in his lifetime? How is this different from how they sell today?

2 How does the **image** of stars in van Gogh's work differ from the traditional representation of stars as white dots in a black sky?

💡**On Your Own**
Do you like van Gogh's paintings? Why or why not?

Reading 1 **389**

Stars

Sara Teasdale

Alone in the night
On a dark hill
With **pines** around me
Spicy and still,

And a heaven full of stars
Over my head,
White and **topaz**
And misty red;

Myriads with beating
Hearts of fire
That **aeons**
Cannot **vex** or tire;

Up the dome of heaven
Like a great hill,
I watch them marching
Stately and still,
And I know that I
Am honored to be
Witness
Of so much **majesty**.

> ✔ **LITERARY CHECK**
> *How many stanzas
> are in this poem?*

---

pines, tall trees common in
    North America
topaz, yellow-brown
myriads, uncountable
    numbers
aeons, very long periods
    of time
vex, bother
majesty, impressive or
    beautiful quality

ABOUT THE POET

Sara Teasdale (1884–1933) most often composed poetry about love, the beauty of nature, and death. Her poems became especially popular during the early twentieth century. In 1918, Teasdale's work was recognized, and she was awarded the Columbia University Poetry Society Prize, later known as the Pulitzer Prize for Poetry.

Escape at Bedtime

Robert Louis Stevenson

The lights from the **parlour** and kitchen shone out
Through the **blinds** and the windows and bars;
And high overhead and all moving about,
There were thousands of millions of stars.
There **ne'er** were such thousands of leaves on a tree,
Nor of people in church or the Park,
As the crowds of the stars that looked down upon me,
And that **glittered** and winked in the dark.
The Dog, and the **Plough**, and the Hunter, and all,
And the star of the **sailor**, and Mars,
These shown in the sky, and the pail by the wall
Would be half full of water and stars.
They saw me at last, and they chased me with cries,
And they soon had me packed into bed;
But the glory kept shining and bright in my eyes,
And the stars going round in my head.

---

parlour, living room
blinds, objects that cover windows
ne'er, never
glittered, were very shiny
plough, farmer's tool
sailor, person who works on a ship

ABOUT THE POET

Robert Louis Stevenson (1850–1894) was a Scottish poet, novelist, and essayist. Some of his best-known works are *Treasure Island* and *Kidnapped* (novels) and *A Child's Garden of Verses* (a collection of poetry).

✔ **LITERARY CHECK**
Read the last four lines of the poem. Which words **rhyme**? *Do you notice a pattern?*

BEFORE YOU GO ON

1 How does the person in the poem "Stars" feel about stars?

2 In the poem "Escape at Bedtime," what are the Dog, the Plough, and the Hunter?

💡**On Your Own**
How do you feel when you look at stars?

Reading 1 **391**

Review and Practice

➤ DRAMATIC READING

One of the best ways to understand a poem is to memorize it. Work in groups of four. Reread, discuss, and interpret "Stars," giving one another feedback and support. Then work together to interpret any difficult words or phrases in the poem. Use a dictionary or ask your teacher for help if necessary.

  After you have examined the poem carefully, assign one of the poem's stanzas to each member of the group. Memorize your assigned stanza. Then come back together as a group to recite the entire poem. Comment on one another's oral recitation and make helpful suggestions for improvements. You can even hold a contest in which each group within your classroom competes for the best oral recitation.

➤ COMPREHENSION  Workbook Page 205

Recall

1. Where and when was Vincent van Gogh born?

2. How old was van Gogh when he became a painter?

Comprehend

3. Name two different van Gogh paintings.

4. In van Gogh's letter to his sister, what colors does he claim to use in his most recent painting?

Analyze

5. Why do you think van Gogh was not able to sell more than one painting in his lifetime?

6. Why do you think his paintings sell for millions of dollars today?

Connect

7. Have you ever seen a van Gogh painting at a museum? If so, which one?

8. Van Gogh thought that the night is more richly colored than the day. Would you agree? Explain.

▶ DISCUSSION

Discuss in pairs or small groups.

1. How are the two van Gogh paintings you read about similar? Give your own brief **interpretation** of one of these paintings.

2. Analyze the two poems "Stars" and "Escape at Bedtime." How are they different? Are they similar in any way?

Q How does the sky influence us? Would you rather talk to a scientist who studies the stars or a poet who writes about them? Why?

▶ RESPONSE TO LITERATURE

Workbook
Page 205

Utilize You read two poems that describe stars. Now, with a partner, write your own poem about the night sky. Your poem should contain three stanzas and words that rhyme. Read your completed poem aloud to your classmates.

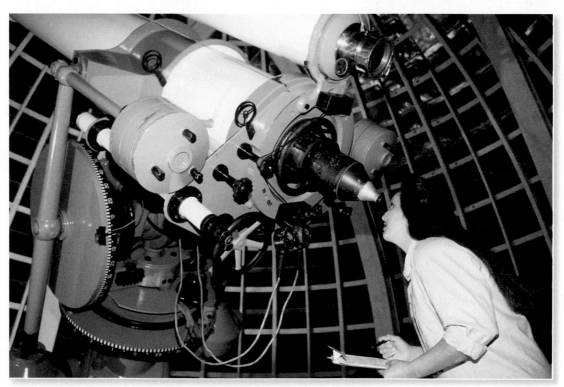

▲ An astronomer looking at the night sky through a telescope

Grammar

Punctuation: Semicolons

A semicolon (;) can be used instead of a period or a coordinating conjunction to connect two independent clauses (complete sentences) that are closely related. When a semicolon is used, the coordinating conjunction is usually dropped. Often a semicolon is used before a clause that begins with a conjunctive adverb or transition. Remember to use a comma after the adverb or transition.

> In 1853, van Gogh was born**;** in his twenties, he became a painter.
> He believed night was rich with colors**; therefore**, he didn't use black in *Starry Night*.
> He suffered from mental illness**; as a result**, he was confined to mental hospitals.

Items in lists are usually separated with commas. However, if the items themselves contain commas, then semicolons can be used.

> He painted the stars yellow, pink, and green**;** the sky blue and violet**;** and the trees green.

Practice  Workbook Page 206

Work with a partner. Rewrite the sentences below, adding semicolons.

Example: He was very hungry, so he finished the chicken.
He was very hungry; he finished the chicken.

1. Our cat ran away this morning, and we looked for her all afternoon.

2. Pia exercises a lot. Consequently, she's in great shape.

3. Frank heard a car. However, it wasn't **visible**.

4. I felt sick. Therefore, I stayed home.

5. He loves school. He never misses class.

Apply

Work with a partner. Look at the first two paragraphs of the reading on page 388. Find sentences that you can combine with semicolons. Write them in your notebook using semicolons.

Punctuation: Colons

A colon (:) must come after an independent clause (complete sentence), never in the middle. A colon is often used before a list.

Grammar SKILL

When a colon is used before a list, the list begins with a lowercase letter.

> independent clause
>
> He painted the sky with many colors: yellow, pink, green, blue, and violet.
>
> NOT He painted the sky with: yellow, pink, green, blue, and violet.

A colon is also used when an appositive, or explanation, is introduced. The appositive may be a word, phrase, or a clause. If it is an independent clause, it begins with a capital letter.

> Van Gogh wanted to paint the sky in a different way: He painted without using black.

Practice

Work with a partner. Put a check (✓) next to the sentences that contain correct punctuation. Put an X next to the incorrect sentences. Add proper punctuation and capitalization to the incorrect sentences and write them in your notebook.

✔ **GRAMMAR CHECK**

Give one example of a situation in which you might use a colon.

Example: ___X___ My favorite subjects are: biology, math, and English.
These are my favorite subjects: biology, math, and English.

1. _____ You have only one choice finish your test.
2. _____ In the bag were the following: a pen, a notebook, and a cell phone.
3. _____ There are two students left: Mary and Jack.
4. _____ We need three kinds of drinks, juice, mineral water, and soda.
5. _____ Spain is very clean country, there is no trash on the beaches.

Apply

Work with a partner. Copy the independent clauses with colons into your notebook. Then complete the sentences with your own ideas.

Example: There are three sports I love: *swimming, running, and skiing.*

1. There are three sports I love: _____.
2. I have to do one thing today: _____.
3. These are my favorite desserts: _____.
4. I've learned one thing this year: _____.

Writing

Write an Introductory Paragraph

At the end of this unit, you will write a research report. First, you will learn how to begin such a report. Then you will conduct research and write an introductory paragraph.

   After you have completed your research, you can write the introductory paragraph for your report. The paragraph should introduce the research topic with an interesting question or fact.

> **Writing Prompt**
>
> Select a topic related to space. Narrow the topic and ask a question to guide your research. After conducting your research, write an introductory paragraph. Be sure to use correct punctuation.

1 **PREWRITE** Begin by choosing a topic related to space.

- Make a list of topics and choose one that is most interesting to you. For example, you might choose to write about stars.

- To narrow your topic further, ask a question: *How do stars form?*

- After you identify the question you want to answer, begin your research.

- Write your ideas in a graphic organizer such as an inverted pyramid.  **Workbook Page 208**

Here's a pyramid created by a student named Ari. He is writing an introductory paragraph to a research report about the life of a star.

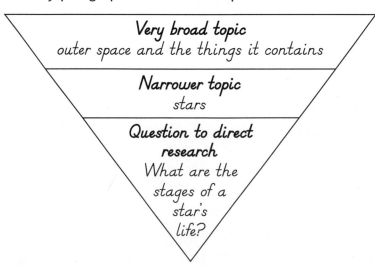

Very broad topic
outer space and the things it contains

Narrower topic
stars

Question to direct research
What are the stages of a star's life?

2 DRAFT Use your pyramid to help you write a first draft.

- Keep in mind your purpose for writing.
- Begin with an interesting question.
- Explain why your research topic is interesting.
- Explain what your research report will be about.
- Remember to check punctuation.

3 REVISE Read over your draft. Look for places where the writing is unclear or needs improvement. Use the Writing Checklist to help you identify problems. Then revise your draft, using the editing and proofreading marks listed on page 458.

4 EDIT Check your work for errors in grammar, usage, mechanics, and spelling. Trade papers with a partner to obtain feedback. Use the Peer Review Checklist on Workbook page 208. Edit your final draft in response to feedback from your partner and your teacher.

5 PUBLISH Prepare a clean copy of your final draft. Share your introductory paragraph with the class. Save your work. You'll need to refer to it in the Writing Workshop at the end of the unit.

Writing Checklist

ORGANIZATION:
☑ I began by introducing the question that directed my research.

CONVENTIONS:
☑ I used semicolons and colons correctly.

Here is Ari's introductory paragraph to a research report about the life of a star. Notice how he begins his paragraph with an interesting question.

Ari Janoff

The Life of a Star

This question has always interested me: What are the stages of a star's life cycle? Because the stars look the same night after night, you might not know that they change at all. In fact, a Greek philosopher named Aristotle believed that stars were made of a special, unchanging material that was found only in space. However, within the last hundred years, astronomers have learned that, like people, stars do experience a limited life cycle: All stars are born in the same way, they may shine for millions or billions of years, and then they die. The size of a star determines how long it will live; size also determines the stages it will experience. These stages are described in detail within the paragraphs that follow.

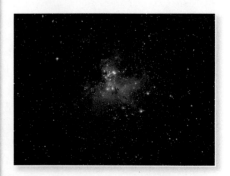

Prepare to Read

What You Will Learn

Reading
- Vocabulary building: *Literary terms, word study*
- Reading strategy: *Read for enjoyment*
- Text type: *Literature (myth)*

Grammar
Capitalization and punctuation of titles; Punctuation: hyphens and dashes

Writing
Include paraphrases and citations

 THE BIG QUESTION

How does the sky influence us? What would life be like for humans without the sun? How do both the sun and the moon influence life on Earth? Use your prior knowledge to discuss these questions with a partner.

➤ **BUILD BACKGROUND**

In this section, you will read a myth called **"The Girl Who Married the Moon."** Myths are very old, fictional stories that are passed down from one generation to the next. They were often created to explain things about the natural world.

"The Girl Who Married the Moon" is about a group of people called the Alutiiq, also known as Eskimo people. The early Alutiiq lived in large villages on Kodiak Island, near Alaska. The women of these villages were responsible for gathering food and sewing clothes. Women were therefore thought to be important to their group's survival.

The Alutiiq were also known for masking, or carving the likenesses of ancestors, animals, and mythological beings into wood or bark.

As you read "The Girl Who Married the Moon," pay attention to how these cultural features are reflected in the story.

◀ A man carves a traditional Native Alaskan mask.

➤ VOCABULARY

Learn Literary Words

A **myth** is a short fictional tale. Myths explain the origins of elements of nature. Their purpose is to entertain and instruct. Every ancient culture has its own mythology that is passed from generation to generation as part of the oral tradition. Read the myth below. Try to determine which natural event it tries to explain.

Literary Words
myth
personification

> Once there was a Mexican people who loved the sun. The sun liked to be near them, and every day he slowly moved closer to Earth. Soon, Earth became too hot for the people on Earth to bear. They begged the sun to move higher into the sky, but he did not want to leave them.
>
> Then, one day, a boy offered to travel high into the sky with the sun, so that he would not be lonely. Soon, the pair were traveling higher and higher into the sky together, and that is where they have been ever since.

Sometimes, **personification** is used in myths. Personification gives human qualities to nonhuman animals or things. What nonhuman thing is personified in the myth above? What human qualities does it have?

Practice

Workbook
Page 209

Work with a partner. Take turns reading the examples of personification below. Identify the object being personified and the human qualities it has.

1. The sunflowers nodded their yellow heads in the summer breeze.
2. Throughout the night, thunder grumbled and growled.
3. The trees shivered in the winter cold.
4. I can hear raindrops dancing on the rooftop.
5. The moon peeked over the treetops.
6. I saw the lamp as it winked at me through the window.

Listening and Speaking: Academic Words

Study the **red** words and their meanings. You will find these words useful when talking and writing about literature. Write each word and its meaning in your notebook, then say the words aloud with a partner. After you read "The Girl Who Married the Moon," try to use these words to respond to the text.

ignored = did not pay attention to someone or something	→	I **ignored** the noisy students as I read the story.
instructed = taught or showed someone how to do something	→	Our teacher **instructed** us to visualize the events as they happened in the story.
job = a particular duty or responsibility that you have	→	My **job** is to research the origins of the myth online. My partner will write the report.
restricted = not allowed to do something	→	Students are **restricted** from using the computer for more than one hour at a time.

Practice

Workbook
Page 210

Write the sentences in your notebook. Choose a **red** word from the box above to complete each sentence. Then take turns reading the sentences aloud with a partner.

1. Her _____ was to collect the books after class and return them to the library.

2. The librarian _____ her to place the books on the counter.

3. She was _____ from using the books for more than one class period at a time.

4. She _____ the rules and kept the book for two days.

Word Study: Spelling Long *i*

In "The Girl Who Married the Moon," you will read many words that have the long *i* sound. There are several ways to spell this sound. Read the information in the chart below for some examples.

Spelling Long *i*			
i_e	-igh	-y	i
like	night	sky	island
wife	brightly	why	climb
admire	might	cycle	kind
mile	high	rely	final

Practice

Work with a partner. Copy the chart above into your notebook. Say a word from the chart, and ask your partner to spell it aloud. Then have your partner say the next word. Continue until you can spell all of the words correctly. Now practice spelling these words with your partner: *side, blind, fry, fright*. Add them to the chart under the correct headings.

READING STRATEGY | **READ FOR ENJOYMENT**

Reading for enjoyment is important because it gives you a purpose for reading and improves your ability to read for specific information. When you read for fun, you may learn new words and ideas that you will see again in nonfictional texts. To read for enjoyment, follow these steps:

- Before you read, remember that your main purpose is reading for enjoyment. You will be learning, too, but this is mainly for fun.
- Pay attention to the characters, settings, and illustrations. Think about how they increase your enjoyment of the text.
- Stop from time to time and think about the reason you enjoyed a particular passage or chapter.

As you read "The Girl Who Married the Moon," focus on the characters and setting. Ask yourself, "How does the author make this fun, interesting, or exciting for me to read?"

Set a purpose for reading As you read, pay attention to the characters' **jobs**. How do these **jobs** influence us?

The Girl Who Married THE MOON

Retold by Joseph Bruchac and Gayle Ross

Long ago, in the village of Chiniak, on the island of Kodiak, there were two **cousins**.

They had reached the age when they could choose a husband. Both of them had just been given the chin **tattoos** that showed they were now women. Both of them were strong and good-looking, and they were so well liked that almost any young man would have agreed to marry them. In fact, some **elders** said that these girls might easily choose—as did some of the women—to each have two husbands. Yet none of the young men in the village of Chiniak or any of the other villages on the island or even the nearby mainland interested those cousins.

---

cousins, relatives whose parents are siblings
tattoos, designs that are permanently put onto the skin
elders, rulers of a village or tribe

When the night had come and the work of the day was done, those two girls would always go down to the beach to play together in the sand and watch for the rising Moon above the water. As soon as he began to show his face, they would turn over their **kayak** and sit, leaning back against it, admiring the moon's beauty. They spent all their time at night staring at the sky. Whether it was winter or summer, they could always be found there on the beach.

One night, one of the girls said, "I have fallen in love with the Moon."

"I have fallen in love with the Moon, too," said the other girl. "If he ever comes down to earth, I will marry him."

Their parents worried about them when they heard that the two girls wished to marry the Moon. But no one told them to stop going to the beach at night.

---

kayak, canoe

BEFORE YOU GO ON

1 Describe the cousins. Why do they go to the beach every night?

2 How do the girls feel about the Moon?

On Your Own
The girls were given chin tattoos to symbolize their becoming young adults. Was there a particular way in which you celebrated this occasion? Explain.

Reading 2 **403**

As they watched the Moon crossing the sky one night,
it disappeared behind some heavy clouds.

"Why does the Moon have to hide his face so early
in the night?" one cousin complained.

"Yes," said the other cousin, "I wish he would show himself again.
I wish he would come here and choose one of us to marry him."

Suddenly they heard the sounds of footsteps on the gravel of the
beach and the voice of a young man.

"You have been saying that you love me," the voice said. "I have
come to marry you."

The two girls leapt to their feet. A tall, handsome man wearing
a beautiful mask on his face stood before them. That mask shone
brightly, and they knew they were looking at the Moon.

"Yes," said the girls. "We will marry you."

"My work is hard," Moon said, "and I can take only one wife.
I will take the one who is the most **patient**."

"We have always done everything together," said the girls.
"You must take us both."

"Then you must close your eyes," Moon said. "Do not open them
until I tell you."

The girls closed their eyes and waited. Moon reached down and
held each of them by the long hair on their head, lifting them up
into the air. The two cousins felt their feet leave the ground and they
felt the wind whistling by them. They kept their eyes closed as they
had been told, but when a long time passed, one of the girls
became impatient.

---

patient, willing to wait for something

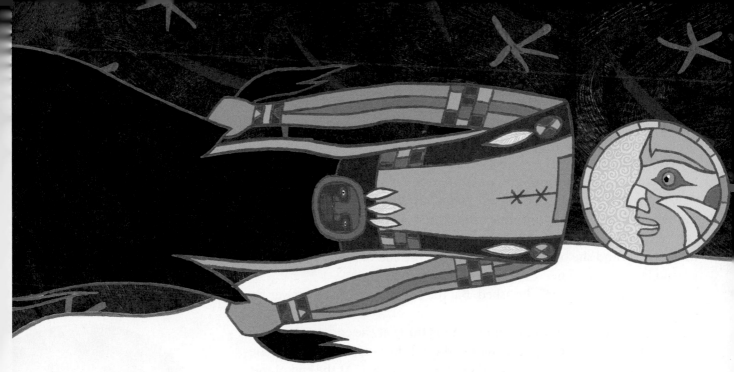

I must see where we are going, she thought. I will just open one eye a little.

But as soon as she opened her eye, she found herself falling down and landing back on the beach alone. Her long hair was gone from her head, and her cousin was gone from her forever.

The other girl, though, did not open her eyes. All through the night, she kept her eyes closed as Moon crossed the sky. When he told her to open her eyes at last, she found herself standing in Moon's house on the other side of the sky.

At first, she was happy to be the wife of Moon.

"Go wherever you wish," her husband told her. "Only do not look behind the blanket and go into my storehouse."

Moon's wife agreed. She would do as her husband said. She settled down to her new life in the land on the other side of the sky, but it was not always easy. Sometimes her husband would spend a long time with her. Sometimes he would be gone all night and then sleep all day after he came home. She never knew when he was going to go or how long he would be gone. Soon she became **bored**.

---

bored, tired and impatient

BEFORE YOU GO ON

1 Whom did Moon drop? Why?

2 Moon **instructed** his wife not to go into his storehouse. Why doesn't she obey him?

On Your Own
Are you a patient person? Explain.

"Why must you always leave me?" She said to her husband. "Why is it that you come and go in such a strange way?"

"It is the work I must do," said Moon. "That is why I cannot always be with you."

"Can I go with you when you do your work?"

"No," said Moon, "my work is too hard. You must stay home and be happy when I am with you."

Moon's wife listened, but she was not happy. That night when her husband left, she began to **wander** about the land on the other side of the sky. She walked farther and farther and came to a place where she saw many trails, and she began to follow one. At the end of that trail, she saw a person lying facedown.

"What are you doing?" she asked. But the person would not answer her or look her way.

She tried more trails and found the same thing at the end—a person lying facedown. And each time she asked what the person was doing, she received no answer. At last she could stand it no longer. At the end of the next trail she took, when she found a person lying down, she began to **poke** the person with her foot.

"Answer me," she said. "Answer me, answer me. What are you doing?"

Finally the person turned and looked at her. She saw he had only one bright eye, sparkling in the middle of his face. "I am working," the person said. "Do not bother me."

When Moon's wife returned home, her husband had not come back. She sat down to wait, but she was still bored. She looked around and saw his **storeroom**, with a dark woven blanket covering the door.

---

wander, walk slowly without having a clear direction or purpose
poke, quickly push someone or something
storeroom, room where goods are kept

✔ **LITERARY CHECK**
*What examples of **personification** exist in this story?*

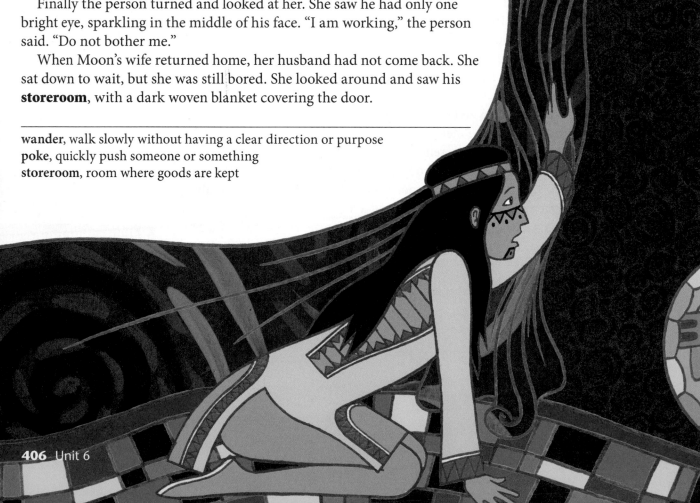

"It will not hurt to take one small look," she said. "Moon is my husband, and I should be able to go wherever I want in our house."

Then she went to the floor and pulled aside the blanket. There in the storeroom were the pieces of light her husband wore when he crossed the sky. There was a half-moon, a **quarter** moon, and all the other phases. The only one missing was the full moon, which her husband had worn when he left that evening. The pieces of light were so beautiful that Moon's wife could not resist.

---

quarter, one-fourth

BEFORE YOU GO ON

1 Why does Moon's wife become impatient?

2 What does Moon's wife find in the forbidden room?

On Your Own
If you were Moon's wife, would you disobey his orders? Explain.

Reading 2 **407**

"I must try on one of them," she said, "to see how my husband feels when he is carrying them across the sky."

She reached down and picked up the one that was almost full and placed it on her face. As soon as she did so, it stuck there. She tried to remove it, but it would not budge. Although she wept and cried, the piece of moon would not come off. Then she heard her husband's steps coming across the sky.

She climbed into their bed and covered her head with a blanket.

"What is wrong?" Moon asked.

"I have a pain on my face," said his wife. "I do not feel well. Leave me alone."

But Moon became **suspicious**. He went to his storeroom and saw that one of the pieces of light was gone. He went back to his wife and pulled the covers from her head.

"Husband," Moon's wife said, "I became bored while you were gone. I tried on this piece of moon and now it is stuck."

Then Moon laughed. He laughed and laughed. And with careful hands, he pulled that piece of moon from her face.

"What else have you done today?" Moon said, still laughing.

His wife told him about following the many trails that led to people lying with their faces down and with a single bright eye in each of their heads.

"Those people are the stars," Moon said. "They should not be bothered while they are doing their work. It is clear to me that you need work to do also, my wife. Since you have shown that you are able to carry the moon you can help me. From now on, I will carry the pieces of moon each **cycle** until it is full, and then you can carry the pieces of moon until it is dark. That way, we will both have time to rest and neither of us will grow bored."

So it is to this day. The man of the moon carries the pieces of light from the time of the moon's first quarter until it is full, and the woman of the moon carries them from the time it is full until the moon grows dark. So they share the **duty** of carrying light across the sky.

✔ **LITERARY CHECK**
What event in nature does this myth explain?

---

suspicious, doubtful
cycle, series of the moon's phases
duty, task

ABOUT THE **AUTHORS**

Joseph Bruchac grew up in Upstate New York with his Native American grandparents, from whom he learned traditional stories and the art of storytelling. Today, in addition to writing and storytelling, he works to preserve the culture of his people, the Abenaki.

Gayle Ross learned the art of storytelling from her grandmother. Today Ross writes about those myths and legends and shares them at schools and colleges across the country. Most often, she tells the stories of her father's people, the Cherokee. Ross is directly related to John Ross, who was chief of the Cherokee nation during the "Trail of Tears."

BEFORE YOU GO ON

1 How does Moon react when he learns his wife entered the storeroom?

2 Who were the people Moon's wife spoke to during her walk? What were they doing?

On Your Own
Did you like this myth? Why or why not?

▶ READER'S THEATER

Act out the following scene with a partner.

Audio

Moon: What's wrong?

Wife: My face hurts. I don't feel good.

Moon: Why? What happened while I was gone?

Wife: [*covering her face with her hands*] I was bored while you were away, so I tried on this piece of moon and now it won't come off.

Moon: [*laughing as he pulls the piece of moon off his wife's face*] What else did you do today?

Wife: I took a walk, and I saw the strangest thing—there were people with only one eye that sparkled in the middle of their faces.

Moon: Those people are the stars—you shouldn't bother them when they're working. It seems like you need some work to do. From now on, you'll help me carry the moon across the sky.

Workbook
Page 213

Did you understand the myth? If not, reread it with a partner. Then answer the questions below.

Recall

1. Where did the two cousins live?

2. Why was Moon's wife unhappy?

Comprehend

3. What did Moon's wife do when she became bored?

4. Which two pieces of light were not in the storeroom when Moon returned home?

Analyze

5. Why do you think Moon told his wife that she was **restricted** from going into his storeroom?

6. What do you think the authors' purpose was in telling this story?

Connect

7. Can you name all of the moon's phases? If not, which ones do you know?

8. What other myths do you know? What are they about? How do they explain objects or events in the natural world?

➤ DISCUSSION

Discuss in pairs or small groups.

1. Moon's wife **ignored** one aspect of Moon's job when she first married him. What was this, and how did it affect her?

2. Do you think patience is a good quality for a person to have? Explain.

Q How does the sky influence us? Why do you think ancient peoples had myths about natural occurrences?

Workbook Page 213

➤ RESPONSE TO LITERATURE

Utilize Like "The Girl Who Married the Moon," many myths explain natural events and occurences. Write your own myth. Illustrate your story. Then share it with the class.

»))) *Listening* TIP

As you listen, think about how your classmates' ideas are similar to or different from your own.

◄ The phases of the moon

Grammar

Capitalization and Punctuation of Titles

Capitalize all words in a title, except for articles (*a, an, the*), prepositions of three letters or fewer (*of, in, for,* etc.), the *to* in an infinitive. Always capitalize the first word of a title and any proper nouns.

> "The Girl Who Married the Moon"
> "No Need to Establish a Moon Base"

Grammar SKILL

If you write by hand, indicate italics with underlining. Underlining should be continuous, not broken.

There are specific punctuation rules for titles when you refer to them in your writing. Some titles are enclosed in quotation marks; others are italicized. Note that there is usually no punctuation within a title, except when the title includes a subtitle. A colon is used between the title and subtitle, which is usually capitalized.

Use quotation marks	Italicize
Short stories "Somebody's Son"	**Novels** *Riding Freedom*
Short poems "Quilt"	**Collections** *Salsa Stories*
Myths "The Girl Who Married the Moon"	**Long poems** *The Lotus Seed*
Legends "Blue Willow"	**Plays** *The Diary of Anne Frank: The Play*
Songs "Follow the Drinking Gourd"	**Paintings** *Café Terrace*
Interviews "An Interview with Gary Paulsen"	**Movies** *A Woman Called Moses*
Informational texts "César Chavez: We Can Do It!"	**Magazines** *Time*
	Newspapers *The New York Times*

Practice

Work with a partner. Copy the sentences into your notebook. Correct the punctuation and capitalization in the boldfaced titles.

Example: My favorite novel is <u>Hatchet</u>.

1. I've just finished reading the novel **war and peace**.
2. Have you ever read the poem **stars** by Sara Teasdale?
3. We saw Miller's play **the crucible** last night.
4. T.S. Elliot's poem **the wasteland** was long and difficult.
5. My father favorite newspaper is **the washington post**.

✔ GRAMMAR CHECK

*What **punctuation** do you use with **titles** of short stories?*

Apply

Work with a partner. Tell your partner the titles of five of your favorite novels, poems, plays, songs, magazines, or movies. Write each other's titles down with the proper punctuation and capitalization. Check each other's work.

Punctuation: Hyphens and Dashes

Use a hyphen with a two-word adjective before a noun, but never after the noun. You can also use a hyphen with some compound words, including numbers.

> The Moon disappeared behind a **heavy-clouded** sky.
> She married her husband when she was **twenty-one**.

Grammar SKILL

Don't confuse hyphens and dashes: Hyphens are shorter than dashes.

You can use dashes (—) to draw attention to an interruption in a sentence. A single dash can be used to set off an appositive, or an explanation of a preceding noun or noun phrase. The appositive can be a noun, phrase, or clause. Note there are no spaces before or after a dash.

> Some elders said that these girls might easily choose—as did some of the women—to each have two husbands.
> She tried more trails and found the same thing at the end—a person lying facedown.

Practice

Work with a partner. Copy the sentences below into your notebook. Then add dashes or hyphens to each.

Example: The light-footed cat brought me her catch—a tiny mouse.

1. He was a kind looking man.
2. The well known scientist accepted her award a medal.
3. Roy got a much needed haircut.
4. They entered the store a convenience store and then immediately left.
5. I passed the test granted, it was easy but I passed.

Apply
Work with a partner. Think of some other compound adjectives. Write them in your notebook. Then use them in sentences.

Writing

Include Paraphrases and Citations

The paragraphs following an introduction should each have a main idea that is supported by details. A paraphrase, or a restatement of someone else's idea in your own words, can be used to support a main idea. You should highlight paraphrased text by providing an "in-text citation," or the source of the information you are using (the author or title of the piece, and the page number, if known, in parentheses). The citation should also be included in an alphabetized "Works Consulted List." (See www.LongmanKeystone.com for how to cite various sources.)

> **Writing Prompt**
>
> Write a paragraph about another myth. Be sure to include the main idea and supporting details. Paraphrase information you have found in other sources and provide an in-text citation. Use capitalization in titles and hyphens and dashes correctly.

1 **PREWRITE** Begin by choosing a myth that you know.

- Use the library or the Internet to research information.
- Write the main idea of your paragraph.
- Select information from your research to support your main idea.
- Paraphrase the information in your own words.
- Provide an in-text citation and a "Works Consulted List."
- Use a source chart like the one below to manage your citations.

Workbook Page 216

Here's a source chart created by a student named Madeline for a paragraph about a Choctaw Myth.

Paraphrase	Source
According to the myth, when a solar eclipse occurs, it's because a black squirrel is eating the sun. Therefore, whenever the Choctaw saw a black squirrel, they would try to frighten it away, hoping to protect the sun.	"Eclipse of the Sun Blamed on Black Squirrel." Choctaw Legends and Stories. 13 September 2007. http://www.tc.umn.edu/~mboucher/ mikebouchweb/Choctaw/legends2.htm.

2 DRAFT Use your source chart to help you write a first draft.

- Include your main idea and support it with details.
- Paraphrase information from sources to support your main idea.
- Provide in-text citations.
- Make a "Works Consulted List" (see below).

3 REVISE Read over your draft. Look for places where the writing is unclear or needs improvement. Use the Writing Checklist to help you identify problems. Then revise your draft, using the editing and proofreading marks listed on page 458.

4 EDIT Check your work for errors in grammar, usage, mechanics, and spelling. Trade papers with a partner to obtain feedback. Use the Peer Review Checklist on Workbook page 216. Edit your final draft in response to feedback from your partner and your teacher.

5 PUBLISH Prepare a clean copy of your final draft. Share your paragraph with your class. Save your work. You'll need to refer to it in the Writing Workshop at the end of the unit.

Writing Checklist

IDEAS:
☑ I used paraphrased information from other sources to support the main idea.

CONVENTIONS:
☑ I correctly cited sources.

Here is Madeline's paragraph about a Choctaw Myth. Notice how she uses details to support the main idea.

Madeline Shaw

A Choctaw Myth

To Native Americans, the natural world is very important and must be treated with respect. In the past, Native Americans also believed that most natural occurrences did not have simple explanations. They used myths to explain how and why things occurred. One Choctaw myth tries to explain the reason for solar eclipses, or times when the moon passes between the earth and the sun, briefly blocking the sun's light. According to the myth, when a solar eclipse occurs, it's because a black squirrel is eating the sun. Therefore, whenever the Choctaw saw a black squirrel, they tried to frighten it away, hoping to protect the sun (Choctaw Legends and Stories).

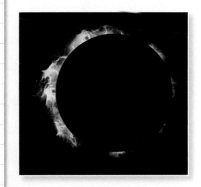

Works Consulted List

"Eclipse of the Sun Blamed on Black Squirrel." Choctaw Legends and Stories. 13 September 2007 <http://www.tc.umn.edu/~mboucher/mikebouchweb/Choctaw/legends2.htm>.

Prepare to Read

What You Will Learn

Reading

■ Vocabulary building:
*Context, dictionary
skills, word study*

■ Reading strategy:
Take notes

■ Text type:
*Informational text
(science)*

Grammar
Parentheses, brackets
and ellipses; Quoting
sources

Writing
Include quotations and
citations

➤ ⓠ THE BIG QUESTION

How does the sky influence us? Look at the picture below.
Does the thought of traveling to space interest you? If you were
given the opportunity to accompany astronauts on a space mission,
would you accept? Discuss with a partner.

➤ BUILD BACKGROUND

In this section, you will read two persuasive articles. The first is
called **"Return to the Moon."** It presents an argument in favor
of American astronauts returning to the moon. The second article,
"No Need to Establish a Moon Base," argues against manned
space flights and the construction of a permanent moon base.
As you read, notice how both authors present clear opinions and
support their views with facts.

An astronaut on
a space walk near
the International
Space Station ▶

➤ VOCABULARY

Listening and Speaking: Key Words

Read and listen to these sentences. Use the context to figure out the meaning of the highlighted words. Use a dictionary to check your answers. Then write each word and its meaning in your notebook.

Key Words

base
crater
lunar
mine
universe
voyage

1. Some people want the United States to build a base on the moon. From there, astronauts could travel to Mars.

2. The meteorite left a crater on the moon's surface.

3. We used a telescope to see craters on the lunar surface.

4. One day, scientists hope to mine the moon's surface for water and oxygen.

5. Our moon is one of many in the vast universe.

6. The voyage resulted in the successful landing of a man on the moon.

Practice

Workbook Page 217

Write the sentences in your notebook. Choose a key word from the box above to complete each sentence. Then take turns reading the sentences aloud with a partner.

1. The spaceship's _____ from Earth to the moon took three days.

2. The spaceship landed on the _____ surface.

3. While on the moon, the astronauts stayed at the _____, where their food was stored.

4. The astronauts walked near a deep _____.

5. They plan to _____ the lunar surface for additional materials.

6. Scientists want to know what is necessary to live on the moon. This information could help humans explore the rest of the _____.

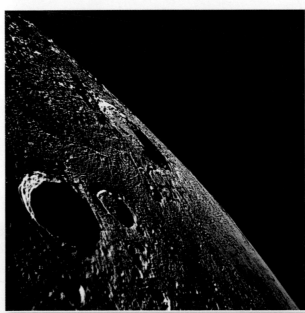

◀ Lunar craters

Listening and Speaking: Academic Words

Study the **red** words and their meanings. You will find these words useful when talking and writing about informational texts. Write each word and its meaning in your notebook. After you read "Return to the Moon" and "No Need to Establish a Moon Base," try to use these words to respond to the texts.

investigate = try to find out the truth about something	➡	Scientists **investigate** the moon and planets to learn more about the universe.
issues = subjects or problems that people discuss	➡	The government considers many **issues** when funding the space program.
promote = help something develop and be successful	➡	After considering the issues, the government decided to **promote** the construction of a permanent moon base.
research = serious study of a subject that is intended to discover new facts about it	➡	Astronauts conduct **research** both on Earth and in space.

Audio

Practice

Workbook
Page 218

Work with a partner to answer these questions. Try to include the **red** word in your answer. Write the sentences in your notebook.

1. What aspects of space travel would you want to **investigate** if given the opportunity?

2. What **issues** would concern you if you were traveling to another planet?

3. What do you feel is the best way to **promote** a return to the moon?

4. What kind of **research** would you want to perform on a space mission?

◀ A NASA scientist analyzing research data at a campsite

Word Study: Acronyms

Acronyms and initials are used frequently in many forms of communication. An acronym is formed by adding the first letters or syllables of several words together. For example, the acronym NASA is made from the first letters of these words: *National Aeronautics and Space Administration*. Read additional examples of acronyms in the chart below.

Acronym	Words that Form Acronyms
NATO	**N**orth **A**tlantic **T**reaty **O**rganization
laser	**l**ight **a**mplification by **s**timulated **e**mission of **r**adiation
asap	**a**s **s**oon **a**s **p**ossible

Practice

Work with a partner. Use a dictionary to find the definition of each acronym in the box below. Write the acronym and the words that form it in your notebook.

CD-ROM	radar	RAM	scuba	UFO	UNICEF

READING STRATEGY TAKE NOTES

Earlier in this book, you learned how to identify main ideas and details (see Identify Main Ideas and Details on page 359). Expand your use of this strategy as you take notes. Taking notes keeps you focused on what you're reading. It also helps you understand and remember new information. To develop this new strategy, follow these steps:

- Think about your purpose for reading the text.
- Scan the text for the key information you need.
- Look for dates, names, places, and events.
- Write notes about the main ideas, not the details.
- Don't write in complete sentences. Use short notes, for example: *landed 6/21/69*.

As you read "Return to the Moon" and "No Need to Establish a Moon Base," think about the information you want to remember. Take notes while you read. Review your notes and check that they're correct.

Set a purpose for reading As you read, think about whether or not we should return to the moon. Is there a need to establish a moon base? Compare the two sides of this issue.

Return to the Moon

Audio

Christy Brownlee

On July 21, 1969, millions of television viewers around the world tuned in to the news to watch an amazing event. For the first time ever, people were walking on the moon! The now-famous moon walkers were American astronauts Buzz Aldrin and Neil Armstrong.

Since that first moon walk, 10 more people have set foot on the gray globe's chalky surface. But no one has walked on the moon for more than thirty-four years. Now, the National Aeronautics and Space Administration (NASA) is gearing up to send astronauts back to the moon— eventually, to stay!

Why send astronauts back? Because our nearest neighbor in space is a great place to learn more about Earth and the rest of the universe. It could also serve as a launching pad for destinations farther than people have ever traveled.

Old Pals

Scientists believe that 4 billion years ago, a small planet the size of Mars smashed into Earth. The crash was so powerful that it chipped off a gigantic chunk of our planet and kicked it into space. That chunk is now the moon.

Since the moon is made of ancient Earth, some scientists think that studying it up close will tell us what our home planet was like long ago.

The moon could also give scientists a better look at what the rest of our universe is like. Earth's **atmosphere** and city lights can **alter** the images that scientists see in **telescopes**. By setting up telescopes on the moon's surface, researchers could get a clearer view of space.

---

atmosphere, air
alter, change
telescopes, instruments that allow people to see things that are very far away

▲ Astronaut Buzz Aldrin stands on the moon's surface during the first American lunar landing in 1969.

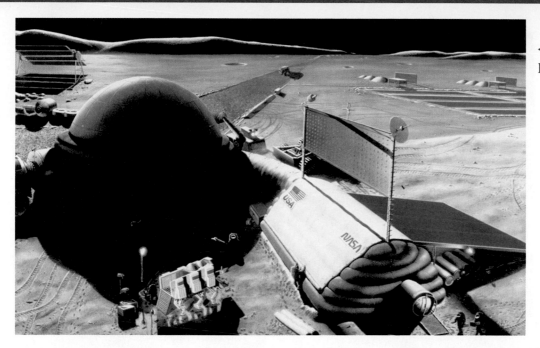

◀ A model lunar base

Home Base

Eventually, the moon could also act as a training camp for trips to planets. A trip to the moon takes a spacecraft only two and a half days. A **trek** to Mars could take almost nine months. "That lengthy time makes it much more difficult to go back if something goes wrong or there's something that we forgot," explains scientist Chris McKay, who works at NASA's Ames Research Center.

After it sends four astronauts to the moon for a brief period in 2018, NASA will have other astronauts visit it for longer stretches of time. Eventually, colonies of astronauts could live there for six months.

But the moon has no food or oxygen, a gas that humans must breathe to stay alive. So how can astronauts remain there for such long periods? On their first few trips, astronauts will take some supplies, such as oxygen packs and tasty meals, with them in separate **cargo vehicles**. But eventually, they plan to mine some supplies from the moon's surface itself. Some researchers believe that there's oxygen buried in the moon's dirt and water hidden in its deep craters.

Figuring out how to live on the moon could teach scientists the skills needed to keep exploring the rest of the universe. Says McKay: "A moon base is the first step to an essentially endless voyage into space."

---

trek, long, difficult journey

cargo vehicles, vehicles that are used to carry additional supplies

BEFORE YOU GO ON

1 In what ways do scientists think **research** about the moon could be beneficial to people on Earth?

2 How many years have passed since American astronauts last walked on the moon?

💡**On Your Own**
Do you think astronauts should return to the moon? Why or why not?

▲ An unmanned robot

No Need to Establish a Moon Base

Audio

Matt Kachur

When Americans landed on the moon in 1969, it was considered to be an American triumph. Today, there is talk of sending American astronauts back to the moon and constructing a permanent base there. However, both actions are unnecessary, dangerous, and expensive.

In truth, the need for manned space flights has decreased as the use of robots has increased. In fact, today's robots can perform most of the tasks previously assigned to humans and can do so in a more **precise** way. Recent achievements in space—such as discovering more than 100 planets outside our solar system and finding **evidence** of water on Mars—have come from unmanned space telescopes or robots.

Furthermore, unmanned space missions **pose** a smaller threat to human life than manned space missions. We often forget how dangerous manned space flights can be. Since 1967, they have been responsible for the deaths of seventeen people.

precise, exact

evidence, proof
pose, present

In addition to the cost in human life, manned space missions are expensive. One space shuttle launch alone can cost $360 million. Much of that money is used to create systems that keep humans alive in space. This, added to the cost of building a moon base, would require hundreds of billions of dollars. In order to meet this need, the U.S. government would have to cut important social programs or raise taxes.

It is for these reasons that it makes sense to **abandon** the idea of a return to the moon and the construction of a permanent base. Instead, we should **invest** our time, money, and energy into additional robotic projects.

---

abandon, leave behind
invest, spend

▲ The Hubble Space Telescope

The launch of the space shuttle *Discovery* ▶

BEFORE YOU GO ON

1 Why has the need for manned space flights decreased?

2 What have robots achieved in space?

On Your Own
Do you think robots should replace humans in space? Explain.

Reading 3 **423**

► COMPREHENSION

Workbook Page 221

Recall

1. Who were the first astronauts to walk on the moon?

2. How many people have walked on the moon?

Comprehend

3. Why should NASA build a moon base?

4. Name three reasons why NASA should not build a moon base.

Analyze

5. Although he opposes a moon base, do you think the author of "No Need to Establish a Moon Base" thinks space exploration is important? Explain by analyzing information in the text.

6. How could the moon's location be helpful to astronauts who are going to Mars?

Connect

7. Do you think it is important for humans to **investigate** space? Explain.

8. What benefits do you think further space exploration could bring?

► IN YOUR OWN WORDS

Work with a partner. Copy the T-chart below into your notebook. Write the **issues** presented in "Return to the Moon" and "No Need to Establish a Moon Base" beneath the corresponding heads. Try to use as many new vocabulary words as possible. Then summarize one of the articles for your partner.

"Return to the Moon"	"No Need to Establish a Moon Base"

➤ DISCUSSION

Discuss in pairs or small groups.

1. What do you think would happen if astronauts were able to find the supplies they needed to live on the moon?

2. Do you think there could be other forms of life in outer space? Why or why not?

Q **How does the sky influence us?** Do you think it is important to **promote** space travel in the United States? Why or why not?

Listening SKILL

When you listen to your classmates debate an issue, take notes. This will help you evaluate other people's points of view.

➤ READ FOR FLUENCY

When we read aloud to communicate meaning, we group words into phrases, pause or slow down to make important points, and emphasize important words. Pause for a short time when you reach a comma and for a longer time when you reach a period. Pay attention to rising and falling intonation at the end of sentences.

Work with a partner. Choose a paragraph from the reading. Discuss which words seem important for communicating meaning. Practice pronouncing difficult words. Take turns reading the paragraph aloud and give each other feedback.

➤ EXTENSION

Workbook Page 221

Utilize You read about robots in space. Work with a partner. Use the Internet or go to the library to research one particular space robot. Try to find the following information: the name of the robot, a picture of the robot, and a description of the robot's job(s) in space. Use as many new academic words as possible. Then present this information to your class.

LEARNING STRATEGY

To better acquire and understand new academic language, use and reuse these words in meaningful ways in your writing.

◀ Robotic hands completing a task

Grammar

Parentheses, Brackets, and Ellipses

Parentheses (( )) are used to show extra information or to set off an abbreviation.

> The astronauts (**Buzz Aldrin and Neil Armstrong**) are now world-famous.
> The National Aeronautics and Space Administration (**NASA**) is gearing up to send astronauts back to the moon—eventually, to stay!

Brackets ([ ]) are used to show changes made to original text.

> **Original:** It could also serve as a launching pad for destinations farther than people have ever traveled.
> **Changed:** **[Sending astronauts back to the moon]** could also serve as a launching pad for destinations farther than people have ever traveled.
> **Changed:** It could also serve as a launching pad for **[farther]** destinations.

Ellipses (. . .) are used when a word or phrase is missing from a statement.

> Recent achievements in space . . . have come from unmanned space telescopes or robots.

Practice

Workbook Page 222

Work with a partner. Use parentheses, brackets, or ellipses with the boldfaced information. Write the sentences in your notebook.

Example: Scientists believe **that 4 billion years ago**, a small planet **the size of Mars** smashed into the Earth. (*ellipses*)
Scientists believe . . . a small planet . . . smashed into the Earth.

1. The moon has no oxygen, **a gas that humans must breathe**. (*parentheses*)
2. Astronauts will take supplies. Eventually, **they** plan to mine some supplies from the moon's surface. (*brackets*)
3. It was **considered to be** an American triumph. (*ellipses*)
4. Unmanned space missions are, **in my opinion**, unnecessary. (*ellipses*)
5. Today's robots can perform most of the tasks, **and do so in a more precise way**, that were previously assigned to humans. (*parentheses*)

Apply

Work with a partner. Find other examples in the reading "Return to the Moon" on pages 420–421 where you can use parentheses, brackets, and ellipses. Write the sentences in your notebook.

426 Unit 6

Quoting Sources

In a research paper, you can use direct or reported speech to quote a source. If you use just a phrase from a quotation, the phrase is set off with quotation marks and begins with a lowercase letter.

Direct Speech: McKay stated, "It is the first step to an essentially endless voyage."
Reported Speech: McKay stated that it was the first step to an essentially endless voyage.
Phrase of Reported Speech: McKay said that it begins "an essentially endless voyage."

When you want to quote several sentences from a source, set them off in block quotations. Block quotations are indented, do not have quotation marks, and are usually introduced with a colon.

Matt Kachur contends:

    In truth, the need for manned space flights has decreased as the use of robots has increased. In fact, today's robots can perform most of the tasks previously assigned to humans and can do so in a more precise way.

Grammar **SKILL**

When you use block quotations or quotation marks around a quote, the quote must be word for word from the original text.

Practice
Workbook Page 223

Work with a partner. Look at the first page of "Return to the Moon" on page 420 and "No Need to Establish a Moon Base" on page 422. Follow the instructions below to quote from the source. Write the sentences in your notebook.

Example: Page 420: Quote the first sentence of the sixth paragraph directly.
According to Brownlee, "The moon could also give scientists a better look at what the rest of our universe is like."

1. Page 420: Quote the first sentence of the first paragraph directly.
2. Page 421: Report what the first sentence of the fourth paragraph says.
3. Page 422: Block quote the first two sentences of the first paragraph.

Apply
Look at one of the sources you've chosen for your research paper. In your notebook, write down a direct quotation, a reported quotation, and a block quotation from the source.

Writing

Ongoing
Writing
Skills
Practice

Include Quotations and Citations

You learned that a research report contains paragraphs with main ideas supported by facts, details, and paraphrases. An effective research report will also include quotations from people who are experienced and knowledgeable about the research topic. Remember that whenever you copy another person's writing or speech word for word, you must put the text in quotation marks. After the quotation, you must provide an in-text citation. (See www.LongmanKeystone.com for guidelines on citing various sources.)

> **Writing Prompt**
>
> Write a paragraph that includes quotations and citations. Be sure to punctuate them correctly.

1 PREWRITE Begin by choosing a topic for your paragraph.

- Use the library or the Internet to find information about your topic.

- Write the main idea of your paragraph.

- Decide which information from your sources you can use to support your main idea.

- Include quotations and citations and make a "Works Consulted List."

- Use a graphic organizer like the one below to list your quotations and sources.

Workbook
Page 224

Here's a source chart created by a student named Andrew for a paragraph about space tourism.

Quotation	Source
"Private companies in Russia, Europe, and the United States are competing to become future leaders of space tourism."	"All about Space Tourism." Space.com 25 October 2007. http://www.space.com/space-tourism/

2 DRAFT Use your source chart to help you write a first draft.

- Explain the main idea and support it with facts and details.
- Include quotations and citations.
- Create a "Works Consulted List."

3 REVISE Read over your draft. Look for places where the writing is unclear or needs improvement. Use the Writing Checklist to help you identify problems. Then revise your draft, using the editing and proofreading marks listed on page 458.

4 EDIT Check your work for errors in grammar, usage, mechanics, and spelling. Trade papers with a partner to obtain feedback. Use the Peer Review Checklist on Workbook page 224. Edit your final draft in response to feedback from your partner and your teacher.

5 PUBLISH Prepare a clean copy of your final draft. Share your paragraph with the class. Save your work. You'll need to refer to it in the Writing Workshop at the end of the unit.

Writing Checklist

SENTENCE FLUENCY:

☑ I made sure quotations flowed smoothly within paragraphs.

CONVENTIONS:

☑ I correctly punctuated my quotations and Works Consulted List.

Here is Andrew's paragraph. Notice that he includes an in-text citation and a "Works Consulted List."

Andrew Denkus

Space Tourism

In 2001, the first space tourist, Dennis Tito, flew into space aboard a Russian spacecraft. Since that successful experience, several others have also paid enormous amounts of money, more than $20 million per trip, for the chance to spend time on the International Space Station. Experts predict that this new industry, space tourism, is sure to grow in the future. In fact, "private companies in Russia, Europe, and the United States are competing to become future leaders of space tourism" ("All about Space Tourism"). Company leaders believe that as space tourism becomes more affordable, it will also become more common. They envision the creation of new vehicles, similar to airplanes, that would be used to transport people into space. They even foresee luxury hotels orbiting Earth!

Works Consulted List

"All about Space Tourism." 2007. Space.com 25 October 2007 <http://www.space.com/space-tourism/>.

Prepare to Read

What You Will Learn

Reading
- Vocabulary building: *Context, dictionary skills, word study*
- Reading strategy: *Connect ideas*
- Text type: *Informational text (science)*

Grammar
More transitions; Transitional clauses

Writing
Support the main idea

▶ THE BIG QUESTION

How does the sky influence us? What do you know about the sky and the solar system? What do you know about the sun? Do you know about solar power? Use your prior knowledge to answer these questions with a partner.

Copy the chart below into your notebook. Complete the K column with what you already know about solar energy. Write your reasons for wanting to learn more about solar energy in the W column. After reading the text, complete the L column with the new information you have learned, and the H column with a description about how you learned it.

LEARNING STRATEGY

Use your prior knowledge. Relating what you already know to a new topic will make it easier to understand new meanings in English.

K What do I **Know**?	W What do I **want** to know?	L What did I **learn**?	H **How** did I learn it?

▶ BUILD BACKGROUND

Throughout history, the sun has been an object of intense interest for scientists in many different cultures. By studying the sun, we have learned to mark time and understand the changes in seasons. In this section, you will read a science article entitled **"Solar Energy—Help from the Sky."** Radiant energy comes from the sun. It travels through space to reach Earth. In this article, you will learn how scientists have harnessed the sun's energy to provide power for homes and businesses.

➤ VOCABULARY

Listening and Speaking: Key Words

Read and listen to the sentences. Use the context to figure out the meaning of the highlighted words. Use a dictionary to check your answers. Then write each word and its meaning in your notebook.

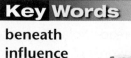

Key Words

beneath
influence
positive
potential
renewable
solar

1. We put the bags beneath the table so they were out of the way.

2. He was a bad influence, so we stopped spending time with him.

3. He was a positive influence on children. They were always well behaved.

4. The student had potential. Her teacher said that with hard work, she could be a great writer one day.

5. Wind is a renewable energy source. It can replace itself naturally and is never used up.

6. The calculator runs on solar power. It is charged by energy from the sun.

Practice  **Workbook Page 225**

Write the sentences in your notebook. Choose a key word from the box above to complete each sentence. Then take turns reading the sentences aloud with a partner.

1. The _____ energy from the sun helped to heat the house.

2. Because it is natural and _____, wind is a clean form of energy.

3. The boss's calm approach had a good _____ on the employees.

4. She dove under the water to find out what was _____ the surface.

5. The building was in a sunny area. It had _____ to run on solar energy.

6. The teacher was a good person and had a _____ influence on his students.

Solar panels on a home ▶

Listening and Speaking: Academic Words

Study the **red** words and their meanings. You will find these words useful when talking and writing about informational texts. Write each word and its meaning in your notebook. After you read "Solar Resources—Help from the Sky," try to use these words to respond to the text.

consists = is made up of	→	Our galaxy **consists** of billions of stars, one of which is the sun.
criteria = facts or standards used in order to help you judge or decide something	→	The sun is a star because it does not meet the necessary **criteria** to be a planet.
features = important, interesting, or typical parts of something	→	One of the **features** of the sun is its spots.
located = in a particular place or position	→	The sun is **located** at the center of our solar system.

Audio

Practice  Workbook Page 226

Write the sentences in your notebook. Choose a **red** word from the box above to complete each sentence. Then take turns reading the sentences aloud with a partner.

1. I want to learn more about the sun. Do you know where the planetarium is _____?

2. What _____ do scientists use to classify stars?

3. A star _____ of hot fiery gases.

4. One of the _____ of solar energy is that it is clean.

Word Study: Greek and Latin Roots

Many words in English have Greek and Latin roots. Understanding the meaning of a word root can help you understand the English words that are formed from them.

Greek or Latin Root	Meaning	Words and definitions
-gram	write or record	**telegram:** a transmitted message
photo-	light	**photograph:** an image formed by exposing film to light
-poly	many	**polymer:** many linked molecules

Practice  Workbook Page 227

Copy the chart below into your notebook. Find the definition of each word in a dictionary. Write the definition in the chart. Then use each word in a sentence. Read your sentences to a partner.

Word	Definition	Sentence
radiogram		
photocell		
polygram		

READING STRATEGY | CONNECT IDEAS

Earlier in this book you learned how to take notes (see Take Notes on page 419). Expand your use of this strategy as you connect ideas in an informational text. When you connect ideas, look for the main idea in each paragraph and see how it fits with all of the other ideas. To develop your use of this new strategy, follow these steps:

- Read the section headings. Do they give you any clues about the main ideas in the text?
- Read each paragraph and take notes about the main idea.
- Review your notes. How are the ideas similar? What connects them to each other?

As you read "Solar Energy—Help from the Sky," look for ideas that are similar. Think about what connects each idea to the next.

 Workbook Page 228

Set a purpose for reading As you read, look for examples of how people through the centuries have viewed the sun and its power. How does the sun influence earth? Why is the Sun Belt a good place for solar power?

Solar Energy Help from the Sky

An Ancient Idea

In ancient Greece, people thought of the sun as a god, Helios. According to legend, Helios was a very busy god. He drove a **chariot,** pulled by many horses. In the morning, he would drive across the sky, and it would be daylight. At night, he would drive back again, letting his horses rest beneath Earth, and it would be dark.

We now know that the sun is a fiery sphere at the center of our solar system. Civilizations throughout history had many different ideas about the sun. Some believed the sun traveled around Earth. Some **civilizations** prayed to the sun. Others used its position in the sky to tell time.

Ancient civilizations learned how to use energy from the sun in a positive way. One example of this is the way they built their homes. The Greeks and Romans knew that if they built their homes to face the rising sun, the sun would be a source of heat and light.

The sun is a powerful influence in our lives. All life on Earth depends on the energy from the sun. Without the sun, plants would not be able to make food. Animals, who eat plants or other animals, would not have food, either. Earth would be cold and **uninhabited.**

Plants have always used energy from the sun. However, humans have not. Humans are finally recognizing the great potential of solar energy.

When houses are built facing the sun, they can take advantage of the sun's energy without any special equipment. This is called **passive** solar energy use.

> **Reading Skill**
>
> To help you understand the reading, study the title and headings. This will help you identify the most important ideas.

▼ Radiant energy from the sun warms our Earth.

---

chariot, a vehicle with two wheels pulled by a horse
civilizations, societies that are well organized and developed
uninhabited, having no life
passive, without machinery

Research and Experimentation

Over time, many people realized that the sun had energy—solar energy—and that this energy could be useful. Scientists in the nineteenth century tried to find ways to **harness** the sun's energy with little success.

Auguste Mouchout was a French scientist. He worried about Europe's **dependence** on coal. He felt certain that the sun could provide the energy people needed. In 1860, he used sunlight to boil water and produce steam. He added **reflectors** to increase the amount of steam. He was able to connect his steam engine to another machine to make ice. But he was not able to produce enough energy to have a substitute for coal.

During the early days of the space program, scientists needed ways to power objects in space. Because of this, many advances were made in the area of solar energy. Today, the International Space Station gets some of its power from solar **cells**.

The amount of attention given to solar energy often depends on the price and availability of other fuels. Fuels are substances such as coal and oil that are burned to give heat, light, and power. In the 1970s, oil was expensive and in short supply. More research went into making solar cells that people could afford to use. Interest in solar energy research during that time was very high, but it was still expensive.

---

harness, control and use
dependence, need for something
reflectors, surfaces that reflect light, heat, or sound
cells, devices that generate electrical energy (also photovoltaic cell)

▲ For boiling to occur, water must absorb enough energy to raise the temperature to 100°C.

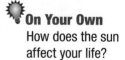

BEFORE YOU GO ON

1 Who was Helios?
2 How did some ancient civilizations tell time?

On Your Own
How does the sun affect your life?

Reading 4 **435**

The Idea Becomes a Reality

Today, there is renewed interest in solar technology for a variety of reasons. Oil is currently very expensive and supplies are limited. Oil is a nonrenewable resource. Once the supply runs out, there is no more left. Coal is more plentiful, but people worry about the effects of burning coal. Though there have been improvements, burning coal is not **ideal** for the environment.

Solar energy is a renewable resource. It will not run out for a very long time. Companies continue to improve on the amount of useable energy a solar cell can provide. A solar panel consists of an **array** of solar cells. As the technology improves, solar panels are becoming less expensive. People use solar panels to collect energy for their homes and **appliances.** They like solar power because it is clean. Also, solar energy is easily stored, and it does not harm the environment. However, because of their cost, solar panels are still not as commonly used as fuels like coal and oil.

You may have seen solar panels on roofs, or perhaps your school uses solar power. You've probably seen solar power in action in one way, at least: Many calculators have small solar cells.

▲ Solar-powered calculator

---

ideal, best that something can be
array, large grouping
appliances, equipment used in people's homes to make a job easier

Solar panels consist of arrays of solar cells. ▶

The Sun Belt

The Sun Belt is a region across the southern United States. This region has long, hot summers and short, mild winters. The states in the Sun Belt are Arizona, New Mexico, Texas, Louisiana, Mississippi, Alabama, Georgia, South Carolina, Florida, and the southern parts of California and Nevada.

These states are ideal for solar power use. They have many sunny days each year, so there is great potential to use solar energy for many different purposes. Even though these states can use oil as an energy source, many people realize that **alternative** sources of energy are better for the environment.

Today, more and more buildings in the Sun Belt are using solar technology. Active solar energy systems use panels or cells to collect the sun's energy. These panels provide the power to heat water and air.

Many cities have special programs that focus on increasing solar energy use. However, using the sun's energy to provide enough power for an entire town or city is not yet possible. Making a solar power plant requires a lot of land to be set aside for panels. Because this is not always possible, it is still more efficient to use fuels as the main source of energy.

---

alternative, different; other

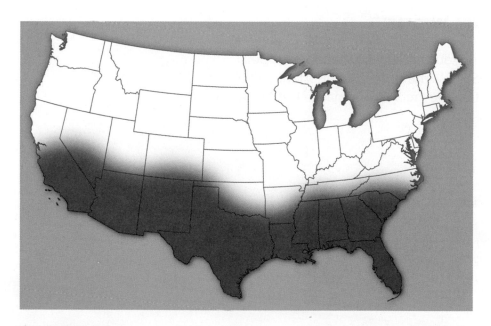

▲ The Sun Belt

BEFORE YOU GO ON

1 What is a renewable resource?

2 Name some states in the Sun Belt.

On Your Own
What things have you seen at home or school that run on solar power?

Review and Practice

► COMPREHENSION

Workbook
Page 229

Recall

1. What does a solar panel **consist** of?
2. What **features** of the Sun Belt make it an ideal region to use solar power?

Comprehend

3. Where are solar panels **located** on a building?
4. Why is solar power a renewable resource?

Analyze

5. How does a building with an active solar energy system differ from one that uses passive solar energy?
6. Why is solar energy research so important for the environment?

Connect

7. How could you convince a classmate to use solar energy?
8. What **criteria** will make solar energy important in the future?

► IN YOUR OWN WORDS

Copy the chart below into your notebook. Then reread "Solar Energy—Help from the Sky." Write the most important fact about each topic in the chart. Use the facts to summarize the article for a partner.

Topic	Facts
Early beliefs about the sun	
Research and experimentation	
Uses of solar energy	
The Sun Belt	

➤ DISCUSSION

Discuss in pairs or small groups.

1. Discuss the potential of solar power.
2. What electronic devices, or modern conveniences, would you most like to see run by solar power? Explain.

Q How does the sky influence us? How does the sun influence Earth? What would life on Earth be like without the sun?

Speaking SKILL

Think about the topic in question. Offer ideas about only that topic and not something else.

➤ READ FOR FLUENCY

It is often easier to read a text if you understand the difficult words and phrases. Work with a partner. Choose a paragraph from the reading. Identify the words and phrases you do not know or have trouble pronouncing. Look up the difficult words in a dictionary.

Take turns pronouncing the words and phrases with your partner. If necessary, ask your teacher to model the correct pronunciation. Then take turns reading the paragraph aloud. Give each other feedback on your reading.

➤ EXTENSION

Workbook Page 229

Utilize Go to the library or use the Internet to research other ways in which solar energy is used today. Think of ways you could use solar energy in your everyday life. What objects do you use that could be powered by the sun? Share your ideas with the class.

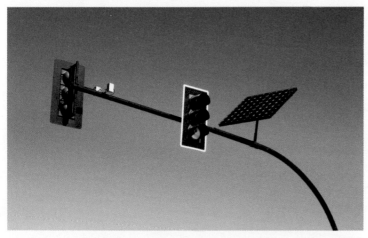

▲ How is solar power being used in this photo?

Grammar

More Transitions

Transitions help your reader make logical connections between sentences, paragraphs, and sections of your writing. You don't need a transition between every idea, just when you want to draw your reader's attention to a specific idea. Different transitions are used for different purposes.

Grammar SKILL

The transitions presented here are interchangeable within their categories.

To Add Information: furthermore, in addition	Some believed the sun traveled around Earth. Some civilizations prayed to the sun. **Moreover,** others used its position in the sky to tell time.
To Contrast: rather, alternatively	Many people don't want to rely on oil. **Instead,** they are looking for other sources of energy.
To Show Cause & Effect: hence, accordingly	Solar power is clean, not like burning fuels. **As a result,** people like it.
To Clarify: to illustrate, that is	You may have seen solar power; **for example,** your calculator may have small solar cells.
To Emphasize a Point: indeed, in fact	Solar panels are still expensive. **For this reason,** they are not as common as burning fuels for energy.
To Summarize: finally, in conclusion	Humans are recognizing the power of that relationship. **In summary,** solar energy will become more important.

Practice  Workbook Page 230

Work with a partner. Copy the sentences below into your notebook. Circle the transition that best completes each sentence.

Example: She works in that bank. (As a result /(In fact)), she's working now.

1. The school doesn't have an auditorium. (Rather / That is), it has a library.
2. Max studies hard. (Indeed / Finally), he gets good grades.
3. Brett plays baseball; (in fact / in addition), he plays soccer.
4. Sid loves animals. (In conclusion / Hence), he has three cats and a dog.
5. Solar energy is renewable. (In conclusion / That is), we can't use it all up.

Apply

Work with a partner. Copy the sentence starters into your notebook. Finish them with your own ideas.

1. I enjoy . . . As a result, . . .
2. I love . . . In fact, . . .
3. I hate . . . Instead, . . .
4. I never . . . Hence, . . .

Transitional Clauses

A transition is a conjunctive adverb or an adverbial phrase that connects two independent clauses. When a transition connects two complete sentences, use a period. When a transition connects two independent clauses, use a semicolon.

   The clause with the transition is called a transitional clause. Transitions are always used with pairs of sentences or independent clauses. The transitional clause is always the second of the pair.

Grammar **SKILL**

When a transition begins a sentence or clause, use a comma after the transition.

Ancient civilizations learned to use the energy from the sun.

transitional clause

   For example, the Greeks and Romans built their houses facing the rising sun.

Auguste Mouchout used sunlight to boil water and produce steam;

transitional clause

   moreover, he added reflectors to increase the amount of steam.

Practice

Workbook
Page 231

Work with a partner. Copy the sentences into your notebook. Then complete each transitional clause with an appropriate transition from the box.

moreover	for example	instead	accordingly	in fact	in conclusion

Example: More people will be using solar power. *In conclusion*, solar power will be the energy of the future.

1. Portugal is beautiful. _____, it's my favorite European country.
2. Many of the stoplights in town are dangerous; _____, the one at Main and King is terrible.
3. Traffic is increasing in the city. _____, the Traffic Commissioner is taking steps to improve public transport.
4. I don't enjoy playing baseball; _____, I like playing basketball.
5. He's going to college. _____, he's working two jobs.

✔ **GRAMMAR CHECK**

*What punctuation do you use before a **transitional clause** when connecting two complete sentences?*

Apply

Work with a partner. Look at the reading. Find three pairs of sentences that you can combine with transitions. Write them in your notebook and underline the transitional clause in each.

Writing

Support the Main Idea

You learned that a research report begins with an introductory paragraph. Following the introduction, each main idea is presented and expanded upon within its own paragraph.

The main idea is the most important point a writer tries to make in a paragraph. Details, including facts and examples, support the main idea. For example, imagine that the main idea of a paragraph is the following: *Neptune is a gas giant.* Your supporting details might include: *Neptune does not have a solid surface. Neptune has rings.*

> ### Writing Prompt
>
> Write a paragraph that includes a main idea and supporting details. Use transitional clauses to connect ideas.

1 PREWRITE Begin by choosing a topic for your paragraph.

- Use the library or the Internet to research information.
- Write the main idea of your paragraph.
- Write details you can use to support your main idea.
- Write your ideas in a graphic organizer. **Workbook Page 232**

Here's a main-idea-and-details web created by a student named Pablo. He is writing about why Pluto is no longer a planet.

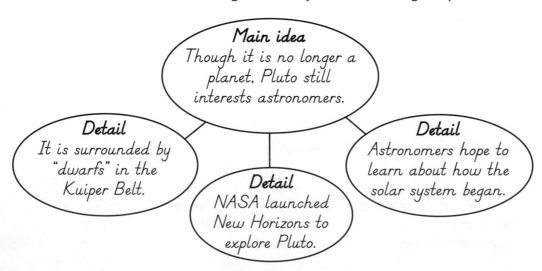

Main idea
Though it is no longer a planet, Pluto still interests astronomers.

Detail
It is surrounded by "dwarfs" in the Kuiper Belt.

Detail
NASA launched New Horizons to explore Pluto.

Detail
Astronomers hope to learn about how the solar system began.

2 **DRAFT** Use your main-idea-and-details web to help you write a first draft.

- Remember to explain the main idea first.
- Support the main idea with details.
- Use transitional clauses to connect ideas.

3 **REVISE** Read over your draft. Look for places where the writing is unclear or needs improvement. Use the Writing Checklist to help you identify problems. Then revise your draft, using the editing and proofreading marks listed on page 458.

4 **EDIT** Check your work for errors in grammar, usage, mechanics, and spelling. Trade papers with a partner to obtain feedback. Use the Peer Review Checklist on Workbook page 232. Edit your final draft in response to feedback from your partner and your teacher.

5 **PUBLISH** Prepare a clean copy of your final draft. Share your paragraph with the class. Save your work. You'll need to refer to it in the Writing Workshop at the end of the unit.

Here is Pablo's paragraph. Notice how he presents the main idea within its own paragraph and uses details to support it.

Writing Checklist

ORGANIZATION:
☑ I used a main-idea-and-details web to organize my notes.

WORD CHOICE:
☑ I included specific examples that explain and support the main idea.

Pablo Espínola

Pluto Is No Longer a Planet

Although it lost its title as the ninth planet in our solar system, Pluto continues to interest astronomers. They are now studying the thousands of rocky, icy chunks, called dwarfs, which surround Pluto. These objects are located in an area called the Kuiper Belt. To learn more about this area, NASA launched a spacecraft in January 2006. The spacecraft, called New Horizons, will reach its destination in 2015. It will collect information about Pluto's surface and atmosphere. The spacecraft will also look for rings and moons. With the information they receive from Pluto and the Kuiper Belt, astronomers hope to learn about the conditions that existed when our solar system began.

Link the Readings

Critical Thinking

Look back at the readings in this unit. Think about what they have in common. They all tell about the sky. Yet they do not all have the same purpose. The purpose of one reading might be to inform, while the purpose of another might be to entertain or persuade. In addition, the content of each reading relates to the sky differently. Now copy the chart below into your notebook and complete it.

Title of Reading	Purpose	Big Question Link
"Starry Nights" "Stars" "Escape at Bedtime"		
"The Girl Who Married the Moon"		*tells about the moon's phases*
"Return to the Moon" "No Need to Establish a Moon Base"	*to inform*	
"Solar Energy—Help from the Sky"		

Discussion

Discuss in pairs or small groups.

- Whose opinion would Sara Teasdale and Robert Lewis Stevenson agree with: the author's for "Return to the Moon" or the author's for "No Need to Establish a Moon Base"? Why?

- **Q How does the sky influence us?** What object in the sky do you think influences us the most? Why?

Media Literacy & Projects

Work in pairs or small groups. Choose one of these projects.

1 Create a skit based on "The Girl Who Married the Moon." Perform the story as a play for the class. Remember that skits of this kind are often informal. You may wish to include simple costumes and music, too.

2 Use the Internet to create a profile of an astronaut or astronomer. Download or copy a picture of the person, or draw one. Display your picture and profile on a class bulletin board.

3 Visit a planetarium. Report your experience to the class.

Further Reading

Choose from these reading suggestions. Practice reading silently for longer periods with increased comprehension.

The War of the Worlds, H. G. Wells
In this Penguin Reader® adaptation, a metal object falls from the sky over the south of England, and strange creatures come out of it. But they are not human—they are fighting machines from Mars. People start to wonder if Martians are trying to take over Earth.

Stars, Seymour Simon
In photo-essay format, *Stars* takes us on a tour of the galaxies. The book describes ordinary stars such as our sun, as well as stars called red giants and white dwarfs. It also explains how stars form, go through various stages of growth, and die.

They Dance in the Sky: Native American Star Myths, Ray A. Williamson and Jean Guard Monroe
This collection of stories includes star myths from Native American tribes. Wolves, bears, eagles, and other animals inhabit the stories and the night sky. The stars themselves tell tales of children who have danced away from home and of the great wounded sky bear, whose blood turns the autumn leaves red.

Put It All Together

LISTENING & SPEAKING WORKSHOP

Oral Report

You will give an oral report on a topic related to the sky.

1 **THINK ABOUT IT** Think about the poems, informational texts, and the myth you read about in this unit. The authors of these texts looked at the sky from many different perspectives. Which readings did you find most interesting? Why? Discuss your thoughts in small groups.

With your group, develop a list of topics related to the sky. For example:
- Space travel
- Constellations
- Weather
- The moon
- Clouds

2 **GATHER AND ORGANIZE INFORMATION** Choose a topic from your group's list. Decide how you want to approach your topic: for example, from a scientific, literary, artistic, or mythological perspective. Fill in the first two columns of a K-W-L chart as you brainstorm ideas for an oral report on this topic.

Research Go to the library or search the Internet to find information about your topic. Record what you find in the third column of your K-W-L chart. Choose the main points you want to include in your oral report, and make sure you have facts, details, and examples to support them.

Order Your Notes Copy your main points and supporting information onto note cards. Then arrange your cards in a logical order. Be prepared to share your sources with the audience.

Use Visuals Make or find photos, drawings, and/or other visuals that will help the audience understand your main points.

3 PRACTICE AND PRESENT Practice giving your oral report to friends or family members. Make sure your listeners can hear and understand you. Ask if your ideas are clear and easy to follow. Revise or rearrange your note cards if necessary. Keep practicing until you can speak confidently, looking at your audience and glancing occasionally at your note cards. Remember to show your visuals at the appropriate times.

Deliver Your Oral Report Before you begin, make sure your note cards and visuals are in order. Remember that an oral report is a formal presentation. Speak at a good pace, not too quickly or too slowly, and pronounce each word carefully. At the end of your report, ask your listeners if they have any questions.

4 EVALUATE THE PRESENTATION

You will improve your skills as a speaker and a listener by evaluating each presentation you give and hear. Use this checklist to help you judge your oral report and the reports of your classmates.

- ☑ Was the topic of the oral report clear?
- ☑ Did the speaker present the main points in a logical order?
- ☑ Were the main points supported by facts, examples, and details?
- ☑ Did the speaker use formal or informal language? Was it appropriate?
- ☑ What suggestions do you have for improving the oral report?

Speaking SKILL

Think of a way to grab the audience's attention and introduce your topic. You might use a quote, make a startling statement, or ask a question.

Listening SKILLS

As you listen, identify the speaker's topic. Listen for the general meaning, main ideas, and details. After each presentation, exchange this information with a partner to confirm that you have understood it correctly.

Take notes on the most important points. If you have questions, write them down, and ask them at the end of the presentation.

Listen for the speaker's sources. Do you think his or her information is reliable?

STRENGTHEN YOUR SOCIAL LANGUAGE

In your classes, you will need to be able to communicate with your teacher and classmates. Go to www. LongmanKeystone.com and do the activity for this unit. This activity will help you to learn and use routine language necessary for classroom communication.

WRITING WORKSHOP

Research Report

Write a Research Report

In this workshop, you will write a research report. In a research report, you present information about a topic you have studied in depth. Your purpose is to give readers a thorough understanding of the topic. You include research gathered from a variety of different sources and list all your sources at the end of the report. A good research report begins with a paragraph that introduces the writer's topic and states a controlling idea or focus. Each body paragraph presents a main idea supported by facts, details, and examples. A concluding paragraph sums up in a memorable way the information that the writer has explained.

> **Writing Prompt**
>
> Write a five-paragraph research report about a topic related to the sky. You might write about clouds and weather, stars and planets, astronauts and space travel, images of the sky in painting or poetry, or beliefs about the sky held by people in the past.

1 **PREWRITE** Review your previous work in this unit. Brainstorm a list of possible topics for your research report in your notebook.

- Choose the issue that most interests you.
- Ask yourself: "What do I want to know about my topic?"
- Use this question to narrow your focus and to guide your research.
- Consult sources such as books, magazines, encyclopedias, and websites. Take notes on note cards.
- Create an outline to organize your ideas.  **Workbook Page 233**

Here is an outline created by a student named Haley.

> I. Introduce the United States Space Program
>   A. Headed by NASA
>   B. Understanding of space shaped by endeavors
> II. Projects Mercury and Gemini
>   A. To see if humans could live in space
>   B. To make longer distance space travel possible
> III. Project Apollo
>   A. To land humans on moon
>   B. Alan Shepard first person to walk on moon
> IV. Space Shuttles
>   A. Useful in launch of Hubble Telescope
>   B. Also put satellites in space for cell phones and TV
> V. Conclude with U.S. Space Exploration
>   A. Understanding of space has been expanded
>   B. New information gained as technology advances

2 **DRAFT** Use your outline and the model on pages 453–454 to help you write a first draft.

- Remember to introduce your topic in the first paragraph. Say why it is important.

- Make sure each paragraph has a main idea and supporting details.

- Write a concluding paragraph that sums up the information in a memorable way.

- Include quotations and citations correctly.

- List all your sources accurately at the end of your report. Look at the style, punctuation, and order of information in the following sources. Use these examples as models.

Book

Stanchak, John. <u>Civil War</u>. New York: Dorling Kindersley, 2000.

Magazine article

Kirn, Walter. "Lewis and Clark: The Journey That Changed America Forever." <u>Time</u> 8 July 2002: 36–41.

Internet website

Smith, Gene. "The Structure of the Milky Way." <u>Gene Smith's Astronomy Tutorial</u>. 28 April 1999. Center for Astrophysics & Space Sciences, University of California, San Diego. 20 July 2009 <http://casswww.ucsd.edu/public/tutorial/MW.html>.

Encyclopedia article

Siple, Paul A. "Antarctica." <u>World Book Encyclopedia</u>. 1991 ed.

3 REVISE Read over your draft. Think about how well you have addressed questions of purpose, audience, and genre. Your purpose is to inform. Is your essay clearly organized? Is it appropriate in content and tone for the intended audience? Does it give the reader a thorough understanding of the topic? Keep these questions in mind as you revise your draft. Use the Writing Checklist below to help you identify additional issues that may need revision. Mark your changes on your draft using the editing and proofreading marks listed on page 458.

SIX TRAITS OF WRITING CHECKLIST

☑ **IDEAS:** Does my first topic introduce my topic and focus?

☑ **ORGANIZATION:** Do I support main ideas with facts, details, and examples?

☑ **VOICE:** Is my tone serious and suited to the topic?

☑ **WORD CHOICE:** Do I use specific words that make the information clear?

☑ **SENTENCE FLUENCY:** Do my sentences vary in length and type?

☑ **CONVENTIONS:** Does my writing follow the rules of grammar, usage, and mechanics?

Here are the revisions Haley plans to make to her first draft.

The Space Program of the United States

The National Aeronautics and space Administration (NASA) is the
U.S. gover~n~mental branch responsible for space exploration. There have
been many important endeavors that have helped shape the U.S. space
program⊙Knowledge about the moon, planets, *such as Mars* and the rest of our
galaxy continues to add to our research about living in space.

Project Mercury was the first space program in the United States.
The goal of Project Mercury was to learn whether or not humans
could endure space flight. In May 1961, Alan Shepard became the
first American astronaut to travel into space. In February 1962,
John Glenn became the first American astronaut to orbit planet Earth.

¶The Gemini Project, which followed Project Mercury, was implemented
to discover ways of enabling longer distance space travel.

Then, In 1961, President John F. Kennedy announced the goal of "landing
a man on the moon and returning him safely to the Earth" ("Man on
the Moon"). This ~was~ *became* the aim of NASA's next mission, Project Apollo.
On June 20, 1969 Apollo 11 succeeded in its mission. Neil Armstrong,
the commander of the three-man crew, was the first person to walk
on the moon. As he stepped onto the moon, Armstrong famously said,
"That's one small step for man, one giant leap for mankind" ("The Apollo
11 Mission").

Revised to include an example.

Revised to improve paragraph organization.

Revised to include a transition word and to improve word choice.

Reusable launch ships, also known as space shuttles, are now used for space exploration. Space shuttle missions have been very helpful in the launch and maintenance of the Hubble Telescope. it takes pictures that reach far out into space to increase our understanding about living in space. Space shuttles ^are also important because they put satellites in place that are used for cell phones and television. In addition, ^since space shuttles are able to orbit close to Earth. ̮They have been able to aid in the repairing and replenishment of the International Space Station.

Revised to improve sequence of ideas and to use a more complex sentence pattern.

In all of these missions, communication has been strengthened, and our understanding of space has been expanded. <u>g</u>reat strides in exploring space have been made through the space program of the United States. Throughout the twenty first century, the United States will strive to learn more about space as technology advances.

Revised to correct an error in mechanics.

Works Consulted List

Kerrod, Robin, and Giles Sparrow. <u>The Way the Universe Works</u>. New York: Dorling Kindersley, 2002.

"Man on the Moon: Kennedy Speech Ignited the Dream." <u>CNN.com/space</u>. 25 May 2001. Cable News Network. 08 October 2009 <http://archives.cnn.com./2001/TECH/space/Kennedy.moon>.

"The Apollo 11 Mission." <u>Human Space Flight</u>. 17 November 2005. National Aeronautics and Space Administration. 6 October 2009 <http://spaceflight1.nasa.gov/history/apollo/apollo11/>.

4 **EDIT** Check your work for errors in grammar, usage, mechanics, and spelling. Then trade essays with a partner and use the Peer Review Checklist to give each other feedback. Edit your final draft in response to feedback from your partner and your teacher.

Workbook
Page 233

Here are the additional changes Haley plans to make to her final draft as a result of her peer review.

Haley Coy

The Space Program of the United States

The National Aeronautics and space Administration (NASA) is the U.S. governmental branch responsible for space exploration. There have been many important endeavors that have helped shape the U.S. space program. Knowledge about the moon, planets such as Mars, and the rest of our galaxy continues to add to our research about living in space.

Revised to correct an error in mechanics.

Project Mercury was the first space program in the United States. The goal of Project Mercury was to learn whether or not humans could endure space flight. In May 1961, Alan Shepard became the first American astronaut to travel into space. In February 1962, John Glenn became the first American astronaut to orbit planet Earth.

The Gemini Project, which followed Project Mercury, was implemented to discover ways of enabling longer distance space travel. Then, in 1961, President John F. Kennedy announced the goal of "landing a man on the moon and returning him safely to the Earth" ("Man on the Moon"). This became the aim of NASA's next mission, Project Apollo. On June 20, 1969, Apollo 11 succeeded in its mission. Neil Armstrong, the commander of the three-man crew, was the first person to walk on the moon. As he stepped onto the moon, Armstrong famously said, "That's one small step for man, one giant leap for mankind" ("The Apollo 11 Mission").

Reusable launch ships, also known as space shuttles, are now used for space exploration. Space shuttle missions have been very helpful in the launch and maintenance of the Hubble Telescope. it takes pictures that reach far out into space to increase our understanding about living in space. Space shuttles are also important because they put satellites in place that are used for cell phones and television. In addition, since space shuttles are able to orbit close to Earth, they have been able to aid in the repairing and replenishment of the International Space Station.

In all of these missions, communication has been strengthened, and our understanding of space has been expanded. Great strides in exploring space have been made through the space program of the United States. Throughout the twenty-first century, the United States will strive to learn more about space as technology advances.

Revised to correct an error in mechanics.

5 **PUBLISH** Prepare a clean copy of your final draft. Share your essay with the class.

Workbook
Page 234

Test Preparation

PRACTICE

Read the following test sample. Study the tips in the boxes. Work with a partner to answer the questions.

Chinese New Year

1   Everyone is invited to celebrate the Year of the Tiger in Chinatown on February 19 and 20. The two-day event is fun for the whole family.

2   Friday the festival starts with a fashion show. Local musicians will play traditional Chinese tunes in front of the Hong Kong Market. Dancers will take the stage at 5:00 PM. Children are invited to make tiger masks in honor of the Year of the Tiger.

3   On Saturday, visitors will enjoy the traditional dragon dance. Again, bands will entertain visitors throughout the day. Chefs from several restaurants in Chinatown will offer free samples of food. The evening will end with a huge fireworks display.

1 According to the selection, what is the first event?
- **A** Musicians on stage
- **B** The dragon dance
- **C** A fashion show
- **D** Children making masks

2 Where would you most likely find this passage?
- **F** In a local newspaper
- **G** On a highway billboard
- **H** In a restaurant menu
- **J** On a map of Chinatown

3 When will the dancers perform?
- **A** Saturday at 12:00 noon
- **B** During the dragon dance
- **C** After the fireworks display
- **D** Friday at 5:00 PM

Taking Tests
· You will often take tests that help show what you know. Study the tips below to help you improve your test-taking skills.

Tip
Your first choice is usually right unless you find you have misread the question.

Tip
When a test asks for specific information, skim the selection for key words. For question 3, skim for the word *dancers* to find what time they perform.

Workbook
Pages 235–238

Capturing Cosmic Beauty

*M*any of us live in urban areas where there are a lot of lights on at night, so we do not get a good look at the stars. But if you sit in a dark field where there are no city lights, you can see the sky the way our ancestors saw it: a great area filled with countless stars. Artists often try to capture the beauty and mystery of the sky in their artwork.

Alma Thomas, *The Eclipse* (1970)

The moon moved in front of the sun during an eclipse that Alma Thomas once saw. She captures this eclipse with a dark, solid blue circle that sits off-center in her painting. Small painted blocks of cooler colors, such as green and light blue, spread out from the center. By the time she got to the edge of the canvas, Thomas was working in warmer oranges and yellows, which run right off the borders. Despite its cool center, the entire painting gives off a joyful celebration of color and light.

"A world without color would seem dead," Thomas once said. "Color is life. Light is the mother of color. Light reveals to us the spirit and living soul of the world."

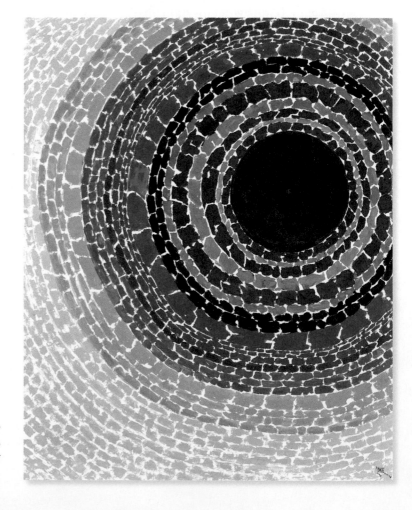

Alma Thomas, *The Eclipse*,
1970, acrylic, 62 x 49¾ in.,
Smithsonian American Art Museum ▶

◀ Charles Burchfield,
Orion in December, 1959,
watercolor and pencil, 39⅞ × 32⅞ in.,
Smithsonian American Art Museum

Charles Burchfield, *Orion in December* (1959)

One December night, artist Charles Burchfield could not sleep. He looked out of his bedroom window and watched the clouds sweep across the sky. Then suddenly he saw three stars in a row. He knew at once that it was Orion, a famous constellation. Orion was named after a Greek mythical figure who was a hunter. The three brightest stars represent his belt, and the three smaller stars that drop down from the belt represent his sword.

In *Orion in December,* Burchfield uses few colors to capture not only the coldness of that evening but also the beauty and sense of calm he felt. The stars in Orion rest in the center of the painting and form an upside-down V of dots above the point of a treetop. Burchfield outlined the trees with strong black lines, which gives them a ghostly appearance. He also outlined each star with a strong black circle, but added a white glow around those circles to give them a soft light.

Artists usually appreciate light and shadow that we never really notice. They are drawn to the dramatic play of light in the sky as the sun and moon rise and set each day.

Discuss What You Learned

1 Both artists capture light in different ways. What is similar about the two paintings, and what is different?

2 Do you agree with Alma Thomas that "color is life [and] light is the mother of color"? Explain your answer.

Big Question
Why do you think the sky is such a popular topic for so many artists?

Workbook
Pages 239–240

Editing and Proofreading Marks

To:	Use This Mark	Example:
add something	$\wedge$	We ate rice, bean^s and corn.
delete something	℘	We ate rice, beans, and corns.
close space	⌣	We ⌣ ate rice, beans, and corn.
start a new paragraph	¶	¶ We ate rice, beans, and corn.
add a comma	$\wedge$,	We ate rice, beans,and corn.
add a period	⊙	We ate rice, beans, and corn⊙
switch letters or words	∿	We ate rice, baehs, and corn.
change to a capital letter	_a_	we ate rice, beans, and corn.
change to a lowercase letter	⁄E	WE ate rice, beans, and corn.
let the marked text stand	(stet)	We ate rice, beans, and corn. (stet)

Glossary

academic relating to work done in schools, colleges, or universities

accompanied went somewhere with someone

accomplish do something successfully

achieved in doing something, especially by working hard

affects produces a change in someone or something

aid help or support given to someone

analyze examine or think about something carefully in order to understand it

approach a way of doing something or dealing with a problem

assisted helped someone

assumed thought that something was true without having proof

athletes people who are good at sports and take part in sports competitions

attached emotionally connected to

attitudes thoughts or feelings about something or someone

authoritative respected and trusted as being true, or making people respect or obey you

author's influences different factors that affect what an author writes about

available able to be used or seen

barriers things, such as rules or problems, that prevent you from doing something

base the main place where the work of a company or expedition is done

beneath under or below something

beneficial good or useful

benefit something that helps you or gives you an advantage

boundaries lines that divide two places

carbon dioxide the gas produced when people and animals breathe out

challenge something difficult that you need skill or ability to do

character motive a reason that explains a character's thoughts, feelings, actions, or speech

characters the people or animals that take part in the action of a story

chemicals substances, especially those made by or used in chemistry

climax the high point in the action of a story's plot

code a way to use words, letters, or numbers to send secret messages

communicate express your thoughts or feelings so other people understand them

community all the people living in one place

conflict a struggle between opposing forces

confrontation an argument or fight

consent permission to do something

conservation the protection of natural things such as animals, plants, forests, etc.

consists is made of or contains a number of different things

correspond write to someone and receive letters from him or her

crater a round hole in the ground made by something that has fallen on it or exploded on it

created made or invented

criteria facts or standards used in order to help you judge or decide something

crops plants such as wheat, corn, fruit, etc., that a farmer grows

cultivate try to develop a friendship with someone

cultural relating to a particular society and its way of life

demand to say or ask (something) in a forceful way

designer a person whose job is to make plans or patterns for clothes, furniture, equipment, etc.

device a thing that you use for a particular purpose

dialogue a conversation between characters

diary a book in which you write about the things that happen to you each day

discriminate treat unfairly

discrimination unfair treatment of some people because of their race, ethnic group, religion, or gender

disease an illness or unhealthy condition

distributes gives something to different people or places

drama a story written to be performed by actors

elements simple chemical substances

encounter an occasion when you meet someone without planning to

endangered species a type of animal or plant that soon might not exist

enemies people or countries that are not friendly to you or want to harm or fight you

environment the land, water, and air in which people, animals, and plants live

exhibit a public show of objects such as paintings, photographs, etc.

experiment a careful test you do to see if something is true

external conflict conflict between a character and an outside force

features the important, interesting, or typical parts of something

fever an illness which causes an increase in your body's temperature

focus pay special attention to a particular person or thing instead of others

foreshadowing the author's use of clues to hint at what might happen later in a story

founded established a business, organization, school, etc.

fugitive someone who is trying to avoid being caught

function the purpose of something

generation all of the people born at roughly the same time

goal something you want to do in the future

hearing impaired unable to hear well, or unable to hear at all

heritage the traditional beliefs, values, customs, etc., of a family, group of people, or country

hypothesis an idea that is suggested as an explanation of something, but that has not yet been proven to be true

ignored did not pay attention to someone or something

illegal not allowed by law

image a picture that you can see through a camera, on a television, in a mirror, etc.

imagery the use of words or phrases to describe ideas or actions in literary works

immigrants people who enter another country in order to live there

impact the effect that an event or situation has on someone or something

indicate say or do something that shows what you want or intend to do

individuals people; not a whole group

influence someone or something that has an effect on other people or things

injured hurt

inspectors officials whose jobs it is to visit places and see if there is anything wrong with them

instructed taught or showed someone how to do something

interact talk to other people and work together with them

interaction the activity of talking with other people and working together with them

interpretation an explanation of the meaning or significance of something

invention something completely new that is made for the first time

investigate try to find out the truth about something

involved included in a project or situation

irony a situation that is unusual or amusing because something strange happens, or the opposite of what is expected happens

issues subjects or problems that people discuss

items things in a set, group, or list

job a particular duty or responsibility that you have

labor work that requires a lot of physical effort

legend a widely told story about the past that may or may not be true

located in a particular place or position

lunar relating to the moon

migrant workers people who go to another area or country in order to find work

migration the act of moving from one place to another

mine dig into the ground for coal, iron, gold, etc.

mission the purpose or the most important aim of an organization

monitor carefully watch, listen to, or examine something over a period of time, to check for any changes or developments

mosquitoes flying insects that drink blood from people or animals and that can spread disease from one person to another

myth a fictional story that explains natural events such as wind or rain

native growing, living or produced in a particular area

nature everything that exists in the world that is not made or controlled by humans, such as animals, plants, etc.

neighborhood a small area of a town and the people who live there

network a group of people, organizations, etc. that are connected or that work together

objective something that you are working hard to achieve

obstacle something that makes it difficult for you to succeed

occupants people who live in a building, room, etc.

occurs happens

opponent someone who tries to defeat someone else in a game or competition

oral tradition stories passed along by word of mouth from one generation to the next

outcome the final result of a meeting, process, etc.

oxygen a gas in the air that all plants and animals need in order to survive

patent a special document that says you have the right to make or sell a new invention or product and that no one else is allowed to do so

participate take part in an activity or event

partnership a relationship in which two or more people, organizations, etc. work together to achieve something

perceive understand or think about something in a particular way

periodic table a specially arranged list of the elements

persistence the determination to do something even though it is difficult or other people oppose it

personification the representation of a thing or a quality as a person

plot a sequence of connected events in a fictional story

point of view the perspective from which a story is written

policy a plan that is agreed to by a political party, government, or organization

political relating to the government or politics of a country

population the number of people or animals living in a place

positive good or useful

potential a natural ability that could develop to make someone very good at something

preserved kept something from being harmed or damaged

principal someone who is in charge of a school

prior before

professional relating to a job for which you need special education or training

promote help something develop and be successful

published printed and distributed

rare not happening or seen very often

reacted behaved in a particular way because of what someone has said or done

reaction the way you behave in response to someone or something

refuge a safe place

region large area

regulations official rules or orders

rejected decided not to do something

removed took something away from where it was

renewable able to be replaced by natural processes so that it is never used up

research serious study of a subject that is intended to discover new facts about it

residents the people who live in a place

resources a supply of materials used to complete a task

response something that is said, written, or done as a reaction or reply to something else

responsibilities things that you have a duty to do or take care of

restricted controlled something or kept it within limits

rhyme when a word ends in the same sound as another

role the position or job that something or someone has in a particular situation or activity

route the way from one place to another

runaway someone who has left the place where he or she is supposed to be

sacrifice to not do something so that you can do something more important

setting the time and place of a story's action

shelter place that protects you from bad weather or danger, or the protection that is given to you

sign language a language that consists of hand movements instead of spoken words

significant noticeable or important

similarities the qualities of being similar or the same

solar relating to the sun or the sun's power

source where something comes from

speaker the imaginary voice a poet uses when writing a poem

stage directions notes in a drama that tell the actors what they should do and how they should do it

stanza a group of lines in poetry that are usually similar in length and pattern and are separated by spaces

strike a time when people stop working, usually because they want more money or better conditions

structure a building or something that has been built

substitute someone who does someone else's job

survive continue to live after an accident or illness

suspense the feeling of uncertainty about what will happen next in a literary work

symbiotic cooperative, depending on one another

symbol a picture, letter, or sign that means or stands for something else

symbolize represent a quality or a feeling against another group in a sport, game, etc.

team a group of people who compete against another group in a sport, game, etc.

technology all the knowledge and equipment used in science

tenement a large building divided into apartments, especially one that is located in a poor area

theme the central message, concern, or purpose in a literary work

tradition a belief or custom that has existed for a long time

transmit pass from one person to another

transportation the process or business of moving people or goods from one place to another

Underground Railroad network of secret routes that escaping slaves followed to freedom

uniforms particular types of clothing worn by members of a group, such as a sports team

union a group of workers who have joined together to protect their pay and working conditions

universe all of space, including all the stars and planets

violence behavior that hurts someone in a physical way

virus a very small living thing that causes illness, or the illness caused by a small living thing

visible able to be seen

volunteer a person who offers to do something without expecting to be paid

voyage a long trip, especially by ship or in a space vehicle

Index of Skills

Index of Authors, Titles, Art, and Artists

Acknowledgments

UNIT 1

Excerpt from *Riding Freedom* by Pam Muñoz Ryan, Scholastic Inc./Scholastic Press. Copyright © 1998 by Pam Muñoz Ryan. Used by permission.

Excerpt from *1000 Inventions and Discoveries* edited by Roger Bridgeman. Copyright © Dorling Kindersley, 2006. Reprinted by permission of Penguin Books, Ltd.

Excerpt from *Seedfolks* by Paul Fleischman. Copyright © 1997 by Paul Fleischman. Used by permission of HarperCollins Publishers.

"From Refugees to Fugees" by Jane Schwartz. Copyright © Pearson Longman, One Lake Street, Upper Saddle River, NY 07458.

UNIT 2

"The Train to Freedom." Copyright © Pearson Longman, One Lake Street, Upper Saddle River, NY 07458.

"The Drinking Gourd." Public domain.

"Five New Words at a Time" by Yu-Lan (Mary) Ying, *The New York Times* Op-ed, March 6, 1993. Copyright © 1993 The New York Times Company. Reprinted by permission.

"Quilt" from *A Suitcase of Seaweed and Other Poems* by Janet S. Wong. Copyright © 1996 Janet S. Wong. Reprinted with the permission of Margaret K. McElderry Books, an Imprint of Simon & Schuster Children's Publishing Division.

Excerpt from the interview with Gary Paulsen in *Author Talk*, compiled and edited by Leonard S. Marcus. Copyright © 2000 by Leonard S. Marcus. Used by permission of the author.

Excerpt from *Hatchet* by Gary Paulsen. Reprinted with permission of Atheneum Books for Young Readers, an Imprint of Simon & Schuster Children's Publishing and by permission of Flannery Literary Agency. Copyright © 1987 Gary Paulsen.

"The Great Fever." Copyright © Pearson Longman, One Lake Street, Upper Saddle River, NY 07458.

UNIT 3

"Aguinaldo" (adapted) from *Salsa Stories* by Lulu Delacre. Scholastic Inc./Scholastic Press. Copyright © 2000 by Lulu Delacre. Used by permission.

"Marilia's Besitos de Coco Recipe" from *Salsa Stories* by Lulu Delacre. Scholastic Inc./Scholastic Press. Copyright © 2000 by Lulu Delacre. Used by permission.

"Sowing the Seeds of Peace" by Mandy Terc. In memory of the founder of Seeds of Peace, John Wallach, for his vision, and the campers of Seeds of Peace, for their courage. Reprinted by permission of the author.

"Seeds of Peace: Cultivating Friendships." Copyright © Pearson Longman, One Lake Street, Upper Saddle River, NY 07458.

Excerpt from *Blue Willow* by Pam Conrad. Copyright © 1991 by Pam Conrad. Reprinted by permission of Maria Carvainis Agency.

"The Ladybird and the Wildflowers." Copyright © Pearson Longman, One Lake Street, Upper Saddle River, NY 07458.

UNIT 4

"97 Orchard Street" and "The Pros and Cons of Tenement Life." Adapted from *Cobblestone*, "Tenement Life," February 2004, Copyright © 2004 Carus Publishing Company, published by Cobblestone Publishing, 30 Grove Street, Suite C, Peterborough, NH 03458. All rights reserved. Used by permission of the publisher.

"Somebody's Son" by Richard Pindell. Reprinted by permission of the author.

Excerpt from "I years had been from home" from *The Poems of Emily Dickinson*, edited by Thomas H. Johnson. Copyright © 1951, 1955, 1979, 1983 by the President and Fellows of Harvard College. Reprinted by permission of the publishers and the Trustees of Amherst College, Cambridge, MA and The Belknap Press of Harvard University Press.

Excerpt from *The Lotus Seed*. Copyright © 1993 by Sherry Garland, reprinted by permission of Harcourt, Inc.

Credits

Smithsonian American Art Museum List of Artworks

UNIT 1 Invention and Change
Page 74
Hans Hofmann
Fermented Soil
1965
oil on canvas
48 x 60 in.
Smithsonian American Art Museum, Gift of S. C. Johnson & Son, Inc.

Page 75
Samuel Colman
Storm King on the Hudson
1866
oil on canvas
32⅛ x 59⅞ in.
Smithsonian American Art Museum, Gift of John Gellatly

UNIT 2 The Challenge of Illness
Page 150
Alice Eugenia Ligon
Embroidered Garment
about 1949
embroidered muslin and cotton crochet
43¾ x 38½ in.
Smithsonian American Art Museum, Gift of Herbert Waide Hemphill Jr.

Page 151
J. Bond Francisco
The Sick Child
1893
oil on canvas
32 x 48 in.
Smithsonian American Art Museum, Museum purchase

UNIT 3 Embracing Family, Friends, and Neighbors
Page 228
Franz Kline
Merce C
1961
oil on canvas
93 x 74⅝ in.
Smithsonian American Art Museum, Gift of S. C. Johnson & Son, Inc.

476

Page 229
Charles "Chaz" Bojórquez
Placa/Rollcall
1980
acrylic on canvas
68¼ x 83⅛ in.
Smithsonian American Art Museum, Gift of the artist
© Smithsonian American Art Museum

UNIT 4 Acknowledging the Past, Reaching for the Future
Page 300
Carmen Lomas Garza
Camas para Sueños
1985
gouache on paper
28⅛ x 20½ in.
Smithsonian American Art Museum, Museum purchase through the Smithsonian Latino
Initiatives Pool and the Smithsonian Institution Collections Acquisition Program
© 1985 Carmen Lomas Garza

Page 301
Hung Liu
The Ocean Is the Dragon's World
1995
oil on canvas, painted wood panel, and metal bird cage
96 x 82½ in.
Smithsonian American Art Museum, Museum purchase in part through the Lichtenberg Family Foundation
© Smithsonian American Art Museum

UNIT 5 Everyday Obstacles, Everyday Courage
Page 380
Residents of Bourbon County, Kentucky
Fan Quilt, Mt. Carmel
1893
cotton, wool, silk, velvet, lace, paint, chromolithographic paper, and canvas
85 x 72¼ in.
Smithsonian American Art Museum, Gift of Herbert Waide Hemphill Jr.

Page 381
Daniel Chester French
Spirit of Life
1914
bronze
51 x 28 x 30 in.
Smithsonian American Art Museum, Museum purchase through
the Luisita L. and Franz H. Denghausen Endowment

Michael Olszewski
Speaking to Hear
1989
silk with acid dyes
parts A and B: both 22½ x 21¼ in.
Smithsonian American Art Museum, Gift of KPMG Peat Marwick
© 2007 Smithsonian American Art Museum

UNIT 6 Capturing Cosmic Beauty
Page 456
Alma Thomas
The Eclipse
1970
acrylic on canvas
62 x 49¾ in.
Smithsonian American Art Museum, Gift of the artist

Page 457
Charles Burchfield
Orion in December
1959
watercolor and pencil on paper
39⅞ x 32⅞ in.
Smithsonian American Art Museum, Gift of S. C. Johnson & Son, Inc.